A·N·N·U·A·L EDITIONS

American History, Volume 2

Reconstruction Through the Present

Nineteenth Edition

D0222870

EDITOR

Robert James Maddox (Emeritus)

Pennsylvania State University
University Park

Robert James Maddox, distinguished historian and professor emeritus of American history at Pennsylvania State University, received a B.S. from Fairleigh Dickinson University in 1957, an M.S. from the University of Wisconsin in 1958, and a Ph.D. from Rutgers in 1964. He has written, reviewed, and lectured extensively and is widely respected for his interpretations of presidential character and policy.

 **Contemporary Learning Series**

2460 Kerper Blvd., Dubuque, IA 52001

Visit us on the Internet
http://www.mhcls.com

Credits

1. **Reconstruction and the Gilded Age**
   Unit photo—Library of Congress, Prints and Photographs Division [LC-USZ62-13016]
2. **The Emergence of Modern America**
   Unit photo—Courtesy of National Archives.
3. **From Progressivism to the 1920s**
   Unit photo—Library of Congress, Prints and Photographs Division [LC-USZ62-53212]
4. **From the Great Depression to World War II**
   Unit photo—Courtesy of the Library of Congress.
5. **From the Cold War to 2006**
   Unit photo—Library of Congress, Prints and Photographs Division [LC-USZ62-117122]
6. **New Directions for American History**
   Unit photo—© Getty Images/PhotoLink

Copyright

Cataloging in Publication Data
Main entry under title: Annual Editions: American History Vol. 2: Reconstruction Through the Present. 19/E.
1. United States—History—Periodicals.   2. United States—Historiography—Periodicals.   3. United States—Civilization—
Periodicals. I.   1. Maddox, Robert James, comp. II   Title: American History, Vol. Two: Reconstruction Through the Present.
ISBN-13: 978–0–07-3511601–1   ISBN 0–07-351601-5   973'.05   74-187540   ISSN 0733–3560

Nineteenth Edition

Cover image © Stockbyte/PunchStock and Library of Congress
Printed in the United States of America   1234567890QPDQPD9876   Printed on Recycled Paper

Editors/Advisory Board

Members of the Advisory Board are instrumental in the final selection of articles for each edition of ANNUAL EDITIONS. Their review of articles for content, level, currentness, and appropriateness provides critical direction to the editor and staff. We think that you will find their careful consideration well reflected in this volume.

Preface

In publishing ANNUAL EDITIONS we recognize the enormous role played by the magazines, newspapers, and journals of the public press in providing current, first-rate educational information in a broad spectrum of interest areas. Many of these articles are appropriate for students, researchers, and professionals seeking accurate, current material to help bridge the gap between principles and theories and the real world. These articles, however, become more useful for study when those of lasting value are carefully collected, organized, indexed, and reproduced in a low-cost format, which provides easy and permanent access when the material is needed. That is the role played by ANNUAL EDITIONS.

This volume begins with an article on post-Civil War Reconstruction, a period that ended in 1877. It was a very different world from the one we are living in today. The United States remained primarily a rural, agricultural nation. People for the most part lived much the same as they had 100 years earlier. They read by candle, lantern, or gaslight at night, they traveled by foot or by wagon, and they rarely ventured far from their home towns.

The following decades brought vast changes in all aspects of American life. Automobiles, expanding railroad systems, and airplanes enabled people to routinely travel to places they would only have dreamed about earlier. Massive population shifts, from farms and small towns to cities and suburbs, and from one section of the nation to another, radically altered the face of the nation. Immigration brought with it a host of opportunities and problems. At home, people could listen to the radio, watch television, or, more recently, explore new worlds of information via their computers. Diseases that once were almost certainly fatal or at least debilitating have now been virtually eliminated, resulting in life expectancies unheard of in the past.

With all of these "improvements," one would be hard put to argue that people in modern society are happier or more content than they were in the past. Extreme poverty is still with us in a land of untold wealth. Television and motion pictures, furthermore, encourage frustration by allowing even the poorest souls to glimpse those with lifestyles that only the wealthiest few would have enjoyed a century earlier. Other issues we face today also have echoes in the past: race relations, gender roles, domestic terrorism, and environmental problems, to name just a few. Some people fear that we are destroying the very planet on which we live. At least one new epidemic— AIDs—has become a scourge just as smallpox once was. Some fear that a pandemic of Avian Flu might break out that could be as devastating as the flu epidemic of 1918–1919 that cost as many as 40 million lives. Studying history will provide no "answers" to our modern troubles, but perhaps can provide some helpful guidelines.

Someone once said that historians wrote about "chaps," meaning white males who enjoyed positions of power or influence. Older history books tended to concentrate on presidents, titans of industry or finance, and military leaders. Women usually were mentioned only in passing, and then primarily as the wives or lovers of important men. Minority groups were treated, if at all, as passive objects of social customs or legislation. Mention of sexual orientation was simply out of the question.

Now virtually everything that has happened is considered fit for study. Books and articles tell us about the lives of ordinary people, about groups previously ignored or mentioned only in passing, and about subjects considered too trivial or commonplace to warrant examination. History "from the bottom up," once considered innovative, has become commonplace. Welcome as these innovations are, they often are encumbered by two unfortunate tendencies: many are freighted down with incomprehensible prose (one of the criterion for inclusion in this volume is that articles be written in standard English), and many are produced to advance agendas the authors try to fob off as scholarship.

Traditional history is still being written. For better or worse, there *have* been men and women who have exercised great power or influence over the lives and deaths of others. They continue to fascinate us. Presidents such as Franklin D. Roosevelt and Harry S. Truman had to make decisions that affected enormous numbers of people at home and abroad. Thomas Alva Edison changed millions of lives with his inventions, one of which, the incandescent light bulb, is treated in this volume. Reformer Jacob Riis, also profiled in these pages, shocked many middle-class readers with his descriptions of how the poor lived. Neither Rosa Parks nor Edith Galt Wilson ever held official positions of power, but both deeply affected the ways people perceived a number of issues.

Annual Editions: American History, Volume 2, constitutes an effort to provide a balanced collection of articles that deal with great leaders and great decisions, as well as with ordinary people at work, at leisure, and at war. Practically everyone who uses the volume will think of one or more articles he or she considers would have been preferable to the ones actually included. Some readers will wish more attention had been paid to one or another subject, others will regret the attention devoted to matters they regard as marginal. That is why we encourage teachers and students to let us know what they believe to be the strengths and weaknesses of this edition.

Annual Editions contains a number of features designed to make the volume "user friendly." These include a *topic guide* to help locate articles on specific individuals or subjects; the *table of contents extracts* that summarize each article with key concepts in boldface; and a comprehensive index. The essays are organized into six units. Each unit is preceded by an overview that provides background for informed reading of the articles, briefly introduces each one, and presents Key Points questions. Please let us know if you have any suggestions for improving the format.

There will be a new edition of this volume in two years, with approximately half the readings being replaced by new ones. By completing and mailing the postpaid article rating form included in the back of the book, you will help us judge which articles should be retained and which should be dropped. You can also help to improve the next edition by recommending (or better yet, sending along a copy of) articles that you think should be included. A number of essays included in this edition have come to our attention in this way.

Robert James Maddox

Robert James Maddox
Editor

Contents

UNIT 1
Reconstruction and the Gilded Age

The concepts in bold italics are developed in the article. For further expansion, please refer to the Topic Guide and the Index.

UNIT 2
The Emergence of Modern America

UNIT 3
From Progressivism to the 1920s

The concepts in bold italics are developed in the article. For further expansion, please refer to the Topic Guide and the Index.

UNIT 4
From the Great Depression to World War II

The concepts in bold italics are developed in the article. For further expansion, please refer to the Topic Guide and the Index.

UNIT 5
From the Cold War to 2006

The concepts in bold italics are developed in the article. For further expansion, please refer to the Topic Guide and the Index.

UNIT 6
New Directions for American History

The concepts in bold italics are developed in the article. For further expansion, please refer to the Topic Guide and the Index.

The concepts in bold italics are developed in the article. For further expansion, please refer to the Topic Guide and the Index.

Topic Guide

This topic guide suggests how the selections in this book relate to the subjects covered in your course. You may want to use the topics listed on these pages to search the Web more easily.

On the following pages a number of Web sites have been gathered specifically for this book. They are arranged to reflect the units of this *Annual Edition*. You can link to these sites by going to the student online support site at *http://www.mhcls.com/online/*.

ALL THE ARTICLES THAT RELATE TO EACH TOPIC ARE LISTED BELOW THE BOLD-FACED TERM.

xi

Internet References

The following internet sites have been carefully researched and selected to support the articles found in this reader. The easiest way to access these selected sites is to go to our student online support site at *http://www.mhcls.com/online/*.

AE: American History, Volume 2

The following sites were available at the time of publication. Visit our Web site—we update our student online support site regularly to reflect any changes.

General Sources

American Historical Association
http://www.theaha.org

This is the logical first visitation site for someone interested in virtually any topic in American history. All affiliated societies and publications are noted, and AHA links present material related to myriad fields of history and for students with different levels of education.

Harvard's John F. Kennedy School of Government
http://www.ksg.harvard.edu/

Starting from this home page, click on a huge variety of links to information about American history, ranging from data about political parties to general debates of enduring issues.

History Net
http://www.thehistorynet.com/

Supported by the National Historical Society, this frequently updated site provides information on a wide range of topics. The articles are of excellent quality, and the site has book reviews and even special interviews.

Library of Congress
http://www.loc.gov/

Examine this Web site to learn about the extensive resource tools, library services/resources, exhibitions, and databases available through the Library of Congress in many different subfields that are related to American history.

National Archives and Records Administration
http://www.nara.gov/nara/nail.html

It is possible to access over 125,000 digital images from this National Archives and Records site. A vast array of American subjects are available.

Smithsonian Institution
http://www.si.edu/

This site provides access to the enormous resources of the Smithsonian, which holds some 140 million artifacts and specimens in its trust for "the increase and diffusion of knowledge." Here you can learn about American social, cultural, economic, and political history from a variety of viewpoints.

The White House
http://www.whitehouse.gov/

Visit the home page of the White House for direct access to information about commonly requested federal services, the White House Briefing Room, and the presidents and vice presidents. The "Virtual Library" allows you to search White House documents, listen to speeches, and view photos.

UNIT 1: Reconstruction and the Gilded Age

Anacostia Museum/Smithsonian Institution
http://www.si.edu/archives/historic/anacost.htm

This is the home page of the Center for African American History and Culture of the Smithsonian Institution. Explore its many avenues. This is expected to become a major repository of information.

American Memory
http://memory.loc.gov/ammem/ammemhome.html

American Memory is a gateway to rich primary source materials relating to the history and culture of the United States. The site offers more than 7 million digital items from more than 100 historical collections.

Gilded Age and Progressive Era Resources
http://www2.tntech.edu/history/gilprog.html

General Resources on the Gilded Age and Progressive Era including numerous links for research and further reading.

BoondocksNet.com
http://www.boondocksnet.com

Jim Zwick's site explores the often-forgotten Filipino revolt against U.S. acquisition of the Philippines after the Spanish-American War. Zwick also discusses anti-imperialist crusades within the United States during the Gilded Age.

UNIT 2: The Emergence of Modern America

The Age of Imperialism
http://www.smplanet.com/imperialism/toc.html

During the late nineteenth and early twentieth centuries, the United States pursued an aggressive policy of expansionism, extending its political and economic influence around the globe. That pivotal era in the nation's history is the subject of this interactive site. Maps and photographs are provided.

Anti-Imperialism in the United States, 1898–1935
http://boondocksnet.com/ail98-35.html

Jim Zwick created this interesting site that explores American imperialism from the Spanish-American War years to 1935. It provides valuable primary resources on a variety of related topics.

William McKinley 1843-1901
http://lcweb.loc.gov/rr/hispanic/1898/mckinley.html

Browse through this Library of Congress site for insight into the era of William McKinley, including discussion of the Spanish-American War.

American Diplomacy: Editor's Corner - If Two By Sea
http://www.unc.edu/depts/diplomat/AD_Issues/amdipl_15/edit_15.html

This essay provides a brief biography of Alfred Thayer Mahan and reviews his contributions and influence towards expansionism in American foreign policy.

Great Chicago Fire and the Web of Memory
http://www.chicagohs.org/fire/

This site, created by the Academic Technologies unit of Northwestern University and the Chicago Historical Society, is interesting and well constructed. Besides discussing the Great

www.mhcls.com/online/

Chicago Fire at length, the materials provide insight into the era in which the event took place.

UNIT 3: From Progressivism to the 1920s

International Channel
http://www.i-channel.com/
Immigrants helped to create modern America. Visit this interesting site to experience "the memories, sounds, even tastes of Ellis Island. Hear immigrants describe in their own words their experiences upon entering the gateway to America."

World War I—Trenches on the Web
http://www.worldwar1.com/
Mike Lawrence's interesting site supplies extensive resources about the Great War and is the appropriate place to begin exploration of this topic as regards the American experience in World War I. There are "virtual tours" on certain topics, such as "Life on the Homefront."

World Wide Web Virtual Library
http://www.iisg.nl/~w3vl/
This site focuses on labor and business history. As an index site, this is a good place to start exploring these two vast topics.

Temperance and Prohibition
http://prohibition.history.ohio-state.edu/Contents.htm
From Ohio State University's Department of History, this Web page covers in depth inquiry into the origins and course of the American temperance movement and prohibition.

The Roaring 20's and the Great Depression
http://www.snowcrest.net/jmike/20sdep.html
An extensive anthology of Web links to sites on the Roaring 20's and the Great Depression.

UNIT 4: From the Great Depression to World War II

Japanese American Internment
http://www.jainternment.org/
This site, which focuses on the Japanese American internment during World War II, is especially useful for links to other related sites.

Works Progress Administration/Folklore Project
http://lcweb2.loc.gov/ammem/wpaintro/wpalife.html
Open this home page of the Folklore Project of the Works Progress Administration (WPA) Federal Writers' Project to gain access to thousands of documents on the life histories of ordinary Americans from all walks of life during the Great Depression.

World War II WWW Sites
http://www.besthistorysites.nte/WWWII.shtml
Visit this site as a starting point to find research links for World War II, including topics specific to the United States' participation and the impact on the country.

World War II Timeline
http://history.acusd.edu/gen/WW2Timeline/start.html
A detailed and interactive timeline covering 1917 through 1945 and includes many photographs.

Hiroshima Archive
http://www.lclark.edu/~history/HIROSHIMA/
The Hiroshima Archive was originally set up to join the on-line effort made by many people all over the world to commemorate the 50th anniversary of the atomic bombing. It is intended to serve as a research and educational guide to those who want to gain and expand their knowledge of the atomic bombing.

The Enola Gay
http://www.theenolagay.com/index.html
The offical Web site of Brigadier General Paul W. Tibbets, Jr. (Ret.) Offers a wealth of historical analysis and photographs of the events surrounding the use of atomic weapons on Japan in 1945.

UNIT 5: From the Cold War to 2006

Coldwar
http://www.cnn.com/SPECIALS/cold.war
This site presents U.S. government policies during the cold war. Navigate interactive maps, see rare archival footage online, learn more about the key players, read recently declassified documents and tour Cold War capitals through 3-D images.

The American Experience: Vietnam Online
http://www.pbs.org/wgbh/amex/vietnam/
Vietnam Online was developed to accompany Vietnam: A Television History, the award-winning television series produced by WGBH Boston.

The Federal Web Locator
http://www.infoctr.edu/fwl
Use this handy site as a launching pad for the Web sites of federal U.S. agencies, departments, and organizations. It is well organized and easy to use for informational and research purposes.

Federalism: Relationship between Local and National Governments
http://www.infidels.org/~nap/index.federalism.html
Federalism versus states' rights has always been a spirited topic of debate in American government. Visit this site for links to many articles and reports on the subject.

The Gallup Organization
http://www.gallup.com/
Open this Gallup Organization home page to access an extensive archive of public opinion poll results and special reports on a huge variety of topics related to American society, politics, and government.

STAT-USA
http://www.stat-usa.gov/stat-usa.html
This site, a service of the Department of Commerce, contains daily economic news, frequently requested statistical releases, information on export and international trade, domestic economic news and statistical series and databases.

U.S. Department of State
http://www.state.gov/
View this site for an understanding into the workings of what has become a major U.S. executive-branch department. Links explain what exactly the department does, what services it provides, what it says about U.S. interests around the world, and much more.

UNIT 6: New Directions for American History

American Studies Web
http://www.georgetown.edu/crossroads/asw/
This eclectic site provides links to a wealth of Internet resources for research in American studies, from agriculture and rural development, to history and government, to race and ethnicity.

National Center for Policy Analysis
http://www.public-policy.org/web.public-policy.org/index.php
Through this site, click onto links to read discussions of an array of topics that are of major interest in the study of American history, from regulatory policy and privatization to economy and income.

www.mhcls.com/online/

The National Network for Immigrant and Refugee Rights (NNIRR)
http://www.nnirr.org/

The NNIRR serves as a forum to share information and analysis, to educate communities and the general public, and to develop and coordinate plans of action on important immigrant and refugee issues. Visit this site and its many links to explore these issues.

STANDARDS: An International Journal of Multicultural Studies
http://www.colorado.edu/journals/standards

This fascinating site provides access to the *Standards* archives and a seemingly infinite number of links to topics of interest in the study of cultural pluralism.

Supreme Court/Legal Information Institute
http://supct.law.cornell.edu/supct/index.html

Open this site for current and historical information about the Supreme Court. The archive contains many opinions issued since May 1990 as well as a collection of nearly 600 of the most historic decisions of the Court.

We highly recommend that you review our Web site for expanded information and our other product lines. We are continually updating and adding links to our Web site in order to offer you the most usable and useful information that will support and expand the value of your Annual Editions. You can reach us at: *http://www.mhcls.com/annualeditions/.*

UNIT 1

Reconstruction and the Gilded Age

Unit Selections

1. **The New View of Reconstruction**, Eric Foner
2. **1871 War on Terror**, David Everitt
3. **Little Bighorn Reborn**, Tony Perrottet
4. **The Spark of Genius**, Harold Evans
5. **Lockwood in '84**, Jill Norgren
6. **A Day to Remember: November 18, 1883**, Charles Phillips

Key Points to Consider

- Radical Reconstruction failed to achieve its goal of ensuring full citizenship to freed people. Could this attempt have succeeded in view of the fierce Southern resistance? How?

- Why have American Indians been dissatisfied with the popular presentation of what used to be called "Custer's Last Stand?" How does changing the name from the Custer Battlefield to the Little Bighorn Battlefield National Monument symbolize efforts at reconciliation?

- What alternatives did mine workers have to forming secret organizations to protect their interests? Were the Molly Maguires given fair trials?

Student Website

www.mhcls.com/online

Internet References

Further information regarding these websites may be found in this book's preface or online.

Anacostia Museum/Smithsonian Institution
http://www.si.edu/archives/historic/anacost.htm

American Memory
http://memory.loc.gov/ammem/ammemhome.html

Gilded Age and Progressive Era Resources
http://www2.tntech.edu/history/gilprog.html

BoondocksNet.com
http://www.boondocksnet.com

Abraham Lincoln had wanted to reunite the nation as quickly as possible after four years of war. During the last months of his life, he had instituted simple procedures through which Southern states could resume their positions within the union. Only a few high-ranking Confederate officials were prohibited from participating. But what of the former slaves? Lincoln's version of reconstruction would result in the South being ruled by essentially the same people who had brought about secession. Those who became known as "Radical" or "Extreme" Republicans refused to abandon Freedpeople to their former masters. They wished to use the power of the federal government to ensure that former slaves enjoyed full civil and legal rights. At first they thought they had an ally in Vice President Andrew Johnson, who assumed the presidency after Lincoln's assassination. When this proved untrue, a gruelling struggle ensued that resulted in Johnson's impeachment and the Radicals in command of recostruction. The South was divided into five military districts and federal troops were sent to protect the rights of Freed people. White

Southerners used every means possible to keep blacks "in their place." As discussed in the article "1871 War on Terror," these methods included organizations such as the Ku Klux Klan and the Knights of the White Camelia. Eric Foner's "The New View of Reconstruction" shows how Radical Reconstruction failed to achieve its goals in the short run but provided what he calls an "enduring vision."

The third essay, "Little Bighorn Revisited," recounts how whites and Indians have continued to seek accommodation over what used to be called "Custer's Last Stand." Indians had complained that the battle was celebrated almost entirely from the standpoint of whites: a courageous "Yellowhair" going down with guns blazing against the savage horde. Efforts to that reconciliation are symbolized by the name-change, from the Custer Battlefield to the Little Bighorn Battlefield National Monument.

Thomas Alva Edison's invention of the incandescent light bulb during the 1870s was a boon to millions of people who previously had had to read by candle, lantern, or gaslight. He took out nearly 1,100 patents during his lifetime, many of which wrought enduring changes in the way people lived. "The Spark of Genius" goes beyond Edison's prowess in the laboratory to emphasize his abilities to bring his inventions to practical use.

In "Lockwood in '84," the remarkable story of Belva Lockwood's presidential campaign of 1884. Running on the Equal Rights ticket, her emphasis was on woman's suffrage but she took progressive stands on most of the day's issues.

By the mid-1850s there were some 144 official times in North America. This did not matter much in the horse-and-buggy era. As long as one knew the local time, it mattered little what the clock read in the next county or state. With the growth of railroads, however, regularized times became imperative. People had to know whether a train was scheduled to arrive at Chicago time or Detroit time. In 1883 standard time zones were established, which with minor variations exist to this day.

The New View of Reconstruction

Whatever you were taught or thought you knew about the post-Civil War era is probably wrong in the light of recent study

Eric Foner

In the past twenty years, no period of American history has been the subject of a more thoroughgoing reevaluation than Reconstruction—the violent, dramatic, and still controversial era following the Civil War. Race relations, politics, social life, and economic change during Reconstruction have all been reinterpreted in the light of changed attitudes toward the place of blacks within American society. If historians have not yet forged a fully satisfying portrait of Reconstruction as a whole, the traditional interpretation that dominated historical writing for much of this century has irrevocably been laid to rest.

Anyone who attended high school before 1960 learned that Reconstruction was a era of unrelieved sordidness in American political and social life. The martyred Lincoln, according to this view, had planned a quick and painless readmission of the Southern states as equal members of the national family. President Andrew Johnson, his successor, attempted to carry out Lincoln's policies but was foiled by the Radical Republicans (also known as Vindictives or Jacobins). Motivated by an irrational hatred of Rebels or by ties with Northern capitalists out to plunder the South, the Radicals swept aside Johnson's lenient program and fastened black supremacy upon the defeated Confederacy. An orgy of corruption followed, presided over by unscrupulous carpetbaggers (Northerners who ventured south to reap the spoils of office), traitorous scalawags (Southern whites who cooperated with the new gov-

ernments for personal gain), and the ignorant and childlike freedmen, who were incapable of properly exercising the political power that had been thrust upon them. After much needless suffering, the white community of the South banded together to overthrow these "black" governments and restore home rule (their euphemism for white supremacy). All told, Reconstruction was just about the darkest page in the American saga.

Originating in anti-Reconstruction propaganda of Southern Democrats during the 1870s, this traditional interpretation achieved scholarly legitimacy around the turn of the century through the work of William Dunning and his students at Columbia University. It reached the larger public through films like *Birth of a Nation* and *Gone With the Wind* and that best-selling work of myth-making masquerading as history, *The Tragic Era* by Claude G. Bowers. In language as exaggerated as it was colorful, Bowers told how Andrew Johnson "fought the bravest battle for constitutional liberty and for the preservation of our institutions ever waged by an Executive" but was overwhelmed by the "poisonous propaganda" of the Radicals. Southern whites, as a result, "literally were put to the torture" by "emissaries of hate" who manipulated the "simple-minded" freedmen, inflaming the negroes' "egotism" and even inspiring "lustful assaults" by blacks upon white womanhood.

In a discipline that sometimes seems to pride itself on the rapid rise and fall of his-

torical interpretations, this traditional portrait of Reconstruction enjoyed remarkable staying power. The long reign of the old interpretation is not difficult to explain. It presented a set of easily identifiable heroes and villains. It enjoyed the imprimatur of the nation's leading scholars. And it accorded with the political and social realities of the first half of this century. This image of Reconstruction helped freeze the mind of the white South in unalterable opposition to any movement for breaching the ascendancy of the Democratic party, eliminating segregation, or readmitting disfranchised blacks to the vote.

Nevertheless, the demise of the traditional interpretation was inevitable, for it ignored the testimony of the central participant in the drama of Reconstruction—the black freedman. Furthermore, it was grounded in the conviction that blacks were unfit to share in political power. As Dunning's Columbia colleague John W. Burgess put it, "A black skin means membership in a race of men which has never of itself succeeded in subjecting passion to reason, has never, therefore, created any civilization of any kind." Once objective scholarship and modern experience rendered that assumption untenable, the entire edifice was bound to fall.

The work of "revising" the history of Reconstruction began with the writings of a handful of survivors of the era, such as John R. Lynch, who had served as a black congressman from Mississippi after the Civil War. In the 1930s white scholars like Francis Simkins and Robert Woody carried the task forward. Then, in 1935, the black historian and activist W. E. B. Du Bois produced *Black Reconstruction in America,* a monumental revaluation that closed with an irrefutable indictment of a historical profession that had sacrificed scholarly objectivity on the altar of racial bias. "One fact and one alone," he wrote, "explains the attitude of most recent writers toward Reconstruction; they cannot conceive of Negroes as men." Du Bois's work, however, was ignored by most historians.

Black initiative established as many schools as did Northern religious societies and the Freedmen's Bureau. The right to vote was not simply thrust upon them by meddling outsiders, since blacks began agitating for the suffrage as soon as they were freed.

It was not until the 1960s that the full force of the revisionist wave broke over the field. Then, in rapid succession, virtually every assumption of the traditional viewpoint was systematically dismantled. A drastically different portrait emerged to take its place. President Lincoln did not have a coherent "plan" for Reconstruction, but at the time of his assassination he had been cautiously contemplating black suffrage. Andrew Johnson was a stubborn, racist politician who lacked the ability to compromise. By isolating himself from the broad currents of public opinion that had nourished Lincoln's career, Johnson created an impasse with Congress that Lincoln would certainly have avoided, thus throwing away his political power and destroying his own plans for reconstructing the South.

The Radicals in Congress were acquitted of both vindictive motives and the charge of serving as the stalking-horses of Northern capitalism. They emerged instead as idealists in the best nineteenth-century reform tradition. Radical leaders like Charles Sumner and Thaddeus Stevens had worked for the rights of blacks long before any conceivable political ad-

vantage flowed from such a commitment. Stevens refused to sign the Pennsylvania Constitution of 1838 because it disfranchised the state's black citizens; Sumner led a fight in the 1850s to integrate Boston's public schools. Their Reconstruction policies were based on principle, not petty political advantage, for the central issue dividing Johnson and these Radical Republicans was the civil rights of freedmen. Studies of congressional policy-making, such as Eric L. McKitrick's *Andrew Johnson and Reconstruction,* also revealed that Reconstruction legislation, ranging from the Civil Rights Act of 1866 to the Fourteenth and Fifteenth Amendments, enjoyed broad support from moderate and conservative Republicans. It was not simply the work of a narrow radical faction.

Even more startling was the revised portrait of Reconstruction in the South itself. Imbued with the spirit of the civil rights movement and rejecting entirely the racial assumptions that had underpinned the traditional interpretation, these historians evaluated Reconstruction from the black point of view. Works like Joel Williamson's *After Slavery* portrayed the period as a time of extraordinary political, social, and economic progress for blacks. The establishment of public school systems, the granting of equal citizenship to blacks, the effort to restore the devastated Southern economy, the attempt to construct an interracial political democracy from the ashes of slavery, all these were commendable achievements, not the elements of Bowers's "tragic era."

Unlike earlier writers, the revisionists stressed the active role of the freedmen in shaping Reconstruction. Black initiative established as many schools as did Northern religious societies and the Freedmen's Bureau. The right to vote was not simply thrust upon them by meddling outsiders, since blacks began agitating for the suffrage as soon as they were freed. In 1865 black conventions throughout the South issued eloquent, though unheeded, appeals for equal civil and political rights.

With the advent of Radical Reconstruction in 1867, the freedmen did enjoy a real measure of political power. But black supremacy never existed. In most states blacks held only a small fraction of political offices, and even in South Carolina, where they comprised a majority of the state legislature's lower house, effective power remained in white hands. As for corruption, moral standards in both gov-

ernment and private enterprise were at low ebb throughout the nation in the postwar years—the era of Boss Tweed, the Credit Mobilier scandal, and the Whiskey Ring. Southern corruption could hardly be blamed on former slaves.

Other actors in the Reconstruction drama also came in for reevaluation. Most carpetbaggers were former Union soldiers seeking economic opportunity in the postwar South, not unscrupulous adventurers. Their motives, a typically American amalgam of humanitarianism and the pursuit of profit, were no more insidious than those of Western pioneers. Scalawags, previously seen as traitors to the white race, now emerged as "Old Line" Whig Unionists who had opposed secession in the first place or as poor whites who had long resented planters' domination of Southern life and who saw in Reconstruction a chance to recast Southern society along more democratic lines. Strongholds of Southern white Republicanism like east Tennessee and western North Carolina had been the scene of resistance to Confederate rule throughout the Civil War; now, as one scalawag newspaper put it, the choice was "between salvation at the hand of the Negro or destruction at the hand of the rebels."

At the same time, the Ku Klux Klan and kindred groups, whose campaign of violence against black and white Republicans had been minimized or excused in older writings, were portrayed as they really were. Earlier scholars had conveyed the impression that the Klan intimidated blacks mainly by dressing as ghosts and playing on the freedmen's superstitions. In fact, black fears were all too real: the Klan was a terrorist organization that beat and killed its political opponents to deprive blacks of their newly won rights. The complicity of the Democratic party and the silence of prominent whites in the face of such outrages stood as an indictment of the moral code the South had inherited from the days of slavery.

By the end of the 1960s, then, the old interpretation had been completely reversed. Southern freedmen were the heroes, the "Redeemers" who overthrew Reconstruction were the villains, and if the era was "tragic," it was because change did not go far enough. Reconstruction had been a time of real progress and its failure a lost opportunity for the South and the nation. But the legacy of Reconstruction—the Fourteenth and Fifteenth Amendments—endured to inspire future efforts for civil rights. As Kenneth Stampp wrote in *The Era of Reconstruction,* a superb summary of revisionist findings published in 1965, "if it was worth four years of civil war to save the Union, it was worth a few years of radical reconstruction to give the American Negro the ultimate promise of equal civil and political rights."

Under slavery most blacks had lived in nuclear family units, although they faced the constant threat of separation from loved ones by sale. Reconstruction provided the opportunity for blacks to solidify their preexisting family ties.

As Stampp's statement suggests, the re-evaluation of the first Reconstruction was inspired in large measure by the impact of the second—the modern civil rights movement. And with the waning of that movement in recent years, writing on Reconstruction has undergone still another transformation. Instead of seeing the Civil War and its aftermath as a second American Revolution (as Charles Beard had), a regression into barbarism (as Bowers argued), or a golden opportunity squandered (as the revisionists saw it), recent writers argue that Radical Reconstruction was not really very radical. Since land was not distributed to the former slaves, the remained economically dependent upon their former owners. The planter class survived both the war and Reconstruction with its property (apart from slaves) and prestige more or less intact.

Not only changing times but also the changing concerns of historians have contributed to this latest reassessment of Reconstruction. The hallmark of the past decade's historical writing has been an emphasis upon "social history"—the evocation of the past lives of ordinary Americans—and the downplaying of strictly political events. When applied to Reconstruction, this concern with the "social" suggested that black suffrage and office-holding, once seen as the most radical departures of the Reconstruction era, were relatively insignificant.

Recent historians have focused their investigations not upon the politics of Reconstruction but upon the social and

economic aspects of the transition from slavery to freedom. Herbert Gutman's influential study of the black family during and after slavery found little change in family structure or relations between men and women resulting from emancipation. Under slavery most blacks had lived in nuclear family units, although they faced the constant threat of separation from loved ones by sale. Reconstruction provided the opportunity for blacks to solidify their preexisting family ties. Conflicts over whether black women should work in the cotton fields (planters said yes, many black families said no) and over white attempts to "apprentice" black children revealed that the autonomy of family life was a major preoccupation of the freedmen. Indeed, whether manifested in their withdrawal from churches controlled by whites, in the blossoming of black fraternal, benevolent, and self-improvement organizations, or in the demise of the slave quarters and their replacement by small tenant farms occupied by individual families, the quest for independence from white authority and control over their own day-to-day lives shaped the black response to emancipation.

The Civil War raised the decisive questions of American's national existence: the relations between local and national authority, the definition of citizenship, the balance between force and consent in generating obedience to authority.

In the post–Civil War South the surest guarantee of economic autonomy, blacks believed, was land. To the freedmen the justice of a claim to land based on their years of unrequited labor appeared self-evident. As an Alabama black convention put it, "The property which they [the planters] hold was nearly all earned by the sweat of *our* brows." As Leon Litwack showed in *Been in the Storm So Long,* a Pulitzer Prize–winning account of the black response to emancipation, many freedmen in 1865 and 1866 refused to sign labor contracts, expecting the federal government to give them land. In some localities, as one Alabama

overseer reported, they "set up claims to the plantation and all on it."

In the end, of course, the vast majority of Southern blacks remained propertyless and poor. But exactly why the South, and especially its black population, suffered from dire poverty and economic retardation in the decades following the Civil War is a matter of much dispute. In *One Kind of Freedom* economists Roger Ransom and Richard Sutch indicted country merchants for monopolizing credit and charging usurious interest rates, forcing black tenants into debt and locking the South into a dependence on cotton production that impoverished the entire region. But Jonathan Wiener, in his study of postwar Alabama, argued that planters used their political power to compel blacks to remain on the plantations. Planters succeeded in stabilizing the plantation system, but only by blocking the growth of alternative enterprises, like factories, that might draw off black laborers, thus locking the region into a pattern of economic backwardness.

If the thrust of recent writing has emphasized the social and economic aspects of Reconstruction, politics has not been entirely neglected. But political studies have also reflected the postrevisionist mood summarized by C. Vann Woodward when he observed "how essentially nonrevolutionary and conservative Reconstruction really was." Recent writers, unlike their revisionist predecessors, have found little to praise in federal policy toward the emancipated blacks.

A new sensitivity to the strength of prejudice and laissez-faire ideas in the nineteenth-century North has led many historians to doubt whether the Republican party ever made a genuine commitment to racial justice in the South. The granting of black suffrage was an alternative to a long-term federal responsibility for protecting the rights of the former slaves. Once enfranchised, blacks could be left to fend for themselves. With the exception of a few Radicals like Thaddeus Stevens, nearly all Northern policy-makers and educators are criticized today for assuming that, so long as the unfettered operations of the marketplace afforded blacks the opportunity to advance through diligent labor, federal efforts to assist them in acquiring land were unnecessary.

Probably the most innovative recent writing on Reconstruction politics has centered on a broad reassessment of black Republicanism, largely undertaken by a new generation of black historians. Scholars like Thomas Holt and Nell Painter insist that Reconstruction was not simply a matter of black and white. Conflicts within the black community, no less than divisions among whites, shaped Reconstruction politics. Where revisionist scholars, both black and white, had celebrated the accomplishments of black political leaders, Holt, Painter, and others charge that they failed to address the economic plight of the black masses. Painter criticized "representative colored men," as national black leaders were called, for failing to provide ordinary freedmen with effective political leadership. Holt found that black officeholders in South Carolina most emerged from the old free mulatto class of Charleston, which shared many assumptions with prominent whites. "Basically bourgeois in their origins and orientation," he wrote, they "failed to act in the interest of black peasants."

In emphasizing the persistence from slavery of divisions between free blacks and slaves, these writers reflect the increasing concern with continuity and conservatism in Reconstruction. Their work reflects a startling extension of revisionist premises. If, as has been argued for the past twenty years, blacks were active agents rather than mere victims of manipulation, then they could not be absolved of blame for the ultimate failure of Reconstruction.

Despite the excellence of recent writings and the continual expansion of our knowledge of the period, historians of Reconstruction today face a unique dilemma. An old interpretation has been overthrown, but a coherent new synthesis has yet to take its place. The revisionists of the 1960s effectively established a series of negative points: the Reconstruction governments were not as bad as had been portrayed, black supremacy was a myth, the Radicals were not cynical manipulators of the freedmen. Yet no convincing overall portrait of the quality of political and social life emerged from their writings. More recent historians have rightly pointed to elements of continuity that spanned the nineteenth-century Southern experience, especially the survival, in modified form, of the plantation system. Nevertheless, by denying the real changes that did occur, they have failed to provide a convincing portrait of an era characterized above all by drama, turmoil, and social change.

Building upon the findings of the past twenty years of scholarship, a new portrait of Reconstruction ought to begin by viewing it not as a specific time period, bounded by the years 1865 and 1877, but as an epi-

sode in a prolonged historical process—American society's adjustment to the consequences of the Civil War and emancipation. The Civil War, of course, raised the decisive questions of America's national existence: the relations between local and national authority, the definition of citizenship, the balance between force and consent in generating obedience to authority. The war and Reconstruction, as Allan Nevins observed over fifty years ago, marked the "emergence of modern America." This was the era of the completion of the national railroad network, the creation of the modern steel industry, the conquest of the West and final subduing of the Indians, and the expansion of the mining frontier. Lincoln's America—the world of the small farm and artisan shop—gave way to a rapidly industrializing economy. The issues that galvanized postwar Northern politics—from the question of the greenback currency to the mode of paying holders of the national debt—arose from the economic changes unleashed by the Civil War.

Above all, the war irrevocably abolished slavery. Since 1619, when "twenty negars" disembarked from a Dutch ship in Virginia, racial injustice had haunted American life, mocking its professed ideals even as tobacco and cotton, the products of slave labor, helped finance the nation's economic development. Now the implications of the black presence could no longer be ignored. The Civil War resolved the problem of slavery but, as the Philadelphia diarist Sydney George Fisher observed in June 1865, it opened an even more intractable problem: "What shall we do with the Negro?" Indeed, he went on, this was a problem "*incapable* of any solution that will satisfy both North and South."

As Fisher realized, the focal point of Reconstruction was the social revolution known as emancipation. Plantation slavery was simultaneously a system of labor, a form of racial domination, and the foundation upon which arose a distinctive ruling class within the South. Its demise threw open the most fundamental questions of economy, society, and politics. A new system of labor, social, racial, and political relations had to be created to replace slavery.

The United States was not the only nation to experience emancipation in the nineteenth century. Neither plantation slavery nor abolition were unique to the United States. But Reconstruction was. In a comparative perspective Radical Reconstruction stands as a remarkable experiment, the only effort of a society experiencing abolition to bring the former

slaves within the umbrella of equal citizenship. Because the Radicals did not achieve everything they wanted, historians have lately tended to play down the stunning departure represented by black suffrage and officeholding. Former slaves, most fewer than two years removed from bondage, debated the fundamental questions of the polity: what is a republican form of government? Should the state provide equal education for all? How could political equality be reconciled with a society in which property was so unequally distributed? There was something inspiring in the way such men met the challenge of Reconstruction. "I knew nothing more than to obey my master," James K. Greene, an Alabama black politician later recalled. "But the tocsin of freedom sounded and knocked at the door and we walked out like free men and we met the exigencies as they grew up, and shouldered the responsibilities."

Y ou never saw a people more excited on the subject of politics than are the negroes of the south," one planter observed in 1867. And there were more than a few Southern whites as well who in these years shook off the prejudices of the past to embrace the revision of a new South dedicated to the principles of equal citizenship and social justice. One ordinary South Carolinian expressed the new sense of possibility in 1868 to the Republican governor of the state: "I am sorry that I cannot write an elegant stiled letter to your excellency. But I rejoice to think that God almighty has given to the poor of S.C. a Gov. to hear to feel to protect the humble poor without distinction to race or color.... I am a native borned S.C. a poor man never owned a Negro in my life nor my father before me.... Remember the true and loyal are the poor of the whites and blacks, outside of these you can find none loyal."

Few modern scholars believe the Reconstruction governments established in the South in 1867 and 1868 fulfilled the aspirations of their humble constituents. While their achievements in such realms as education, civil rights, and the economic rebuilding of the South are now widely appreciated, historians today believe they failed to affect either the economic plight of the emancipated slave or the ongoing transformation of independent white farmers into cotton tenants. Yet their opponents did perceive the Reconstruction governments in precisely this way—as representatives of a revolution that had put the bottom rail, both racial and economic, on top. This perception helps explain the ferocity of the attacks leveled against them and the pervasiveness of violence in the post-emancipation South.

In the end neither the abolition of slavery nor Reconstruction succeeded in resolving the debate over the meaning of freedom in American life.

The spectacle of black men voting and holding office was anathema to large numbers of Southern whites. Even more disturbing, at least in the view of those who still controlled the plantation regions of the South, was the emergence of local officials, black and white, who sympathized with the plight of the black laborer. Alabama's vagrancy law was a "dead letter" in 1870, "because those who are charged with its enforcement are indebted to the vagrant vote for their offices and emoluments." Political debates over the level and incidence of taxation, the control of crops, and the resolution of contract disputes revealed that a primary issue of Reconstruction was the role of government in a plantation society. During presidential Reconstruction, and after "Redemption," with planters and their allies in control of politics, the law emerged as a means of stabilizing and promoting the plantation system. If Radical Reconstruction failed to redistribute the land of the South, the ouster of the planter class from control of politics at least ensured that the sanctions of the criminal law would not be employed to discipline the black labor force.

An understanding of this fundamental conflict over the relation between government and society helps explain the pervasive complaints concerning corruption and "extravagance" during Radical Reconstruction. Corruption there was aplenty; tax rates did rise sharply. More significant

than the rate of taxation, however, was the change in its incidence. For the first time, planters and white farmers had to pay a significant portion of their income to the government, while propertyless blacks often escaped scot-free. Several states, moreover, enacted heavy taxes on uncultivated land to discourage land speculation and force land onto the market, benefiting, it was hoped, the freedmen.

As time passed, complaints about the "extravagance" and corruption of Southern governments found a sympathetic audience among influential Northerners. The Democratic charge that universal suffrage in the South was responsible for high taxes and governmental extravagance coincided with a rising conviction among the urban middle classes of the North that city government had to be taken out of the hands of the immigrant poor and returned to the "best men"—the educated, professional, financially independent citizens unable to exert much political influence at a time of mass parties and machine politics. Increasingly the "respectable" middle classes began to retreat from the very notion of universal suffrage. The poor were not longer perceived as honest producers, the backbone of the social order; now they became the "dangerous classes," the "mob." As the historian Francis Parkman put it, too much power rested with "masses of imported ignorance and hereditary ineptitude." To Parkman the Irish of the Northern cities and the blacks of the South were equally incapable of utilizing the ballot: "Witness the municipal corruptions of New York, and the monstrosities of negro rule in South Carolina." Such attitudes helped to justify Northern inaction as, one by one, the Reconstruction regimes of the South were overthrown by political violence.

In the end, then, neither the abolition of slavery nor Reconstruction succeeded in resolving the debate over the meaning of freedom in American life. Twenty years before the American Civil War, writing about the prospect of abolition in France's colonies, Alexis de Tocqueville had written, "If the Negroes have the right to become free, the [planters] have the incontestable right not to be ruined by the

Negroes' freedom." And in the United States, as in nearly every plantation society that experienced the end of slavery, a rigid social and political dichotomy between former master and former slave, an ideology of racism, and a dependent labor force with limited economic opportunities all survived abolition. Unless one means by freedom the simple fact of not being a slave, emancipation thrust blacks into a kind of no-man's land, a partial freedom that made a mockery of the American ideal of equal citizenship.

Yet by the same token the ultimate outcome underscores the uniqueness of Reconstruction itself. Alone among the societies that abolished slavery in the nineteenth century, the United States, for a moment, offered the freedmen a measure of political control over their own destinies. However brief its sway, Reconstruction allowed scope for a remarkable political and social mobilization of the black community. It opened doors of opportunity that could never be completely closed. Reconstruction transformed the lives of Southern blacks in ways unmeasurable by statistics and unreachable by law. It raised their expectations and aspirations, redefined their status in relation to the larger society, and allowed space for the creation of institutions that enabled them to survive the repression that followed. And it established constitutional principles of civil and political equality that, while flagrantly violated after Redemption, planted the seeds of future struggle.

Certainly, in terms of the sense of possibility with which it opened, Reconstruction failed. But as Du Bois observed, it was a "splendid failure." For its animating vision—a society in which social advancement would be open to all on the basis of individual merit, not inherited caste distinctions—is as old as America itself and remains relevant to a nation still grappling with the unresolved legacy of emancipation.

Eric Foner is Professor of History at Columbia University and author of Nothing but Freedom: Emancipation and Its Legacy.

From *American Heritage*, October/November 1983, pp. 10–15. Reprinted by permission of American Heritage, Inc., a division of Forbes, Inc.

1871 War on Terror

In the aftermath of the Civil War, America's federal authorities took unprecedented action to crack down on the Ku Klux Klan.

By David Everitt

Secret cells of violent zealots target civilians in their homes and workplaces. When not carrying out terrorist acts, they conceal themselves among the general population, aided by local officials. As waves of fear spread, an American president decides the time has come to strike back.

A description of recent world events? Not necessarily. The scenario also fits another time in America's history. The campaign against Al Qaeda and its allies is not the United States' first war on terror. In the American South during the aftermath of the Civil War, a terrorist organization emerged. Cloaked in ghostly disguise, it sought to murder and maim in the dead of night as it set out to impose its ideological agenda. For several years the governmental response was ineffectual. Finally, in 1871, the U.S. Congress and President Ulysses S. Grant took action and initiated a new policy in South Carolina, where the organization was especially brazen. The government took extraordinary—some said excessive—measures to crack down on the brutal crimes of this terrorist group, the Reconstruction-era Ku Klux Klan.

Some of the issues surrounding this 19th-century war on terror are reminiscent of those we face now. Like George W. Bush's today, Grant's administration was criticized for overstepping its authority and for not understanding the true nature of the problem. In the end, the offensive that Grant launched against the Klan produced some very tangible results, but the ultimate success of his effort is still open to debate.

Terrorism thrives on great turmoil, and in the conquered and humiliated South it found an ideal breeding ground. Reconstruction upended society as white Southerners knew it, not only freeing blacks from slavery but also providing opportunity for their advancement in both business and government. Enraged by those developments, many Southern white men looked for some way to lash out at emancipated slaves and their white supporters. More than that, they hoped to restore the old order. For them, the Ku Klux Klan was the answer.

In 1868, the Klan was imported to South Carolina from Tennessee, where it had originated earlier that same year. The organization immediately demonstrated it would not tolerate former slaves exercising their right to vote. During the 1868 South Carolina election campaign, the Klan murdered eight blacks, two of them state congressmen.

The state government controlled by Republicans—the party of Abraham Lincoln—met the terrorist threat by raising a special militia and filling its ranks with black citizens. That proved to be dramatic enough to inflame the Klan, but not strong enough to defeat it.

During the 1870 election campaign, the new militia countered the Klan's intimidation tactics to some extent, and the ballot results enraged Klan members even further when the Republican governor, Robert Scott, was re-elected. The next day, South Carolina's wave of terror truly began.

South Carolina was by no means the only state plagued by Klan violence—the organization was active throughout the South—but in portions of South Carolina the acts of terror were especially alarming between the fall of 1870 and the summer of 1871. A public Klan proclamation announced that the organization's targets were "the scum of the earth, the scrapings of creation" and that they intended to do everything possible to oppose "negro rule, black bayonets, and a miserably degraded and thievish set of lawmakers." Over a nine-month period in South Carolina's York County alone, six murders were attributed to the Ku Klux Klan, while whippings and beatings might have numbered in the hundreds.

One of the most notoriously brutal cases was the murder of a black man named Tom Roundtree. The Klan shot him to death, then mutilated his body and sank it in a nearby stream. Other infamous crimes involved the black militia, an especially hated target of the Klan. In one instance, in Unionville, Klansmen lynched 10 black militiamen who had been jailed for the murder of a whiskey peddler. In another case, in the town of Yorkville, a black militia captain named Jim Williams allegedly issued a threat against whites in the area. The Klan dragged him from his house and hanged him. On his dangling body they left a card on which they had written "Jim Williams on his big muster."

The Klan cast a wide net and showed little mercy for those unlikely to be able to defend themselves. One of their whipping victims was a 69-year-old white man who had offended the Klan by acting as a Republican election officer, and another was a black preacher, incapacitated from birth by stunted arms and legs, who was charged with rabble-rousing from the pulpit. At times the Klansmen also took it upon themselves to punish what they considered domestic offenses. In an incident that would have pleased today's religiously fanatic terrorists, for example, Ku Kluxers in Spartanburg County once whipped a woman for the crime of leaving her husband.

As indefensible as the Klan's actions surely were, apologists for those acts were plentiful, and they did not necessarily come from the South.

As indefensible as the Klan's actions surely were, apologists for those acts were plentiful, and they did not necessarily come from the South. Sometimes their statements echo reactions to modern terrorism that we've heard in recent years. Certain pundits in the early 1870s, for instance, offered the terrorists-as-freedom-fighters rationalization. On the floor of the U.S. Congress, Representative S.S. Cox from New York argued that "South Carolina has been infested by the worst local government ever vouchsafed to a people." Comparing the Klan to the Carbonari, which fought for constitutional government in Italy during the early 1800s, Cox concluded, "All history shows that such societies grow by persecution and that they are the bitter fruits of tyranny." Even those in the South who criticized Klan excesses only did so because they considered them counterproductive as opposed to immoral, similar to the way some Middle Easterners today have criticized suicide bombers because they don't help the Palestinian cause, not because the acts themselves are unspeakable.

In the North, newspapers often minimized the Klan threat. A *New York Times* editorial stated that when there weren't enough real Klan atrocities to report, "the matter was put into the hands of literary gentlemen who thereupon started armed bands in all directions through the newspaper woods, dragged out newspaper negroes from newspaper homes, and, tying them up to trees of the mind, lashed their newspaper backs till blood ran down, awful to behold."

With little support for a forceful response, Governor Scott tried appeasing the South Carolina Klan. In February 1871, he disarmed York County's black militia, hoping that this would persuade the Klan to stop its raids. But the Ku Kluxers responded to that gesture as if it were a sign of weakness—they resorted to even more violence. At his wits' end, Scott requested help from Washington, and in March President Grant sent in federal troops.

The soldiers assigned to South Carolina belonged to the 7th Cavalry, Lt. Col. (Brevet Maj. Gen.) George Armstrong Custer's regiment, which had recently fought the Cheyennes on the Great Plains. The troops were headquartered in York County, the center for much of the Klan activity in the state, and they were commanded by 37-year-old Major Lewis M. Merrill. At first skeptical of the seemingly alarmist accounts of the KKK, Merrill soon became convinced of the basic truth of the allegations and would go on to play a crucial role in combating terrorism in the state.

Merrill quickly discovered that he faced great obstacles. Like terrorist organizations today, the Klan was highly compartmentalized. Klan chiefs had no direct contact with underlings, making it difficult for the Army to collect evidence against ringleaders. And even after Merrill and his men collected information on subordinates, local authorities sabotaged any effort to win a conviction in court. As Merrill later described it, "I never conceived of such a state of social disorganization being possible in any civilized community." Still, he continued to investigate in the hope that the federal government would find a way to bring the terrorists to justice.

In May 1870, Congress had passed the Enforcement Act, which had attempted to prevent the Klan from violating citizens' constitutional protections, but the law produced little result. Now, in 1871, Republicans in Congress considered passing a much stronger bill.

The Ku Klux Act, as it came to be called, targeted people who "conspire together, or go in disguise upon any public highway, or upon the premises of another" for the purpose of depriving any citizens of their legal rights. The bill authorized President Grant to dismantle those conspiracies in no uncertain terms: He could, in effect, place an area under martial law and suspend the writ of habeas corpus, which would allow authorities to imprison suspected Klansmen for extended periods of time without bringing them to court to face formal charges.

Democrats charged that the methods of enforcement amounted to tyrannical, unconstitutional powers. In rebuttal, Representative Robert B. Elliott, a black Republican from South Carolina, drew his fellow legislators' attention to more basic Constitutional protections. He pointed out that the Constitution states, "The United States shall guarantee to every State in the Union a republican form of government." States like South Carolina were denied this type of government, Elliott's argument went, as long as terrorists threatened citizens' right to vote. Strong as his case might have been, it could not overcome the congressional bickering that gridlocked the bill. What was needed was the moral authority of President Grant. The Ku Klux Act finally became law on April 20, only after Grant publicly urged Congress to ratify it.

Now, Major Merrill's efforts had a chance of making a difference. That summer, he testified before a congressional subcommittee that arrived in South Carolina to investigate the extent of Klan outrages in the state. The intelligence Merrill had gathered on whippings, beatings and murders painted a disturbing portrait for the congressmen.

'I never conceived of such a state of social disorganization being possible in any civilized community.' —Major Lewis M. Merrill

During their four-week tour of the state, the congressmen could see for themselves how desperate the situation had become. Refugees from Klan violence congregated wherever the subcommittee convened. Many of them, both white and black, had been spending their nights in the woods for months to avoid Ku Klux attacks. According to a *New York Times* report, "It was found impossible for the Committee to examine more than a small part of the crowds of whipped, maimed, or terror-stricken wretches who flocked in upon hearing of their coming."

Pressing the case for forceful action was Grant's attorney general, Amos T. Akerman. A scalawag, according to conventional Southern wisdom of the day, Akerman was a transplanted Northerner who had spent his adult life as a citizen of Georgia and was now a staunch supporter of Reconstruction. He went to South Carolina to conduct his own investigation in late September and concluded that the Klan could be smashed quickly if the government took decisive steps that would rattle rank-and-file Ku Kluxers and convince them to confess. As Klan raids continued, Akerman met with Grant in early October and helped persuade him that the time had come to activate the Ku Klux Act's enforcement measures.

On October 12, Grant ordered the South Carolina Klan to disperse and disarm in five days. The warning was ignored. On October 17, Grant proclaimed that "in my judgment the public safety especially requires that the privileges of the writ of habeas corpus be suspended." The suspension applied to all arrests made by U.S. marshals and federal troops in nine of the state's western counties.

Akerman immediately met with Merrill to assemble a list of Klansmen to be arrested, based on information gathered by the major over the previous seven months. Their strategy was to hit several towns suddenly and simultaneously, with teams of federal marshals backed up by the 7th Cavalry, in order to instill panic throughout the organization. The plan could not have worked better.

Within 10 days of Grant's proclamation, marshals and troops made 100 arrests in York and Spartanburg counties. Many more Klansmen came in on their own, and by the end of November federal officials in South Carolina had made 600 arrests in all. A large number of those were very willing to "puke," the colorful slang term in those days for confess. There were 160 confessions in York County alone, and in the process investigators learned of five murders that had previously gone unreported. The federal crackdown had such a profound effect that York's county seat had "the

look of a town in wartime recently captured by an invading army," according to a *New York Tribune* correspondent.

Louis F. Post, an aide to Merrill, contended that the mass confessions were the direct result of the suspension of habeas corpus. "For a time the prisoners were silent," he wrote. "But as hope of release died out and fears of hanging grew stronger, the weaker ones sought permission to tell Major Merrill what they knew."

Some editorialists saw grave dangers in the government's actions. Similar to some of today's critics of the war on terrorism, these people claimed that the government's aggressiveness was only making more enemies. "I shudder to think," wrote a *New York Herald* correspondent, "what the retaliation will be [from the Klan] for the imprisoning of two hundred white men and the driving from their homes of three or four hundred others."

To be precise, hundreds of South Carolinians were not driven from their homes—they fled to avoid prosecution. This was both good news and bad. True, the flight of so many Ku Kluxers disrupted the organization, but the fugitives included some of the most prominent Klan chiefs. Federal prosecutors would only be able, for the most part, to press charges against the organization's underlings. Still, Akerman believed that convictions of these men would send a strong warning to anyone considering further Klan raids.

The Ku Klux court cases began November 27, 1871, in the U.S. Circuit Court in the South Carolina capital of Columbia. The first to go on trial was farmer Robert Hayes Mitchell, an ordinary, subordinate Klansmen whose case provided an extraordinary glimpse into the inner workings of the KKK and two of its most notorious crimes.

Like other defendants who followed, Mitchell was charged with conspiracy to prevent black citizens from voting. To illustrate the nature of the conspiracy, prosecutors called on one witness to outline the elaborate series of signs and passwords that Ku Kluxers used to identify one another and maintain security. The government also presented testimony on the Klan constitution. Acquired at Merrill's instigation, the document revealed the organization's deadly oath of secrecy: Anyone breaking this oath, the constitution stated, "shall meet the fearful penalty and traitor's doom, which is death, death, death."

Specific instances of conspiracy included the murder of Captain Jim Williams of the black militia. Klan supporters maintained that the organization's raids had been provoked by militia excesses, which typically amounted to arrogant, intimidating behavior. Federal prosecutors, though, established in court that the Klan had first resorted to violence two years before the black militia was formed in 1870.

Another count of conspiracy against Mitchell involved the assault against a black man named Amzi Rainey who had offended the Klan by voting for radical Republicans. The victim's testimony dramatized the savagery of the attack. Crashing into Rainey's house around midnight, the Klan beat not only Rainey but also his wife. At one point Rainey's little daughter ran at the Klansmen, yelling, "Don't kill my pappy; please don't kill my pappy!" One of the attackers responded by firing a shot that grazed the little girl's forehead.

'In my judgement the public safety especially requires that the privileges of the writ of habeas corpus be suspended.' —U.S. Grant

In his summation for the defense, attorney Reverdy Johnson saw no point in trying to dispute the charges of Klan violence, conceding that the outrages "show that the parties engaged were brutes, insensible to the obligations of humanity and religion." Instead, he argued that the Enforcement Act of 1870 and the Ku Klux Act were unconstitutional. The argument made little impression on the jury of 10 blacks and two whites who took only 38 minutes to bring in a guilty verdict.

Through the month of December, similar verdicts followed, along with a procession of guilty pleas. In pronouncing sentences, Judge Hugh L. Bond brought a finely tuned moral voice to the proceedings, showing both leniency for unsophisticated men pressured into the Klan ranks and severity for those who exercised some degree of authority. The most common of the 58 prison sentences ranged from three to six months, while others entailed both prison time and some sort of fine.

The most severe was a combination of five years and $1,000, reserved for the likes of Klan chief John W. Mitchell, a prominent member of his community and somebody, Judge Bond asserted, who should have known better. In his sentencing, the judge stressed Mitchell's abdication of responsibility: "Knowing all this [about the Klan's activities], hearing of the ravishing, murders and whipping going on in York County, you never took any pains to inform anybody; you never went to the civil authorities and you remained a chief till they elected somebody else."

The federal crackdown did not stop there. Through 1872, Major Merrill continued to make arrests, and in April the federal court in Charleston delivered 36 more convictions. At the same time, though—as critics branded Grant a dictator—the government began to back off.

Attorney General Akerman resigned in January 1872, and though his exit was amicable on the surface, some have speculated that he was frustrated by the lack of funding for ongoing Klan prosecutions. His replacement was less concerned with Klan violence, even though a federal marshal was killed in South Carolina while enforcing the Ku Klux Act, and a prosecution witness had his throat slit. Further impeding the anti-Klan campaign was Congress' decision in 1872 to restore habeas corpus rights. By August,

the federal government began pardoning convicted Ku Kluxers. The government's war on Ku Klux Klan terror came to a definitive end in 1877, when President Rutherford B. Hayes ordered the end of Reconstruction.

Looking back upon this episode, we can see that the Grant administration faced two especially difficult questions that confront us today as once again we wage a war on terror. First, how much should the government limit constitutional rights when fighting an enemy that does not respect the rights of others? By imposing federal authority on local jurisdictions and suspending the writ of habeas corpus, the Grant administration was taking unprecedented measures in peacetime to deal with a dire crisis. In 1876, five years after the first Klan prosecutions, the U.S. Supreme Court ruled that the Enforcement Act of 1870 and the Ku Klux Act were indeed unconstitutional, that they had improperly superceded the rights of the states.

The second question is: How does one know when a war on terror is truly won? Although the Klan prosecutions did not last long, some historians maintain that they accomplished their immediate goal. According to Allen W. Trelease, author of *White Terror*, "The federal government had broken the back of the Ku Klux Klan throughout most of the South." And it is true that the Klan did not rise again until after World War I, some 50 years later. But the Grant administration left larger goals unrealized. Even though the outer trappings of the Klan might have disappeared, its attitudes and the willingness to impose those attitudes through violence remained. And once Reconstruction ended and the passage of repressive Jim Crow laws began, white supremacy reigned once again throughout the South. Jim Crow would continue to rule for another 80 years, until the dawn of the modern civil rights movement.

Union forces won the Civil War against the Confederacy. President Grant's marshals and troops won the battle against the Reconstruction-era Klan. Nevertheless, the federal government failed to see its war on terror as a long-term commitment, and it failed to come up with a practical plan for rebuilding the South and bringing the Old Confederacy into the modern, fully democratic age. As a consequence, some might say that the North ultimately failed to win the peace.

Little Bighorn Reborn

With a new Indian memorial, the site of Custer's last stand draws descendants of victors and vanquished alike

Tony Perrottet

"**A** BEAUTIFUL PLACE...," I murmured to no one in particular, gazing down from a hilltop to cottonwood forests on both sides of a lazy river. A woman at my side finished the thought: "...to die."

A touch morbid for an exchange between strangers? Perhaps, but this was not just any hill top or any day. We were part of a small crowd gathered on Last Stand Hill on the 128th anniversary of the West's most famous battle. A few feet away, in the gently swaying grass, dozens of bone-white headstones mark the military's best guesstimates of where 42 of the Seventh Cavalry soldiers fell that June 25, 1876, some having held out behind a breastwork made of their dead horses. In the center of the markers, next to a small American flag, lay the headstone of their flamboyant, controversial leader, Lt. Col. George Armstrong Custer.

Still, on that clear, sunny summer morning, it seemed hard to believe that this quiet corner of Montana had been the scene of desperate hand-to-hand combat, when Custer and 209 men under his command were wiped out by the combined forces of the Sioux, Cheyenne and Arapaho Indians.

And then a voice rang out in the distance: "Here they come!"

Suddenly, the earth began to quiver, and the breeze carried shrill cries—*yip, yip, yip*. Bursting from behind Battle Ridge thundered 100 Lakota on horseback. Several were carrying wooden staffs adorned with colored tassels and eagle feathers, the sacred war standards of the Sioux (a name assigned to several Indian tribes, including the Lakota, who find the term offensive). For a moment, 128 years dissolved, and we were given a pale glimpse of the emotions those U.S. cavalrymen must have felt when they realized what Custer, hoping to attack an Indian camp before it could scatter, had led them into. On that fateful morning—a suffocatingly hot day—the entire valley ba-

sin had been covered with tepees, part of the largest Indian force on record. Custer and the five companies he was leading were surrounded and annihilated.

The news of Custer's defeat reached American cities just after jubilant Fourth of July centennial celebrations had concluded, stunning the nation. How could a group of "uncivilized" Indians have wiped out a modern military force, killing even a decorated Civil War hero?

Now, as I stood on Last Stand Hill, history seemed to have come full circle. Another 27 Lakota horsemen, these led by descendants of Crazy Horse, the most revered of the Sioux warriors at the 1876 battle, had ridden 360 miles in two weeks from their South Dakota reservation. They had followed the same route as their ancestors, and were now praying for their dead killed at the battle at an impressive new Indian memorial, just 50 yards northwest of Last Stand Hill. Dedicated in 2003, the memorial is a circular earth-and-stonework balustrade, with a weeping wall, interpretive panels and an elegant sculpture of Spirit Warriors—spirits of the Indian soldiers that were protecting the village that day

UNTIL RECENTLY, the Great Sioux Nation Victory Ride—let alone the crowds of Native Americans participating in the anniversary festivities—would have been hard to imagine here. Indians "used to believe they weren't really welcome," said Tim McCleary, 42, a historian formerly at the battlefield who now teaches at Little Bighorn College. "And not surprisingly. All the interpretation was from the U.S. cavalry point of view." Kenneth Medicine Bull, a member of the Northern Cheyenne Nation visiting the battlefield, nodded in agreement. "Before, this place felt like it was a tribute to Custer," he said. "Nothing even mentioned the Cheyenne and Sioux."

Today, for Indians and whites alike, the June anniversary has become a three-day extravaganza of religious services, academic symposia and general whooping it up. (There is not one but two reenactments of the battle, held by rival groups.) After the Sioux had ridden off, John Doerner, the park's official historian, told me that there are still visitors who believe Custer was an American martyr who died to tame the Indians as well as Custerphobes who consider him a war criminal. But the arguments over the site no longer carry the same venom they did in the 1970s, when the American Indian Movement disrupted memorial services here by carrying a flag upside down across the battlefield, singing "Custer Died for Your Sins."

"The shouts have died down to whispers now," Doerner said. "Time heals all."

BACK IN 1876, the first U.S. Army reports of the site sanitized the grisly fate of Custer's men. Lt. James H. Bradley arrived two days after the battle to help identify the slain officers and bury the dead. Not wishing to further upset the families of the fallen, he described for the *Helena Herald* an almost pastoral scene where few soldiers had been scalped and Custer's body was "that of a man who had fallen asleep and enjoyed peaceful dreams." But another eyewitness, Gen. Edward S. Godfrey, privately admitted that the reality was "a sickening, ghastly horror." Some soldiers had been stripped, scalped and mutilated. Many had had their genitals severed, some say in retaliation for the genital mutilation of Indian men and women by soldiers in previous battles. The burial party was not only sickened by the carnage but feared further attacks. With only a handful of shovels, the men hastily threw dirt over the dead, dug a shallow grave for Custer and beat a hasty retreat.

A year would pass before a second detail would come to remove the bodies of 11 officers and 2 civilians and send them to Eastern graveyards. (Indians had removed their dead shortly after the battle.) By now, as Lt. John G. Bourke noted, "pieces of clothing, soldiers' hats, cavalry coats, boots with the leather legs cut off, but with the human feet and bones still sticking in them, strewed the hill." Custer's shallow grave had been disturbed. After misidentifying one skeleton as Custer's—a blouse upon which the remains were lying identified it as belonging to a corporal—the party chose another. "I think we got the right body the second time," one member of the detail, Sgt. Michael Caddle, recalled in a letter to a historian; but another eyewitness remembered the commanding officer muttering: "Nail the box up; it is alright as long as the people think so."

The first actual sightseers at Little Bighorn were Indians. In the winter of 1876, Wooden Leg, a Cheyenne warrior and a veteran of the battle, led a nine-man hunting party to the desolate spot. Acting as tour guide, he and the group rode through hills still strewn with unexpended gun cartridges, spears, arrows and the bleached bones of cavalrymen.

Two years later, 25 recently surrendered Sioux and Cheyenne veterans provided a battlefield tour for Col. Nelson A. Miles, commander of Fort Keogh, in Montana, and a personal friend of the Custer family; who sought "the attainment of the Indian narrative of the engagement." As 400,000 visitors a year learn today, the battle involved more than just the cinematic debacle on Last Stand Hill. Early in the afternoon of June 25, Custer sent one of his three battalions, led by Maj. Marcus Reno, to attack the Indian encampment from the south. Repulsed, Reno retreated across Little Bighorn River to the bluffs beyond to be joined by a second battalion led by Capt. Frederick Benteen. The force dug in four miles southwest of Last Stand Hill, where they held out overnight against Indian attacks. After a harrowing siege, tormented by thirst and picked at by sniper fire, the soldiers saw the Indians withdraw the next afternoon; the battalions had suffered 53 killed and 52 wounded. Some 380 survived.

In 1879, the battle site fell under the jurisdiction of the War Department, and that year troops from the nearby Fort Custer erected a rough log memorial on the crest of Last Stand Hill. Native American visitation waned. The Indians who had won the battle had lost the war, and with it the right to interpret the past. Back East, Custer was turned into a hero.

It was not until 1881 that the bones of the remaining cavalrymen and their horses were finally gathered by hand into a mass grave, over which a 36,000-pound granite memorial was erected. Even then, the job was hardly thorough: in 1925, a decapitated skeleton of a trooper in Reno's command was found near the modern-day hamlet of Garryowen; another, wearing an Army tunic, was exposed in a shallow grave on Reno Hill in 1958.

The memorial, and the growing popularity of the automobile, brought more tourists to Little Bighorn. But it was not until the 1926 semicentennial of the battle that a major event was staged at the site: 50,000 people showed up, including western film star William S. Hart, to participate in services and watch a reenactment. There was an official burying of the hatchet ceremony in which General Godfrey, who had fought with Benteen and White Bull, Sitting Bull's nephew, came together to erase old hatreds. Bull gave Godfrey a blanket, and Godfrey gave White Bull an American flag. The tomahawk was buried in the grave of the soldier found the year before, as a symbolic gesture. But to some in the predominantly white audience, the ceremony suggested that the Indians had accepted domination by the white man.

About this time, Nellie Beaverheart, daughter of possibly the only Indian chief killed at the battle, Lame White Man, asked for a marker from the War Department at the place where he died. The request was ignored until the 1950s, when the National Park Service, now administering the site, erected a wooden marker. Still, it took until the 1970s—with the publication of works such as Dee Brown's poignant *Bury My Heart at Wounded Knee*—for the winds of cultural change to stir the battlefield. In 1991, Barbara Sutteer, the first Native American superintendent of the site, oversaw the name change, long requested by Indians, from Custer Battlefield to Little Bighorn Battlefield National Monument. An 11-member Indian memorial design committee, authorized by the same legislation, oversaw the design and content of a memorial. A sculpture, in an opening in the north wall of the memorial, was based on the pictograph drawings of White Bird, a Cheyenne warrior who had participated in the battle at age 15. It consists of three horsemen crafted from thick black wire, representing warriors riding out to defend the Indian village from Custer's attack; a fourth figure, a woman running alongside and passing up a shield to one of the soldiers, emphasizes the importance of women in Indian life. Within the circular earthworks of the memorial, designed by Philadelphians John R. Collins and Allison J. Towers, are interpretive panels about the Native American groups. A symbolic "spirit gate" welcomes the Indians' and soldiers' spirits.

I met Sutteer, who works today as a consultant on Native American issues, at the Hardin Dairy Queen. A soft-spoken woman in her 60s, she told me she had received death threats for wanting to introduce Native American viewpoints to the site. "Of course, the battlefield has been sacred to the Indians far longer than for white people," she told me. "The quality of the grass made it an excellent hunting place. That's one reason the groups had camped here in 1876."

The attention to Indian history at the monument has highlighted some complexities of Native American culture. "White people often take Native Americans as a single monolithic culture," says Tim McCleary. The Crow and Arikara were actually on Custer's side, working as scouts. They regarded the Sioux, Cheyenne and Arapaho as invaders of their homeland. "The opportunity to kill Sioux with the assistance of the U.S. military was really inviting," McCleary goes on, adding that the Arikara remain proud of their role as U.S. Army allies. To the Cheyenne and Sioux, on the other hand, the Battle of Little Bighorn climaxed long resistance to white incursions, and to this day they resent the favoritism they believe the government showed the Crow. (They also resent that the site of their greatest victory is on Crow land, adds McCleary, which allows Crow guides to give "Native American" tours. As for the Crow, they felt that the reservation they were given after the battle was too small and regard the creation of the Northern Cheyenne reservation right next door to their traditional home—with a slice of their original reservation carved off for their enemies—as a pointed insult.

These ancient rivalries still spill onto the battlefield today. Since 1999, five red-granite headstones have been placed to mark spots where Sioux and Cheyenne warriors fell, counterparts to white tablets erected for the men of the Seventh Cavalry in 1890. But their inscriptions, saying that each warrior "Died in Defense of His Homeland," enrage the Crow, who argue that the battle was actually on *their* homeland. "The Sioux and Cheyenne were migrating onto our land from the east and the Arapaho from the south," says Marvin Dawes, a Crow Indian historian.

"Shall we say, they were passing through. They were visitors in the area."

WHEN I GOT TO HARDIN, a lonely looking, hard-bitten prairie town with a string of boarded-up bars, the place was getting ready for the anniversary that keeps its economy alive. Every hotel room was booked, and reenactors wearing bluecoats and war paint thronged the streets.

The day of the anniversary, I got to the battlefield before dawn to see, along with about 50 others, seven Cheyenne elders in cowboy hats and dark glasses conduct a peace ceremony at the Indian memorial. Donlin Many Bad Horses lit a wooden pipe and said: "When things were bad for us, we could not do this. There were times when we could not come in here. But now a door has opened to us. We can come in and worship and pray. I hope this opening will continue to grow."

One morning a couple of days later, I met Ernie Lapointe, a great-grandson of Sitting Bull. "For many years," he said, "the Lakota, Cheyenne, Arapahos, everyone didn't like the Crow. We're natural enemies. But it's time now to settle those differences, to heal all those wounds." He told me that Sitting Bull had had a vision before the battle that "told him our warriors shouldn't take the spoils of war, or injure the dead—but they did. That's why we're oppressed to this day—by the losers in the battle!"

"WHO WANTS TO SEE Custer get killed?" a man with a loudspeaker asked the thousand-strong crowd at the longest-running reenactment of the battle, hosted by the mostly white businesses of Hardin on a dusty plain just outside town. "Y–e-s-s-s!" came the roar from the bleachers, as bluecoats on horseback rode out from a wooden fort. Next to me sat Joy Austin, the wife of Tony Austin, a 50-year-old postman now living in British Columbia who plays Custer. I asked how she felt about watching her husband die three times a day. "It's OK," she answered. "The only place I get choked up is when he leads the column of soldiers over the hill. You know that he and everyone else who rides with him won't be returning."

A Crow Indian, Joe Medicine Crow, wrote the script for this reenactment. It is based, he says, on interviews with a Cheyenne veteran of the battle, with echoes of the 1940 Errol Flynn film *They Died With Their Boots On*, and emphasizes reconciliation. "In this Battle of the Little Bighorn, there were no victors. …We red men and white men live in a united fortress of democracy, the United States of America."

Afterward, I went to the rival reenactment—hosted by the Real Bird family of Crow Indians by the Little Bighorn River—where I ran into Jason Heitland, who portrayed a federal soldier. "I'm going to fight here every year until I'm too old to do it," he told me breathlessly as we wandered among replica military tents by a shady creek.

"You're fighting on the actual battlefield! You sleep where the actual Indian camp was, where the Cheyenne dog soldiers slept. And the battle itself is totally unscripted. You've got whooping Indians coming from all directions. It's quite a thrill."

"And the horses don't know it's fake," added Nicola Sgro, a coffee salesman from Michigan in his late-30s. "That's why it's so dangerous!"

By dusk on Sunday, after the last shot had been fired and the last memorial wreath had been laid, the battlefield had returned to its eerie silence. Visiting the site one last time, I was left with a sense of sadness for those on both sides—cavalrymen who were paid $13 a month to risk their scalps in an alien land, and Indian warriors desperately trying to preserve their nomadic way of life. "This was Custer's last stand," said John Doerner, "but it was also the last stand of the Indians. Within a year after the Little Bighorn, there wasn't a truly free Indian left on the plains."

Tony Perrottet, a New York-based travel writer, is the author of Pagan Holiday *and* The Naked Olympics.

THE SPARK OF GENIUS

Thomas Edison created the first light bulb 125 years ago. But he was not only America's greatest inventor. He was also a master entrepreneur

HAROLD EVANS

It sits in isolation on a slope in the middle of a cow pasture, a two-story white clapboard house surrounded by a picket fence. Approached from the front, it looks like an ordinary home, with high sash windows, a gracefully arched porch ascended by sagging wooden steps, and a little balustraded balcony above. The first surprise is how far back the house extends. From the modest 30-foot facade, it runs at least 100 feet to the fringe of a virgin forest.

It is late on a winter's night in 1876. There is snow on the ground, and wood smoke curls from two brick chimneys. Inside, up the dark, uncarpeted stairs, a big bare-boarded room lit by gas jets and kerosene lamps stretches the building's full 100 feet. Its ceiling is laced with wire and piping, its walls lined floor to roof with jars of liquids and bottles of powder of every color. A rack in the center of the room is stacked with galvanic batteries, and every other nook and surface is covered with bits of copper, brass, lead, and tinfoil; crucibles, phials, and small darkened panes of glass; microscopes, spectrometers, telegraph keys, and galvanometers; rubber tubing and wax and small disks of some obscure material. At scattered workbenches and heaped-up tables there are a dozen young men engrossed in what they are doing: A bearded pair observe a spark jumping from an electromagnet to a metal lever; another boils a smelly chemical; another has his ear to some kind of telephone receiver; another, chewing tobacco, bends his head to frown at the needle on an instrument. In the far corner, stretched out on the floor amid a score of open books, is a pale young man with a mop of brown hair and stains on his hands, entirely lost to this world because he is concentrating on making a new one.

This is Thomas Alva Edison at 30. If we stay long enough, we will see him uncoil his shabby 5 feet, 8 inches and, stooping slightly, move slowly among the workbenches, cupping an ear to listen to observations on the night's work, reaching over to tweak an instrument, breaking out in laughter as one of the fellows makes a joke at his expense. His black frock coat and waistcoat are dusty, and a white silk handkerchief around his neck is tied in a careless knot over the stiff bosom of a white shirt rather the worse for wear, but what stands out is the extreme brightness of his eyes.

Around midnight he and his comrades in discovery will settle in front of a blazing fire for pie, ham, crackers, smoked herring, and beer. There is as likely to be a competition in mocking doggerel or crude cartoons as a debate on the proper expression of Newton's law of gravitation. Someone, maybe Edison himself if he has had a good day, will blast out a melody on a huge pipe organ at the end of the big room and they will raise the rafters singing sentimental (and censorable) ditties. Then they will all go back to their benches and books until the early hours while down the hill in Edison's farmhouse home, Mary Edison, his wife and the mother of two of his children, will have given up and gone to sleep with a revolver under her pillow. One late night soon a disheveled Edison will forget his keys, climb onto the roof, and let himself in through an open bedroom window. Mary, ever fearful of intruders, will nearly shoot him with her .38 Smith & Wesson. In the words of his journal, he will again "resolve to work daytimes and stay home nights," but he cannot keep a promise to himself when his head is filled working out the complexities standing between a panoramic vision and the steps to its realization.

Thomas Edison was America's most productive inventor in the 19th century and remains so into the 21st. His 1,093 patents are by no means the proper measure of the man. To Edison, the patents were the easy part, before "the long, laborious trouble of working them out and producing apparatus which is commercial"—and then fighting off the pirates. Edison's greatness lies not in any single invention, not even in the whole panoply, but in what he did with his own and other men's cleverness.

The invention for which he is most remembered, the incandescent bulb, is emblematic. The technology was a marked advance over the work of other inventors, but the piercing vision—and it was Edison's alone—was how he would bring light and power to millions of homes and offices. The historian Ruth Cowan writes that Edison from the beginning wanted to build a technological system *and* a series of businesses to manage that system. By the time he applied for any patent, Edison had already envisaged how he could translate the invention into a tangible, commercial product; indeed, he would not begin the research otherwise. Still, he was a classic innovator. "Only Leonardo da Vinci evokes the inventive spirit as impressively," writes the historian Thomas Hughes, "but, unlike Edison, Leonardo actually constructed only a few of his brilliant conceptions." Purists might respond that Leonardo was on his own whereas Edison had clever men at his beck and call—but what a sensible notion that was! One man could hardly hope to keep up with the efflorescence of knowledge in the sciences and the profusion of new techniques and new materials. In the decades after 1870, when industrialization in manufacturing superseded the machine-shop culture, it was quite brilliant to

finance and focus multidisciplinary research in an organized manner with the deliberate intention of manufacturing the results. The momentum by which the United States surpassed Britain as the greatest industrial power near the turn of the century was in significant part due to the culture of research and development. In the year Edison was born, 1847, only 495 inventors won patents; in the year of his 40th birthday, he had more than 20,000 lesser mortals for company.

LITTLE AL, AS HE WAS CALLED then, did not do well at school. At the age of 8, in 1855, Edison was described by a teacher as "a little addled." Edison himself recalled, "I was always at the foot of the class. I used to feel that the teachers did not sympathize with me." Part of the trouble was that he missed years of lessons because of a series of infections, one of which seriously damaged his hearing. He was also ill-suited to rote learning; he could reach understanding only by doing and making.

His father, Sam, was a handsome jack-of-all-trades of Dutch extraction who became a lighthouse keeper on moving his family to Port Huron, Mich., in 1854. He had endless schemes for getting rich that never quite came off, but the little family was comfortable by the standards of the day, if erratically in debt. But it was Al's very protective mother, Nancy, a devout Presbyterian (who always dressed in black in memory of three children dead in infancy), who would be the boy's salvation. She divined that Al had a visual imagination and unusual powers of reasoning, and made it her business to take him out of the school that found him defective. She read him classics like Gibbon's *Decline and Fall of the Roman Empire* and Sear's *History of the World*, and when he kept asking questions she could not answer (*What is electricity? What is pitch made of?*) she put into his hands, at the age of 9, R. G. Parker's *A School Compendium of Natural and Experimental Philosophy*. It illustrated simple home experiments in chemistry and electricity, and Al attempted every one of them. When he left school for good at 13, a boy with a large head and jutting jaw, Alva was "dead set on being an engineer of a locomotive."

His first job was to climb aboard a train at Port Huron at 7 a.m. with copies of the Detroit *Free Press* to sell to passengers on the three-hour journey to Detroit and back. The budding entrepreneur persuaded the conductor to let him store berries, fruit, and vegetables, as well as sandwiches and peanuts, and deputized two other boys to sell the food for him. He also made a cheeky habit of walking into the composing room of the *Free Press* to find out what the next day's headlines would be, and a year into the Civil War, on April 6, 1862, he scored a coup. A proof of next day's sensational front page reported that as many as 60,000 might be dead in a battle at Shiloh (actual deaths were 24,000). He had enough money to buy only 300 papers but talked his way into the sanctum of the fierce managing editor, Wilbur F. Storey, and got 1,000 copies on credit. Edison had already bribed officials at the railroad office to telegraph the fact that there had been a battle to every train station on the way back to Port Huron. He was mobbed at the first stop, raised prices at every station thereafter, and ended with a sell-out auction—and the princely sum of around $150. "I determined at once to be a telegrapher," he recalled later.

His luck was in. Late that summer, he plucked a 3-year-old boy from the path of a boxcar, and the grateful father—the railroad's stationmaster—offered telegraph lessons as a reward. Five months later, Al—now to be called Tom—began wandering Middle America as one of the hundreds of young "tramp" telegraph operators. In demand because so many telegraphers had been called into the armies on both sides, the tramps were fond of gambling, cursing, drinking, smoking, playing jokes, and carousing with women. Edison chewed tobacco ceaselessly, gambled a little, and played practical jokes, but he spent most of his spare time reading in lonely boardinghouse rooms and fiddling with telegraph equipment in railway stations on his preferred night shifts.

By the time he arrived in Boston in 1868, after jobs with Western Union and the military, Edison was a haunted man. The little sleep he had was populated by polarized magnets, springs, cylinders, rotating gears, armatures, batteries, and rheostats, all dancing intricate patterns with labyrinthine strands of wire to make the most marvelous advances in telegraphy, and all vanishing as soon as he awoke. He rented a corner of Charles Williams Jr.'s instrument workshop (the same workshop where Alexander Graham Bell encountered his collaborator Thomas A. Watson). Here Edison improved on the standard stock telegraph tape printer and went into business with other telegraphers to sell his machine and a stock-and-gold quotation service.

But there was not enough money for all his ideas in Boston, so Edison decamped for New York. Soon after his arrival in Manhattan in June 1869, at the age of 22, he was in the office of Dr. Sam Laws's Gold Indicator's wire service as a piecework assistant when its machine broke down. Hundreds of brokers' messengers fought at the door for the information while Wall Street came to a stop and the experts responsible for transmission worked themselves into impotent rage.

Edison fixed the machine.

He was now the golden boy in the dizzily evolving telegraph world. When he went before the directors of a Western Union subsidiary to present a device that aligned stock tickers in outside offices with the central station, they offered an astounding $30,000. His confidence, already sublime, came to border on the reckless.

He boldly contracted to deliver private telegraph machines and electrical equipment as well as 1,200 sped-up stock tickers for Western Union, manufacturing them with a machinist in Newark. By working 16 hours at a stretch, living on coffee, apple pie, and cigars, he delivered all the machines, though his bookkeeping mixed up the accounts of rival companies. Then he bought out his machinist partner. He was now his own man. He acted as foreman of 50 or more pieceworkers in the Newark factory, but this was a secondary preoccupation. He set up a laboratory equipped with the latest scientific equipment. One of his associates described seeing him go through a 5-foot-high pile of journals from Europe, eating and sleeping in his chair over six weeks, and conducting hundreds of experiments.

Most important, in the early 1870s, he recruited three men who would be crucial: Charles Batchelor, an English textile machinist; John Kruesi, a Swiss clockmaker; and Edward Johnson, a voluble railroad and telegraph engineer. Batchelor would render a rough Edison sketch into a precise drawing, Kruesi would make a model that could be entered into an application for a patent, and Johnson would organize patent applications, contracts, and payroll. Edison had an instinct for the kind of people he needed to stimulate and service his fertile imagination, and the right people were drawn like moths to his creative flame. His journal of February 1872 had more than 100 sketches; with the help of Batchelor and Krusei, he won 34 patents in that single year.

IN 1875 EDISON GAVE HIS 71-YEAR-OLD father an assignment. Sam had an eye for property, and it was he who found the pasture in New Jersey and oversaw the building of the curiously shaped house where Edison set up his laboratory in March 1876. Thomas Hughes describes Menlo Park as a cross between Camelot and a monastic cloister. Every downstairs room in the lab had a needling quotation from the English painter Joshua Reynolds: "There is no expedient to which a man will not resort to avoid the real labor of thinking." Every clock had its spring removed to show that the place would not be a slave to time as measured by a machine; the length of the days would be fixed by Edison, who would often work for 24 hours, with tiny naps stretched out on floor or bench, and then sleep for 18.

His happy band of brothers knew something big was brewing at the end of August 1878 when a well-tanned Edison bounced into the lab wearing a big black sombrero. His exuberance was so different from July when, sick and exhausted, he had gone off by himself to the Rockies for a vacation, watching the total eclipse of the sun with a group of scientists. One of the scientists, George Barker of the University of Pennsylvania, had enthused about a system of lights the inventor Moses Farmer had installed at an Ansonia, Conn., foundry. They were arc lights, so called because the light was an arch of elongated sparks reaching between two carbon electrodes. Bright as searchlights, they had been familiar since the '60s in British and American lighthouses and a few places of public assembly but were too blinding (and hazardous) for domestic use.

Epiphanies. When he took the train to Ansonia with Barker and Batchelor on Sunday, September 8, it was not so much the eight big arc lamps at the foundry that excited Edison as the system he examined that morning: electric light generated not by batteries but by a primitive little dynamo, the current wired a quarter mile to the foundry. It was a double epiphany. Edison was seeing for the first time practical proof that electric power could be sent a distance—and subdivided between lamps. His next question: Could it be done at a profit? A reporter for Charles Dana's New York *Sun*, who had come along, captured the moment of realization: "Edison was enraptured…. He ran from the instrument to the lights and from the lights back to the instrument. He sprawled over a table with the *simplicity of a child*, and made all kinds of calculations. He estimated the power of the instrument and of the lights, the probable loss of power in transmission, the amount of coal the instrument would save in a day, a week, a month, a year, and the result of such saving on manufacturing."

Edison's intuition was to think small. Instead of sending current to create a leap of light between the electrodes of big arc lamps, useless for domestic lighting, why not send it along the wire and into a filament in a small incandescent lamp? Back at Menlo Park he worked euphorically through two nights. "I discovered the necessary secret, so simple that a bootblack might understand it," he wrote. Edison went public only a week after his visit to Ansonia. His spicy quotes got full play in the newspapers: He had not only found the way to create an incandescent bulb but would be able to light the "entire lower part of New York" with one engine and 15 or 20 dynamos: "I have it now! With a process I have just discovered, I can produce a thousand—aye, ten thousand (lamps) from one machine. Indeed, the number may be said to be infinite…. with the same power you can run an elevator, a sewing machine, or any other mechanical contrivance, and by means of the heat you may cook your food."

It was hot air. The "secret" was something he had visualized but not realized, a thermal regulator to cut off current to the filament before it melted or burned out. The Edison scholars Robert Friedel and Paul Israel underline his audacity: "For Edison, the search for a practical incandescent light was a bold, even foolhardy, plunge into the unknown guided at first more by overconfidence and a few half-baked ideas than by science. To suggest other-

wise is to rob the inventive act of its human dimension and thus to miss an understanding of the act itself."

Other experimenters in both arc and incandescent lighting had pushed a great deal of current along a thick wire to a low-resistance filament. The real secret, Edison found, arguing it out with Charles Batchelor, was to raise the voltage to push a small amount of current through a thin wire to a high-resistance filament. It was an application of the law propounded in 1827 by the German physicist George Ohm, but it was still imperfectly understood. Edison himself said later, "At the time I experimented I did not understand Ohm's law. Moreover, I do not want to understand Ohm's law. It would stop me experimenting." This is Edison in his folksy genius mode. Understanding the relationship linking voltage, current, and resistance was crucial to the development of the incandescent lamp, and he understood it intuitively even if he did not express it in a mathematical formula.

Scientists in America and England who were still thinking of low resistance and thicker and thicker wires (at great cost) dismissed Edison's project to light New York as both scientifically stupid and economically hopeless. But he had to find a filament of high resistance—and heat it up to incandescence in a bulb as close to airless as he could get to hinder oxidization. Edison was not even close to resolving these dilemmas in the early fall of 1878 when his friend and lawyer Grosvenor Lowrey (who had encouraged Edison to fly his colorful kite in the press) moved on his behalf in New York's banking parlors. Lowrey swiftly raised $300,000 to form the Edison Electric Light Co. The filament proved more elusive than Edison had hoped. He had discarded carbon because it burned up so readily. Platinum wire offered only low resistance but did not oxidize and therefore seemed to offer the best prospect. They worked on making long spirals of thin platinum, to increase the resistance, but it was delicate and dangerous work. In mid-April, Lowrey led a group of investors into the darkened lab where Edison had installed 12 lamps with a platinum filament linked in series. Edison told John Kruesi to turn on the current slowly. Francis Jehl, an assistant, recalls: "I can see those lamps rising to a cherry red and hear Mr. Edison saying, 'A little more juice,' and the lamps began to glow. A little more … and then one emits a light like a star after which there is an eruption and a puff, and the machine shop is in total darkness." Batchelor replaced the dud lamp; the same thing happened a few minutes later. Only Lowrey's eloquence and the steadfastness of 42-year-old John Pierpont Morgan held the group together.

The other challenge was the vacuum; nobody had been able to get enough air out of the bulb. Edison did a simple thing. He had put a classified advertisement in the New York *Herald* for a glass blower, which netted an 18-year-old in a little red German student cap. The mechanics were amused by the dainty Ludwig Boehm and his pince-nez, but he blew a better bulb to Edison's design and he helped work out a new way of evacuating a bulb by infusions of mercury. It was laborious, frustrating work, but in September, after weeks of effort, Edison and his team achieved a vacuum of one hundredth of an atmosphere. Edison discovered that at this level they had so reduced the oxygen in the bulb that a carbon stick did not burn up quickly and it gave a better light than platinum ever had. That was the good news; the less good was that resistance to this particular piece of carbon was only around 2 ohms (which would mean more current, more copper). Resistance could be raised by shaping a tiny filament in a small spiral, but the filament would have to be no thicker than 15 thousandths of an inch. Edison set everyone in a frenzy trying to roll carbon into reeds no thicker than thread. Day after day, night after night, the spiral reeds kept breaking.

Success. After two sleepless weeks, Edison relieved the carbon rollers. His new idea was to bake the carbon into a length of plain cotton thread. On the eighth attempt, on October 21, the dexterous Batchelor held his breath carrying a tiny thread bent into the shape of a horseshoe to Boehm's house for insertion in a bulb. "Just as we reached the glass blower's house, the wretched carbon broke," Edison recalled. "We turned back to the main laboratory and set to work again. It was late in the afternoon before we produced another carbon, which was broken by a jeweler's screwdriver falling against it. But we turned back again and before nightfall the carbon was completed and inserted in the lamp. The bulb was exhausted of air and sealed, the current turned on, and the sight we had so long desired to see met our eyes."

Thread No. 9, lit at 1:30 a.m., lasted until 3 p.m.—13½ hours, whereupon Edison added a stronger battery to boost the light to 30 candles, or three times gaslight. They watched the tiny filament struggle with the intense heat. The light continued for 60 minutes. It was a crack in the glass that turned the room back into darkness—amid the cheers of exhausted men. They had proved that a carbon filament in a vacuum would work.

After examining the charred filament under a microscope, Edison launched another search for an organic fibrous material, some form of cellulose that might yield even more resistance than cotton. By November 16, they settled on a piece of common cardboard. Edison records: "None of us could go to bed, and there was no sleep for any of us for 40 hours. We sat and watched it with anxiety growing into elation. The lamp lasted about 45 hours, and I realized that the practical incandescent lamp had been born."

ALREADY, EDISON WAS PREPARING TO ESTABLISH ELECTRIC beachheads in New York, Paris, and London. The lab staff worked frantically making bulbs by hand, one by one, so that on New Year's Eve, when Edison opened Menlo Park to a public exhibition, he had around 300 bulbs. Some 3,000 people came to gaze and put questions to the great man. Still, the experts in America and England refused to be dazzled. Henry Morton of the Stevens Institute, who had been on the Rockies expedition, charged that Edison was perpetrating "a fraud upon the public," provoking Edison to make another promise: He would erect a statue of Morton at Menlo Park and shine an eternal electric light on his gloomy countenance.

What Edison attempted next can be characterized only as awesome, as if having climbed Everest he sprouted wings and flew from the top. "There is a wide difference," he said, "between completing an invention and putting the manufactured article on the market," but marketing an electric light bulb was the least of it. He had to invent the electrical industry. He had to conceive a system down to its very last detail—and then manufacture everything in it. He had to build a central power station; design and manufacture his own dynamos to convert steam power into electrical energy; ensure an even flow of current; connect a 14-mile network of underground wiring; insulate the wiring against moisture and the accidental discharge of electrical charges; install safety devices against fire; design commercially efficient motors to use electricity in daylight hours for elevators, printing presses, lathes, fans, and the like; design and install meters to measure individual consumption of power; and invent and manufacture a plethora of switches, sockets, fuses, distributing boxes, and lamp holders.

Luckily, Edison was worth around half a million dollars by then; Western Union had made big payments for his telegraph and telephone patents. Shuttling between Menlo Park and his grand new headquarters in a double brownstone mansion at 65 Fifth Avenue, Edison the industrialist organized a group of companies from 1880 to 1881, the progenitors of the modern Con Edison and General Electric. For his power station, Edison bought a couple of dilapidated warehouses at 25–257 Pearl Street within sight of the high towers of the unfinished Brooklyn Bridge. In December 1881, he began to dig up cobblestones for conduits radiating symmetrically outward from Pearl Street. He was often down in the trenches in the raw early hours checking the connections made by the wiring runners. It took six months to do the work.

Lights on. Sunday was normally the one day of the week reserved for his neglected wife, Mary, and their two children, but Sunday, Sept. 3, 1882, was different. All day and into the night Edison was on Pearl Street rehearsing every part of the operation for the system's debut due on Monday afternoon. So much might go wrong when he gave the orders for the steam to flow. "The gas companies were our bitter enemies, ready to pounce upon us at the slightest failure," he recalled later. When the chief electrician pulled the switch at 3 p.m., only one of the six dynamo sets worked and the steam engine was wobbly. But Edison, over at the offices of Drexel, Morgan & Co., ready for the big moment when he would ceremonially connect the 106 lamps there, was not disappointed. They all came on! They came on, too, at the offices of the *New York Times,* "in fairy tale style," said the paper, 52 filaments appearing to glow stronger as the night drew in.

Edison's success was at once a vindication and an incitement. His patent was swiftly challenged, his ideas stolen. But Edison would not sue; he would out-invent and undersell them all. When Pearl Street went on line in 1882, no fewer than 200 companies across America had already signed up with the Edison Company for Isolated Lighting, using 45,000 lamps a day: companies like Marshall Field's dry goods store in Chicago, George Eastman's Photographic company in Rochester, N.Y., the Stetson Hat Co. in Philadelphia, and Dillard's Oregon Railway and Navigation Co. The electrical evangelists Edison had sent overseas had done their work well. A London newspaper summed up the acclaim: "There is but one Edison."

Lockwood in '84

In 1884, a woman couldn't vote for the president of the United States, but that didn't stop activist lawyer Belva Lockwood from conducting a full-scale compaign for the office. She was the first woman ever to do so, and she tried again for the presidency in 1888. It's time we recognized her name.

by Jill Norgren

In 1884, Washington, D.C., attorney Belva Lockwood, candidate of the Equal Rights Party, became the first woman to run a full campaign for the presidency of the United States. She had no illusion that a woman could be elected, but there were policy issues on which she wished to speak, and, truth be told, she welcomed the notoriety. When challenged as to whether a woman was eligible to become president, she said that there was "not a thing in the Constitution" to prohibit it. She did not hesitate to confront the male establishment that barred women from voting and from professional advancement. With the spunk born of a lifelong refusal to be a passive victim of discrimination, Lockwood told a campaign reporter, "I cannot vote, but I can be voted for." Her bid for the presidency startled the country and infuriated other suffrage leaders, many of whom mistakenly clung to the idea that the Republican Party would soon sponsor a constitutional amendment in support of woman suffrage.

In the last quarter of the 19th century, Lockwood commanded attention, and not just from the columnists and satirists whom she led a merry chase. Today she is virtually unknown, lost in the shadows of the iconic suffrage leaders Elizabeth Cady Stanton and Susan B. Anthony. That's an injustice, for Belva Lockwood was a model of courageous activism and an admirable symbol of a woman's movement that increasingly invested its energies in party politics.

Lockwood was born Belva Ann Bennett in the Niagara County town of Royalton, New York, on October 24, 1830, the second daughter, and second of five children, of Lewis J. Bennett, a farmer, and Hannah Green Bennett. Belva was educated in rural schoolhouses, where she herself began to teach at the age of 14. In her first profession she found her first cause. As a female instructor, she received less than half the salary paid to the young men. The Bennetts' teenage daughter thought this treatment "odious, an indignity not to be tamely borne." She complained to the wife of a lo-

cal minister, who counseled her that such was the way of the world. But bright, opinionated, ambitious Belva Bennett would not accept that world.

From her avid reading of history, Belva imagined for herself a life different from that of her mother and her aunts—the life, in fact, of a great man. She asked her father's permission to continue her education, but he said no. She then did what she was expected to do: On November 8, 1848, she married Uriah MeNall, a promising young farmer. She threw herself into running their small farm and sawmill, wrote poetry and essays, and determined not to let marriage be the end of her individuality. She wanted to chart her own course, and tragedy gave her an opportunity to do so. In April 1853, when she was 22 and her daughter, Lura, three, Uriah McNall died.

The young widow had a second chance to go out into the world. She resumed her teaching and her education. In September 1854, she left Lura with her mother and traveled 60 miles east to study at the Genesee Wesleyan Seminary in Lima. The seminary shared a building with the newly coeducational Genesee College, which offered a more rigorous program. Belva transferred to the college (becoming its third woman student), where she took courses in science and politics. She graduated with a bachelor's degree (with honors) on June 27, 1857, and soon found a position teaching high school in the prosperous Erie Canal town of Lockport. Four years later, she took over a small school in the south-central New York town of Owego. In 1866, Belva McNall traveled to Washington and began to reinvent herself as an urban professional. She was neither flamboyant nor eccentric. Indeed, had she been a man, it would have been apparent that her life was following a conventional 19th-century course: Talented chap walks off the farm, educates himself, seeks opportunities, and makes a name. But because Belva strove to be that ambitious son of ordinary people who rises in the world on the basis of his wits and his work, she was thought a radical.

In Washington, Belva taught school and worked as a leasing agent, renting halls to lodges and organizations. She tutored herself in the workings of government and the art of lobbying by making frequent visits to Congress. In 1868 she married Ezekiel Lockwood, an elderly dentist and lay preacher who shared her reformist views. We do not know precisely when she fell in love with the law. In antebellum America the profession belonged to men, who passed on their skill by training their sons and nephews and neighbors' boys. After the Civil War a handful of women, Lockwood among them, set out to change all that. She believed from her reading of the lives of great men that "in almost every instance law has been the stepping-stone to greatness." She attended the law program of Washington's National University, graduated in 1872 (but only after she lobbied for the diploma male administrators had been pressured to withhold), and was admitted to the bar of the District of Columbia in 1873 (again, only after a struggle against sex discrimination). When the Supreme Court of the United States refused to admit her to its bar in 1876, she single-handedly lobbied Congress until, in 1879, it passed, reluctantly, "An act to relieve the legal disabilities of women." On March 3, 1879, Lockwood became the first woman admitted to the high Court bar, and, in 1880, the first woman lawyer to argue a case before the Court.

From her earliest years in Washington, Lockwood coveted a government position. She applied to be a consul officer in Ghent during the administration of Andrew Johnson, but her application was never acknowledged. In later years, she sought government posts—for women in general and for herself in particular—from other presidents. Without success. When Grover Cleveland passed over Lockwood and appointed as minister to Turkey a man thought to be a womanizer, she wrote to compliment the president on his choice: "The only danger is, that he will attempt to suppress polygamy in that country by marrying all of the women himself." A year later, in 1886, in another communication to Cleveland, she laid claim to the position of district recorder of deeds and let the president know in no uncertain terms that she had a "lien" on the job. She did not give up: In 1911 she had her name included on a list sent to President William Howard Taft of women attorneys who could fill the Supreme Court vacancy caused by the death of Justice John Marshall Harlan.

What persuaded Lockwood that she should run for the highest office in the land? Certainly, she seized the opportunity to shake a fist at conservatives who would hold women back. And she was displeased with the enthusiasm for the Republican Party shown by suffrage leaders Susan B. Anthony and Elizabeth Cady Stanton. More than that, however, campaigning would provide an opportunity for her to speak her mind, to travel, and to establish

herself on the paid lecture circuit. She was not the first woman to run for president. In 1872, New York City newspaper publisher Victoria Woodhull had declared herself a presidential candidate, against Ulysses Grant and Horace Greeley. But Woodhull, cast as Mrs. Satan by the influential cartoonist Thomas Nast, had to abandon her campaign barely a month after its start: Her radical "free love" views were too much baggage for the nascent women's movement to bear, and financial misfortune forced her to suspend publication of *Woodhull & Claflin's Weekly* at the very moment she most needed a public platform.

Years later, Lockwood—and the California women who drafted her—spoke of the circumstances surrounding her August 1884 nomination, their accounts colored by ego and age. Lockwood received the nod from Marietta Stow, a San Francisco reformer who spoke for the newly formed, California-based Equal Rights Party, and from Stow's colleague, attorney Clara Foltz. Foltz later insisted that Lockwood's nomination amounted to nothing more than a lighthearted joke on her and Stow's part. But Stow's biographer, Sherilyn Bennion, has made a strong case that the nomination was, in fact, part of a serious political strategy devised by Stow to deflect attention from the rebuff given suffrage leaders that year at the Republican and Democratic conventions, and to demonstrate that "the fair sex" could create its own terms of engagement in American party politics. Women were becoming stump speakers, participants in political clubs, candidates for local office, and, in a handful of places, voters. (By 1884 the Wyoming, Utah and Washington Territories had fully enfranchised women, who in 14 states were permitted to vote in elections dealing with schools.) Marietta Stow began the Equal Rights Party because she had long been interested in matters of public policy and because readers of her newspaper, *The Women's Herald of Industry*, had expressed an interest in a "new, clean, uncorruptible party."

In July 1884 Stow urged Abigail Scott Duniway, an Oregon rights activist and newspaper editor, to accept the Equal Rights Party's nomination. But Duniway declined, believing, as Bennion writes, that "flaunting the names of women for official positions" would weaken the case for equal rights and provide "unscrupulous opponents with new pretexts and excuses for lying about them." Undiscouraged, Stow continued her search for a candidate. In August, she hit her mark.

Belva Lockwood, *Women's Herald* reader, had already begun to think of herself as a standard-bearer. On August 10 she wrote to Stow in San Francisco and asked rhetorically, and perhaps disingenuously, "Why not nominate women for important places? Is not Victoria Empress of India? Have we not among our country-women persons of as much talent and ability? Is not history full of precedents of women rulers?" The Republicans, she commented, claimed to be the party of progress yet had "little else but insult for women when [we] appear before its conventions." (She had been among those rebuffed that summer by the Republicans.) She was exasperated with the party of Lincoln and maddened by Stanton and Anthony's continuing faith in major-party politics: "It is quite time that we had our own party, our own platform, and our own nominees. We shall never have equal rights until we take them, nor respect until we command it."

Stow had her candidate! She called a party convention on August 23, read Lockwood's letter to the small group, and proposed her as the party's nominee for president of the United States, along with Clemence S. Lozier, a New York City physician, as the vice presidential nominee. Acclamation followed, and letters were sent to the two women. The dispatch to Lockwood read as follows: "Madam: We have the honor to inform you that you were nominated, at the Woman's National Equal-Rights Convention, for President of the United States. We await your letter of acceptance with breathless interest."

Lockwood later said that the letter took her "utterly by surprise," and she kept it secret for several days. On September 3, she wrote to accept the nomination for "Chief Magistrate of the United States" from the only party that "really and truly represent the interests of our whole people North, South, East, and West.... With your unanimous and cordial support ... we shall not only be able to carry the election, but to guide the Ship of State safely into port." Lockwood went on to outline a dozen platform points, and her promptness in formulating policy signaled that she (and the party) intended to be taken seriously about matters of political substance.

Forecasters in '84 were predicting another close presidential race. Four years earlier, James Garfield had defeated Winfield Hancock by just 40,000 votes (out of nine million cast), and people were again watching the critical states of New York and Indiana. The nearly even division of registered voters between the two major parties caused Democratic candidate Grover Cleveland and Republican candidate James G. Blaine to shy away from innovative platforms. Instead, the two men spent much of their time trading taunts and insults. That left the business of serious reform to the minor parties and their candidates: Benjamin Butler (National Greenback/Anti-Monopoly), John St. John (Prohibition), and Samuel Clarke Pomeroy (American Prohibition). Butler, St. John, and Pomeroy variously supported workers' rights, the abolition of child and prison labor, a graduated income tax, senatorial term limits, direct election of the president, and, of course, prohibition of the manufacture, sale, and consumption of alcohol. Lockwood joined this group of nothing-to-lose candidates, who intended to promote the public discussion of issues about which Blaine and Cleveland dared not speak.

The design of Lockwood's platform reflected her practical savvy. The platform, she said, should "take up every one of the issues of the day" but be "so brief that the newspapers would publish it and the people read it."

(She understood the art of the sound bite.) Her "grand platform of principles" expressed bold positions and comfortable compromise. She promised to promote and maintain equal political privileges for "every class of our citizens irrespective of sex, color or nationality" in order to make America "in truth what it has so long been in name, 'the land of the free and home of the brave.'" She pledged herself to the fair distribution of public offices to women as well as men, "with a scrupulous regard to civil service reform after the women are duly installed in office." She opposed the "wholesale monopoly of the judiciary" by men and said that, if elected, she would appoint a reasonable number of women as district attorneys, marshals, and federal judges, including a "competent woman to any vacancy that might occur on the United States Supreme Bench."

Lockwood's views extended well beyond women's issues. She adopted a moderate position on the contentious question of tariffs. In her statement of September 3, she placed the Equal Rights Party in the political camp that wanted to "protect and foster American industries," in sympathy with the working men and women of the country who were organized against free trade. But in the official platform statement reprinted on campaign literature, her position was modified so that the party might be identified as middle-of-the-road, supporting neither high tariffs nor free trade. Lockwood urged the extension of commercial relations with foreign countries and advocated the establishment of a "high Court of Arbitration" to which commercial and political differences could be referred. She supported citizenship for Native Americans and the allotment of tribal land. As was to be expected from an attorney who earned a substantial part of her livelihood doing pension claims work, she adopted a safe position on Civil War veterans' pensions: She argued that tariff revenues should be applied to benefits for former soldiers and their dependents; at the same time, she urged the abolition of the Pension Office, "with its complicated and technical machinery," and recommended that it be replaced with a board of three commissioners. She vowed full sympathy with temperance advocates and, in a position unique to the platform of the Equal Rights Party, called for the reform of family law: "If elected, I shall recommend in my Inaugural speech, a uniform system of laws as far as practicable for all of the States, and especially for marriage, divorce, and the limitation of contracts, and such a regulation of the laws of descent and distribution of estates as will make the wife equal with the husband in authority and right, and an equal partner in the common business."

Lockwood's position paper of September 3 was revised into the platform statement that appeared below her portrait on campaign flyers. The new version expanded on certain points, adopted some sharper rhetoric, and added several planks, including a commitment that the remaining public lands of the nation would go to the "honest yeomanry," not the railroads. Lockwood stuck to her radical positions of support for women's suffrage and the reform of domestic law, but, in a stunning retreat, her earlier promises of an equitable allotment of public positions by sex and any mention of the need for women in the judiciary were absent from the platform.

Armed with candidate and platform, the leaders and supporters of the Equal Rights Party waited to see what would happen. A great deal depended on the posture adopted by the press. Fortunately for Lockwood and the party, many of the daily newspapers controlled by men, and a number of weeklies owned by women, took an interest in the newest contender in the election of '84. A day after she accepted the nomination, *The Washington Evening Star* made her candidacy front-page news and reprinted the entire text of her acceptance letter and platform of September 3. The candidate told a *Star* reporter that she would not necessarily receive the endorsement of activist women. Indeed, leaders of the nation's two top woman suffrage associations had endorsed Blaine, and Frances Willard had united temperance women with the Prohibition Party. "You must remember," Lockwood said, "that the women are divided up into as many factions and parties as the men."

On September 5, an editorial in the *Star* praised Lockwood's letter of acceptance: "In all soberness, it can be said [it] is the best of the lot. It is short, sharp, and decisive.... It is evident that Mrs. Lockwood, if elected, will have a policy [that] commends itself to all people of common sense." Editor Crosby Noyes rued the letter's late appearance: Had it existed sooner, "the other candidates might have had the benefit of perusing it and framing their several epistles in accord with its pith and candor." Newspaper reporting elsewhere was similarly respectful.

Abigail Duniway's warning that women candidates would meet with "unpleasant prominence" and be held up "to ridicule and scorn" proved correct, but Lockwood actually encountered no greater mockery than the men in the election. She had to endure silly lies about hairpieces and sham allegations that she was divorced, but Cleveland was taunted with cries of "Ma, Ma Where's My Pa" (a reference to his out-of-wedlock child). Cartoonists for *Frank Leslie's Illustrated* and *Puck*, mass-circulation papers, made fun of all the candidates, including Lockwood. This was a rite of passage and badge of acceptance. *Leslie's* also ran an article on Lockwood's campaign and contemplated the entrance of women into party politics with earnest good wishes: "Woman in politics. Why not?.... Twenty years ago woman's suffrage was a mere opinion. To-day, it is another matter."

After establishing campaign headquarters at her Washington home on F Street, Lockwood wrote to friends and acquaintances in a dozen states asking that they arrange ratification meetings and get up ballots containing the names of electors (as required by the Constitution) pledged to her candidacy. This letter to a male friend in

Philadelphia was a typical appeal: "That an opportunity may not be lost for the dissemination of Equal Rights principles, cannot, and will not the Equal Rights Party of Philadelphia hold a ratification meeting for the nominee, put in nomination a Presidential Elector, and get up an Equal Rights ticket? Not that we shall succeed in the election, but we can demonstrate that a woman may under the Constitution, not only be nominated but elected. Think of it."

Closer to home, party supporters organized a ratification meeting in mid-September at Wilson's Station, Maryland. (They bypassed the District to make the point that, under federal law, neither men nor women could vote in the nation's capital.) Lockwood delivered her first speech as a candidate at this gathering of about 75 supporters and journalists, and two Lockwood-for-president electors were chosen. She did not disclose at the rally that Clemence Lozier had declined the nomination for vice president—and not until September 29 did Marietta Stow decide to run in the second spot and complete the ticket.

Throughout September the national press spread the story of the Equal Rights Party and its candidate, and letters poured in to the house on F Street. They contained "earnest inquiries" about the platform, nasty bits of character assassination, and, from one male admirer, the following poem, which so amused Lockwood that she gave it to a reporter for publication:

> O, Belva Ann!
> Fair Belva Ann!
> I know that thou art not a man;
> But I shall vote,
> Pull off my coat,
> And work for thee, fair Belva Ann.
> For I have read
> What thou hast said,
> And long I've thought upon thy plan.
> Oh no, there's none
> Beneath the sun
> Who'd rule like thee, my Belva Ann!

The letters also brought invitations to speak in cities across the East and the Midwest. In late September, Lockwood prepared to go on the stump, her expenses covered by sponsors. Many of the lectures she gave were paid appearances; indeed, she claimed to be the only candidate whose speeches the public paid to hear. She was a widowed middle-class woman (her second husband, who was more than 30 years her senior, had died in 1877), and her livelihood depended on the earnings of her legal practice. So the time she devoted to politics had to pay. When the election was over, she told reporters that she had a satisfaction denied the other candidates: She had come out of the campaign with her expenses paid and "$125 ahead."

Lockwood took to the field in October. She made at least one full circuit in October, beginning in Baltimore,

Philadelphia, and New York. Mid-month she delivered speeches in Louisville and in Cleveland, where she appeared at the Opera House before 500 people. In a loud and nasal voice, she attacked the high-tariff position of the Republicans on the grounds that it would injure American commerce, But she also assailed the free-trade policy of the Democrats, arguing that they were "willing to risk our manufacturing interests in the face of the starving hordes of pauper labor in other countries." She applauded the good that capital had done and said that "capital and labor did not, by nature, antagonize, and should not by custom."

If the people who came to hear Lockwood expected nothing but women's rights talk, they were disappointed. She and her party colleagues believed that the Equal Rights Party should not run a single-issue campaign. Of course, the platform introduced "feminist" ideas. But it also allowed Lockwood to address many other issues that preoccupied Americans. So she directed only a small part of her talk to describing how women had helped to make the country "blossom as a rose." She intended her candidacy to make history in the largest sense—by demonstrating that the Constitution did not bar women from running in elections or serving in federal elective office.

People who saw her for the first time said that her campaign photographs did not do her justice: The lady candidate had fine blue eyes, an aquiline nose, and a firm mouth, and she favored fashionable clothes. The cartoonists naturally focused on her sex, and the public had its own fun by creating dozens of Belva Lockwood Clubs, in which men meaning to disparage Lockwood paraded on city streets wearing Mother Hubbard dresses, a new cut of female clothing with an unconstructed design that freed movement and was considered improper to wear out of doors.

On November 3, the day before the election, Lockwood returned from a campaign tour of the Northwest. She had stayed "at the best hotels; had the best sleeping berths." Her last stop was Flint, Michigan, and she told a Washington reporter that 1,000 people had attended her (paid) talk there, a larger number than Ohio congressman Frank Hurd drew the following night. When asked on November 4 where she would await the election news, she replied that her house would be open throughout the evening, "the gas will be lighted," and reporters were welcome to visit. The historic first campaign by a woman for the presidency of the United States had ended, though in politics, of course, nothing is ever over.

When the ballots were tallied, Cleveland was declared the winner, with an Electoral College vote of 219 to 182. In the popular vote, he squeaked by with a margin of 23,000.

In 1884 the United States had yet to adopt the "Australian" ballot, which has the names of all candidates for office printed on a single form. The system then in effect, dating from the beginning of the Republic, required that each political party in a state issue ballots that contained the names of that party's slate and the electors pledged to them. A supporter cast his vote by depositing the ballot of his chosen party in a box. Some states required that voters sign the back of their ballot, but the overall allocation of ballots was not controlled by polling place officials, and stuffing the box was not impossible. It was also possible for officials in charge of the ballot boxes to discount or destroy ballots. And that, Lockwood claimed, is precisely what happened.

In a petition sent to Congress in January 1885, she wrote that she had run a campaign, gotten up electoral tickets in several states, and received votes in at least nine of the states, only to determine that "a large vote in Pennsylvania [was] not counted, simply dumped into the waste basket as false votes." In addition, she charged that many of the votes cast for her—totalling at least 4,711—in eight other states ("New Hampshire, 379 popular votes; New York, 1,336; Michigan, 374; Illinois, 1008; Iowa, 562; Maryland, 318; California, 734 and the entire Electoral vote of the State of Indiana") had been "fraudulently and illegally counted for the alleged majority candidate."

She asked that the members of Congress "refuse to receive the Electoral returns of the State of New York, or count them for the alleged majority candidate, for had the 1,336 votes which were polled in said state for your petitioner been counted for her, and not for the one Grover Cleveland, he would not have been awarded a majority of all the votes cast at said election in said state." (Cleveland's margin of votes in New York was 1,149). Lockwood also petitioned Congress for the electoral vote of Indiana, saying that at the last moment the electors there had switched their votes from Cleveland to her. In fact, they had not; it was all a prank by the good ol' boys of Indiana, but either she did not know this or, in the spirit of political theater, she played along with the mischief and used it to her advantage.

The electoral votes of New York (36) and Indiana (15) had been pivotal in the 1880 presidential race. With her petition and credible evidence, Lockwood—perhaps working behind the scenes with congressional Republicans—hoped to derail Cleveland's victory and keep him from becoming the first Democratic president since James Buchanan in 1856. She failed when the legislators ignored her petition, which had been referred to their Committee on Woman Suffrage. On February 11, Congress certified the election of New York governor Grover Cleveland as the 22nd president of the United States.

Subsequent interviews suggest that Lockwood was satisfied with the campaign, if not with the vote counting. The U.S. Constitution had betrayed women in the matter of suffrage, but it did not, as she said, prohibit women's speech and women's candidacies. As a celebration of the First Amendment, Lockwood's campaign was a great success. It served the interests of women (though it angered Susan B. Anthony), the candidate, and the country. Lockwood ran as an acknowledged contender and was allowed to speak her mind. American democracy was tested, and its performance did not disappoint her.

After the election, while maintaining her law practice, Lockwood embarked on the life of travel that she had long sought—and that she continued until her early eighties. Not unlike 21st-century politicians, she capitalized on the campaign by increasing her presence on the national lecture circuit; she even made at least one product endorsement (for a health tonic). She had long worked as a pension claims attorney, and, while traveling as a lecturer, she used the publicity surrounding her appearances to attract clients who needed help with applications and appeals. In 1888, the Equal Rights Party again nominated her as its presidential candidate. She ran a more modest campaign the second time around, but she still offered a broad domestic and foreign policy platform and argued that "equality of rights and privileges is but simple justice."

Lockwood always spoke proudly of her campaigns, which were important but not singular events in a life that would last 87 years. She was a woman of many talents and interests. Blocked from political office or a high-level government position because of her sex, she sought new realms after the campaigns of 1884 and 1888 where she might raise questions of public policy and advance the rights of women. Representing the Philadelphia-based Universal Peace Union, she increased her work on behalf of international peace and arbitration at meetings in the United States and Europe. She participated in an often-interlocking network of women's clubs and professional organizations. And she maintained a high profile

in the women's suffrage movement, which struggled throughout the 1890s and the first two decades of the 20th century to create a winning strategy. In the spring of 1919, the House of Representatives and the Senate acted favorably on legislation to amend the Constitution to give women the right to vote; the proposed Nineteenth Amendment went out to the states in a ratification process that would not be completed until August 1920. But Belva Lockwood never got the right to vote. She died in May 1917.

Lockwood remains the only woman to have campaigned for the presidency right up to Election Day. (In 1964, Senator Margaret Chase Smith of Maine entered several Republican primaries and received 27 delegate votes; in 1972, Representative Shirley Chisholm of New York ran in a number of Democratic primaries and won 151 delegates.) In 1914 Lockwood, then 84 years old, was asked whether a woman would one day be president. The former candidate answered with levelheaded prescience and the merest echo of her former thunder: "I look to see women in the United States senate and the house of representatives. If [a woman] demonstrates that she is fitted to be president she will some day occupy the White House. It will be entirely on her own merits, however. No movement can place her there simply because she is a woman. It will come if she proves herself mentally fit for the position."

JILL NORGREN, *a former Wilson Center fellow, is professor of government and legal studies at John Jay College and the University Graduate Center, City University of New York. She is writing the first full biography of Belva Lockwood, to be published in 2003. Copyright © 2002 by Jill Norgren.*

A DAY TO REMEMBER

November 18, 1883

Charles Phillips

Before the coming of the railroads, American towns kept their own time, using some form of local solar time maintained by a well-located clock—in a church steeple, perhaps, or prominently displayed in a jeweler's window. Most folks simply ignored the fact that solar time changed as the earth rotated and the sun crossed new longitudinal meridians. Thus in the Delaware Valley it might be only 11:55 a.m. as 60 miles to the east the midday whistle blew in lower Manhattan. A New York or a Chicago could impose its timekeeping on a few nearby areas, but "official" times proliferated as municipalities jealously defended their own as the only true reckoning. By the mid-1800s there were some 144 official times in North America. So long as people lived mostly in towns and villages, and so long as traffic between them traveled relatively slowly, by buggy and barge, competing times seemed to hardly matter. But once the railroads began crisscrossing the country, the keeping (and scheduling) of time grew considerably more critical.

By 1848, the British government had established a railroad standard time based on the prime meridian at Greenwich, England, but American railroad barons flinging tracks across the continental United States in the wake of the Civil War were highly skeptical of any kind of government regulation. They preferred keeping their own time. An American railroad passenger entering one of the larger stations to transfer to another line might be faced with a row of clocks behind the ticket counter, labeled not for places as they would be today—"New York," "Chicago" and "Cincinnati"—but instead for railroad lines: "New York Central," "Chicago, Milwaukee & St. Paul," and "Baltimore & Ohio." Each discreet time reflected the clock back at the railroad company's headquarters. Along Penn Central's lines, the schedules were keyed to time in Philadelphia. The "Vanderbilt time" of the New York Central line was set at Grand Central Station in New York City. It was up to the

ticket holder to know who ran on what time, to convert that into local time, and hop on the right train.

To complicate matters further, some towns boasted more than one official time, such as Buffalo, N.Y., which displayed three, one for each of the three railroads that served the city. Little wonder that many passengers were bewildered. Competing times were not merely disconcerting, they were dangerous. Inevitably, trains employing different times on the same tracks ran into each other, and train wrecks were frequent. Passengers traveling by rail became by necessity obsessively conscious of the time, which, along with everything else, made travel even more nerve-racking.

The absurd time conflicts at Buffalo so outraged the principal of a small women's college in upstate New York that he came up with what he hoped would be a solution. In 1869 Professor Charles Dowd of Temple Grove Ladies' Seminary (now Skidmore College) in Saratoga Springs made the first proposal for standard time, based on the Washington, D.C., meridian, as a way of simplifying the Byzantine complications of American railroad schedules. Referring to the three "official" railroad clocks in the Buffalo station (reflecting Albany, Columbus and Buffalo time), he wrote, "The traveler's watch was to him but a delusion; clocks at stations staring each other in the face defiant of harmony either with one another or with surrounding time and wildly at variance with the traveler's watch, baffled all intelligent interpretations."

In 1872 he revised his original proposal. A graduate of Yale, marked by his fellows as an outstanding scholar, Dowd had done his homework. He was now dropping the Washington meridian for the Greenwich. He knew, of course, that there were 10 official prime meridians then currently in use, all of them historically justified, and the United States was free to adopt any of them. But the U.S. Navy and the American commercial fleet, along with Britain and its colonies, all used Greenwich charts, as did all but about 10 percent of the world. Then, too, as Dowd read in *Atlantic Monthly*, Benjamin Peirce, a Harvard mathematician and astronomer, had proposed similar reforms based on the Greenwich meridian. As it happened, the system Dowd proposed for North American railroads—five time zones, each varying by an hour, each zone spreading across 15 degrees of longitude in leaps westward from Greenwich—is remarkably similar to the one we use today.

William F. Allen, secretary of the American Railroad Association, and any number of other railroad trunk managers did take heed of the proposals from the persistent professor, but Dowd was ahead of his time and an outsider to the railroad fraternity. To them, he appeared a dotty professor, while true railroad men, real astronomers, established theorists, diplomats—in short, people who they believed knew what they were talking about—were only just beginning to take up the cause of reform, meeting in a series of conferences around the world. Standard time, opposed by religious bigots, agrarian reactionaries, even the contented, nontraveling populace, was only now becoming a cause—a symbol, actually, of progress and rationality. Those with the real power to change railroad timekeeping, however, shelved Dowd's proposals for more than a decade.

Among the reformers was Sandford Fleming, a Scottish emigrant to Canada, who upon his arrival in 1845 began training as an engineer. By 1857, he had become chief engineer for the Ontario, Simcoe, and Huron Railway (now part of the Canadian National Railway, the CNR). In 1863 the Canadian government hired him to conduct a survey for the initial stretch of the railway that was ultimately to connect Canada's Atlantic and Pacific lines. He became chief engineer for the construction of the Intercolonial Railway as part of the CNR. In 1871 he was appointed engineer-in-chief of the proposed Canadian Pacific Railway. But political infighting and squabbling among his staff led him to take a leave of absence, during which he first pursued new ideas on the standardization of time in a series of articles and presentations at professional conferences.

In 1878 Fleming proposed the system of worldwide time zones that we use today. He recommended that the world be divided into 24 time zones, each spaced 15 degrees of longitude apart. Since the earth rotates once every 24 hours and there are 360 degrees of longitude, each hour the earth rotates one-twenty-fourth of a circle or 15 degrees of longitude. Fleming's time zones were heralded as a brilliant solution to a chaotic problem worldwide. Nevertheless, in 1880 Fleming lost his job with the Canadian National Railway. He took a position as chancellor of Queen's University in Kingston, Ontario, and devoted himself to his scientific projects and his writing.

Although Fleming's arguments for the establishment of time zones met with some resistance, railroad men like William Allen were certainly aware of his proposals and the growing ferment for reform. Allen dusted off Professor Dowd's proposals, revised them a little and introduced them as a new plan of action at the semiannual meeting of the General Time Convention of the American Railroad Association. On April 8, 1883, the 50 managers of grand-trunk railroads voted to accept the changes.

Reducing the number of time standards used by American railroads from almost 50 to only four, Allen called them Eastern, Central, Mountain and Pacific—the same names, though not precisely the same zones, we use today. (A fifth zone for Canada's maritime provinces—called the Intercolonial zone—was added some months later.) On Sunday morning, November 18, 1883, railroad standard time was established across North America. It became known as "the Sunday of two noons" because towns along the eastern edges of the four American time zones had to turn their clocks back half an hour, thus creating a second noon, to get in synch with those towns along the western edges. Skeptics sneered and dubbed the startling commercial innovation "Vanderbilt time," but up in Canada, Fleming hailed the change as a "quiet revolution."

Within a few days, 70 percent of North America's schools, courts and local governments had adopted railroad time as their official standard, though some towns—Bangor, Maine, and Savannah, Ga., to name two—refused, mostly for religious reasons, to go along, and Detroit, at the edge of the Eastern and Central times, voted itself in and out of each before finally settling on the Eastern zone. Probably much to Allen's and the railroads' relief, the federal government did not sign up. It would take 35 years for Congress to recognize the benefits of a standard time and write it into law in 1918. Meanwhile, President Chester A. Arthur, in one of the few acts that distinguished his administration, called for a Prime Meridian Conference in Washington, D.C., to set standard time for the whole world.

Delegates from the 25 countries then labeled "civilized" (meaning not colonies) showed up less than a year later in October 1884 at the conference, at which the American and British delegates browbeat the others, especially the French, into adopting Fleming's time zone scheme but with Greenwich as the prime meridian. Thus the conference's protocols owed much to Charles Dowd, though Professor Dowd was not invited to Washington and his name was not even mentioned in the proceedings. William Allen was there, of course, and so was Sandford Fleming. Together they became celebrated as the creators of modern standard time. Although recognized today for his role in creating standard time, Charles Dowd was less honored in his lifetime despite his pioneering. He died, mostly unheralded, in a railroad crossing accident in Saratoga Springs in 1904.

UNIT 2

The Emergence of Modern America

Unit Selections

7. **Where the Other Half Lived**, Verlyn Klinkenborg
8. **The Murder of Lucy Pollard**, Caleb Crain
9. **Our First Olympics**, Bob Fulton
10. **T.R.'s Virtuoso Performance**, Henry J. Hendrix II
11. **And Still Champion**, Gary Cartwright

Key Points to Consider

- Discuss the kinds of conditions Jacob Riis found in the slums. What combination of factors made it difficult for individuals to escape this environment?

- What does the article "The Murder of Lucy Pollard" tell us about race relations in the South during the 1890s? What were "Jim Crow" laws?

- Discuss Teddy Roosevelt's part in securing the rights to build a canal through the Panamanian section of Colombia. Were his actions justified? Or did he simply go after what he wanted?

- Jack Johnson would have been resented by many whites simply because he, a black man, won the heavyweight boxing championship. What was there about his conduct that further enraged his critics?

Student Website

www.mhcls.com/online

Internet References

Further information regarding these websites may be found in this book's preface or online.

The Age of Imperialism
http://www.smplanet.com/imperialism/toc.html

Anti-Imperialism in the United States, 1898–1935
http://boondocksnet.com/ail98-35.html

William McKinley 1843-1901
http://lcweb.loc.gov/rr/hispanic/1898/mckinley.html

American Diplomacy: Editor's Corner - If Two By Sea
http://www.unc.edu/depts/diplomat/AD_Issues/amdipl_15/edit_15.html

Great Chicago Fire and the Web of Memory
http://www.chicagohs.org/fire/

The United States underwent enormous changes during the 1880s and 1890s. Millions of people continued to live on family farms or in small towns. Millions of others flocked to the cities in search of a better life. It was a period of huge immigration, most of which landed in the poorer parts of cities. Most of these people came from from Southern and Eastern Europe, and became known as the "new" immigration (previous waves had come from Ireland and Germany). Because their dress, their languages, and their customs differed so markedly from native-born Americans, they were seen by many as inferior peoples. One of the essays in this section, "Where the Other Half Lived," shows the incredible poverty and crowded conditions some of these people had to endure.

Small and medium sized businesses continued to exist, but corporations on a scale previously unheard of came to dominate the marketplace. Though the gross national product increased dramatically, the gap between rich and poor steadily widened. Corporate leaders, on the one hand, amassed unprecedented fortunes on which they paid no income taxes. Urban working families, on the other, often lived in unhealthy squalor even

though all their members, including young children, worked in some shop or factory. Depressions, one beginning in 1873 and another in 1893, threw more people out of work than ever before. Farmers had to sell what they produced in markets that fluctuated widely, but had to purchase equipment and other necessities at prices often fixed by the large companies. They also had to contend with the monopolistic practices of railroads, which charged "all the traffic would bear" for shipping and storing farm products. Minority groups, such as Indians and blacks, continued to suffer socially and economically through good times as well as bad.

Two articles in this unit treat the lives of black people. "The Murder of Lucy Pollard" tells the story of three Southern black women and a black man who were arrested on charges of a murder they almost certainly did not commit, and of a crusading black journalist who was determined to expose this travesty of justice. The essay uses the incident to depict conditions in the South during the 1890s, when blacks were increasingly denied the right to vote and lynchings were at an all-time high. "And Still Champion" treats prizefighter Jack Johnson, who won the heavyweight title in 1908. Bad enough that he was black, many whites believed, but worse that he refused to conform to any stereotypes about how black people should act.

"Our First Olympics" is about the first modern Olympic games that were held in Greece in 1896. The Frenchman who organized the event hoped they would contribute to international harmony. In contrast with the enormous hoopla that now surrounds the Olympics; the early games were neither well-attended nor widely publicized. Organized American athletic groups tended to ignore the occasion with the result that the United States sent a rag-tag contingent that nonetheless performed surprisingly well.

American foreign policy became more assertive during the 1880s and 1890s. Various theories were put forward to justify American expansion into the Pacific: the need for Asian markets, the acquisition of coaling stations for merchant and naval vessels, and taking up the "white man's burden" among them. The Spanish-American War provided opportunity to put these ideas in practice. Although events in Cuba provided the immediate cause of the war, by its end the United States acquired the Philippines, and other Pacific islands. Although it lasted only a few months and casualties were relatively low, what a contemporary referred to as a "splendid little war" actually had very significant consequences."

America's thrust into the Pacific brought to the fore front what some people believed was crucial to future development: the need for a canal in Central America that would permit free passage of ships from one ocean to the other. This was vital, they argued, for both strategic and commercial reasons. "T.R.'s Virtuoso Performance" analyzes President Theodore Roosevelt's role in securing the rights to build a canal through the Panamanian section of Colombia. We have long since turned the canal over to the Panamanians, despite one senator's complaint that "we stole it fair and square."

The Conscience of Place
MULBERRY BEND

Where the Other Half Lived

The photographs of Jacob Riis confronted New Yorkers with the misery of Mulberry Bend—and helped to tear it down.

By Verlyn Klinkenborg

A BLOCK BELOW CANAL STREET in lower Manhattan, just a few hundred yards from City Hall, there is a small urban oasis called Columbus Park. Early on a spring morning, the sun rises over an irregular threshold of rooftops to the east of the park—a southern spur of Chinatown—and picks out details on the courthouses and state office buildings looming over the west side of the park. Carved eagles stare impassively into the sunlight. Incised over a doorway on the Criminal Courts Building is a strangely senseless quotation from Justinian. "Justice is the firm and continuous desire to render to every man his due," it says, as though justice were mainly a matter of desire.

Beneath the sun's level rays high overhead, Columbus Park seems almost hollow somehow, and since it is open ground—open playground, to be accurate—it exposes the local topography. The land slopes downward from Bayard Street to Park Street, and downward from Mulberry to Baxter. At the north end of the park, temporary fencing surrounds an ornate shelter, the sole remnant of the park's original construction in 1897, now given over to pigeons. Plane trees lean inward around the perimeter of the asphalt ball field, where a tidy squadron of middle-aged and elderly Asian women stretches in unison, some clinging to the chain-link fence for balance. One man wields a tai chi sword to the sound of Chinese flutes from a boom box. A gull spirals down out of the sky, screeching the whole way. All around I can hear what this city calls early morning silence,

an equidistant rumble that seems to begin a few blocks away.

I watch all of this, the tai chi, the stretching, the old men who have come to sit in the cool spring sunshine, the reinforced police vans delivering suspects to the court buildings just beyond it all, and as I watch I try to remember that Columbus Park was once Mulberry Bend. Mulberry Street still crooks to the southeast here, but the Bend proper is long gone. It was the most infamous slum in 19th-century New York, an immeasurable quantity of suffering compacted into 2.76 acres. On a bright April morning, it's hard to believe the Bend ever existed. But then such misery always inspires disbelief.

The Bend was ultimately torn down and a park built on its site in 1897 after unrelenting pressure from Jacob Riis, the Danish-born journalist and social reformer. In *How the Other Half Lives*, an early landmark in reforming literature whose title became a catchphrase, Riis provides some numbers for Mulberry Bend, which he obtained from the city's Registrar of Vital Statistics. In 1888, he wrote, 5,650 people lived on Baxter and Mulberry streets between Park and Bayard. If Riis means strictly the buildings within the Bend, as he almost certainly does, then the population density there was 2,047 persons per acre, nearly all of them recent immigrants.

By itself, that's an almost meaningless figure. But think of it this way: In Manhattan today, 1,537,195 persons live on 14,720 acres, a density of slightly more than 104 per acre. (In 1890, the average

density within the built-up areas of Manhattan was about 115 per acre.) If Manhattan were peopled as thickly today as the Bend was in 1888, it would have more than 30 million inhabitants, an incomprehensible figure, the equivalent of nearly the whole of California jammed onto a single island. To put it another way, if the people who live in Manhattan today were packed as tightly as the immigrants in Mulberry Bend were, they could all live in Central Park with room to spare. But these are suppositions, imaginary numbers. The truly astonishing figure, of course, is 5,650 persons—actual human beings, every one of them—living in Mulberry Bend, among the highest population density ever recorded anywhere.

Now consider a final set of numbers: According to Riis and the city statistician, the death rate of children under five in Mulberry Bend was 140 per 1,000, roughly 1 out of 7. This is likely to be an underestimate. (Citywide, the number was just under 100 per 1,000 and falling fast.) Today, Mulberry Bend would rank between Lesotho and Tanzania in under-five mortality and worse than Haiti, Eritrea, Congo, and Bangladesh. Last year, the under-five mortality rate for the United States was 8 per 1,000, or 1 out of 125.

Numbers, even numbers as striking as these, do not do a good job of conveying horror. But when the horror is literally fleshed out, it begins to make an impression, as it did on Riis himself. After coming to America in 1870, at age 21, and enduring a vagrant existence for a few years, he found work at the *New York Tri-*

bune as a police reporter and was sent to the office at 303 Mulberry Street, a few blocks north of the Bend and across from police headquarters. Night after night, Riis visited the Bend, sometimes in police company, often not, and he reported what he saw—especially the extreme overcrowding—to the Board of Health. "It did not make much of an impression," Riis wrote in *The Making of an American.* "These things rarely do, put in mere words."

So Riis put them in pictures. With a flashgun and a handheld camera, invented just a few years earlier, Riis began to take photographs of what he found in the Bend. "From them," he wrote, "there was no appeal." They made misery demonstrable in a way that nothing else had. No political or economic or cultural theory could justify the crowding his photographs document. There was no explaining away the sense of oppression and confinement they reveal. In picture after picture you see not only the poverty and the congestion of the Bend—the stale sweatshops and beer dives and five-cent lodging houses—but the emotional and psychological consequences of people living on top of each other.

Since the mid-20th century, Riis has been considered one of the founders of documentary photography. Over the years, his photographs of Mulberry Bend and other New York slums have become a part of the city's conscience. But his approach to photography was flatly utilitarian. "I had use for it," Riis wrote of the camera, "and beyond that I never went." Printing technology at the time meant that in books and articles his pictures had to be redrawn as wood engravings, considerably reducing their impact. The actual photographs were seen only in lantern slides accompanying his lectures. What mattered was not aesthetics but what the pictures showed. Riis had a similar use for words and statistics. They were merely tools to persuade New Yorkers to witness what was right in front of their eyes.

In one of his many articles on tenement housing, Riis printed a map of the Bend drawn from overhead, a silhouette showing the proportion of open space to buildings. Looking at that map is like looking at an old-fashioned diagram of a cell, a hieroglyphic of dark and light. It's hard to know what to call the spaces depicted by the white areas on Riis's map. *Yard* is too pastoral and *air shaft* too hygienic. Riis calls them "courts" and "alleys," but even those words are too generous. What the white spaces really portray are outdoor places where only a single layer of humans could live, many of them homeless children who clustered in external stairwells and on basement steps. In the tenements of the Bend—three, four, and five stories each—families and solitary lodgers, who paid five cents apiece for floor space, crowded together in airless cubicles. "In a room not thirteen feet either way," Riis wrote of one midnight encounter, "slept twelve men and women, two or three in bunks set in a sort of alcove, the rest on the floor."

For reformers, Riis included, the trouble with the Bend wasn't merely the profits it returned to slumlords and city politicians, nor was it just the high rents that forced tenants to sublet floor space to strangers. The problem was also how to portray the Bend in a way that conveyed its contagious force, the absence of basic sanitation, of clean water and fresh air, the presence of disease, corruption, and crime, the enervation and despair. It was, for Riis, the problem of representing an unrepresentable level of defilement. The power of his silhouette map, for instance, is flawed by its white margins, which falsely imply that conditions improved across the street, when, in fact, the entire Sixth Ward was cramped and impoverished. Even the grimmest of Riis's photographs show only a few people, at most, in the back alleys and basement dives. Powerful as they are, these pictures fail to convey the simple tonnage of human flesh in those dead-end blocks.

But the problem of Mulberry Bend was also how to interpret it. On a bright spring morning in the 1880s or early 1890s, a New Yorker—curiosity aroused, perhaps, by one of Riis's articles—might have strolled over to Mulberry or Baxter Street to see for himself. What he found there would depend on his frame of mind. It might have been, as photographs suggest, a bustling streetfront crowded with people going rather shabbily about the ordinary sorts of business, much as they might in other neighborhoods. Such a New Yorker—disinclined to push through to the dark inner rooms a few flights up or to the dismal courts and alleys behind or to the dank beer dives below—might conclude that perhaps Riis had exaggerated and that perhaps all there was to see here was a people, immigrants nearly all of them, who were insufficiently virtuous or cleanly or hardworking or American. It would be possible for such a person to blame Mulberry Bend on the very people who were its victims. But when the tenements were condemned and their inhabitants moved into decent housing, particularly in Harlem, they blended imperceptibly into the fabric of the city.

Riis has been faulted for his glib descriptive use of racial and ethnic stereotypes, a convention of his time that sounds raw and coarse to us now. In his defense, he came to understand that the power of a place like Mulberry Bend was enough to corrupt its residents, no matter who they were, as it had the Irish, and then the Italians who were their successors in the Bend. No iniquity within the Bend was as great, to Riis, as the political and financial iniquity that sustained the tenements there.

But the tragedy of Mulberry Bend isn't only that it came to exist and, once in existence, to be tolerated. It was also that when the city finally tore down the Bend and at last built the park that Calvert Vaux had designed for the site, a kind of forgetfulness descended. A New Yorker coming to the newly built Mulberry Bend Park in 1897, or to its renaming in 1911, or merely to watch the sun rise on a bright spring morning in 2001, might never know that there had been such a place as the Bend. The park that stands in its place is some kind of redemption, but without memory no redemption is ever complete. And without action of the kind that Riis undertook, justice remains only a matter of desire.

From *Mother Jones,* July/August 2001, pp. 54-57. © 2001 by Foundation for National Progress. Reprinted by permission.

The Murder of Lucy Pollard

Caleb Crain

On July 12, 1895, in Lunenburg County, Virginia, a retired farmer complained to his diary that the state was spending $300 a day to keep four blacks accused of murder safe in jail. "They should and ought to have been promptly lynched at once," wrote Robert Allen, who had recently been elected to his twentieth consecutive term as a justice of the peace, "for there is not the least shadow of doubt about the guilt of all four of them."

In *A Murder in Virginia: Southern Justice on Trial*, Suzanne Lebsock, a historian, has chronicled the efforts that frustrated Allen and other would-be lynchers in Lunenburg County. The prisoners, three women and one man, were being held for the murder and robbery of a white woman named Lucy Pollard. The story is full of suspense and complex characters, with a plot so rich in incident and irony that Lebsock is puzzled that the case vanished from history for nearly ninety years. After all, Lebsock writes, "it had bedeviled some of Virginia's most prominent politicians, engaged its best legal minds, and inspired some of the state's most creative investigative reporting."

In a footnote, she names the historian who broke the silence. Ann Field Alexander, who wrote her 1973 Ph.D. dissertation on John Mitchell Jr., the editor of the black newspaper *The Richmond Planet*, who covered the trials and their aftermath. With *Race Man: The Rise and Fall of the 'Fighting Editor' John Mitchell Jr.*, a book based on Alexander's dissertation, readers may supplement Lebsock's account of the case with a biography of the journalist who was largely responsible for its surprising outcome.

The body of Lucy Pollard, a white planter's daughter, was discovered by her husband at dusk on Friday, June 14, 1895, lying between her house and her chicken coop. A nearby meat ax accounted for the wounds to her face and head, while a struggle with her killer was the likely cause of the bruises on her neck and wrists. A lens had been knocked out of her glasses, and a dozen eggs had fallen from her basket and were lying broken beside her on the ground.

Lucy had married down. Her husband, Edward Pollard, a former peddler, had, thanks in part to the land brought to him by a series of wives, become a farmer and moneylender. When he came upon the body he rang the alarm bell twice, then stopped to check the liquor cabinet, where he kept his cash, and found that he had been robbed as well as widowed. His bell-ringing and shouting brought neighbors to the scene, including two black women, Mary Abernathy and Pokey Barnes, who kept vigil over the body through the night while Edward slept beside it. The next day, the women were arrested as suspects by the local constable. Soon Mary Barnes, a black woman who worked in Pollard's garden and was the mother of Pokey Barnes, was also arrested. Mary Abernathy and Mary Barnes were the last people known to have seen Lucy Pollard alive. They had shared a drink of water with her and Edward at four o'clock, and after Edward had left, they had stayed behind for a few minutes to chat. Pokey Barnes, meanwhile, admitted to having been in the vicinity at the time.

Edward Pollard thought that some of his wife's clothes were missing and, as Lebsock explains, stealing clothes was considered to be a crime characteristic of black women. All of this evidence was circumstantial, and it failed to convince a coroner's jury. On Monday, three days after the murder, the women were released. But shortly afterward they were fingered as accomplices in the murder by a fourth suspect, a mulatto laborer named William Henry "Solomon" Marable, who had been seen the day after the murder spending twenty-dollar bills, then a large denomination, in nearby Chase City. The women were rearrested.

Despite angry crowds carrying ropes, the suspects were not lynched. Local officials smuggled them from one jail to another until they reached the relative safety of the city of Richmond, where they fell under the protection of the new governor, Charles O'Ferrall. During the last weeks of O'Ferrall's 1893 election campaign, an unemployed black laborer had been hanged, shot, and burned in Roanoke before an audience of four thousand onlookers, and in response, O'Ferrall had committed himself politically to the suppression of lynching. At the request of Lunenburg County's sheriff, O'Ferrall ordered two infantry units to escort the suspects back to Lunenburg for their trials. There a captain in the militia named Frank Cunningham pacified the crowds outside the courthouse by organizing baseball games and concerts and offering free medical care. Marable and the three women were safely tried. They were convicted and sentenced, and it looked as if Marable and two of the women would unjustly but legally hang, until a young black newspaper editor, John Mitchell Jr., involved himself in the case.

Mitchell was born in 1863 at Laburnum, an estate outside Richmond, the property of James Lyons, a genteel and well-connected attorney. Lyons was a close friend of Jefferson Davis, owned more than two dozen slaves, and decried Lincoln's Emancipation Proclamation as "inhuman and atrocious." Among his possessions were Mitchell's mother, a seamstress, and his father, a coachman. Alexander suggests that young Mitchell studied his master's grand manner, which he later used to social advantage. As an adolescent, Mitchell took advantage of the schools that opened for blacks during the early years of Reconstruction and was educated to become a teacher. While teaching in Richmond's schools, he began in 1883 to write for the black press. His first column, for *The New York Globe*, the most prominent black newspaper in the country, narrated the hanging of a black murderess in Henrico County, Virginia, in a suspenseful and sentimental style.

When a new black weekly, *The Richmond Planet*, was founded in December 1883, Mitchell and several other teachers began to write for it. No clippings from the paper's first two years have survived. A few months after the Planet's inception, white Democrats ousted blacks and their allies from the Richmond school board, and many of the city's black teachers were purged, among them Mitchell and ten others who had been moonlighting for the *Planet*. Unable to find any other work that satisfied him, at the end of 1884, Mitchell, at age twenty-one, took over the paper.

Under Mitchell's leadership, the *Planet* had an exuberant, even militant tone. In every issue, beneath an image of a hanged black man, Mitchell published a list of lynching victims. He urged blacks to arm themselves against lynch mobs, writing that "the best remedy for a lyncher or a cursed mid-night rider is a 16-shot Winchester rifle in the hands of a dead-shot Negro who has nerve enough to pull the trigger." He presented himself in his articles as a swashbuckling character, and at times he was. In 1886, when his articles about a recent lynching provoked an anonymous death threat, Mitchell printed the letter and then toured the scene of the lynching, sporting a pair of Smith & Wesson revolvers. In 1889 he saved a fifteen-year-old from hanging by riding all night to hand-deliver the governor's stay of execution. In 1893 he helped obtain the acquittal and release from jail of a black farmhand who had miraculously survived a beating, shooting, and hanging by a white mob. He became well known for his bravado, and in 1888 he was elected to the lower house of Richmond's city council. In 1890 he was elected alderman.

Mitchell made his newspaper a financial success. He found odd outside jobs to keep his printing press running. Alexander suggests that the *Planet* may have been subsidized by the local Republican Party in return for its support. Most important, black readers responded to its appeal. Alexander quotes an ad for subscribers that ran in the *Planet* in 1891:

Do you want to see what the Colored People are doing? Read the *Planet*. Do you want to know what Colored People think? Read the *Planet*. Do you want to know how many Colored People are hung to trees without due process of law? Read the *Planet*....

Anti-lynching was the principal cause of the *Planet*, but by the time of the Lunenburg cases, Mitchell realized that he had to press the *Planet*'s campaign further. Even when blacks received due process in the courts, they could be the victims of racism in the community. The threat of lynching could function as blackmail, intimidating judges and juries into disregarding evidence, or the lack of it.

For righting this subtler injustice, Mitchell realized, the murder of Lucy Pollard was an opportune case. As he must have suspected when he read accounts in the white press of the four Lunenburg trials, and as he recognized as soon as he interviewed the four prisoners in Richmond in late July 1895, the case against the women was extremely thin. The principal witness against them was Solomon Marable, who had confessed to the murder and, under a surprisingly vigorous cross-examination by Pokey Barnes herself, had also confessed to perjury. Moreover, only one of the women, Mary Abernathy, had been represented by a lawyer. He had represented her only for as long as it took to request a change of venue; as soon as the request was denied, he quit.

During his first jailhouse interview, Mitchell learned from Mary Abernathy that a local white man whose last name was Thompson had threatened to kill Edward Pollard the day of the murder, calling him "a thief in every degree"—a fact that had gone unmentioned in all four trials. In the Lunenburg courtroom there had been such flagrant disregard of the facts—lack of interest in them, really—that it was clear to Mitchell that the trials' outcome was the result of pressure on the part of lynch-hungry people like the justice of the peace and diarist Robert Allen, the lack of mob violence notwithstanding. Mitchell at once hired three conservative white lawyers to appeal the verdicts against the women. To pay their fees, he appealed to the generosity of readers of the *Planet*.

Thompson's threat to "squash [Edward Pollard] in hell" turned out to be only the first in a series of revelations that undermined the case against Mary Abernathy,

Pokey Barnes, and Mary Barnes. The case further unraveled when Solomon Marable began to tell a new story: not three black women but a white man had enlisted him to help with the killing, and that man's name was also Thompson. But the Thompson who had threatened to "squash" Edward Pollard turned out to be William G. Thompson, Edward Pollard's stepson, whereas the Thompson accused by Solomon Marable was David James Thompson, the son of one of Lucy Pollard's cousins. Neither Thompson was charged with murder, although Solomon continued to repeat the name of David James Thompson to the press, until Thompson took the precaution of suing one of Richmond's white newspapers for libel.

Was David James Thompson the murderer? Lebsock leads the reader through a thicket of conflicting theories and irreconcilable testimony. Since David James Thompson was never tried, there isn't enough evidence to judge him in retrospect. But Marable's story about Thompson was more credible than his story about the three women had been. He made his accusation against Thompson in court only once, and retracted it almost immediately, but it must have helped to sow doubt, especially in the minds of the judges, who later granted retrials in the women's cases.

Doubt over the identity of the killer persists. No one ever found the eight hundred dollars stolen from Edward Pollard, or at least no one ever admitted to finding it. And in his last statement before hanging, Solomon Marable insisted that authorities were executing the wrong man.

At the end of her narrative, Lebsock speculates on who the murderer or murderers might have been. She suggests that the crime may have been the work of David James Thompson's brother, Herbert Thompson, and that Cass Gregory, an amateur detective, may have encouraged Solomon to name the right family but the wrong man, so that Gregory could blackmail Herbert Thompson. This strikes me as somewhat too complex to be likely. But unresolved murders are tempting, and it is one of the merits of Lebsock's book that readers acquire so detailed a knowledge of the case that they can invent theories of their own.

I myself was struck by an odd bit of dialogue that Marable repeated almost every time he blamed the murder on David James Thompson. According to Marable, just before Thompson murdered Lucy Pollard, he asked her, "Do you know me?" and she replied, "You are a white man." While Lebsock observes that "the statement is just strange enough to ring true," her explanation doesn't quite account for its strangeness. Was Marable struggling to make up a story about a killer unlike himself, while also struggling riot to pin the crime on a real and identifiable person, as his story about the three black women had done? As an invented line of dialogue, "You are a white man" would have been such a story, though not a very convincing one. On the other hand, what if Marable was telling the truth? Perhaps he reported Lucy Pollard's statement accurately but misunderstood what she had said. Perhaps when the killer had asked, "Do you know me?" Mrs. Pollard had answered, "You are a Whiteman." She would have been replying that she did know him, by giving his family name. Therefore, having robbed her, Mr. Whiteman would have had to kill her.

The 1890 census records for Virginia were destroyed in a fire long ago, but the names "Whiteman" and "Whitman" appear in Richmond city directories for 1889 and 1890. But unless there are descendants of people named Whiteman with pertinent information, my theory isn't any more susceptible of proof than Lebsock's.

Alexander points out that the close of the nineteenth century has been called "the nadir" of African-American history. In the 1890s, lynching in the United States was at its peak, with 161 cases reported in 1892. Virginia had a better record than most Southern states. Racial violence there tapered off steeply around the time of the Lunenburg cases. Yet even in Virginia, the situation of African-Americans continued to be bleak for years to come. In 1896, flush with his success in exonerating the three black women, Mitchell failed to win reelection as an alderman when white election officials obstructed the voting in the polls in black districts and discarded many black ballots on the grounds that they were incorrectly marked.

The disfranchisement of blacks soon became systematic; after Mitchell's defeat, there would be no blacks on Richmond's city council for the next fifty years. In 1901, Virginia's trains were segregated for the first time. In 1904, Richmond's streetcars were segregated. Indeed, the transit company responsible for the segregation order was represented by one of the lawyers Mitchell had hired to defend the Lunenburg women a decade earlier.

Lebsack believes that the Lunenburg cases were forgotten because few people had both the power and the motive to recall them publicly once white supremacy took hold in Virginia. When blacks lost their political voice, they also lost the ability to keep alive the memory of past victories, and whites found the Lunenburg cases inconvenient to remember, perhaps because, as Lebsock suggests, their story was exceptional, involving "a united and highly mobilized African American citizenry, formidable African American leadership, and a critical mass of whites and blacks who worked in concert to the same end."

Yet the Lunenburg cases coincide with the decline of lynching in Virginia, and so to some degree they reflect the historical moment. Without Mitchell's intervention, Mary Abernathy and Pokey Barnes would no doubt have been hanged, but once Mitchell took up their cause, a number of powerful whites were willing to bend the rules to assist him. When Lunenburg's sheriff would not accept a military escort to prevent the lynching, the governor refused to hand the prisoners over to him, even though he had no legal authority to hold them. In the original trials no one had filed a bill of exceptions on behalf of the defendants, but Virginia's Supreme Court of Appeals nonetheless granted writs that allowed lawyers to request retrials. A commonwealth attorney spontaneously halted his county's prosecution of Pokey Barnes in what seems to have been an act of conscience. In 1896, the year of *Plessy* v. *Ferguson*, the white elite of Virginia seems to have been ready to set aside both lynching and the railroading of juries by the threat of lynching. Why?

Perhaps the state's leaders were able to feel ashamed of these clumsy and brutal tools of oppression because they had taken up a new, bloodless, and more efficient one: disfranchisement. It may be no coincidence that Mitchell was turned out of office just as he was winning the Lunenburg cases. White supremacy had shifted its strategy. The shift was never a complete one. Lynching survived, side by side with denying blacks the vote, until the 1960s, and it would turn out that in order to end lynching, one had to allow black people to vote.

The shift does not make Mitchell's part in the Lunenburg cases any the less heroic, but it does complicate the story's ending. In the difficult decades that followed, he seems to have become demoralized. "We find as we grow older that nothing speaks so loud as money," he wrote in 1905. Although he kept his newspaper, he turned most of his attention to banking, insurance, and real estate speculation, and in the pursuit of financial success, he ceased to challenge the people he began to call "quality white folks." After his bank failed in 1922, he was found guilty of fraud and theft. The conviction was overturned on technicalities, but his career was over. A. Philip Randolph's journal, *The Messenger*, did not regret Mitchell's fall from grace: "When one loses his courage and devotes most of his time [to] urging the victims of oppression to be polite to the persecutors, it is time for him to go." Perhaps we remember the Lunenburg cases now because we can appreciate a victory in a cause that did not achieve everything that had been hoped for.

OUR FIRST OLYMPICS

A CENTURY AGO a tiny American team arrived in Athens drained from an awful journey and proposing to take on the champions of Europe with—among other handicaps—a discus thrower who had never seen a real discus

BY BOB FULTON

THERE WERE SURELY MOMENTS during the long journey to Greece when James Connolly was seized with foreboding, convinced this antic venture was doomed to failure. Connolly and a dozen countrymen, who constituted America's first Olympic team, certainly had cause for misgivings as they sailed toward Athens and the revival of the long-dormant Games in 1896. These thirteen competitors—an unlucky thirteen, it seemed—had received no financial support from the nation they were to represent. The general public regarded the reborn Olympics with an utter lack of interest, and even their fellow athletes didn't care; only one of the Americans was a national champion in the event he had entered.

Now, it turned out, they were due to arrive in Athens the day before the competition commenced, woefully out of shape after a wearing sixteen-day journey from Hoboken, New Jersey. Failure appeared as inevitable as the next morning's sunrise.

No one viewed the American team's plight more bleakly than Connolly, who had dropped out of Harvard to take part in the Games. The fact that he had managed to lose his wallet in Italy seemed emblematic of the whole doleful enterprise.

SEVEN HUNDRED AMERICANS will participate in the 1996 centennial Games in Atlanta, a figure that dwarfs the tiny U.S. contingent of 1896. But the contrast between the first modern Olympics and the upcoming Games transcends mere numbers, for no American team has ever encountered as much adversity as our first.

The hardships faced by the pioneers of a century ago were the result of indifference. All the prominent athletic groups in the United States turned their backs on the Olympics and, by extension, on Pierre de Coubertin, the French baron who was the driving force behind the Olympic renaissance. His grand revival barely drew a glance from an America that thought the Games a relic best left buried under the dust of the ages—especially given their checkered history.

The ancient Olympics came to an ignominious end. They had originated as a local festival in 776 B.C., but as their popularity grew, athletes journeyed to Olympia from the far margins of the known world. Increasingly elaborate prizes fomented increasingly widespread cheating. In time an avalanche of abuses buried the ideals that guided the earliest competitors. A disgusted Emperor Theodosius abolished the Games in A.D. 393.

Coubertin believed that resuscitating the Games in their old grandeur would foster international harmony. He first proposed his idea in 1892 during a lecture at the Sorbonne: "Let us export oarsmen, runners, fencers; there is the free trade of the future. And on the day when it shall take its place among the customs of Europe, the cause of peace will have received a new and powerful support."

His vision of a multinational gathering came to fruition two years later, when the International Athletic Congress voted to hold the first modern Olympics in Greece, where the Games had been born. But while Olympic fervor burned on the Continent, American sportsmen dismissed the revival as a European creation designed for European athletes. In fact, the prestigious New York Athletic Club, which included many national track and field champions among its membership, snubbed the Games completely.

So the American presence at the first modern Olympics was utterly extemporaneous; our pioneer Olympians were spurred by personal impulse to be the representatives of a nation that didn't care whether it was represented or not.

James Connolly was a twenty-seven-year-old Harvard undergraduate when he got wind of the Games. He applied for a leave of absence from school to participate only to have a dean deny him out of hand, citing Connolly's poor academic standing. His only recourse, the dean informed him, was to resign from Harvard and then take his chances on being readmitted later. Connolly was indignant.

"I am not resigning and I am not making application to re-enter," he told the dean. "But I *am* going to the Olympic Games, so I am through with Harvard right now."

Connolly never did return to school and, in fact, still held a grudge years after he had gained renown as a war correspondent for *Collier's* magazine and as the author of twenty-five novels. Offered an honorary degree by Harvard, he summarily refused it.

Robert Garrett, a twenty-year-old captain of the Princeton track team and the scion of a wealthy Baltimore banking family, learned of the revival Games from his history professor, who wholeheartedly endorsed Coubertin's efforts.

Garrett persuaded three schoolmates to accompany him—after agreeing to pay their way. His largess enabled the sprinter Francis Lane; Herbert Jamison, a middle-distance runner; and the pole vaulter Albert Tyler to carry Princeton's black and orange colors overseas (official Olympic uniforms would not be mandated until 1906).

The Boston Athletic Association sent five representatives to Greece, in no small measure because of a facetious remark uttered by the distance runner Arthur Blake three months earlier. Congratulated on winning a 1,000-yard race, Blake joked, "Oh, I am too good for Boston. I ought to go over and run the Marathon at Athens in the Olympic Games." A stockbroker named Arthur Burnham overheard him and offered to bankroll a BAA contingent. Blake was joined by Thomas Burke, the defending U.S. champion in the 440-yard run; the hurdler Thomas Curtis; Ellery Clark, a jumper; and the pole vaulter William Welles Hoyt.

Gardner Williams, a swimmer, and two marksmen, the brothers John and Sumner Paine, rounded out an American team that was really nothing more than a glorified pickup squad. After all, no trials had been held to determine the most qualified representatives, and only Burke was a national champion in his event.

Prospects for success in Athens were abysmal and declined from there when the star-crossed competitors began their odyssey on March 20 aboard the tramp steamer *Fulda*. The ship was ill equipped to carry passengers, but it was cheap. With little room to exercise, the athletes were reckoning on the benefits of two weeks' worth of workouts in Athens prior to the start of the Olympics.

But when the *Fulda* docked in Naples, twelve dreary days later, on April 1, they discovered to their horror that the Games were scheduled to begin on April 6, not April 18 as they had supposed; the Greeks observed the Julian calendar, not the Gregorian. Time was running out.

After crossing Italy by train, the team sailed to Patras, a Greek port on the Ionian Sea. The weary Americans disembarked and immediately boarded a train for a ten-hour trip to Athens. They arrived on April 5 utterly dispirited.

An official reception in the capital, while hospitable, served only to deplete the team further. Curtis recalled: "We were met with a procession, with bands blaring before and behind, and were marched on foot for what seemed miles to the Hôtel de Ville. Here speech after speech was made in Greek, presumably very flattering to us, but of course entirely unintelligible. We were given large bumpers of the white-resin wine of Greece and told by our advisors that it would be a gross breach of etiquette if we did not drain these off in response to the various toasts. As soon as this ceremony was over, we were again placed at the head of a procession and marched to our hotel. I could not help feeling that so much marching, combined with several noggins of resinous wine, would tell on us in the contests the following day."

Fortunately Curtis proved a poor prophet. Only two finals were held on the opening day, and the wrung-out, hung-over Americans won them both.

Connolly gained a landmark victory—and acclaim as the first Olympic champion since the fourth-century athlete Varastades—with a leap of 44 feet 11 3/4 inches in the triple jump. In a matter of hours he had completed a stunning metamorphosis from unknown to celebrity.

THE JUDGES PRESENTED CONNOLLY WITH A tangible link to his predecessors. "The olive crown that was awarded the victors," wrote the New York *Herald's* correspondent, "will be made from material furnished from the same grove from which were taken the leaves and sprigs that formed the crowns of victory more than 15 centuries ago."

Connolly also received a diploma and a medal—a *silver* medal. Although Olympic records list gold, silver, and bronze recipients back to 1896, gold medals were not actually given champions until the 1908 London Games (for clarity's sake, winners have been referred to throughout this article as gold medalists). Runners-up were awarded bronze medals and diplomas.

Connolly's historic victory in the triple jump notwithstanding, the opening-day highlight was unquestionably Robert Garrett's performance with the discus. Garrett had never even seen a real discus before his arrival in Athens—the event was still all but unknown in the United States—but "having noticed on the program

the throwing of the discus, [he] decided in youthful fashion to have a try at it merely for the sake of competing in an event that belonged to antiquity.… "

Unable to locate a genuine discus with which to practice at Princeton, Garrett commissioned a local blacksmith to forge one, patterned on a description he unearthed in the works of the second-century Greek writer Lucian: "A lump of brass, circular and not unlike a small shield." The finished product weighed twenty pounds. Discouraged by his inability to throw this monster any distance at all, Garrett abandoned his plan to compete in the discus throw.

He reconsidered only after making a fortuitous discovery in Athens. While strolling to the Panathenaic Stadium, Garrett happened upon a discarded discus, picked it up, and was astonished to find that it weighed less than five pounds. After several experimental throws, he decided to enter the event after all.

It seemed a reckless choice. He was up against Panagiotis Paraskevopoulos, the reigning Greek champion, the prohibitive favorite whose countrymen called him a "discus demigod."

"Garrett entered the arena unknown and unheralded," said the *Herald*. "His hair was not as dark or curly as his antagonist's, nor his nose as straight. He was scantily clad and looked hungry. The Athenians gazed with pity."

ENTERING AN OLYMPIC EVENT, as Sumner Paine demonstrated by joining (and winning) one on a whim, was simple proposition in 1896: Just show up.

Soon they were gazing with wonder. "We all held our breath as he carefully prepared for the last throw," recalled Albert Tyler, Garrett's Princeton classmate. "By this time he had caught the knack … and had complete confidence in himself. He put all his energy into the last cast, and as the discus flew through the air the vast concourse of people were silent as if the structure were empty. When it struck, there was a tremendous burst of applause from all sides." The spindly American had spun the discus 7½ inches beyond Paraskevopoulos's best toss to snatch the gold medal from his adversary. Although the distance was modest by modern standards—95 feet 7½ inches (the existing Olympic record is 225 feet 9 inches)—it was a "throw considered something phenomenal," the *Herald* reported.

Garrett humbled another Greek star the next day. He heaved the shot put 36 feet 9¾ inches to dethrone Miltiades Gouskos before an estimated hundred thousand spectators. "Even Garrett was hailed with enthusiasm when he defeated Gouskos," wrote the *Herald* reporter, "although the Greeks were surprised and disappointed by the downfall of their champion."

Garrett's victories doubtless surprised those back home too. "Captain Robert Garrett was up to a year ago little known as an athlete, even at Princeton," noted the New York *Herald*. "In his freshman year young Garrett showed some ability in the weights and jumps and was taken on the track team largely because of his promise to make an athlete with training. George Goldie, the trainer, took him in hand, trained him, especially in putting in the shot, and has now succeeded in putting him very close to the first rank of college athletes."

Of world-class athletes, for that matter. Garrett won four medals at the revival Olympics—a total eclipsed only by the German gymnast Hermann Weingartner's seven—and added two more at the Paris Games four years later.

Thomas Burke joined Garrett in the winner's circle on the second day, having coasted to victory in the 400-meter run. Then Ellery Clark attempted the long jump.

Like Connolly, Clark had requested a leave of absence from Harvard to participate in the Games; unlike Connolly, he received permission, because of his superior grades. But after fouling on his first two jumps, Clark lamented ever having petitioned his dean for time off. "I was little short of agony," he wrote later. "I shall never forget my feelings as I stood at the end of the path for my third— and last—try. Five thousand miles, I reflected, I had come; and was it to end in this? Three fouls and then five thousand miles back again, with that for my memory of the Games."

He gathered himself, ran, leaped—and touched the ground 20 feet 10 inches later to claim the championship. He and his Boston Athletic Association teammates burst forth with their distinctive victory cheer, "B-A-A, rah, rah, rah." While most of the startled Greeks considered this outburst "barbaric," some spectators found the display of enthusiasm refreshing; King George, a frequent visitor to the stadium, asked the BAA members to repeat their cheer on several occasions. Even discounting royal requests, the Bostonians' shouts were heard regularly in Athens: Of the twelve track and field events, BAA athletes won half.

After posting victories on the second day, Clark and Burke returned to claim additional honors. Clark followed his gold-medal performance in the long jump with a winning leap of 5 feet 11¼ inches in the high jump. Burke, fresh off his 400-meter success, captured the 100-meter championship in 12.0 seconds, aided by a "crouch" start then foreign to the Europeans. Curtis collected a gold medal with a 17.6-second effort in the 110-meter hurdles, and Hoyt soared 10 feet 10 inches to win the pole vault.

Not all the U.S. victories came in track. The Paine brothers had traveled to Athens independently of the American team and thus been spared the claustrophobic miseries of the *Fulda*. Sumner was working at a Paris art gallery when John passed through en route to Athens and persuaded his brother to accompany him. Sumner did more than tag along; he entered the free-pistol event on a whim and won. He also finished second in the military-revolver competition— to John.

Entering an Olympic event, as Sumner Paine demonstrated, was a simple proposition in 1896: Just show up. An Oxford student named John Boland, for instance, traveled to the Olympics as a spectator, then impulsively entered the tennis competition and wound up winning gold medals in the singles and doubles competitions.

Conversely, one American athlete underwent a transformation from competitor to spectator in Greece—quite unintentionally. Williams, a champion swimmer accustomed to the tepid water of indoor pools, was not prepared for the 100-meter freestyle event, held in the frigid Bay of Zea. Curtis described his teammate's all-too-brief performance: "… as he poised with the others on the edge of the float, waiting for the gun, his spirit thrilled with patriotism and determination. At the crack of the pistol, the contestants dived head first into the water. In a split second his head reappeared. 'Jesu Christo! I'm freezing!' he cried. With that shriek of astonished frenzy he lashed back to the float. For him the Olympics were over."

The fifty-five-degree water temperatures fazed even the hardiest of participants. "The icy water almost cut into our stomachs," said Alfréd Hajós of Hungary, the champion, who later entered—and won—the 1,500-meter freestyle, having this time taken the precaution of smearing a layer of grease over his body as insulation.

Swimming, as it turned out, was the only sport U.S. athletes entered but did not win. Indeed, the ad hoc team captured more gold medals than any other nation in the showcase sport of track and field; it won nine of the twelve events and demoralized several Greek champions. Overall, the United States claimed eleven gold medals to outstrip more established European rivals, such as Greece (ten), Germany (seven), France (five), and Great Britain (three).

Admittedly, THE QUALITY OF THE COMPETITION was watered down; a multitude of elite athletes—not just U.S. champions— spurned Coubertin's revival, which accounts for the mediocre winning times and distances. In fact, not a single world record fell in Athens. Casper Whitney of *Harper's* declared Spiridon Louis's climactic victory in the marathon "the only remarkable performance at the Games."

Maybe so (although Panagiotis Paraskevopoulos probably wouldn't have agreed), but that shouldn't diminish the achievements of America's first Olympians. These intrepid pioneers who weathered adversity en route to Greece and surpassed every expectation once they got there could celebrate not only victories but a pre-eminent role in a momentous event—the rebirth of the Olympic Games.

"Nothing could equal this first revival," Clark wrote afterward. "The flavor of the Athenian soil—the feeling of helping to bridge the gap between the old and the new—the indefinable poetic charm of knowing one's self thus linked with the past, a successor to the great heroic figures of olden times. There is but one first time in everything, and that first time was gloriously, and in a manner ever to be remembered, the privilege of the American team of 1896."

Bob Fulton is the author of The Summer Olympics: A Treasury of Legends and Lore, *recently published by Diamond Communications, South Bend, Indiana.*

T.R.'s Virtuoso Performance

Speaking softly but wielding a big stick, Theodore Roosevelt orchestrated the independence of Panama and gained U.S. rights to build the canal.

Henry J. Hendrix II

President Theodore Roosevelt was furious. On August 17, 1903, the senate of Colombia surprisingly rejected the carefully negotiated Hay-Herran Treaty, an agreement that would have leased the United States a narrow strip of land across the Central American isthmus and allowed the U.S. to purchase the legal right of way and equipment of a French-based construction consortium established in the area. With the treaty already ratified by the U.S. Senate, an affirmative vote by the Colombians would have authorized construction to begin on one of the greatest engineering feats in history: the long-awaited canal across the Isthmus of Panama, the northern province of Colombia.

Creation of a canal connecting the Atlantic and Pacific oceans to expedite the delivery of products from Asia and the U.S. West Coast to eastern metropolitan markets and shorten the delivery time for American products and raw resources to overseas markets (not to mention the quick transfer of Navy ships from one ocean to the other) was the centerpiece of Roosevelt's foreign policy. When word of the vote reached Washington, it had all the appearances of a badly disguised Colombian shakedown of both the United States and the French-based New Panama Canal Company for more money. Displaying his characteristic cultural chauvinism, Roosevelt raged that the "jack rabbits" in Bogotá must not be allowed to unilaterally "bar one of the future highways of civilization." Clearly, Colombia's attempt to gain more in terms of fiscal compensation struck a discordant note in the symphony of Roosevelt's foreign policy.

In the days following the Colombian vote, Roosevelt mulled over his options. Some advisers urged shifting the planned canal route north to Nicaragua, while others recommended the outright seizure of the isthmus, citing the United States' responsibilities under the 1846 treaty with New Grenada (Colombia) to keep commercial traffic flowing. T.R. waited, composing a plan.

More than 50 revolutions or uprisings had occurred on the isthmus in the previous 50 years. Ironically, Colombia had requested American assistance in squelching disturbances no less than six times, including as recently as 1901 and 1902. In short, the United States had repeatedly acted, in the interest of maintaining safe transit through the isthmus, as Colombia's policeman in Panama. Based upon these historical trends, T.R. fully expected another disturbance to occur during his presidency, and he was correct.

On October 9, 1903, Roosevelt conducted a carefully scored meeting with Philippe Bunau-Varilla, an accomplished engineer and major stockholder in the New Panama Canal Company, which held the contract for building the canal (but had so far been stymied in its efforts by engineering challenges, corrupt politicians and mostly the jungle). Bunau-Varilla, who had met repeatedly with leaders of the Panamanian opposition as well as members of Roosevelt's government, audaciously predicted a revolution would soon occur in Panama. Roosevelt affected surprise but remained noncommittal when Bunau-Varilla asked if the United States would take action either for or against the revolutionaries. The president, however, could not (or, more likely, would not) conceal his disgust with the Colombian leadership. His "accidental" indiscreet allusion to "a plan," caused Bunau-Varilla to bolt from the room confident of American support. Days later, two American Army officers, returning from the isthmus, provided T.R. with firsthand intelligence that Panama's local population deeply resented the Bogotá government and that a revolution would indeed occur at the end of October. This report may have given some comfort to the president, for he had already triggered a plan to ensure the success of the looming revolution. Like a musician instinctively reaching for his favorite instrument, Roosevelt ordered the U.S. Navy into action.

At the beginning of the 20th century, Theodore Roosevelt and the Isthmian canal were intrinsically linked in the public consciousness. T.R.'s wish for a canal lay at the center of a new American foreign policy. The United States had spent its first century conquering a continent. Now, with the closing of the frontier, Roosevelt, along with naval strategist Alfred T. Mahan and Senator Henry Cabot Lodge of Massachusetts, promoted a vision of the nation's future that expanded outward across the oceans. In 1903 the American people knew that Theodore Roosevelt was a Navy man.

The salt in Roosevelt's veins flowed from his mother's line. Martha Bulloch Roosevelt, the sister of two Confederate sailor-heroes, delighted her son with exciting tales, as he later remembered, of "ships, ships, ships and the fighting of ships till they sank into the depths of my soul." His first major accomplishment as an adult came with the publication of a history research project he had begun in college. *The Naval War of 1812* appeared in Roosevelt's 24th year and earned the young man reputations both as a first-rate historian and a talented strategist. He quickly emerged as one of the great minds of his generation. The impact of *The Naval War* and later writings led to T.R.'s appointment as assistant secretary of the Navy (a leading policy position in that day) at the age of 38. Working out of the gothic State, War, and Navy Building next to the White House, T.R. called upon prodigious reserves of energy and took full advantage of his boss' frequent absences to incrementally (at first) and then dramatically alter American foreign policy. In a single day in February 1898, following the explosion of USS *Maine* in Havana Harbor, the young subcabinet appointee nearly single-handedly catapulted his country into a war with Spain, sending multiple cables placing components of the American fleet on war footing. Roosevelt subsequently resigned from the Navy Department to go to Cuba as an Army volunteer. His heroism there ultimately led to national acclaim and the presidency.

The Naval War of 1812 appeared in Roosevelt's 24th year and earned him reputations both as a first-rate historian and a talented strategist.

Theodore Roosevelt knew the internal workings of the Navy, but more important as a young president, he knew how to orchestrate United States naval power to shift the tempo of the international environment in such a way as to facilitate American interests. In the winter of 1902, Roosevelt sent the combined Atlantic Fleet into the Caribbean to persuade Germany and Great Britain not to occupy Venezuela following defaulted loan payments. Many observers, convinced that Roosevelt hungered for the opportunity to prove himself as a wartime com-

mander in chief, expected another demonstration of overwhelming force near Colombia. T.R. surprised them all.

The Navy had ensured the success of a revolution and would soon be called upon to defend it.

The Navy and the Marine Corps, Roosevelt observed, had often served as the boot on the neck of revolution in Central America. So long as Colombia had acted in harmony with United States objectives, Roosevelt had remained willing to enforce the peace. Now faced with a situation out of tune with his U.S. interests, Theodore Roosevelt made a subtle yet effective shift in his use of American power. He decided to lift his boot and ignore rebel activities while at the same time denying Colombia the opportunity to land troops in Panama or transport those already there to centers of insurrection.

As darkness settled on Washington after Roosevelt's October meeting with Bunau-Varilla, a steady drumbeat of deployment orders resonated from the office of the secretary of the Navy. The gunboat USS *Nashville*, operating near Colón (the Caribbean port of the Panamanian province), had been scheduled to sail to St. Andrew's Island, off the coast of Nicaragua. Navy headquarters directed *Nashville*'s captain, Commander John Hubbard, to go ahead with his visit to the island, but to cut short his stay and proceed with all haste to Kingston, Jamaica, for coal and then return to Colón.

USS *Dixie*, an auxiliary cruiser attached to the North Atlantic Squadron, was reassigned to the Caribbean Squadron on October 15 and ordered to League Island, Pa., to take aboard 500 Marines. Stopping at Guantánamo and Kingston for supplies and coal, it expeditiously proceeded to Panama. Other ships soon followed, taking up station on both the Atlantic and Pacific approaches to the isthmus. Commanding officers received no specific instructions on their mission, but knew they were to hold their ships and crews in high readiness in this very unstable region.

Aboard *Nashville*, Hubbard arrived off Colón on November 2. That evening the Colombian transport *Cartegena* anchored with nearly 500 troops on board. Telegrams instructing Hubbard not to let Colombian troops ashore had not reached his ship, and the Colombians disembarked from *Cartegena* unopposed. They proceeded to the Colón train station with the intention of boarding a train bound for Panama City to put down the rebellion. Local Panamanian officials conspired to delay transportation of the troops, but graciously allowed their commanders to board a special train and proceed ahead of their force, which they were assured would be permitted to follow. In the interim, a telegram from the White House caught up with *Nashville*. Sent the day before, it instructed Hubbard to "make every effort to prevent the Colombian troops at Colón from proceeding to Panama ... secure special train if necessary." Invoking the broad language of the 1846 treaty, the Navy commander halted all trains "in order to preserve peace and good order." Declaring his neutrality, he denied rail use to both the Colombians and the rebellious Panamanians. By then, however, the Panamanians had already had time to optimally position their forces. The Colombians found themselves strategically and tactically isolated.

The Colombian troops reacted strongly. Deprived of their leadership, yet aware of the events transpiring around them, they threatened American property and citizens in Colón. Hubbard moved American women and children aboard *Nashville* and other American-flagged vessels, while the men and a force quickly assembled from the ship's crew took up a defensive position at an American warehouse.

A standoff ensued. Colombians attempted to provoke the Americans into action, but discipline prevailed. Two days passed as opposing commanders negotiated for advantage. The Americans offered money if the Colombians returned home. The Colombians demanded the return of their leaders. Both sides struggled to maintain civility. Hubbard, numerically out-numbered, knew that if he backed down the way could be cleared for the Colombians to board the train west, quickly ending Panamanian dreams of independence.

Just as the situation appeared untenable, the second movement of Roosevelt's composition began when USS *Dixie* appeared on the horizon with its complement of Marines. The Colombians boarded the steamer *Orinoco* the next morning, bound for the Colombian port Cartegena. Hubbard and the other commanders received instructions to allow no other Colombian troops to land. On November 18, Rear Adm. Thomas Glass, commander in chief of the Pacific Squadron, having previously recognized the new government in Panama, paid a visit to its leaders. The Navy had ensured the success of a revolution and would soon be called upon to defend it.

Two days later, the French mail steamer *Trent* entered Colón Harbor. Her passenger, General Rafael Reyes, was an envoy of the Colombian government. In a clear indication of the shadow Theodore Roosevelt cast over the events in Panama, Reyes asked the new senior American officer present, Navy Rear Adm. Joseph Bullock Coghlan, to host a conference on "political affairs." Coghlan demurred, citing a lack of "authority to enter into such subjects." Reyes somewhat reluctantly (and unsuccessfully) met with the Panamanians before declaring his intention to proceed on to Washington, D.C. Before leaving, he asked Coghlan the extent of Roosevelt's protection of the new republic. Reyes' worst fears were realized when the admiral replied that he had orders to prohibit any outside force from landing anywhere within the province of Panama. After the envoy's departure, the Colombian army chief of staff issued a blistering declaration, calling upon all Colombians to defend their nation's honor against Theodore Roosevelt's infamy.

T.R. expected Colombian attempts to regain Panama. Within a week of the initial declaration, Washington forwarded intelligence reports to the American commanders on the scene relating to Colombian troop movements. There were estimates that as many as 15,000 men arrived in Panama City and Colón. In reality, an expedition of 1,100 Colombians did set out via an overland route, only to be turned back by weather, hunger, disease and the jungle. The route itself had been deemed impossible, but the Colombians felt it had to be attempted because the American Navy unquestionably barred access to the isthmus along seaward approaches. American sailors and Marines established fortified observation posts along the land frontier of Panama, but by mid-December orders to American commanders in Panama had been modified to authorize only the defense of the railroad line. The statements implying total American defense of the new nation may have been a bluff, but if so Roosevelt was never called on it. Colombia protested, probed and negotiated, but it never regained its former province. Roosevelt later remarked that he "took the Canal Zone," and with the help of the Navy he had.

Despite the aggressive timbre of his modern reputation, Theodore Roosevelt remains one of two United States chief executives consistently ranked by historians as "great" that never led the nation in war or significant domestic strife (Thomas Jefferson is his companion). Close examination reveals T.R. as a sophisticated practitioner of statecraft who instinctively seemed to know the exact amount of pressure to apply to achieve his ends without descending into outright war. In Venezuela in 1902 he had concentrated American naval power to "shock and awe" his opponents. In Panama he systematically introduced naval units, utilizing the minimum power necessary to achieve his aims. In later conflicts, Roosevelt repeatedly demonstrated an uncanny understanding of the use of coercive force as an instrument of diplomacy in the maritime environment. If the diplomatic interactions between nation-states can be accurately described as a concert, then Theodore Roosevelt's chosen instrument was the U.S. Navy, and his handling of Panama's emergence as an independent nation upholds his reputation as a virtuoso.

And Still Champion

Galveston's Jack Johnson was the first black man to wear boxing's heavyweight crown—and white America has never forgiven him for it. A presidential pardon for a trumped-up crime would right a century-old wrong.

Gary Cartwright

While researching a history of Galveston in the late eighties, I came across an abstract sculpture in a small park on Seawall Boulevard. Its steel spirals were a representation of Jack Johnson, the first black heavyweight champion of the world. The sculpture was perforated with small round holes that had to have been made by bullets. Someone had deliberately tried to destroy it. I knew the story of how Johnson had won the championship in 1908: He had battered the reigning titleholder—a cocky, loudmouthed, money-hungry Canadian named Tommy Burns—so savagely that the final moments of the newsreel footage of the fight were cut to protect the public from the spectacle of a white man getting knocked silly by a black man. White America never forgave Johnson for that victory. Standing by the statue, looking at those bullet holes, I realized that that hatred had endured. I was reminded of that mindless vandalism last fall at the Texas Book Festival, in Austin, when I viewed a short film clip of Ken Burns's documentary on Johnson that will be shown this month on PBS. The title, *Unforgivable Blackness: The Rise and Fall of Jack Johnson*, includes an ironic phrase coined by black writer W. E. B. DuBois, explaining white America's attitude toward the black champion. What people failed to appreciate about Johnson, then and now, is that he was the fire-breathing embodiment of the American spirit. He refused to settle for being a second-class citizen. He was a "pure-blood American," he insisted, whose forebears had arrived in this country long before there was a United States. Jack and

his four siblings were the first generation of American blacks born after Emancipation. He grew up fighting in a street gang on east Broadway and quit school in his early teens to work as a stable hand and as a stevedore, picking up extra change fighting other black dockworkers in makeshift matches.

His first ring experience was in fighting exhibitions known as battles royal—in this version, a white man's joke in which eight or more black fighters were thrown into a ring together, sometimes blindfolded, sometimes with their wrists or ankles tied together, sometimes naked. They were urged to maim one another until the last man was standing. Johnson left home for keeps when he was about 21, hopping freight trains and moving from city to city—Springfield, Denver, Chicago, St. Louis, Baltimore, Boston, fighting in small arenas for smaller purses, mostly against other blacks. He turned professional in 1895, the same year that the *New York Sun* warned readers that black athletes—boxers in particular—were a threat to white supremacy. No black man had ever been permitted to fight for the heavyweight title, whose holder has been described as the "Emperor of Masculinity."

For two decades, as a contender and a champion, Johnson never once climbed into the ring against a white opponent except in front of an overwhelmingly hostile crowd. Newspapers referred to him as "De Big Coon" and "Texas Watermelon Pickaninny"; a reporter for the *Baltimore American* wrote that Johnson appeared as "happy and carefree as a plantation darky in watermelon time." Contenders sug-

gested that he was too black to have the heart of a fighter, which served as their excuse for refusing to fight him.

Johnson endured the slander with maddening calm, always grinning, always cool and in control. A boxer's first task, it has been said, is to "turn his opponent into an assistant in his own ass-whipping," and few did it as well as Jack Johnson. He may have been the best defensive fighter of all time, waiting for opponents to get close and then cutting them to pieces. Johnson's easygoing manner lulled opponents into mistakes, and his sharp tongue destroyed their composure. "Poor little Tommy. Who ever told you you were a fighter?" he snickered as Burns chased him around the ring in Australia, challenging Johnson to "fight like a white man." Though the memory of that fight has dimmed with the ages, the phrase that identified every subsequent challenger who took on and lost to the new champion is still with us—the Great White Hope, which was also the title of a Broadway play and a 1970 film based on Johnson's life, both starring James Earl Jones.

Historian Geoffrey C. Ward, who researched and wrote the script for Burns's four-hour documentary and later wrote a book with the same title, told me that Johnson's career was characterized by three qualities: personal courage, masterful boxing, and a refusal to let anyone else do his thinking for him. "Jack Johnson was a very complex man," Ward explained. "He read, he loved opera, he played the bass fiddle. Above all, he believed that a black man need not limit his horizons." As his reputation (and bank account) grew,

Johnson became a notorious bon vivant, partial to pricey call girls, fine wine, and games of chance. Always the fashion plate, he wore expensive suits; high, modish collars; diamond stickpins; and patent leather boots with spats and carried suede gloves and an ivory-handled cane. People were furious when he moved into a white neighborhood and struck temporarily aphonic when he announced that henceforth he would date only white women. He bedded them with wild abandon and even married three of them. His other passion was fancy racing cars, which he bought like candy. There were fewer than half a million cars in the United States in 1909, Ward told me, and Johnson owned five of them. Stopped for speeding in some Southern town, he supposedly tossed a roll of $100 bills to the sheriff, explaining that he would be driving even faster when he returned. The consummate showman, he loved making his ring entrance garbed in gaudy bathrobes and trunks; one outfit was described by a reporter as "screaming, caterwauling, belligerent pink."

Americans had always accorded their heavyweight champion the right to drink, gamble, chase whores, and spend staggering amounts of money—"Gentleman" Jim Corbett and John L. Sullivan were hardly choirboys—but Johnson was judged by a different standard. When he dared buckle up the champion's belt, the white world went crazy. An outraged media launched a desperate search for a Great White Hope to reclaim the title. Sullivan personally groomed a former wrestler named Kid Cutler, hoping he might wipe the smile off Johnson's face. The champ put Cutler to sleep in the first round; then he looked across the ring at the crestfallen Sullivan and quipped, "How do you like that, Cap'n John?"

Writer Jack London, among others, begged former champ Jim Jeffries to come out of retirement and avenge the white man. Jeffries had sworn that he would never climb into the ring with a black man, but the lure of the biggest payday in ring history (over $100,000) caused a change of heart. Boxing experts were certain that Jeffries would regain the crown, but in the fifteenth round of what was scheduled to be a 45-rounder, the unimaginable happened: Jeffries sank to the canvas, one arm draped helplessly over the bottom rope, knocked off his feet for the first time in his career. A great silence fell across the crowd; it was as if the sun had set on the white race. Riots broke out across America. "On Canal Street, in New Orleans," Ward writes, "a ten-year-old paperboy named Louis Armstrong was warned to run for his life." Johnson had become the hero of blacks everywhere, both for what he had done in the ring and the bold way he lived his life. To Jeffries's credit, the ex-champ later admitted to a reporter: "I could never have whipped Jack Johnson at my best. I couldn't have reached him in a thousand years."

By 1912 the relentless pressure was taking its toll on the aging Johnson. His wife, Etta, who had suffered for years from depression, killed herself. He married again, but by now the Justice Department was after him for twice violating the Mann Act, the so-called white slavery law that made transporting a woman across a state line for immoral purposes a crime. It didn't matter that the law was applied retroactively or that, in one case, the woman had become his wife. Sentenced to a year in prison, Johnson, by his own account, bribed federal authorities to look the other way while he escaped to Europe.

He remained abroad for seven years, making numerous stage appearances, touring with vaudeville companies, and fighting exhibitions, dealing handily with all challengers. But in 1915, under a blazing hot sun in Havana, Johnson finally met a white hope he couldn't beat, a Kansas giant named Jess Willard. By the twenty-sixth round, heat, age, exhaustion—and Willard's paralyzing right hand—proved too much for the champ, and he crumpled to the canvas. A famous photograph of Johnson sprawled on his back, one arm apparently shading his eyes, helped spread a rumor that he had thrown the fight. Truth was, time had finally caught up with Jack Johnson, who had been fighting professionally for twenty years and was 37, far past his prime. By 1920 he was running a saloon in Tijuana, Mexico, and putting on strong-man shows and exhibition matches before small crowds in Mexican border towns. Eventually, he returned voluntarily to the States and served ten months in Leavenworth, finishing out his old sentence. He spent the next 25 years mostly in Chicago and New York, frequently working as a sparring partner with rising young boxers. In 1946, on his way back east from Texas, where he had performed with a traveling tent show, Johnson lost control of his high-powered Lincoln Zephyr in North Carolina and slammed into a telephone pole. At age 68, he died as he had lived—too fast and without permission.

Twenty-two years elapsed between Johnson's loss to Willard and the emergence of another black heavyweight champion. Joe Louis was polite, nonthreatening, and, as they used to say, "a credit to his race." Twenty-seven years later, another black champion, Cassius Clay—who soon changed his name to Muhammad Ali—got in the face of the white establishment, just as Johnson had. The difference was that he got away with it. Scholars of the sweet science have noted many similarities between Ali and Johnson: their speed and grace and the way they invited challengers to take their best shot. Neither champion felt obliged to step aside for any man, black or white.

Six decades after his death, Americans seem finally ready to admit that Jack Johnson's only real crime was his "unforgivable blackness." A group of U.S. senators, businesspeople, historians, and artists have petitioned George W. Bush to grant a posthumous pardon. I hope the president watches the documentary and understands the injustice done to this great athlete. For me, a presidential pardon would right not only the wrong done to Johnson but also the wrong done to his statue in Galveston years ago. Mark Muhich, the sculptor, tried to patch the bullet holes, but in the weeks and months that followed, the statue was regularly blasted by vandals using high-powered rifles and shotguns and defaced with Ku Klux Klan stickers and racial graffiti. When nothing remained of Muhich's work except a mangled piece of scrap metal, the city carted it away.

UNIT 3

From Progressivism to the 1920s

Unit Selections

Key Points to Consider

- What factors were at work in the trial and ultimate lynching of Leo Frank? That he was Jewish was obvious, but what else did he represent that seemed so threatening?

- Why does the author of the essay on Women's Progressivism claim that the legacies of the movement were "ambiguous?"

- How did Edith Galt Wilson try to protect President Wilson after he suffered several strokes in 1919? How might she have exercised power without anyone else knowing it?

Student Website

www.mhcls.com/online

Internet References

Further information regarding these websites may be found in this book's preface or online.

International Channel
http://www.i-channel.com/

World War I—Trenches on the Web
http://www.worldwar1.com/

World Wide Web Virtual Library
http://www.iisg.nl/~w3vl/

Temperance and Prohibition
http://prohibition.history.ohio-state.edu/Contents.htm

The Roaring 20's and the Great Depression
http://www.snowcrest.net/jmike/20sdep.html

Reform movements in the United States have most often developed in the face of economic dislocation. The Populist crusade in the 1890s and the New Deal in the 1930s are typical. Progressivism was an exception. It developed during a period of relative prosperity. Yet more and more people became dissatisfied with existing conditions. Writers who collectively became known as "muckrakers" published books and articles that revealed the seamier side of American life. One focused on the terrible working conditions in the meat-packing industry, another on corruption and cronyism in the Senate, still another on the "bossism" and "machine politics" he found in a number of cities. The popularity of muckraking in newspapers, journals, and books showed that many segments of the public were receptive to such exposures.

The Progressive movement generally was led by white, educated, middle or upper-middle class men and women. They were not radicals, though their opponents often called them that, and they had no wish to destroy the capitalist system. Instead they wanted to reform it to eliminate corruption, to make it function more efficiently, and to provide what we would call a "safety net" for the less fortunate. The reforms they proposed were modest ones such as replacing political appointees with trained experts, having senators elected directly by the people, and conducting referenda on important issues. The movement arose on local levels, percolated upward to state governments, then into the national arena.

President Teddy Roosevelt responded to progressive sentiment through actions such as his "trust busting." He did not seek a third term in 1908; instead he anointed William Howard Taft as the Republican candidate for the presidency. Taft won the election but managed to alienate both progressives and conservatives during his tenure of office. By 1912, progressivism ran strongly enough that the Democrat party nominated Woodrow Wilson, who had compiled an impressive record as a reform governor in the state of New Jersey. Roosevelt, now counting himself a full-blown progressive, bolted the Republican party when Taft won renomination and formed the Progressive or "Bull Moose" party. Roosevelt was still popular, but he managed only to split Republican support with the result that Woodrow Wilson won the election with just 42 percent of the popular vote.

Those progressives who held or competed for political offices were almost exclusively white males. Women had not yet been granted the right to vote, let alone be elected to positions in government, and the prevailing racism ensured that blacks would be excluded from the power structure. "Jim Crow" laws in the South had virtually pushed blacks out of the political arena altogether. Yet members of both groups were attracted to progressivism. Blacks, at least as much as whites, wanted to change the power structures that kept them down. Female progressives shared these goals as well. "The ambiguous Legacies of Women's Progressivism" points out that, contrary to what one might think, the movement did not always serve to liberate women.

Anti-Semitism was a fact of life during this era and beyond. "The Fate of Leo Frank" describes how a Northern Jew was convicted of the murder of a little girl, and later removed from jail and lynched. He was almost certainly innocent, yet the things he represented enraged those who persecuted him.

That virulent racism continued in this nation can be seen in the article "Uncovering History." The diary of a black soldier who served in France during World War I reveals the petty restrictions and humiliations he had to endure, and the periodic race riots that broke out. Author Pressley nonetheless believes the experience afforded black soldiers an "intellectual freedom" that was missing in their own country by being able to talk to French people "who had no preconceptions about them except they were people like us."

The early years of Woodrow Wilson's presidency saw the enactment of a number of progressive reforms, some of which are now accepted as the norm. It was his fate, however, to be better remembered for his role as leader during the Great War and for his failed attempt to bring the United States into the postwar League of Nations. To a far greater degree than most presidents, Wilson consulted his wife Edith on a wide variety of state matters. He was incapacitated following a series of strokes in 1919, during a critical period in the struggle over League membership. Edith kept him isolated from all but a small group of intimates, and she may have exercised a number of presidential prerogatives on her own.

After numerous crusades against inequities at home and the consequences of waging war abroad, the American people in 1920 yearned to return to what Republican presidential candidate Warren G. Harding referred to as "normalcy." Harding was elected in a landslide. Following a recession brought about by postwar reconversion, prosperity returned again although not equally shared by all. The genial Harding presided over this economic boom and was an extremely popular president at the time of his death in 1923. He was succeeded by his vice president, Calvin Coolidge, who also was disinclined to make any waves.

America's entry into World War I or "The Great War," as people at the time called it, to a great degree stifled the progressive impulse. Furthering the war effort seemed more important than experimenting with this or that reform, and the perceived threat of espionage or sabotage by German agents brought about drastic curtailments of civil liberties. "The Home Front" examines the impact of mobilization, government propaganda, and the drive for "national unity" on the society. The question, according to author Ronald Schaffer, was whether "the United States Government could be strong enough to defend the nation without destroying American freedoms." This issue is very much with us today in the wake of the war on Iraq. "From Front Porch to Back Seat: A History of the Date" discusses how courting practices began to change during the mid-1920s.

The Fate of Leo Frank

He was a Northerner. He was an industrialist. He was a Jew.
And a young girl was murdered in his factory.

By Leonard Dinnerstein

Leo M. Frank, manager and co-owner of National Pencil Company (above), was accused of the murder of Mary Phagan.

On December 23, 1983, the lead editorial in the Atlanta *Constitution* began, "Leo Frank has been lynched a second time." The first lynching had occurred almost seventy years earlier, when Leo Frank, convicted murderer of a thirteen-year-old girl, had been taken from prison by a band of vigilantes and hanged from a tree in the girl's hometown of Marietta, Georgia. The lynching was perhaps unique, for Frank was not black but a Jew. Frank also is widely considered to

have been innocent of his crime. Thus the second "lynching" was the refusal of Georgia's Board of Pardons and Paroles to exonerate him posthumously.

Frank's trial, in July and August 1913, has been called "one of the most shocking frame-ups ever perpetrated by American law-and-order officials." The case became, at the time, a cause célèbre in which the injustices created by industrialism, urban growth in Atlanta, and

fervent anti-Semitism all seemed to conspire to wreck one man.

Until the discovery of Mary Phagan's body in the basement of Atlanta's National Pencil Company factory, Leo Frank led a relatively serene life. Born in Cuero, Texas, in 1884, he was soon taken by his parents to Brooklyn, New York. He attended the local public schools, the Pratt Institute, and Cornell University. After graduation he accepted the offer of an uncle, Moses Frank, to

COURTESY OF THE ATLANTA HISTORY CENTER

Mary Phagan, found dead in the factory's basement.

help establish a pencil factory in Atlanta and become both co-owner and manager of the plant. He married Lucille Selig, a native Atlantan, in 1910, and in 1912 he was elected president of the local chapter of the national Jewish fraternity B'nai B'rith. Then, on the afternoon of April 26, 1913, Mary Phagan, an employee, stopped by Frank's factory to collect her week's wages on her way to see the Confederate Memorial day parade and was murdered.

Hugh Dorsey built a case around Frank's alleged perversions. Four weeks after the murder the grand jury granted the indictment he sought.

A night watchman discovered the girls' body in the factory basement early the next morning. Sawdust and grime so covered her that when the police came they could not tell whether she was white or black. Her eyes were bruised, her cheeks cut. An autopsy would reveal that her murderer had choked her with a piece of her own underdrawers and broken her skull. The watchman, Newt Lee, sum-

moned the police; they suspected that he might have committed the murder, and they arrested him. After inspecting the scene, the officers went to Frank's home and took him to the morgue to see the body. The sight of the corpse unsettled him, and he appeared nervous. He remembered having paid the girl her wages the previous day but could not confirm that she had then left the factory. The police would find no one who would admit to having seen her alive any later.

A number of unsolved murders had taken place in Atlanta during the previous eighteen months, and the police were under pressure to find the culprit. Early newspaper reports erroneously suggested that Mary Phagan had been raped, and crowds of people were soon milling about the police station, anxious to get their hands on whoever had committed the crime. Frank's uneasy behavior and the public's hunger for justice made him a prime suspect. He was arrested two days later.

Shortly thereafter some factory employees told a coroner's jury, convened to determine the cause of death and suggest possible suspects for investigation, that Frank had "indulged in familiarities with the women in his employ." And the proprietress of a "rooming house" signed an affidavit swearing that on the day of the murder Frank had telephoned her repeatedly, seeking a room for himself and a young girl. Both these charges were later proved false (many witnesses recanted their accusations later), but newspapers headlined them, fueling talk of Jewish men seeking Gentile girls for their pleasure. The solicitor general, Hugh Dorsey, built a case for the prosecution around Frank's alleged perversions. Four weeks after the murder the grand jury granted the indictment Dorsey sought.

Unknown to the members of the grand jury, however, another suspect had also been arrested. He was Jim Conley, a black janitor at the factory who had been seen washing blood off a shirt there. He admitted having written two notes found near her body. They read: "Mam that negro hire down here did this i went to make water and he push me down that

hole a long tall negro black that hoo it was long sleam tall negro i wright while play with me" and "he said he wood love me land dab n play like the night witch did it but that long tall black negro did buy his slef."

At first almost all investigators assumed that the author of these items had committed the crime. But Conley claimed to have written them as Frank dictated the words, first the day before the murder occurred, then, according to Conley's second affidavit, on the day of the crime.

Conley ultimately signed four affidavits, changing and elaborating his tale each time. Originally he said he had been called to Frank's office the day before the murder and asked to write phrases like "dear mother" and "a long, tall, black negro did this by himself;" and he claimed to have heard Frank mumble something like "Why should I hang?" But the newspapers found the idea of Frank's having prepared for an apparent crime of passion by asking a black janitor to write notes about it utterly ridiculous. So Harry Scott, the chief detective, said he then "pointed out things in [Conley's] story that were improbable and told him he must do better than that." Another lengthy interrogation led to the second affidavit. It stated that Frank had dictated the notes just after the murder and that Conley had removed the dead body from a room opposite Frank's office, on the second floor, and taken it by elevator to the basement. (Later evidence showed that the elevator had not been in operation from before the time of the girl's death until after her body was discovered.) A third affidavit spelled out in greater detail the steps Conley had allegedly taken in assisting Frank with the disposal of the dead girl. The Atlanta *Georgian* had already protested after the janitor's second statement that with Conley's "first affidavit repudiated and worthless it will be practically impossible to get any court to accept a second one." But Atlantans had been so conditioned to believe Frank guilty that few protested the inconsistencies in the janitor's tale.

Among those who questioned the prosecution's case against Frank were the members of the grand jury that had originally indicted him. They wanted Dorsey to reconvene them so that they could charge Conley instead. Dorsey refused, so the jury foreman did it on his own. It was the first time an Atlanta grand jury had ever considered a criminal case against the wishes of the solicitor general. Then Dorsey came back before the group and pleaded with them not to indict the black man. Exactly what he told them was not made public, but the next day the Atlanta *Constitution* reported that "the solicitor did not win his point without a difficult fight. He went in with a mass of evidence showing why the indictment of the negro would injure the state's case against Frank and stayed with the grand jurors for nearly an hour and a half."

It is difficult to say why the grand jury ultimately supported Dorsey. Perhaps they accepted the Atlanta *Georgian*'s explanation: "That the authorities have very important evidence that has not yet been disclosed to the public is certain." Or, given Southern values, they may have assumed that no attorney would base his case on the word of a black man "unless the evidence was overwhelming." In any case, the solicitor prevailed and prepared to go to trial.

T he trial began on July 28, 1913, and brought forth large and ugly-tempered crowds. The heinous nature of the crime, rumors of sexual misdeeds, newspaper reports of "very important evidence that has not yet been disclosed," the solicitor general's supreme confidence, and anti-Semitism (a Georgia woman had written that "this is the first time a Jew has ever been in any serious trouble in Atlanta, and see how ready every one is to believe the worst of him") combined to create an electric tension in the city. Gossip about Frank had been widespread, and many Georgians wondered if an unbiased jury would be possible. But jury selection was swift, and in an atmosphere punctuated by spontaneous applause for the prosecuting attorney and shouts of "Hang the Jew" from throngs outside the courthouse, the proceedings unfolded.

Solicitor Dorsey opened his presentation by trying to establish where and when the crime had occurred. He elicited testimony from several witnesses about blood spots on the floor and strands of hair on a lathe that Mary Phagan had allegedly fallen against in the room opposite Frank's office. (The state biologist had specifically informed the prosecution that the hair was not Mary Phagan's, and many witnesses testified that the bloodstains could have been merely paint spots; Dorsey ignored them.)

COURTESY OF THE ATLANTA HISTORY CENTER

Frank's wife, Lucille Selig Frank, sits close by him during the murder trial.

The heart of the state's case, however, revolved around Jim Conley's narrative. Although his story had gone through several revisions during the previous weeks—all of them published in the newspapers—his courtroom account mesmerized the spectators. Conley told how he had served as a lookout in the past when Frank "entertained" women in the factory (no such women ever appeared at the trial), how after an agreed-upon signal he would lock or unlock the front door or go up to the superintendent's office for further instruction. He claimed that on the fatal day Frank had summoned him to his office, and when he arrived there, he had found his boss "standing up there at the top of the steps and shivering and trembling and rubbing his hands.... He had a little rope in his hands.... His eyes were large and they looked right funny.... His face was red. Yes, he had a cord in his hands.... After

I got up to the top of the steps, he asked me 'Did you see that little girl who passed here just a while ago?' and I told him I saw one.... 'Well... I wanted to be with the little girl and she refused me, and I struck her and... she fell and hit her head against something, and I don't know how bad she got hurt. Of course you know I ain't built like other men.' The reason he said that was, I had seen him in a position I haven't seen any other man that has got children." Conley did not explain that last sentence; instead he went on to detail how Frank had offered, but never given him, money to dispose of the body. He said Frank had then asked him if he could write and, when he said yes, had dictated the murder notes.

When Dorsey concluded his presentation, *Frost's Magazine* of Atlanta, which had previously made no editorial comment about the case, condemned both the solicitor and Atlanta's chief detective for misleading the public into thinking that the state had sufficient evidence to warrant an accusation against Frank. "We cannot conceive," the commentary read, "that at the close of the prosecution, before the defense has presented one single witness, that it could be possible for any juryman to vote for the conviction of Leo M. Frank."

Frank had retained two of the South's best-known attorneys to defend him: Luther Z. Rosser, an expert at cross-examination, and Reuben R. Arnold, a prominent criminal lawyer. Despite their brilliant reputations, they failed to display their forensic talents when they were most needed. Rosser and Arnold cross-examined Conley for a total of sixteen hours on three consecutive days and could not shake his basic tale. He continually claimed to have forgotten anything that tended to weaken the case against Frank, and some observers thought Conley had been carefully coached by the solicitor general and his subordinates. The murder and disposal of the body would have taken at least fifty minutes to accomplish as the janitor described them, yet witnesses corroborated "Frank's recollection of his whereabouts for all but eighteen minutes of that time. Furthermore, much of Conley's narrative depended on his having removed the body to the basement via the elevator, but floor markings, the absence of blood in the elevator, and other incontrovertible evidence proved that he hadn't. Why Frank's attorneys failed to exploit these facts, and why they also failed to request a change of venue before the trial began, has never been explained. But their inability to break Conley undermined their client's case. A reporter who attended every session of the hearings later observed, "I heard Conley's evidence entire, and was impressed powerfully with the idea that the negro was repeating something he had seen.... Conley's story was told with a wealth of infinitesimal detail that I firmly believe to be beyond the capacity of his mind, or a far more intelligent one, to construct from his imagination."

One juror had allegedly been overheard to say, "I am glad they indicted the God damn Jew. They ought to take him out and lynch him."

Rosser and Arnold's biggest error was probably their attempt to delete from the record Conley's discussion of times he had "watched for" Frank. For a day the two men got the janitor to talk about Frank's alleged relationships with other women, hoping to poke holes in the testimony; then they tried to get the whole discussion stricken. Even one of Dorsey's assistants agreed this information should not have been allowed into the record but added that once Conley had been examined and cross-examined on the subject, it was wrong to try to expunge. "By asking that the testimony be eliminated," the Atlanta *Constitution* noted, the defense "virtually admit their failure to break down Conley."

It did not matter thereafter that witnesses came in to attest to Frank's good character and his whereabouts before, during, and after the murder. It also made little difference that Frank's explanation of his activities on the day of the murder carried, according to the *Constitution*, "the ring of truth in every sentence."

Conley's narrative absolutely dominated the four-week trial.

In their summations Arnold and Rosser accused the police and solicitor general of having fabricated the evidence. Arnold stated that "if Frank hadn't been a Jew, there would never have been any prosecution against him," and he likened the entire case to the Dreyfus affair in France: "the savagry [*sic*] and venom is... the same."

But once again Dorsey emerged the winner. The *Constitution* described his closing argument as "one of the most wonderful efforts ever made at the Georgia bar." The solicitor reviewed the evidence, praised his opponents as "two of the ablest lawyers in the country," and then reemphasized how these men could not break Conley's basic narrative. He went on to state that although he had never mentioned the word *Jew*, once it was introduced he would use it. The Jews "rise to heights sublime," he asserted, "but they also sink to the lowest depths of degradation." He noted that Judas Iscariot, too, had been considered an honorable man before he disgraced himself. The bells of a nearby Catholic church rang, just as the solicitor was finishing. Each time Dorsey proclaimed the word *guilty* the bells chimed, and they "cut like a chill to the hearts of many who shivered involuntarily" in the courtroom.

The jury took less than four hours to find Frank guilty, and the judge, fearing mob violence, asked the defense to keep their client out of court during sentencing. Rosser and Arnold agreed. Solicitor Dorsey requested that they promise not to use Frank's absence as a basis for future appeals—even though barring a defendant from his own sentencing might constitute a denial of his right to due process of law—and the two defense attorneys assented.

Frank's attorneys kept their word and ignored the issue in their appeals for a new trial. According to state law, appeals in a capital case could be based only on errors in law and had to be heard first by the original trial judge. Rosser and Arnold based their appeal on more than 115 points, including the alleged influence of the public on the jury, the admissibility of Conley's testimony about Frank's al-

leged sexual activities, and affidavits from people who swore that two of the jurors were anti-Semitic. (One had allegedly been overheard to say, "I am glad they indicted the God damn Jew. They ought to take him out and lynch him. And if I get on that jury I'd hang that Jew sure.") Dorsey and his associates countered with affidavits from the jurors swearing that public demonstrations had not affected their deliberations. In his ruling, Leonard Roan, the trial judge, upheld the verdict and commented that although he was "not thoroughly convinced that Frank is guilty or innocent. The jury was convinced."

The next appeal, to the Georgia Supreme Court, centered on Roan's doubt of Frank's guilt, but the justices went along with the earlier decision. This court concluded that only the trial judge could decide whether the behavior of the spectators had prevented a fair trial and whether the jurors had been partial. The judges also ruled Conley's testimony relevant and admissible and dismissed Roan's personal expression of doubt.

At this point Frank replaced his counsel. The new attorneys did not feel bound by their predecessors' promise to Dorsey, and they pressed the argument that Frank had been denied due process by being absented from his sentencing. But the state supreme court responded that "it would be trifling with the court to... now come in and... include matters which were or ought to have been included in the motion for a new trial."

The new attorneys went on to try to get the United States Supreme Court to issue a writ of habeas corpus, on the ground that the mob had forced Frank to absent himself from the court at the time of his sentencing, and thus he was being held illegally. The Court agreed to hear arguments on that question and, after two months, rejected the plea by a vote of 7-2.

Justice Mahlon Pitney explained that errors in law, no matter how serious, could not legally be reviewed in a request for a writ of habeas corpus but only in a petition for a writ of error. And Frank's contention of having been denied due process "was waived by his failure to raise the objection in due season...." In a celebrated dissent, Justices Oliver Wendell Holmes and Charles Evans Hughes concluded, "Mob law does not become due process of law by securing the assent of a terrorized jury."

It is difficult for those not well versed in the law to follow the legal reasoning behind such procedural and constitutional questions, especially when judges are not even considering disputes in testimony or blatantly expressed prejudices. Thus many people assumed that the Court was reconfirming the certainty of Frank's guilt. Afterward his attorneys sought commutation to life imprisonment rather than a complete pardon because they concluded that after all the judicial setbacks they would have a better chance with the governor that way.

Once the case came before him, Gov. John M. Slaton moved with dispatch. He listened to oral presentations from both sides, read the records, and then visited the pencil factory to familiarize himself with the scene of the crime. Since the two sides differed in their arguments on where the murder had actually taken place—the metal-lathe room on the second floor versus the factory basement—and whether the elevator had been used, the governor paid particular attention to those parts of the building. Besides the voluminous public records, Slaton received a personal letter written by the trial judge recommending commutation, a secret communication from one of Hugh Dorsey's law partners stating that Jim Conley's attorney believed his own client was guilty, and a note from a federal prisoner indicating that he had seen Conley struggling with Mary on the day of the murder.

For twelve days Slaton wrestled with the materials. On the last day he worked well into the night, and at 2:00 A.M., on June 21, 1915, he went up to his bedroom to inform his wife. "Have you reached a decision?" she asked.

"Yes," he replied, "... it may mean my death or worse, but I have ordered the sentence commuted."

Mrs. Slaton then kissed her husband and confessed, "I would rather be the widow of a brave and honorable man than the wife of a coward."

A ten-thousand-word statement accompanied the governor's announcement. Slaton appeared thoroughly conversant with even the minutiae of the case. He saw inconsistencies in Conley's narrative and zeroed in on them. The first significant discrepancy dealt with the factory elevator. Conley had admitted defecating at the bottom of the shaft on the morning before the murder. When police and others arrived the next day, the feces remained. Not until someone moved the elevator from the second floor was the excrement mashed, causing a foul odor. Therefore, Slaton concluded, the elevator could not have been used to carry Mary Phagan's body to the basement. Furthermore, according to scientific tests, no bloodstains appeared on the lathe or on the second floor—where the prosecution had contended that the murder had taken place—or in the elevator. But Mary's mouth, nostrils, and fingernails had been full of sawdust and grime similar to that in the basement, not on the second floor.

Other details also incriminated Conley. The murder notes found near the body had been written on order pads whose numerical sequence corresponded with those stored in the basement and not at all with those in Frank's office. Another major discrepancy that Slaton noticed concerned the strand of hair found on the metal lathe. Since the state biologist had determined that it could not have come from Mary's head, testimony from Dorsey's witness that "it looked like her hair" had to be dismissed.

Although most of Marietta knew who the killers were, a coroner's jury concluded that Frank had been lynched by persons unknown.

Privately Slaton told friends that he believed Frank was innocent, and he claimed that he would have pardoned him except that he had been asked only for a commutation and he assumed the truth would come out shortly anyway, after which the very people clamoring for Frank's death would be demanding his release. Slaton's announcement of the commutation sent thousands of Atlantans to the streets, where they burned Frank and the governor in effigy; hundreds of others marched toward Slaton's mansion, where state troopers prevented them from lynching him.

A wave of anti-Semitic demonstrations followed. Many Georgians assumed that the governor's "dastardly" actions resulted from Jewish pressures upon him. Atlanta Jews feared for their lives, and many fled the city. Responding to these actions a few days later, Slaton declared: "Two thousand years ago another Governor washed his hands of a case and turned over a Jew to a mob. For two thousand years that Governor's name has been accursed. If today another Jew were lying in his grave because I had failed to do my duty I would all through life find his blood on my hands and would consider myself an assassin through cowardice."

But the mob would not be thwarted. A fellow inmate at the state prison farm cut Frank's throat. While he was recovering in the hospital infirmary, a band of twenty-five men, characterized by their peers as "sober, intelligent, of established good name and character—good American citizens," stormed the prison farm, kidnapped Frank, and drove him 175 miles through the night to Marietta, Mary Phagan's hometown, where, on the morning of August 17, 1915, they hanged him from an oak tree. Although most of the people in Marietta knew who the killers were, a coroner's jury concluded that Frank had been lynched by persons unknown. The Pittsburgh *Gazette* restated that finding: "What the coroner's jury really meant was that Frank 'came to his death by hanging at the hands of persons whom the jury wishes to remain unknown.'"

Many of Frank's friends and later defenders attributed the hanging to unbridled mob passions, but the explanation cannot suffice. "The very best people," a local judge opined at the time, had allowed the Frank case to go through all the courts, letting the judicial process take its course. Then, after every request for a new trial had been turned down, the governor had outrageously stepped in. "I believe in law and order," the judge said. "I would not help lynch anybody. But I believe Frank has had his just deserts."

Obviously, much more than just a wish to carry out the court's decision motivated Frank's killers. The man symbolized all that Georgians resented. He was the Northerner in the South, the urban industrialist who had come to transform an agrarian society, a Jew whose ancestors had killed the Savior and whose co-religionists rejected the truth of Christianity. Thus, despite the fact that the state used a black man as its key witness, something that would have been unthinkable had the accused been a Southern white Christian, Atlantans could easily believe the worst about this particular defendant.

Over the years scores of people have wondered why many Georgians were loath to suspect that a black man might have committed the murder. The answer may have come from the pastor of the Baptist church that Mary Phagan's family attended. In 1942 the Reverend L. O. Bricker wrote: "My own feelings, upon the arrest of the old negro night-watchman, were to the effect that this one old negro would be poor atonement for the life of this little girl. But, when on the next day, the police arrested a Jew, and a Yankee Jew at that, all of the inborn prejudice against the Jews rose up in a feeling of satisfaction, that here would be a victim worthy to pay for the crime."

As time passed, people no longer remembered the specific facts of the case, but they told the story of Mary Phagan and Leo Frank to their children and grandchildren. As with all folktales, some details were embellished, others were dropped; however, as the first three verses of "The Ballad of Mary Phagan" unfold, no listener can have any difficulty knowing what happened:

Little Mary Phagan
She left her home one day;
She went to the pencil-factory
To see the big parade.

She left her home at eleven,
She kissed her mother good-by;

Not one time did the poor child think
That she was a-going to die.

Leo Frank he met her
With a brutish heart, we know;
He smiled and said, "Little Mary,
You won't go home no more."

People have argued the Frank case again and again, but usually without specific knowledge, falling back on hearsay to support their positions. However, in 1982 a dramatic incident put the case back in the public spotlight. Alonzo Mann, who had been a fourteen-year-old office boy in the Atlanta pencil factory in 1913, swore that he had come into the building on the day of the murder and witnessed Jim Conley carrying Mary Phagan's body toward the steps leading to the basement. The janitor had warned him, "If you ever mention this, I'll kill you." Lonnie Mann ran home and told his mother what he had seen and she advised him to "not get involved." He obeyed her but eventually began telling his tale to friends. Finally, in 1982, two enterprising reporters filed the story in the Nashville *Tennessean*.

Mann's revelations stimulated a renewed effort to achieve a posthumous pardon for Leo Frank. Newspapers editorialized on the need to clear his name, public-opinion polls showed a majority in Georgia willing to support a pardon, and the governor of the state announced in December 1983 that he believed in Frank's innocence. But three days before Christmas the Board of Pardons and Paroles denied the request. It asserted that Mann's affidavit had provided "no new evidence to the case," that it did not matter whether Conley had carried the body to the basement or taken it via the elevator, and that "there are [so] many inconsistencies" in the various accounts of what had happened that "it is impossible to decide conclusively the guilt or innocence of Leo M. Frank."

Once again a storm broke as editorials and individuals excoriated the Board of Pardons and Paroles. The *Tennessean* said that "the board turned its back on the chance to right an egregious wrong."

The *Tennessean*, and others that were so certain about what the board should have done, had the advantage of hind-

sight. While this historian believes there is no question that Frank was an innocent man, the fact is that his case was much more complex than those who have read about it afterward recognize. One should not dismiss the impact of Jim Conley's performance on the witness stand or the electrifying effects of the innuendoes and charges in the courtroom that Frank might have engaged in improper sexual activities with the young people who worked in the pencil factory. Aside from the defendant's partisans, most people who heard the evidence or read about it in the newspapers during the summer of 1913 accepted its truthfulness. No reporter who attended the proceedings daily ever wrote of Frank's innocence. Long after the trial ended, O. B. Keeler and Herbert Asbury, newspapermen who covered the case, still regarded him as guilty; Harold Ross, another writer and later the founding editor of *The New Yorker*, stated merely that the "evidence did not prove [Frank] guilty beyond that 'reasonable doubt' required by law."

Another factor is the ineptitude of Frank's counsel. They failed to expose the inaccuracies in Conley's testimony, and they blundered by asking him to discuss occasions when Frank had allegedly entertained young women. This opened the door for a great deal of titillating but irrelevant material and allowed Dorsey to bring in witnesses to corroborate Conley's accusation. The defense attorneys demonstrated their limitations once more by ignoring relevant constitutional questions in their original appeal to the Georgia Supreme Court. Thus a reinvestigation of the case in the 1950s led one observer to write that "the defense of Leo Frank was one of the most ill-conducted in the history of Georgia jurisprudence."

Still another consideration is the environment in which the trial took place. Today judicial standards have been tightened, and it is unlikely that any court proceedings would be conducted in so hostile an atmosphere as that in which Frank met his doom. But that does not necessarily outweigh the effect of the witnesses' testimony and the subsequent cross-examinations. To be sure, many of the jurors feared going against popular opinion, but perhaps they might have reached an identical judgment in a hermetically sealed chamber.

There is no reason to doubt that Alonzo Mann's affidavit is accurate. Had he ignored his mother's advice and gone to the police with his information right away, Conley would surely have been arrested, the police and district attorney would not have concentrated their efforts on finding Frank guilty, and the crime would most likely have been quickly solved. But by the time the trial began, in July 1913, Mann's testimony might hardly have even seemed important.

When reviewing the case, one need not be so one-sided as to ignore the very real gut reactions that Atlantans had to Mary Phagan's murder, the trial, and Leo Frank. Prejudice did exist in Atlanta, some people did lie at the trial, and anti-Semitism did contribute to the verdict.

There were also contradictions in the case that people could not understand. Rational persons believed Conley's tale, and there is no denying that the janitor made a tremendously good impression on the stand. A reporter listening to him wrote that "if so much as 5 per cent" of his story was true, it would suffice to convict Frank.

The struggle to exonerate Leo Frank continued, and in March 1986 the state Board of Pardons and Paroles reversed itself and granted a pardon. It had been granted, said the accompanying document, "in recognition of the state's failure to protect the person of Leo Frank and thereby preserve his opportunity of continued legal appeal of his conviction, and in recognition of the state's failure to bring his killers to justice, and as an effort to heal old wounds."

Not, that is, because Frank was innocent.

In the late 1980s a Georgia citizen, firmly convinced of Frank's guilt, vehemently underscored the point in a letter to the Marietta *Daily Journal:* "The pardon expressly does not relieve Mr. Frank of his conviction or of his guilt. Rather, it simply restored to him his civil rights, permitting him to vote and serve on juries, activities which, presumably, at this date are meaningless."

Meaningless they may be. Still, Leo Frank's unquiet spirit continues to vex the conscience of many Georgians eighty-one years after he died on an oak tree in Marietta.

Leonard Dinnerstein is a professor of history and the director of Judaic Studies at the University of Arizona. His books include The Leonard Frank Case *(available in paperback from the University of Georgia Press),* America and the Survivors of the Holocaust, *and* Antisemitism in America.

From *American Heritage*, October 1996, pp. 99–102, 105–109. © 1996 by Forbes, Inc. Reprinted by permission of *American Heritage* magazine, a division of Forbes, Inc.

The Ambiguous Legacies of Women's Progressivism

Robyn Muncy

Most undergraduates come into my classroom convinced that men have so dominated American political life that they are responsible for all the good and evil in America's public past. The history of progressive reform usually persuades them otherwise. Students discover that black and white women, by the hundreds of thousands—even millions—threw themselves into progressive reform, helping to chart the direction of public policy and American values for the century to come. When they learn this, students want to believe that such activism and power must have tended unambiguously to liberate women. My job is to explain that this is not altogether the case.

The truth is that female progressive activism left a complicated legacy to twentieth-century American women. First, women reformers generally failed to overcome (and white activists often worked to sustain) racial divisions in American life. Second, black and white female progressives changed "the place" of American women in many important senses, especially in winning admittance to the polls and the policymaking table. Third, despite carving out significant public space for women, female progressives—mostly white in this case—embedded in public policy the notion that motherhood and economic independence were incompatible. Women reformers thus empowered successive generations of women in some ways while continuing to deny them the multiplicity of roles open to men.

Most women's activism took place through the many local, regional, and national organizations that women formed around 1900. The sheer number of women participating in these associations boggles the late-twentieth-century mind and suggests an engaged, cohesive female citizenry well before the achievement of women's suffrage. For instance, two hundred local white women's clubs joined together in 1890 to form the General Federation of Women's Clubs (GFWC), which by 1920 claimed over a million members. Along with the National Mothers' Congress (NMC), formed in 1897, the GFWC became a vehicle for moderate white women's political activism. In

similar fashion, one hundred middle-class black women's clubs created the National Association of Colored Women (NACW) in 1896, and by 1914 this group claimed fifty thousand members in one thousand local clubs. Jewish women organized the National Council of Jewish Women in 1893, and black Baptist women founded the Woman's Convention of the National Baptist Convention in 1900. That organization alone embraced over one million members (1).

Although gender and race segregation were the rule among civic organizations early in this century, there were exceptions. Some women participated in gender-integrated groups like the National Child Labor Committee, which targeted child labor as an urgent public problem, and some women helped to found such gender- and race-integrated groups as the National Association for the Advancement of Colored People and the National Urban League. One of the most important progressive organizations, the National Consumers League (NCL), was ostensibly a gender-integrated group, though white women dominated it throughout the period, and thousands of women—overwhelmingly white—invigorated the Progressive party of 1912 (2).

In these organizations, women pursued an agenda that set them squarely in the social justice wing of progressivism. They aimed to ameliorate the worst suffering caused by rapid industrialization, immigration, and urbanization without forsaking capitalism altogether. To do so, they strove to make government at all levels more responsible for the social and economic welfare of citizens, and though many hoped ultimately to improve the lives of America's entire working class or the whole community of color, most women reformers found that they were especially effective when they spoke specifically to the needs of women and children. Their agendas ran the gamut from antilynching campaigns to the prohibition of alcohol, from maximum hours laws to women's suffrage, from improved educational opportunities for African-American children to the

The mansion of the late Chicago businessman Charles Hull served as the original home of Jane Addams's famous social settlement. This photo of Hull House was taken around 1893. (Courtesy of the Jane Addams Memorial Collection, Special Collections, The University Library, The University of Illinois at Chicago, Negative 146.)

abolition of prostitution. A brief article can glimpse only a tiny portion of their work.

One example, the campaign for protective labor legislation, reveals some of the complex meanings of women's progressivism. Although many working-class women believed the solution to workplace problems lay in unionization, some accepted the middle-class preference for legislation as the surest route to job-related improvements. Thus, both groups—organized, for instance, in the National Women's Trade Union League—lobbied their states for guarantees of factory safety, maximum hours laws, and less often, minimum wage provisions as well. Many states passed such laws and even hired women as factory inspectors to enforce them.

These legislative successes were threatened in 1905, when the U.S. Supreme Court handed down its famous *Lochner* decision. In it, the Court struck down a New York law that regulated the hours of bakers, an overwhelmingly male group. The Court ruled that states could interfere in the freedom of contract only if long hours constituted a clear health risk either to the workers themselves or to the general public.

Women reformers would not see their protective laws undone. Indeed, their determination to sustain protective labor legislation led to their participation in a second case, *Muller v. Oregon*. In 1903, Oregon passed a law that limited the hours of women in industrial work to ten per day. Two years later, the state prepared a case against laundry owner Curt Muller for violation of the law. Muller took the case to the U.S. Supreme Court, where he expected the reasoning in *Lochner* to strike down Oregon's law. The NCL, with the fiery Florence Kelley at its head, took up Oregon's fight, leading the charge for protective legislation for women workers.

Kelley, who had fought for and implemented a similar law in Illinois, hired Louis Brandeis to argue against Muller. Kelley's colleague, Josephine Goldmark, aided Brandeis in preparing a precedent-setting brief. Providing over one hundred pages of evidence that showed that women workers were hurt by long hours in ways that men were not, the brief argued that women

workers warranted the state's interference in freedom of contract even when men did not. In 1908, the Supreme Court accepted their arguments, concluding that "woman's physical structure and the performance of maternal functions place her at a disadvantage in the struggle for subsistence" (3).

Women reformers thus won a progressive end—government intervention in the economy on behalf of workers—by perpetuating an older belief in male/female difference and moreover inscribing that difference into law. In this crusade, activist women, mostly middle-class and white, gained public power for themselves while at the same time cementing in public policy a view of working women as peculiarly vulnerable workers. This image of working women, while justifying legislation that genuinely helped many, made it impossible for women to compete effectively with men in many sectors of the labor market. This law created a complicated bequest to later generations of American women. Moreover, these maximum hours laws, antecedents of the Fair Labor Standards Act of 1938, also supported racial difference, not explicitly as in the case of gender, but implicitly, by omitting from coverage the occupations in which African-American women were heavily represented: agricultural labor and domestic service.

Another campaign rooted in a belief in the difference between women and men was the movement for mothers' pensions. Mothers' pensions were public stipends paid to mothers—usually widows—who found themselves without male support. The purpose of these payments was to allow impoverished mothers to remain at home with their children rather than having to put them in an orphanage or neglect them while working for wages. Led especially by the NMC and the GFWC, white activists lobbied their state governments for such programs and won them in virtually every state by the mid 1920s. These programs, unfortunately poorly funded and often unjustly administered, set the precedent for Aid to Dependent Children, a federal program enacted as part of the Social Security Act in 1935 during Franklin Roosevelt's New Deal (4).

African-American women reformers, seeing that social workers often reserved mothers' pensions for white women, lobbied for their extension to qualified African-American women. Simultaneously however, they promoted day care services as an alternative response to mothers' need to work for pay. These services revealed not only black women's suspicion of government programs—based in part on the disenfranchisement of African-American men and spread of Jim Crow laws in the early twentieth century—but also their greater acceptance of working mothers. Poor wages for men were so endemic to African-American communities that black reformers could not so easily envision a world in which mothers were spared paid labor, and so they were more ready than white women to create institutions that allowed women to be both good mothers and good workers (5).

In both black and white neighborhoods, day care services were often provided by other, multifaceted progressive women's institutions. Indeed, the quintessential progressive women's institutions were social settlements and neighborhood unions. Social settlements first appeared in the United States in the 1880s. They were places where middle-class women and

To counter the claim that suffragists deserted their families or disrespected motherhood, suffragists often took their children on parade with them, as some did in this 1912 demonstration in New York City. (Library of Congress, Division of Prints and Photographs.)

men lived in the midst of working-class, largely immigrant neighborhoods. Their purpose was to bridge the gap between the classes. By the turn of the century, settlements existed in most sizable cities. Educated women took the lead in the establishment of settlement communities. Once acquainted with their working-class neighbors, these middle-class women created social services that they believed their neighbors needed. Much of the time, settlement residents piloted local health services, educational series, or recreational programs and then lobbied their municipal, county, or state government to provide permanent funding and oversight. In this way, settlement residents became leaders in progressive reform.

The most famous social settlement was Hull House in Chicago. Founded in 1889 by Jane Addams and Ellen Gates Starr, Hull House set the standard for the hundreds of settlements that subsequently opened in cities all over the country. Beginning with a day nursery (considered a regrettable, stop-gap measure by the white reformers) and evening classes and clubs for its immigrant neighbors, Hull House eventually housed seventy middle-class residents, a library for the neighborhood, a community theater, a gym, playground, labor museum, many classrooms and clubhouses for adults and children, and a coffee house. It offered a visiting nurse and employment counseling to the neighborhood, as well as a meeting ground for unions and political groups. It was a vital hub of neighborhood life and provided the initiative and/or support for much progressive legislation, including protective legislation for women workers and children, women's suffrage, workers' compensation programs, increased funding for public education, and the creation of the U.S. Children's Bureau.

Besides women's suffrage, the Children's Bureau may have been progressive women's most significant national achievement. The idea for a federal agency devoted to child welfare is usually credited to Lillian Wald, founder and head resident of the Henry Street Settlement in New York City. Herself a visiting nurse, Wald joined Jane Addams in creating a female reform network that stretched across the country by 1903. That year Wald first proposed that the U.S. government create a bu-

reau to collect information and propose legislation of benefit to the country's children. In 1912, Congress finally rewarded the women's lobbying efforts by establishing the Children's Bureau in the U.S. Department of Labor.

Addams immediately argued that a woman should head the new agency and proposed in particular Julia Lathrop, a long-time resident of Hull House. To everyone's surprise, President William Howard Taft accepted the recommendation, and Lathrop became the first woman ever to head a federal agency. She quickly hired other women to staff the bureau, which became a female beachhead in the federal government for decades to come. In 1921, Lathrop and her staff drafted and won from Congress the first piece of federal social/welfare legislation: the Sheppard-Towner Maternity and Infancy Act, which sent public health nurses into nearly every corner of America to teach pregnant women how best to care for themselves and their newborns. This set another precedent for New Deal programs (6).

Although African-American women also founded social settlements, as did some interracial groups, more typical of black women's institution building was the neighborhood union. Such entities differed from social settlements mainly in that few reformers actually lived in them, reflecting in part the tendency of black women reformers to be married while their white counterparts often remained unmarried. Many of these progressive institutions called themselves missions, community centers, institutional churches, or even schools, but like settlements, they provided meeting places and services for those living nearby, and they joined the middle and working classes in local political crusades (7).

The most famous such center was the Neighborhood Union in Atlanta. Founded in 1908 by Lugenia Burns Hope, the union provided day care services, health care and health education, and playgrounds. It sponsored clubs and classes for children and adults alike, and organized lobbying campaigns to obtain greater funding for the education of African-American children, as well as improved street lights and sanitation in black neighborhoods. Members urged public relief for the unemployed. The Neighborhood Union's appeals for governmental support remind us that even though black women had less hope for a positive response from government officials than white women, they did not—even in this hour of miserable race relations—give up entirely on obtaining government resources (8).

Just as social settlements and neighborhood unions were usually race-segregated, so were organizations that fought for women's suffrage. Ratification of the Nineteenth Amendment in 1920 stood as a monumental victory for women progressives; it is one of the signal achievements of progressive reform. But even that fight to expand democracy was marked by racial division and hierarchy. Hoping to win support from white southerners, leaders in the North refused to admit black women's clubs to the National American Woman Suffrage Association, which, with two million members in 1917, was the largest suffrage organization in U.S. history. In response, black women formed their own suffrage associations—like the Equal Suffrage League founded by Ida Wells-Barnett in Chicago—or fought for enfranchisement through multi-issue groups like the

Lugenia Burns Hope founded the Neighborhood Union in Atlanta. While white progressives in the South usually pursued policies that assured white dominance, Hope's activism reminds us that southern African Americans were also progressives. (Courtesy of the National Park Service, Mary McLeod Bethune Council House National Historic Site, Washington DC.)

NACW or the black Baptist Women's Convention (9). Complicating black women's struggle for suffrage was their simultaneous fight for the re-enfranchisement of African-American men in the South, whose right to vote was eroding in the face of brutal violence, literacy tests, and poll taxes. When the women's suffrage amendment passed, no state could deny suffrage on the basis of sex, but the same measures that disenfranchised black men in the South also prevented most black women from approaching the polls. Thus, not until the Voting Rights Act of 1965 did women's suffrage achieve a complete victory.

Black and white women were integral to progressivism. No history of progressive reform could possibly be complete without discussing the campaign for women's suffrage, the work of neighborhood unions, or the struggle for protective legislation.

These efforts by millions of American women suggest several conclusions. This history illuminates the source of some-times contradictory views of women embedded in public policy and personal identities since the Progressive Era: while most American women received the vote by 1920, imparting a new parity with men in public life, the same period produced legislation that construed women primarily as mothers rather than as workers and as more vulnerable, weaker workers than men. This ambiguous legacy has reverberated through the twentieth century.

The history of these women reformers moreover reveals some of the ways that race has shaped women's experience and political agendas in the past, and it embodies the ways that racism has crippled democracy and betrayed democratic movements in the United States. It reminds us that the renewed political life we might create in the twenty-first century, if it is to fulfill the promise of democracy, must strive to overcome the racial hierarchy that progressives—and all of their successors—failed to defeat.

END NOTES

1. Karen J. Blair, *Clubwoman as Feminist. True Womanhood Redefined, 1868–1914* (New York: Holmes and Meier, 1980); Evelyn Brooks Higginbotham, *Righteous Discontent. The Women's Movement in the Black Baptist Church* (Cambridge: Harvard University Press, 1993), 8; and Stephanie Shaw, "Black Club Women and the Creation of the National Association of Colored Women," *Journal of Women's History 3* (Fall 1991): 10–25.

2. Dorothy Salem, *To Better Our World: Black Women in Organized Reform, 1890–1920* (Brooklyn: Carlson, 1990), 45–46, 100–14, 146–96, 274; Kathryn Kish Sklar, "The Historical Foundations of Women's Power in the Creation of the American Welfare State, 1830–1930," in *Mothers of a New World: Maternalist Politics and the Origins of Welfare States*, ed. Seth Koven and Sonya Michel (New York: Routledge, 1993), 43–93; and Robyn Muncy, "'Women Demand Recognition': Women Candidates in Colorado's Election of 1912," in *We Have Come to Stay: American Women and Political Parties, 1880–1960*, ed. Melanie Gustafson, Kristie Miller, and Elisabeth Israels Perry (Albuquerque: University of New Mexico Press, 1999), 45–54.

3. Muller v. Oregon, 208 U.S. 412; Nancy Woloch, *Muller v. Oregon: A Brief History with Documents* (Boston: Bedford Books, 1996); Sybil Lipschultz, "Social Feminism and Legal Discourse," *Yale Journal of Law and Feminism 2* (Fall 1989): 131–60; and Kathryn Kish Sklar, "Hull House in the 1890s: A Community of Women Reformers," *Signs* 10 (Summer 1985): 658–77.

4. Molly Ladd-Taylor, *Mother-Work: Women, Child Welfare, and the State, 1890–1930* (Urbana: University of Illinois Press, 1994), 135–66; and Theda Skócpol, *Protecting Soldiers and Mothers: The Political Origins of Social Policy in the United States* (Cambridge: Belknap Press of Harvard University, 1992), 424–79.

5. Linda Gordon, "Black and White Visions of Welfare: Women's Welfare Activism: 1890–1945," *Journal of American History 78* (September 1991): 559–90; Eileen Boris, "The Power of Motherhood: Black and White Activist Women Redefine the 'Political,'" *Yale Journal of Law and Feminism 2* (Fall 1989): 25–49.

6. Robyn Muncy, *Creating a Female Dominion in American Reform, 1890–1935* (New York: Oxford University Press, 1991).

7. Salem, *To Better Our World;* and Elisabeth Lasch-Quinn, *Black Neighbors: Race and the Limits of Reform in the American Settlement House Movement, 1890–1945* (Chapel Hill: University of North Carolina Press, 1993).

8. Jacqueline Anne Rouse, *Lugenia Burns Hope: Black Southern Reformer* (Athens: University of Georgia Press, 1989).

9. Rosalyn Terborg-Penn, "Discrimination Against Afro-American Women in the Woman's Movement, 1830–1920," in *The Afro-American Woman: Struggles and Images*, ed. Sharon Harley and Rosalyn Terborg-Penn (Port Washington, NY: National University Publications, 1978); and Higginbotham, *Righteous Discontent, 226.*

BIBLIOGRAPHY

In addition to the works cited in the endnotes, the following sources are helpful for studying women's activism in the Progressive Era.

Boris, Eileen. *Home to Work: Motherhood and the Politics of Industrial Homework in the United States*. New York: Cambridge University Press, 1994.

Cott, Nancy F. *The Grounding of Modern Feminism*. New Haven: Yale University Press, 1987.

Crocker, Ruth Hutchinson. *Social Work and Social Order: The Settlement Movement in Two Industrial Cities, 1889–1930*. Urbana: University of Illinois, 1992.

Goodwin, Joanne L. *Gender and the Politics of Welfare Reform: Mothers' Pensions in Chicago, 1911–4929*. Chicago: University of Chicago Press, 1997.

Gordon, Linda. *Pitied But Not Entitled: Single Mothers and the History of Welfare, 1890–1935*. New York: Maxwell MacMillan International, 1994.

Hewitt, Nancy A. and Suzanne Lebsock, eds. *Visible Women: New Essays on American Activism*. Urbana: University of Illinois Press, 1993.

Knupfer, Anne Meis. *Toward a Tenderer Humanity and a Nobler Womanhood: African American Women's Clubs in Turn-of-the-Century Chicago*. New York: New York University Press, 1996.

Neverdon-Morton, Cynthia. *Afro-American Women of the South and the Advancement of the Race, 1895–1925*. Knoxville: University of Tennessee Press, 1989.

Scott, Anne Firor. *Natural Allies: Women's Associations in American History*. Urbana: University of Illinois Press, 1991.

Robyn Muncy is an associate professor of history at the University of Maryland. She is the author of Creating a Female Dominion in American Reform, 1880–1935 *(1991) and coauthor with Sonya Michel of* Engendering America: A Documentary History, 1865–The Present *(1999).*

From *OAH Magazine of History*, Spring 1999, pp. 15-19. © 1999 by the Organization of American Historians. Reprinted by permission.

Uncovering History

1918 Diary Opens Window on Black Soldier's World

Sue Anne Pressley

The small, black leather-bound book had remained for decades, forgotten, inside a box stuffed with papers in the venerable old brick house on Irving Street NE in Washington. But when Gretchen Roberts-Shorter stumbled upon it recently, as she packed up the home for her elderly relatives, she soon realized it was something special.

The book was a diary from World War I, and in spare, unemotional language, it tells what it was like to be a young black soldier serving in the U.S. Army in France in 1918 and 1919. Journals detailing the experience of African Americans in that conflict are so rare that the Smithsonian does not have one in its collections, a curatorial specialist there said.

"From World War I, we have some really fine uniforms and photographs and other materials, but not a diary [from a black soldier], which is a very intimate and important artifact," said Margaret Vining of the Smithsonian, who specializes in the military history of women and blacks and has examined the journal. "That's a very rare diary — a day-by-day account, a beautifully written account, of his life in the Army."

The diary belonged to Roy Underwood Plummer, who enlisted in 1917 in the District and, because of his writing skills, worked as a clerk in Company C. He graduated from the Howard University School of Medicine in 1927 and lived a productive, cultured life with his wife, Mary, a District educator for whom Plummer Elementary School in Southeast is named. Until his death in 1966, at the age of 69, he practiced medicine in the District.

Roberts-Shorter, a retired D.C. teacher, never met Roy Plummer, a relative by marriage. But as she began to read his daily entries, she felt she got to know "this gentleman" and admired how he approached his wartime adventure and the realities of official segregation. Through his long-ago words, a young man came alive again.

"When I first started reading, I noticed how well he wrote, and I thought how beautifully he must have spoken," she said. "And I started to notice how evenhanded he was in his documentation of the things he observed.

And then, of course, I had differing emotions as I started to see his descriptions of black-and-white issues."

■

The diary, an early Christmas gift from one of Plummer's friends, opens Dec. 15, 1917, when his company was about to cross the Atlantic to France, and ends June 5, 1919, when he was honorably discharged and armed with a ticket to return home to the District.

Written in a fine, clear hand, the entries are often brief: "Called for first time for guard duty. Bright moonlight," reads the entry for Jan. 26, 1918. "Went to town of Libourne in truck. Saw there a meat market, where nothing but horse meat was sold," he wrote on May 18, 1918.

But over the course of a year and a half, he also recorded the impact of the deadly 1918 flu epidemic on the troops; the sadness of seeing a young Belgian boy on crutches come begging into camp; the bitterness of a Christmastime fight that broke out between some black and white troops.

"Friction between the races," he wrote on Dec. 19, 1918. "Though the colored troops are not equipped with guns, according to reports they behaved themselves most bravely and pluckily against the Marines. It seems that the trouble started in a cafe when a Marine Sgt. made some remark which displeased the colored 'boys' there."

An order posted at the military encampment in France is noted, without comment: "The walking of white soldiers with colored women or colored soldiers with white women within the limits of this camp is strictly prohibited."

There also are moments of pleasure, as when he recorded his pride after a Frenchwoman complimented him on his improving language skills or when he wrote about eating out at a cafe and taking a late-night cab back to the camp.

"I think [the experience] afforded him and probably many of the African American soldiers an intellectual freedom that had been stifled in their own country," Vining said, "learning the language and talking to people who had no preconceptions about them except they were people like us."

■

Roberts-Shorter, who has with time become her family historian, transcribed the 115-page journal late at night, handling it reverently, only after putting on white gloves. She felt a growing interest in Plummer as she typed. She learned that for the rest of his life, he studied French and several other languages. She also was amused to discover, after happening on one of his old patients, that the mature Dr. Plummer was a chain smoker famous for admonishing his patients not to smoke.

Roy and Mary Plummer, who had no children, left the Brookland home they had built in the 1930s to their nephew, Robert L. Plummer, now 86, who is Roberts-Shorter's uncle by marriage. As she and an assistant prepared the house for sale in January, they accumulated more than 50 boxes of old papers, photos and artifacts. With time, she joked, the Plummers became so vivid to her that she began to say regular hellos to the two photographs of them she had framed and placed in her living room.

At some point, Roberts-Shorter said, the family "would very much like" to donate the journal to a museum such as the Smithsonian. She also hopes to see it published someday.

"I want it to be safe and preserved for posterity in an institution that is hopefully timeless," she said. "My other thought is, I want as many people as possible to be aware of it, that it just had so many powerful statements about the times in which he lived."

AMERICAN BIOGRAPHY
Edith Galt Wilson

Colleen Roche

In June of 1915, as World War I raged in Europe, U.S. Secretary of State William Jennings Bryan offered his resignation to his boss, President Woodrow Wilson, with whom he disagreed over how to keep America out of the conflict. Although the loss of the top foreign policy adviser during a time of war should naturally be avoided if possible, Wilson's most trusted adviser felt differently, urging him to accept the secretary's resignation. When the president did just that, the adviser exulted: "Hurrah! Old Bryan is out!" adding in a letter the following week, "I will be glad when he expires from an over dose of peace or grape juice—and I never hear of him again." Wilson's only response to such incautious words was a gentle reply, "What a dear partisan you are." Even more surprising than the president's reaction is the identity of the adviser: his paramour of only a few months, Edith Bolling Galt, who would later become the president's second wife.

When Wilson came to the White House in 1913, he was accompanied by his three grown daughters and his first wife, Ellen Louise Axson. Throughout their 30-year marriage Ellen Wilson had worked alongside her husband, aiding him in his various jobs and supporting his political goals. He not only accepted her advice, he craved it. Indeed, from the very beginning of their courtship Woodrow Wilson made it clear to her that he needed a wife who would share in his work. When she died of a kidney ailment, Bright's disease, in August 1914—18 months after becoming first lady—the president was devastated.

Later that month, Wilson's physician and confidant Dr. Cary Grayson commented on "the heartbreaking loneliness of the President" to his friend, Edith Bolling Galt, widowed as well. At the age of 43, Mrs. Galt cut a striking figure. A tall, well-endowed woman who often sported an orchid on her lapel, she had a charming personality and a lilting Southern voice that revealed her Virginia roots. One of 11 children, Edith Galt had only two years of formal schooling. Her 1895 marriage to Norman Galt, a jeweler in Washington, D.C., had left her a wealthy widow—the jeweler died in 1908, leaving his store and

$125,000 to his wife. Despite having many suitors, it seemed unlikely that she would marry again—until she met the president in early 1915.

Following that encounter—a meeting possibly engineered by Dr. Grayson and the president's cousin Helen Bones—Wilson was smitten with Mrs. Galt. The melancholy widower saw in her a woman who could replace his beloved wife as his lover, companion and work partner. Their correspondence reveals the speed with which their relationship developed. On April 28, a month after their initial meeting, Wilson wrote to "dear Mrs. Galt." Two days later he addressed her as "dear friend"; less than one week after that he told her he loved her and asked her to marry him. Bones later told a relative: "I can't say that I foresaw in that first minute what was going to happen. It may have taken ten minutes...."

Although Mrs. Galt refused that first proposal, she did not discourage the president's attentions. The diary of a White House usher, Irwin Hood Hoover, reveals the depth of Wilson's infatuation. Despite the heavy burdens of his office, the president spent a great deal of his time with his new lady friend, going on car rides and having lunch and dinner with her several times a week. The 58-year-old president was like a schoolboy. He wrote to Edith Galt every day, sometimes two or three times, telling her, "I do not want you to go a single day without a Love message from me...." The intensity of Wilson's emotions was alarming to some who knew him and knew the importance of the affairs he was neglecting. Hoover later wrote: "The President had no time for anything else. What was done would be hurried thru.... The afternoons and evenings were all for her and hers for him."

Considering the strength of his attachment to her, it is not surprising that the president should have shared with Mrs. Galt the burdens of his office, yet her involvement went far beyond casual conversations. Following a pattern he had established with his first wife, Wilson not only confided in Edith Galt, he also sought her advice on his work. By the summer of 1915 he had begun to send her packets of state papers, and he expected her to comment on the issues contained therein. Despite the confidential nature of much of his business, the president showed no restraint in what he shared with her. He discussed the war, his challenges with Congress and his personal opinion on colleagues and foes, and he sought her advice on these and many other problems. Everything was fair game: "Whatever is mine is yours, knowledge of affairs of state not excepted—and that without reserve, except that, as you know, there may be a few things that it would not be wise or prudent to commit to writing." Wilson had a private phone line installed between the White House and Mrs. Galt's home so that they could discuss state business at any hour. He even taught his new love the secret code for emissaries abroad, and for the rest of the war she decoded and encoded confidential messages to and from Europe for him.

Given her lack of formal schooling, Mrs. Galt initially felt ill-equipped for the role into which the president had thrust her. Protesting her lack of knowledge about government, she wrote to him, "I feel so queer…reading all these reports from the different theaters of war…I, an unknown person, one who had lived a sheltered, inconspicuous existence…." In another letter she wondered: "Why should I be chosen among all women to help you in your masterful strength, to serve…. The thought makes me tremble…." Wilson replied that she was "as trustworthy and capable and fit for counsel as any man." Indeed, he seemed to respect her intuition more than the experience of his advisers, writing her: "I have plenty of well informed minds about me. I can get all the wisdom of information that I can make use of. That is not what I need. What I need is what you give me…an insight into the very needs of my heart [and] the support of a great character…."

With the president's constant encouragement, Edith Galt eventually settled happily into the role of partner. Soon, the work that they shared became one of the most important aspects of their relationship to her: "Much as I enjoy your delicious love-letters…I believe I enjoy even more the ones in which you tell me (as you did this morning) of what you are working on… for then I feel I am sharing your work—and being taken in to partnership." Unfortunately, she shared with him a tendency to interpret disagreement as disloyalty, and she rarely contradicted him, even when he was irrational, as he was increasingly as his health declined. Her deficiencies did not discourage Mrs. Galt from sharing her opinions, however, nor prevent Wilson from acting on her advice. The episode with Secretary of State Bryan reveals both Wilson's incredible faith in her as well as her naiveté. When the president asked for her advice on what to do about the secretary of state, Mrs. Galt weighed in eagerly, joking that she would like to take Bryan's place so that she could have daily conferences with the president.

Her role continued following their marriage in December 1915. The new first lady often accompanied the president to the White House in the morning and sat by his desk, listening as he dictated memos or handing him papers to sign. Edith Wilson sat in on important meetings and advised him on his speeches. The president even delegated Mrs. Wilson to meet alone with an administrative official, Secretary of the Navy Josephus Daniels, regarding the arming of American ships. When the president journeyed to Paris for the peace conference following the war, she went with him. There the first lady "acted in [the president's] stead," visiting wounded soldiers and receiving dignitaries.

After coming home from the Paris peace negotiations, and aware that the Treaty of Versailles faced potential defeat in the U.S. Senate, President Wilson embarked on a cross-country tour in the fall of 1919 aimed at persuading Americans to pressure their senators to ratify it. In October, Wilson collapsed and had to return to Washington, where he suffered a stroke that incapacitated him. Given their relationship, it should not be surprising that Mrs. Wilson continued in her capacity as "secret partner" after her husband became ill. Indeed, she undoubtedly believed that the president would have wanted her to do so. In the months following his stroke, the first lady continued to be Wilson's loyal aide, never leaving his side but for one night for the next four years.

One of the most controversial first ladies in history, Edith Wilson for decades has been identified by many historians as "the first woman president of the United States" because of the influence she had in the aftermath of the president's debilitating stroke. Critics claim that Mrs. Wilson ran the government during her husband's illness, fulfilling what one described as "her own ambitions to act as president." However, Mrs. Wilson always denied such charges, benignly describing her role in her official memoir as a "stewardship," adding that she "never made a single decision [other than] what was important and what was not, and the very important decision of when to present matters to my husband." The truth appears to lie somewhere in the middle.

Historian John Milton Cooper has written that Edith Wilson made two fateful choices following the onset of her husband's illness: She refused to disclose the true nature of the president's condition to the public, and she restricted his access to visitors and information. Both decisions had significant consequences. The public was not only uninformed, it was deliberately misled, told for months by the president's doctors that he was suffering from a nervous disorder. Even the cabinet and the vice president did not know the full extent of President Wilson's debilitation. As a result, any effort to persuade Wilson to resign and allow able-bodied Vice President Thomas Marshall to lead the country through the troubled postwar months never gained momentum.

More important, the limitation of the flow of information to the president influenced his ability to govern effectively. In an effort to shelter him, Mrs. Wilson restricted his visitors in the early weeks to medical attendants and family, and she suppressed any news she thought might upset him. Messages were passed back and forth through the first lady, with her decisions as to what to share with the president often based not just on "what was important" but on her personal feelings about the subject or the concerned party. The most serious information concealed from the president concerned the Treaty of Versailles.

As President Wilson lay ill in the White House, the U.S. Senate heatedly debated the treaty, with many senators of both parties arguing for changes that would preserve American neutrality and isolation. Several government officials gave Mrs. Wilson letters urging the president to compromise on the treaty, but few of them got a response, and it was later discovered that some of the letters were never even opened. Knowing the animosity that existed between Wilson and his main Senate opponent, Henry Cabot Lodge, the first lady chose to keep the sick president somewhat removed from the conflict. After months of wrangling, the Senate voted down the treaty. Although it probably would have been defeated anyway—his opponents were unbending, and the president had never shown any interest in compromising—Mrs. Wilson's decision to shield him from the controversy only added to the belief of many that she was running the government during her husband's illness.

Despite the significance of her actions, calling Mrs. Wilson "the first female president" exaggerates her role, for the evidence suggests that she was more of a courier than a policymaker. Indeed, the greatest indication that Mrs. Wilson did not function as president is the tremendous amount of work that was left undone. Appointments went unfilled, diplomats were not received and 28 bills became law without the president's signature. In fact, it was the Cabinet, which met more than 25 times in President Wilson's absence, that was "running things," as Secretary of the Interior Franklin Lane told a friend at the time.

Although Mrs. Wilson did not wield the authority of the chief executive that her detractors have claimed for decades, she was nevertheless an unusually powerful first lady. Edith Wilson was not a feminist, however, nor was she interested in politics. She had nothing but contempt for suffragettes, calling them "disgusting creatures," and she probably never voted. Her reluctance to marry the president while he was still in office contradicts the theories of those historians who believe she was personally ambitious. While it may seem surprising that she took such an active part during Wilson's illness, she was in fact fulfilling the traditional role of a loyal wife—for it was the president himself who had asked her to function as his adviser.

If Mrs. Wilson made fateful decisions about what information to share with her sick husband, her confidence in the propriety of her role is understandable. As she told one of her biographers, Alden Hatch, about her relationship with the president, "I talked with him so much that I knew pretty well what he thought of things." More intriguing than dubious allegations about Mrs. Wilson's political aspirations is the president's own role in grooming his wife to function as what he called his "secret partner," thereby putting her in a position that historian John Garraty noted was "scarcely contemplated by the Constitution."

After the president's death in February 1924, her role changed to that of guardian of his legacy, as she supported every cause that advanced the ideals for which her husband had worked. Mrs. Wilson traveled to Geneva to observe his beloved League of Nations in action, and she worked tirelessly to turn his birthplace in Staunton, Va., into a museum. Ever loyal to his party, she maintained a relationship with every Democratic president from Franklin D. Roosevelt to John F. Kennedy, and, although she personally liked Dwight Eisenhower, she refused to visit Staunton in 1960 when he was there, lest her visit be misinterpreted as political support for the Republicans.

Edith Wilson's work on behalf of her late husband's causes and legacy continued until December 28, 1961, when she died in the night from a respiratory illness. Mrs. Wilson had been scheduled to attend the dedication of the Woodrow Wilson Bridge near Washington, D.C., the following morning. Despite the cold weather and her advanced age of 89, one feels certain that, had she not died, she would have been there.

Evolution on Trial

In 1925 science teacher John Scopes agreed to challenge Tennessee's new anti-evolution law in court. The resulting legal battle pitted two of the country's premier orators against each other and treated newspaper readers worldwide to what Baltimore Sun columnist H.L. Mencken called a "genuinely fabulous" show.

by J. Kingston Pierce

Travelers wandering through Dayton, Tennessee, in mid-July 1925 might have been excused for thinking that the tiny hill town was holding a carnival or perhaps a religious revival. The street leading to the local courthouse was busy with vendors peddling sandwiches, watermelon, calico, and books on biology. Evangelists had erected an open-air tabernacle, and nearby buildings were covered with posters exhorting people to "read your Bible" and avoid eternal damnation.

If there was a consistent theme to the garish exhibits and most of the gossip in Dayton it was, of all things, *monkeys*. Monkey jokes were faddish. Monkey toys and souvenirs were ubiquitous. A soda fountain advertised something called a "monkey fizz," and the town's butcher shop featured a sign reading, "We handle all kinds of meat except monkey."

As comical as this scene sounds, its background was anything but amusing. Sixty-six years after Charles Darwin published his controversial *Origin of Species*, the debate he'd engendered over humankind's evolution from primates had suddenly reached a fever pitch in this hamlet on the Tennessee River. Efforts to enforce a new state statute against the teaching of evolution in public schools had precipitated the arrest of Dayton educator John T. Scopes. His subsequent prosecution drew international press attention as well as the involvement of the American Civil Liberties Union (ACLU). It also attracted two headliners of that era--Chicago criminal attorney Clarence Darrow and former presidential candidate William Jennings Bryan—to act as opposing counsel.

Bryan characterized the coming courtroom battle as a "duel to the death"—one that would pit religious fundamentalists against others who trusted in scientific conclusions, and would finally determine the right of citizens to dictate the curricula of the schools their tax dollars supported. The case rapidly took on a farcical edge, however, as attorneys shouted at each other and outsiders strove to capitalize on the extraordinary publicity surrounding this litigation. (At one point, for instance, a black man with a cone-shaped head who worked New York's Coney Island sideshows as Zip, the "humanoid ape," was offered to the defense as the "missing link" necessary to prove Darwin's scientific claims.) The "Scopes Monkey Trial," as history would come to know it, also included a personal dimension, becoming a hard-fought contest not just between rival ideas, but between Bryan and Darrow, former allies whose political differences had turned them into fierce adversaries.

Crusades to purge Darwinism from American public education began as early as 1917 and were most successful in the South, where Fundamentalists controlled the big Protestant denominations. In 1923, the Oklahoma Legislature passed a bill banning the use of all school texts that included evolutionist instruction. Later that same year, the Florida Legislature approved a joint resolution declaring it "improper and subversive for any teacher in a public school to teach Atheism or Agnosticism, or to teach as true, Darwinism, or any other hypothesis that links man in blood relationship to any other form of life."

To Fundamentalists, for whom literal interpretation of the Bible was central to their faith, there was no room for compromise between the story of God's unilateral creation of man and Darwin's eons-long development of the species. Moreover, these critics deemed evolutionist theories a threat not only to the belief in God but to the very structure of a Christian society. "To hell with science if it is going to damn souls," was how one Fundamentalist framed the debate.

John Washington Butler couldn't have agreed more. In January 1925, this second-term member of the Tennessee House of Representatives introduced a bill that would make it unlawful for teachers working in schools financed wholly or in part by the state to "teach any theory that denies the story of the divine creation of man as taught in the Bible." Violation of the statute would constitute a misdemeanor punishable by a fine of not less than $100 or more than $500 for each offense.

Butler's bill flummoxed government observers but delighted its predominately Baptist backers, and it sailed through the Tennessee House on a lopsided 71 to 5 vote. It went on to the state Senate, where objections were more numerous, and where one member tried to kill the legislation by proposing an amendment to also "prohibit the teaching that the earth is round." Yet senators ultimately sanctioned the measure 24 to 6. As the story goes, many Tennessee lawmakers thought they were safe in voting for this "absurd" bill because Governor Austin Peay, a well-recognized progressive, was bound to veto it. However, Peay—in a prickly political trade-off that won him the support of rural representatives he needed in order to pass educational and infrastructural reforms—signed the Butler Act into law. As he did so, though, he noted that he had no intention of enforcing it. "Probably," the governor said in a special message to his Legislature, "the law will never be applied."

Peay's prediction might have come true, had not the ACLU chosen to make the statute a *cause célèbre*. Worried that other states would follow Tennessee's lead, the ACLU agreed in late April 1925 to guarantee legal and financial assistance to any teacher who would test the law.

John Scopes wasn't the obvious candidate. A gawky, 24-year-old Illinois native, he was still new to his job as a general science teacher and football coach at Rhea County Central High School. Yet his views on evolution were unequivocal. "I don't see how a teacher can teach biology without teaching evolution," Scopes insisted, adding that the state-approved science textbook included lessons in evolution. And he was a vocal supporter of academic freedom and freedom of thought. Yet Scopes was reluctant to participate in the ACLU's efforts until talked into it by Dayton neighbors who hoped that a prominent local trial would stimulate prosperity in their sleepy southeastern Tennessee town.

On May 7, Scopes was officially arrested for violating Tennessee's anti-evolution statute. Less than a week later, William Jennings Bryan accepted an invitation from the World's Christian Fundamentals Association to assist in Scopes' prosecution.

No one who knew the 65-year-old Bryan well should have been surprised by his involvement in the case. Bryan had been trained in the law before being elected as a congressman from Nebraska, and he made three spirited but unsuccessful runs at the presidency on the Democratic ticket. He had served as secretary of state during President Woodrow Wilson's first term but had spent the last decade writing and lecturing more often about theology than politics. With the same silver tongue he'd once used to excoriate Republican office seekers and decry U.S. involvement in World War I, Bryan had since promoted religious ethics over man's exaltation of science. "It is better

to trust in the Rock of Ages than to know the ages of the rocks," Bryan pronounced; "It is better for one to know that he is close to the Heavenly Father than to know how far the stars in the heavens are apart." Ever the rural populist— "the Great Commoner"—Bryan saw religion as the crucial backbone of agrarian America, and he reserved special enmity for accommodationists who struggled to reconcile Christianity and evolution. Such modernism, he wrote, "permits one to believe in a God, but puts the creative act so far away that reverence for the Creator is likely to be lost."

Bryan's role elevated the Scopes trial from a backwoods event into a national story. Clarence Darrow's agreement to act in the teacher's defense guaranteed the story would be sensational. A courtroom firebrand and a political and social reformer, the 68-year-old Darrow was still riding high from his success of the year before, when his eloquent insanity defense of Chicago teenagers Nathan Leopold and Richard Loeb, who had kidnapped and murdered a younger neighbor, had won them life imprisonment instead of the electric chair. The ACLU would have preferred a less controversial and more religiously conservative counsel than Darrow, an agnostic who characterized Christianity as a "slave religion" that encouraged complacency and acquiescence toward injustices. According to biographer Kevin Tierney, the Chicago attorney "believed that religion was a sanctifier of bigotry, of narrowness, of ignorance and the status quo." The ACLU feared that with Darrow taking part, the case would, to quote Scopes, "become a carnival and any possible dignity in the fight for liberties would be lost." In the end, Darrow took part in the Dayton trial only after offering his services free of charge—"for the first, the last, and the only time in my life," the attorney later remarked.

After spending the previous Friday impaneling a jury (most members of which turned out to be churchgoing farmers), all parties gathered for the start of the real legal drama on Monday, July 13, 1925. Approximately 600 spectators—including newspaper and radio reporters, along with a substantial percentage of Dayton's 1,700 residents—elbowed their way into the Eighteenth Tennessee Circuit Court. Presiding was Judge John T. Raulston, who liked to call himself "jest a reg'lar mountin'er jedge." The crowded courtroom made the week's stifling heat even more unbearable. Advocates on both sides of the case quickly resorted to shirtsleeves. The prosecution included Bryan, Circuit Attorney General Arthur Thomas Stewart, and Bryan's son, William Jennings Bryan, Jr., a Los Angeles lawyer. For the defense were Darrow, New York lawyer and co-counsel Dudley Field Malone, ACLU attorney Arthur Garfield Hays, and Scopes' local lawyer, John Randolph Neal.

The prosecution's strategy was straightforward. It wasn't interested in debating the value or wisdom of the Butler Law, only in proving that John Scopes had broken it. "While I am perfectly willing to go into the question of evolution," Bryan had told an acquaintance, "I am not sure that it is involved. The right of the people speaking through the legislature, to control the schools which they create and support is the real issue as I see it." With this direction in mind, Bryan and his fellow attorneys took two days to call four witnesses. All of them confirmed that Scopes had lectured his biology classes on evolution, with two students adding that these lessons hadn't seemed to hurt them. The prosecution then rested its case.

Scopes' defense was more problematic. Once a plea of innocence had been lodged, Darrow moved to quash the indictment against his client by arguing that the Butler Law was a "foolish, mischievous, and wicked act … as brazen and bold an attempt to destroy liberty as ever was seen in the Middle Ages." Neal went on to point out how the Tennessee constitution held that "no preference shall be given, by law, to any religious establishment or mode of worship." Since the anti-evolution law gave preference to the Bible over other religious books, he concluded, it was thus unconstitutional. Raulston rejected these challenges.

From the outset, defense attorneys focused their arguments on issues related to religion and the influences of a fundamentalist morality. Early in the proceedings, Darrow objected to the fact that Judge Raulston's court opened, as was customary, with a prayer, saying that it could prejudice the jury against his client. The judge overruled Darrow's objection. Later the defense examined the first of what were to be 12 expert witnesses—scientists and clergymen both—to show that the Butler Law was unreasonable and represented an improper exercise of Tennessee's authority over education. When the state took exception, however, Raulston declared such testimony inadmissible (though he allowed affidavits to be entered into the record for appeal purposes).

With the defense's entire case resting on those 12 experts, veteran courtroom watchers figured that this decision effectively ended the trial. "All that remains of the great case of the State of Tennessee against the infidel Scopes is the formal business of bumping off the defendant … " harrumphed journalist H.L. Mencken after the sixth day of litigation. "[T]he main battle is over, with Genesis completely triumphant." So sure were they of a swift summation that Mencken and others in the press corps simply packed their bags and left town. Yet Darrow had a surprise up his sleeve. When the court reconvened on Monday, July 20, the ACLU's Arthur Hays rose to summon one more witness—William Jennings Bryan. "Hell is going to pop now," attorney Malone whispered to John Scopes.

Calling Bryan was a highly unusual move, but an extremely popular one. Throughout the trial, the politician-cum-preacher had been the toast of Dayton. Admirers greeted Bryan wherever he went and sat through long, humid hours in court just for the opportunity to hear him speak. He'd generally been silent, listening calmly, cooling himself with a fan that he'd received from a local funeral home, and saving his voice for an hour-and-a-half-

long closing argument that he hoped would be "the mountain peak of my life's effort." But Bryan didn't put up a fight when asked to testify. In fact, he agreed with some enthusiasm, convinced—as he always had been—of his righteous cause.

Judge Raulston, concerned that the crowd massing to watch this clash of legal titans would prove injurious to the courthouse, ordered that the trial reconvene on the adjacent lawn. There, while slouched back in his chair and pulling now and then on his signature suspenders, Darrow examined Bryan for almost two hours, all but ignoring the specific case against Scopes while he did his best to demonstrate that Fundamentalism—and Bryan, as its representative—were both open to ridicule.

Darrow wanted to know if Bryan really believed, as the Bible asserted, that a whale had swallowed Jonah. Did he believe that Adam and Eve were the first humans on the planet? That all languages dated back to the Tower of Babel? "I accept the Bible absolutely," Bryan stated. As Darrow continued his verbal assault, however, it became clear that Bryan's acceptance of the Bible was not as literal as his followers believed. "[S]ome of the Bible is given illustratively," he observed at one point. "For instance: 'Ye are the salt of the earth.' I would not insist that man was actually salt, or that he had flesh of salt, but it is used in the sense of salt as saving God's people." Similarly, when discussing the creation, Bryan conceded that the six days described in the Bible were probably not literal days but periods of time lasting many years.

With this examination dragging on, the two men's tempers became frayed, and humorous banter gave way to insults and fists shaken in anger. Fundamentalists in the audience listened with increasing discomfort as their champion questioned Biblical "truths," and Bryan slowly came to realize that he had stepped into a trap. The sort of faith he represented could not adequately be presented or justly parsed in a court of law. His only recourse was to impugn Darrow's motives for quizzing him, as he sought to do in this exchange:

BRYAN: Your Honor, I think I can shorten this testimony. The only purpose Mr. Darrow has is to slur at the Bible, but I will answer his questions … and I have no objection in the world. I want the world to know that this man, who does not believe in God, is trying to use a court in Tennessee—

DARROW: I object to that.

BRYAN: —to slur at it, and, while it will require time I am willing to take it.

DARROW: I object to your statement. I am examining you on your fool ideas that no intelligent Christian on earth believes.

It was a bleak moment in what had been Bryan's brilliant career. He hoped to regain control of events and the trust of his followers the next day by putting Darrow on the stand. But Attorney General Stewart, who'd opposed Bryan's cross-examination, blocked him and instead convinced the judge to expunge Bryan's testimony from the record.

Before the jury was called to the courtroom the following day, Darrow addressed Judge Raulston. "I think to save time," he declared, "we will ask the court to bring in the jury and instruct the jury to find the defendant guilty." This final ploy by Darrow would ensure that the defense could appeal the case to a higher court that might overturn the Butler Law. The defense also waived its right to a final address, which, under Tennessee law, deprived the prosecution of a closing statement. Bryan would not get an opportunity to make his last grandiloquent speech.

The jury conferred for only nine minutes before returning a verdict of guilty. Yet Bryan's public embarrassment in Dayton would become legend—one that the prosecutor could never overcome, for he died in his sleep five days after the trial ended.

Following the trial, the school board offered to renew Scopes' contract for another year providing he complied with the anti-evolution law. But a group of scientists arranged a scholarship so he could attend graduate school, and Scopes began his studies at the University of Chicago in September. Mencken's *Baltimore Sun* agreed to pay the $100 fine Judge Raulston levied against Scopes. On appeal, the Tennessee Supreme Court ruled that the jury, rather than the judge, should have determined Scopes' fine, but it upheld the Butler Law's constitutionality. Darrow had hoped to take the matter all the way to the U.S. Supreme Court. Any chance of that, though, was foreclosed when Tennessee's chief justice nullified Scopes' indictment and threw what he called "this bizarre case" out of the courts.

Not until April 1967—42 years after the Butler Law was passed, and 12 years after *Inherit the Wind*, a play based on the Scopes Monkey Trial, became a Broadway hit—did the Tennessee Legislature repeal the anti-evolution law.

Since then, a series of court decisions has barred creationists' efforts to have their beliefs taught in public schools. Yet 75 years after the Scopes trial, debate over evolution still continues to simmer as states and education boards struggle with the subject that pits science against religion.

From Front Porch to Back Seat
A History of the Date

Beth Bailey

One day, the 1920s story goes, a young man came to call upon a city girl. When he arrived, she had her hat on. The punch line is completely lost on twenty-first-century readers, but people at the time would have gotten it. He came on a "call," expecting to sit in her parlor, be served some refreshments, perhaps listen to her play the piano. She expected to go out on a date. He, it is fairly safe to surmise, ended up spending a fair amount of money fulfilling her expectations (1).

In fact, the unfortunate young man really should have known better. By 1924 when this story was current, "dating" had almost completely replaced "calling" in middle-class American culture. The term appeared in *The Ladies' Home Journal*, a bastion of middle-class respectability, several times in 1914—set off by quotation marks, but with no explanation of its meaning. One article, written in the then-exotic voice of a college sorority girl, began:

> One beautiful evening in the spring term, when I was a college girl of eighteen, the boy whom, because of his popularity in every phase of college life, I had been proud gradually to allow the monopoly of my 'dates,' took me unexpectedly into his arms. As he kissed me impetuously I was glad, from the bottom of my heart, for the training of that mother who had taught me to hold myself aloof from all personal familiarities of boys and men (2).

Despite the sugarcoating provided by the tribute to motherhood and virtue, dating was a problematic new practice for the middle classes. Its origins were decidedly not respectable; they lay in the practices of "treating" and the sexual exchanges made by "charity girls." The very term "date" came from prostitution. While the urban working class and frankly sexual origins of dating were fairly quickly obscured, not only by such tributes to virtue but also by the increasingly common belief that young people began "going out" because automobiles made it possible, notions of exchange lingered. The same author who re-corded the story about the frustrated caller and the woman in the hat made sense of dating this way: In dating, a man is responsible for all expenses. The woman contributes only her company. Of course, the man contributes his company also, but since he must "add money to balance the bargain," his company must be worth less than hers (3). Thus, according to this economic understanding, she is selling her company to him. Some men declared, flat out, that the exchange was not equitable, that men were operating at a loss. Others, of course, imagined ways to balance the equation: Man's Company + Money = Woman's Company + ?

Dating, which emerged from working class urban culture, became a key ritual of youth culture in the 1920s and was unquestionably the dominant form of "courtship" by the beginning of World War II. Certainly not all American youth participated in the rituals of dating. But those who did not, whether by choice, exclusion, or ignorance of the dominant custom, often still felt the weight of a set of expectations that were enacted in high school peer cultures and even written into school curriculums. For the great majority of youth who did date, the highly personal emotions and experiences of dating were shaped, at least in part, through an increasingly powerful and far-reaching national culture that defined the conventions of dating and lent meaning and coherence to individual experience.

While dating remained "the way of American youth," in the words of one sociologist, it took radically different forms during its roughly forty-five-year heyday from the mid-1920s through the late 1960s. In the years before-World War II, American youth prized a promiscuous popularity, demonstrating competitive success through the number and variety of dates they commanded. After the war, youth turned to "going steady," arguing that the system provided a measure of security from the pressures of the postwar world.

In the 1930s, a sociologist gave the competitive system a name: the dating and rating complex. His study of a college campus revealed that the system was based on notions of popularity. To be popular, men needed outward, material signs: an automobile, the right clothing, and money. Women's popularity depended on building and maintaining a reputation for popularity. They had to *be seen* with many popular men in the right places, indignantly turn down requests for dates made at the "last minute," which could be weeks in advance, and cultivate the impression that they were greatly in demand (4). Thus, in *Mademoiselle's* 1938 college issue, a Smith College senior advised incoming freshmen to cultivate an "image of popularity." "During your first term," she wrote, get "home talent" to ply you with letters, telegrams, and invitations. College men will think, "She must be attractive if she can rate all that attention" (5). At Northwestern University in the 1920s, the competitive pressure was so intense that coeds made a pact not to date on certain nights of the week. That way they could find time to study, secure in the knowledge they were not losing out to others in the race for popularity by staying home (6).

The new conventions held sway well beyond the gates of colleges. The *Woman's Home Companion* explained the modern dating system—with no mention of college campuses—for its non-elite readers: "No matter how pretty you may be, how smart your clothes—or your tongue—if you have no dates your rating is low…. The modern girl ailtivates not one single suitor, but dates, lots of them…. Her aim is not a too obvious romance but general popularity" (7). Writing to *Senior Scholastic*, a magazine for high school classrooms, a girl from Greensboro, North Carolina, summed it all up:

Going steady with one date

Is okay, if that's all you rate (8).

Rating, dating, popularity, and competition: catchwords hammered home, reinforced from all sides until they seemed a natural vocabulary. You had to rate in order to date, to date in order to rate. By successfully maintaining this cycle, you became popular. To stay popular, you competed. In the 1930s and 1940s, this competition was enacted, most publicly, on the dance floor—whether in private dances, college formals, or high school parties. There success was a dizzying popularity that kept girls whirling from escort to escort. One etiquette book advised young women to strive to become "once-arounders" who never completed a turn around the dance floor before another man "cut in" on her partner (9). Dancing and cutting in were governed by strict protocol: The man had to ask the woman to dance and was responsible for her until she was taken over by another partner. On no account could he leave her stranded on the dance floor or alone on the sidelines. "Getting stuck" with a partner was taken quite seriously as a sign of social failure—even if it was with one's escort. Though a 1933 advice book told the story of a girl who, catching her partner waving a dollar bill behind her back as an inducement to cut in, offered, "Make it five and I'll go home"(10), a more serious suggestion for handling

the situation appeared in *Mademoiselle*: "Keep smiling if it kills you" (11).

By 1950, that system had almost completely disappeared. A girl in Green Bay, Wisconsin, reported that her parents were "astonished" when they discovered that she had not danced with anyone but her escort at the high school formal. "The truth was," she admitted, "that I wasn't aware that we were supposed to" (12). This 180-degree reversal signaled not simply a change in dancing etiquette but a complete transformation of the dating system. Definitions of social success as promiscuous popularity based on strenuous competition had given way to new definitions, which located success in the security of a dependable escort.

How did such an entrenched system I change so quickly? It was in large part because of World War II. With virtually all physically fit men between the ages of eighteen and twenty-six inducted into the military by 1943, a system already strained to provide multiple male escorts for every woman foundered. Though some women, near military bases, found an overabundance of men seeking companionship, in much of the nation the complaint was, in the words of the popular song, "There is no available male."

As war disrupted one pattern of courtship, it also changed priorities for many of the nation's youth. During the war, the rate at which Americans married jumped precipitously. That made sense—many young couples, facing an uncertain future, including the possibility the man might not survive the war, married in haste. Marriage rates also rose because the war revived the American economy; many couples had delayed marriage during the Depression, so there was a backlog of couples waiting to marry. But the high rate of marriages continued on well past the end of the war. And most strikingly, the average age at marriage plummeted. In 1939, the average age of marriage for women was 23.3. By 1959, fully 47 percent of brides married before they turned nineteen (13).

Before the war, when discussions of courtship centered on rating and dating, marriage had few cheerleaders. It is not that people did not intend to marry. They did. But marriage and the dating system were two quite different things. Dating was about competition within the peer-culture of youth; marriage was the end, not the culmination, of participation in youth culture. By the time World War II drew to a close, however, American culture had begun celebrating marriage for youth. And the dating system was no longer a competitive struggle for popularity within youth culture, but instead preparation for an early marriage.

This new model had some unusual results. If girls were to marry at eighteen and boys at twenty, the preparation for marriage had to begin earlier than before. Experts told parents to help their children become datable, warning that a late start might doom their marriage prospects. Thirteen-year-olds who did not yet date were called "late daters;" magazines recommended formal sit-down birthday dinners and dances for ten-year old boys and their dates. A 1961 study found that 40 percent of the fifth-graders in one middle-class Pennsylvania district were already dating (14).

In the prewar years, high school students had emulated the dating-rating system of their elders. As conventions changed for older youth, the younger group tried to keep up. As their slightly older peers married, younger teens developed a parallel convention: going steady. In earlier times, "keeping steady company" was understood as a step along the way to marriage (15). Going steady meant something quite different by the 1950s. Few steady couples really expected to marry one another—especially the twelve-year olds—but, for the duration, they acted as if they *were* married. Going steady had become a sort of play marriage, a mimicry of the actual marriage of their older peers (16).

The new protocol of going steady was every bit as strict as the old protocol of rating and dating, with the form of going steady mirroring teenagers' concepts of young marriage. To go steady, the boy gave the girl some visible token—class ring, letter sweater, etc.—or they exchanged identical tokens, often gold or silver friendship rings worn on the third finger of the left hand. Customs varied locally, as *Life* magazine reported: in Birmingham, Michigan, the girl wore the boy's ID bracelet, but never his letter sweater. In rural Iowa, the couple wore matching corduroy "steady jackets," but in the far West, any couple wearing matching clothing was sure to be laughed at (17).

As long as they went steady, the boy had to call the girl a certain number of times a week and take her on a certain number of dates a week—both numbers were subject to local convention. Neither boy nor girl could date anyone else or pay too much attention to anyone of the opposite sex. While either could go out with friends of the same sex, each must always know where the other was and what he or she was doing. Going steady meant a guaranteed date, but it also meant that the girl had to help her boyfriend save up for big events by budgeting "their" money, even if it meant sitting home together. Going steady also implied, as parents quickly figured out, greater sexual intimacy—either more necking or "going further" (18).

Despite the intense monogamy of such relationships, few saw going steady as a precursor to marriage. One study of 565 seniors in a suburban high school in the East found that 80 percent of them—or approximately 452 seniors—had gone or were going steady, but only 11 of them planned to marry their steadies (19). In New Haven, Connecticut, girls wore "obit bracelets": each time they broke up with a boy they added a disc engraved with his name or initials to the chain. So temporary were such arrangements that a teen advice book from the mid-1950s suggested girls engrave a "Puppy Love Anklet" with "Going Steady" on one side and "Ready, Willing, 'n Waiting" on the other (20).

Harmless as this system sounds today, especially compared to the rigors of rating and dating, going steady precipitated an intense generational battle. The key issue, predictably, was sex. A popular advice book for teenage girls argued that going steady inevitably led girls to heavy necking and thus to guilt for the rest of their lives. Better to date lots of strangers, the author insisted, than end up necking with a steady boyfriend (21). Adults who advocated the old system as somehow sexually safer, however, had selective memories. The days of promiscuous popularity were also the days of "petting parties," and young people had worried endlessly about how "far" to go with a date. And who knew whether a stranger, parked on a dark road, would listen to a young woman's "firm but polite" NO (22)?

Promiscuous dating and going steady held different dangers. Consent was the difference. A beleaguered system of sexual control based on the resolve of girls and young women to say no—at least to the final step of sexual intercourse—was further breaking down in the new system of going steady. As going steady was a simulated marriage, relationships could and did develop within its even shortterm security, monogamy, and, sometimes, love. Parents thought it was easier for girls to say no to the rapid succession of boys who were, at some level, markers for popularity—even when the young men insisted, as one did in the pages of *Senior Scholastic*, that the $1.20 he spent on the date should entitle him to at least a little necking (23). Adults were afraid it was harder for girls to say no to a steady.

In some ways parents were right, but it was youth themselves, not parental complaints, that would transform the dating system once again. By the late 1960s, the system of sexual exchange that underlay both dating systems was in tatters, undermined by a widespread sexual revolution. In the 1970s, many young people rejected the artificialities of dating, insisting that it was most important to get to know one another as *people*. And a great many women, recognizing the implied exchange in Man's Company + Money = Woman's Company + ?, rejected that sort of bargain altogether for a variety of arrangements that did not suggest an equation in need of balancing. Since the early 1970s, no completely dominant national system of courtship has emerged, and the existing systems are not nearly so clear in their conventions and expectations as were the old systems of dating. Not always knowing "the rules" is undoubtedly harder than following the clear script of the traditional date, but those critics who are nostalgic for the good old days should first understand the complicated history of the date.

Endnotes

1. Alexander Black, "Is the Young Person Coming Back?" *Harper's*, August 1924, 340. The author of *Ladies' Home Journal's* (*LHJ*) "Good Manners and Good Form" column advised a young woman who had been invited to the theater to greet her escort with her hat on, though without her wrap and gloves. Mrs. Burton Kingsland, *LHJ*, August 1909, 39.
2. "How Maya Girl Know?" *LHJ* January 1914, 9. See also a letter to Mrs. Stickney Parks, 'Girls' Affairs,' *LHJ*, May 1914, 58.
3. Black, 342.
4. Willard Waller, "The Rating and Dating Complex," *American Sociological Review* 2 (1937): 727–34. Women's popularity was described as associational—she received status as the object of men's choice. Undoubtedly, the right clothes, the right connections, and all the intangibles that come from the right background purchased male attention in the first place, but popular and scholarly experts consistently slighted this angle.

5. Mary Ellen Green, "Advice to Freshmen," *Mademoiselle*, August 1939, 8.

6. Paula Fass, *The Damned and the Beautiful* (New York: Oxford University Press, 1977), 200. Fass found the Northwestern arrangement reported in the *UCLA Daily* (November 13, 1925). I found an aprocryphal version of the story in "If Your Daughter Goes to College," *Better Homes and Gardens (BH&G)*, May 1940.

7. Anna Streese Richardson, "Dates in Christmas Socks," *Woman's Home Companion* (WHC), January 1940, 7.

8. "Jam Session," *Senior Scholastic (SS)*, February 28–March 4, 1944, 32.

9. Elizabeth Eldridge, *Co-ediquette* (New York: E.P. Dutton & Company, 1936), 203. The author based her book on personal research and experience at several U.S. colleges and universities.

10. Alice Leone Moats, *No Nice Girl Swears* (New York: Alfred A. Knopf, 1933) 84–5.

11. Virginia Hanson, "Party-Girl—Princeton Style," *Mademoiselle*, May 1938, 46.

12. Jan London, "The Dateline: Every Dance With the Same Boy?" *Good Housekeeping (GH)*, March 1955, 100. In the South, the cut-in system persisted longer, but as *Esquire* noted in 1958, "Cutting is the outer limit of poor form almost everywhere else in America" (Nicholas David, "Courtship on the Campus," *Esquire*, February 1958, 49).

13. See Phyllis I. Rosenteur, *the Single Woman* (Indianapolis, IN: Bobbs-Merrill Co., 1961), 58; James H.S. Bossard, "The Engagement Ring—A Changing Symbol," *New York Times Magazine*, September 14, 1958, 74: "The Family: Woman's World," *Time*, June 14, 1963, 66.

14. Ruth Imler, "The Sub-Deb: The Late Dater," *LHJ*, September 1955, 54: Dorothy Barclay, "When Boy (Age Twelve) Meets Girl," *New York Times Magazine*, January 23, 1955, 39: "The Pre-Teens," *Time*, April 20, 1962, 68. "Going Steady at Twelve," *Newsweek*, December 18, 1961, 90. See also David R. Mace, "Let's Take a Sane Look at the Hysterical Quest for a Husband," *McCall's*, September 1962, 54.

15. See, for example, G. O. Schultz, "Are Our High Schoolers Snobs?" *BH&G*, February 1941, 86; and Henrietta Ripperger, "Maid in America: Going Steady—Going Where?" GH, April 1941, 70. In the 1930s and early 1940s, *Senior Scholastic* argued that going steady would divert teens from achieving their ambitions. A 1939 argument against going steady went: "In our modern, high-speed civilization, it is safe to say that physical maturity usually arrives long before emotional maturity … and before most young men are vocationally established and capable of supporting a wife, let alone a family. The educational process for professional or business success today often requires the full concentration of thought and energies for a long time before love and marriage can be seriously considered" ("Readers' Forum," *SS*, February 11, 1939, 3).

16. Psychologists warned that going steady (unless leading directly to marriage) could have a "permanent emotional effect that makes later marriage anti-climatic, since it is 'make believe'" ("Going Steady … a National Problem," *LHJ*, July 1949, 131.)

17. For descriptions of the protocol of going steady, see "Going Steady," *LHJ*, 44.; Betty Coe Spicer, "If You Don't Go Steady You're Different," *LHJ*, December 1955, 68–9; Cameron Shipp, "The Strange Custom of Going Steady," *WHC*, March 1956, 4; "Profile on Youth: Iowa Teen-agers Step Out," *LHJ*, July 1949, 42; Jan Landon, "The Date Line," *GH*, October 1956, 21; Thomas B. Morgan, producer, "How American Teen-Agers Live," *Look*, July 1957, 21–32.

18. Ibid; see especially the articles in the *Ladies Home Journal*.

19. Maureen Daly, ed., *Profile of Youth* (New York: J .B. Lippincott Co., 1949), 30. Also quoted in E.E. LeMasters, *Modern Courtship and Marriage* (New York: Macmillan, 1957) 123.

20. Jan Landon, "The Date Line," *GH*, June 1957, 20; Landon, "The Date Line," *GH*, October 1954, 18; Beverly Brandow, *Date Data* (Dallas, TX: Banks Upshaw & Co., 1954), 100.

21. Helen Louise Crounse, *Joyce Jackson's Guide to Dating* (Englewood Cliffs, NJ: Prentice-Hall, 1957), 101. Crounse's name appears nowhere on the book—it was supposedly written by teenage Joyce Jackson.

22. For example, see Gay Head, "Boy Dates Girl: Fresh Date," *SS*, February 18, 1939, 31.

23. Gay Head. "Boy Dates Girl Jam Session," *SS*, December 1943, 45.

Beth Bailey is professor of history at Temple University. Bailey is a cultural and social historian, specializing in the study of gender and sexuality in twentieth-century America. Her books include *From Front Porch to Back Seat: Courtship in Twentieth-Century America* (1988) and *Sex in the Heartland* (1999). She is also coauthor of the American history survey text, *A People and A Nation* (7th ed.).

From *OAH Magazine of History*, July 2004, pp. 23-26. Copyright © 2004 by Organization of American Historians. Reprinted by permission.

UNIT 4

From the Great Depression to World War II

Unit Selections

Key Points to Consider

- Discuss the personality and character of Franklin D. Roosevelt. What made him such an effective president?

- Why was the Republican Convention of 1940 so important? How might the nomination of an isolationist such as Robert Taft have affected the campaign and the nation?

- What was the "Second Bill of Rights?" What role did FDR think the federal government should play in seeing that people were free from want and from fear?

- Analyze the situation President Truman faced at the time the atomic bombs were dropped on Japan. What alternatives did he have, and how were they likely to have turned out?

Student Website
www.mhcls.com/online

Internet References
Further information regarding these websites may be found in this book's preface or online.

Japanese American Internment
   http://www.jainternment.org/
Works Progress Administration/Folklore Project
   http://lcweb2.loc.gov/ammem/wpaintro/wpalife.html
World War II WWW Sites
   http://www.besthistorysites.nte/WWWII.shtml
World War II Timeline
   http://history.acusd.edu/gen/WW2Timeline/start.html
Hiroshima Archive
   http://www.lclark.edu/~history/HIROSHIMA/
The Enola Gay
   http://www.theenolagay.com/index.html

Republicans like to proclaim the prosperity of the 1920s as a "New Era." Business was booming, and more people had more surplus money to spend than ever before. Some groups, such as farmers, did not truly share in the affluence but even many of them were purchasing automobiles, radios, and the sundry other consumer goods pouring off assembly lines. When people ran out of things to buy and still had money left over they dabbled in the stock market. As stock prices rose dramatically, a kind of speculative mania developed in the latter half of the decade. In the past most people had bought stocks as investments. That is, they wanted to receive income from the dividends reliable companies would pay over the years. Speculators had no interest in the long run, they bought stocks on the assumption that they would make money when they sold on the market in a matter of months or even weeks. Rumors abounded, some of them true, about individuals who had earned fortunes "playing" the market.

By the end of the 1920s the stock market prices had soared to unprecedented heights. So long as people were confident that they would continue to rise, they did. There were a few voices warning that stocks were overpriced, but they were denounced as doomsayers. Besides, had not the highly regarded President Herbert Hoover predicted that "we are on the verge of a wave of never ending prosperity?" No one can say why this confidence began to falter when it did and not months earlier or later, but on October 24, 1929 the market crashed. "Black Thursday" set off an avalanche of selling as holders dumped their shares at whatever price they could get, thereby driving prices even lower. Some large banks tried to shore up confidence by having representatives appear at the stock exchange where they ostentatiously made large purchase orders. Despite such efforts, prices continued to tumble in the months following.

President Herbert Hoover tried to restore confidence by assuring the public that what had happened was merely a glitch, a necessary readjustment of a market that had gotten out of hand. The economy of America was sound, he claimed, and there was no reason business should not go on as usual. His reassurances met with increasing disbelief as time went on. Businessmen as well as stockholders were worried about the future. In order to protect themselves they laid off workers, cut back on inventory, and put off previous plans to expand or to introduce new products. But their actions, however much sense they made for an individual firm, had the collective result of making the situation worse. "Brother, Can You Spare a Dime" provides a closeup view of the pathetic lives led by those who fell prey to the widespread unemployment.

Hoover endorsed more federal programs than had any of his predecessors to combat the depression, but they failed to stop the downward slide. Just as people tend to credit an incumbent when times are good, they also blame him things go sour. Hoover became the most widely detested man in America: trousers with patches on them were scoffingly referred to as "Hoover" pants and in every city the collection of shacks and shanties in which homeless people lived were called "Hoovervilles." "A Promise Denied" tells how Hoover's stock fell even lower when he ordered federal troops to disperse what was known as "the Bonus army." The discredited Hoover lost by a

landslide to Franklin D. Roosevelt in the presidential election of 1932. Although Roosevelt had compiled an impressive record as governor of New York state, his greatest asset in the election was that he was not Hoover.

Roosevelt assumed the presidency without any grand design for ending the depression. Unlike Hoover, however, he was willing to act boldly and on a large scale. His "first 100 days" in office resulted in passage of an unprecedented number of measures designed to promote recovery and to restore confidence. "A Monumental Man" provides a portrait of Roosevelt as president: his appearance, his confidence, his ability to persuade people that he cared about them.

Eleanor Roosevelt was America's most influential "first lady." Her marriage to Franklin was no love story, especially when she discovered that he was involved with another woman. Their marriage continued, but Eleanor began developing her own interests quite apart from merely being Franklin's wife. When he became president, she served as both his "eyes and ears" and his conscience, particularly with regard to civil rights. They made an effective team: Franklin the pragmatic politician not overly concerned with moral issues, Eleanor the moral uplifter "barging into cocktail hour when he wanted only to relax, cross-examining him at dinner, handing him memos to read late at night." Eleanor was wrong in saying "the story is over" when Franklin died, for her stature and influence actually increased in later years

Roosevelt's "New Deal" mitigated the effects of the depression but did not end it. That came with the onset of war in Europe and America's preparedness program. Unlike Woodrow Wilson, Roosevelt made no effort to remain neutral when conflict engulfed Europe and Asia. He believed the United States ought to cooperate with other nations to stop aggression, but had to contend with a congress and public that was deeply influenced by those who thought the United States should remain aloof. After war broke out, Roosevelt took a decidedly unneutral step when he transferred 50 overage destroyers to Great Britain. A divided nation might have become even more divided had the Republicans nominated an isolationist for president in 1940. "The Greatest Convention" shows how a man who basically endorsed FDR's foreign policies became the Republican candidate. Through 1940 and 1941, Roosevelt tried to use economic pressure to get Japan to back off from its attempt to subdue China. His efforts only stiffened the will of Japanese hard liners who planned and carried out the raid on Pearl Harbor on December 7, 1941. An aroused Congress approved the declaration of war Roosevelt asked for

Pearl Harbor and Germany's declaration of war against the United States a few days later united Americans in their determination to win the war. For the next six months the Japanese ran rampant as they inflicted a string of defeats against British and American forces in the Pacific. The British suffered a humiliating defeat at Singapore, and though American forces fought with greater determination in the Philippines they too had to surrender. The tide of Japanese expansion was halted during the summer of 1942 by the naval battles at the Coral Sea and at Midway. The United States launched its first offensive operations on Guadalcanal in the Solomon Islands. Though much bitter fighting remained, American military and industrial might ensured Japan's ultimate defeat.

Hatred towards the Japanese who had mounted the "sneak attack" on Pearl Harbor extended to those who resided in the United States. Americans who were quite willing to believe there were "good" Germans who had been bamboozled by their Nazi leaders, despised all Japanese as inherently treacherous and savage. Long-standing racism against the Japanese who resided on the west coast crystallized during the months after Pearl. Although not a single case of espionage or sabotage was ever proven, rumors spread that Japanese agents were busily trying to undermine the war effort. Many were placed in detention camps for most of the war.

Roosevelt and his military advisers agreed at the beginning of the war that the European theater should receive top priority. Offensive operations against the Germans and Italians began when US forces invaded North Africa in November 1942—Sicily and Italy during the next year. Still, the main effort against Germany was put off until June 6, 1944, when Allied forces invaded the French beaches at Normandy. "What They Saw After They Landed" provides eyewitness accounts of that historic day.

After tough going against determined German opposition, the invaders broke out across France and began approaching the German border. Some generals predicted that the Germans could not recover and that the war would be over by Christmas. What they did not know was that even as German troops were retreating, Hitler began planning a major counteroffensive that he hoped would split the Allied forces in two. What became known to Americans as the "Battle of the Bulge" began on December 16, 1944, and achieved considerable success before bogging down. That was Germany's last gasp. Following several more months of fighting, with Germany caught between the Western allies and Soviet armies advancing from the east, Adolf Hitler committed suicide and Germany finally surrendered on May 8, 1945.

Meanwhile, American forces in the Pacific were steadily advancing toward the Japanese homeland. Capture of the Mariana Islands enabled the United States to mount massive air attacks against Japanese cities, and naval actions progressively strangled their war machine. Some historians have argued that President Harry S. Truman could have attained a Japanese surrender by the summer of 1945 if only he had assured them that they could retain their sacred emperor. That is incorrect. The Japanese will to resist still ran strong, as the bloody battles of Iwo Jima and Okinawa during the first half of 1945 had shown. Indeed, Japanese generals claimed that they welcomed an invasion of the home islands, where they would inflict such staggering casualties that the United States would settle for a negotiated peace instead of unconditional surrender. "The Biggest Decision: Why We had to Drop the Bomb" shows that Truman used atomic weapons to end a bloody war that would have been far bloodier if an invasion had been necessary.

There is an article dealing with domestic affairs during the war. "We Need to Reclaim the Second Bill of Rights" discusses FDR's State of the Union Address to the congress of January 11, 1944. "Essential to peace is a decent standard of living for all individual men women and children in all nations," Roosevelt proclaimed, "Freedom from fear is eternally linked with freedom from want." Five months later Congress passed what became known as the "GI Bill of Rights."

'Brother, Can You Spare a Dime?'

1930–1940: Making do and trying to forget reality during the Depression

By Henry Allen
Washington Post Staff Writer

It's not like you go out on your porch and see the Depression standing there like King Kong. Most neighborhoods, things look pretty normal, not that different from before the Crash. Paint peels on houses. Cars get old, break down. Nothing you'd notice right away. Kids play with their Buck Rogers ray guns. You go to the movies on Dish Night—you like the Fiesta Ware, very modernistic, red and blue.

Definitely, you read in the papers how in Chicago unemployment hit 50 percent, and men were fighting over a barrel of garbage; or in the Dust Bowl, farmers saying they'll lynch judges who foreclose on their property. That kind of thing. It's terrible.

But most places you don't see it. Roosevelt can say: "I see one-third of a nation ill-housed, ill-clad, ill-nourished." That leaves two-thirds where you don't see the hobo jungles, people lined up for government cheese.

You feel what isn't there: It's like on Sunday afternoon, the quiet. You don't hear carpenters driving nails, you don't hear rivet hammers going in the city.

Fewer cars in town, just the stoplights rocking in the wind. You don't hear as many whistles: factory, railroad. You don't hear as many babies crying. People are afraid to have them.

Down the block there's a man you don't see outside his house on workdays. He doesn't want the neighbors to know he's out of work again. Smoking cigarettes, looking out the window, waiting for "Amos 'n' Andy" to come on the radio.

He was a sales manager for a train wheel company, back when the railroads were buying 1,300 locomotives a year. In 1932, they don't buy any. The company lets him go.

He takes a job selling insurance. Insurance companies know you can sell policies to your family, your friends. When you can't sell any more, they let you go.

He sells vacuums, the encyclopedias, door to door. He ends up spending all day at the movies. He won't let his wife apply for relief. He's too proud. His son quits high school—he's out West building a national park for the Civilian Conservation Corps, $30 a month. He sends most of it home so his mother can get her teeth fixed. And put dimes in the chain letters she mails out.

People write songs about tramps—"Brother, Can You Spare a Dime?"—but you don't see them unless they come to your back door; people say they make a chalk mark on your fence if

Dorothea Lange's photograph of a migrant farm worker and her child has come to symbolize the wrenching poverty that characterized much of the decade.

you're good for a handout. You've never found the mark but they keep coming. You wonder how they survive.

One guy's feet are coming out of his shoes but he's got a new tweed overcoat.

You say: "Glad to see you got a warm coat."

He says: "I got it raking leaves for an undertaker. They're good for clothes."

In 1932, in the depths of the Depression, President Hoover called out troops to roust impoverished World War I veterans—"Bonus Marchers"—from their camp in Washington, D.C. Their burning shanties blackened the skies around the Capitol.

You see the Depression in the papers, the magazines and newsreels: heads getting busted during strikes, dust storms burying cows, Reds parading through Wall Street with their fists in the air, shouting "bread, bread," or Huey Long, the Louisiana Kingfish himself, flapping his arms and shouting about "every man a king," Roosevelt looking over plans for electric power dams in the Tennessee Valley, his cigarette holder pointing up—the columnists say "at a jaunty angle." And the lines: in front of soup kitchens, relief offices, banks that are failing. And cute stuff: Kids hang a sign that says "Depression" on a snowman and throw snowballs at it.

THEN YOU'RE LOOKING AT BLOOD AND BULLET holes from gangster shootouts, a girl drinking a glass of beer at the end of Prohibition, kids jitterbugging to Benny Goodman or Count Basie. Bathing beauties, bathing beauties, bathing beauties, and the glamour girls of cafe society—Brenda Diana Duff Frazier, the debutante of the year, smiling from her table at El Morocco or the Rainbow Room. No Depression there.

The Yankees win the pennant. Jesse Owens makes the Olympic team. Soldiers goose-step in front of Hitler or Mussolini or Stalin. Hemingway in the Spanish Civil War, glamorous in that manly way that took over from everybody wanting to look like boys in the 1920s, including the women.

In the new styles, women have waists and busts again. They aren't supposed to look bored anymore, either. You don't get a job, relief, whatever, looking bored. Hemlines go back down. People say hemlines go up and down with the stock market, but that's hooey. The idea is to look more mature. Women's hats, though—feathers, veils, flowers. You read how a woman in a New York tearoom put a bread basket on her head and nobody knew the difference.

From the Crash until Roosevelt took office in 1933, everybody tried to keep living the way they had been living. It didn't work. Things had to change. Now Fortune magazine says the Flaming Youth of the 1920s are gone and we've got "a generation that will not stick its neck out. It keeps its shirt on, its pants buttoned, its chin up, and its mouth shut."

If you're older, during those good years you felt like a self-made man, so now when you're cleaning out your desk, boarding up your store, you feel like a self-ruined man.

THE PREACHERS AND BUSINESSMEN ALL HAVE SOMEthing to blame: moral breakdown, a natural cycle, the Wall Street short-sellers, the installment plan, high tariffs, low tariffs, the British, the Russians. That didn't use to be the American way, to blame anybody but yourself. Lot of things have changed.

Your father's job was to build towns, raise wheat. Your job is to buy things. A poster shows a guy with a lunch bucket and a paycheck, his wife smiling at him. The words say: "When You BUY an AUTOMOBILE You GIVE 3 MONTHS WORK to Someone Which Allows Him to BUY OTHER PRODUCTS."

If you ain't got the mazuma to spend, you don't count.

You hear a husband and wife arguing.

"Why don't you fix cars?" the wife asks. "Every time I go downtown I see a new garage, everybody's car is breaking down."

"I'm not a car mechanic. I'm a machinist," the husband says.

"It's money," she says.

"That's the sad part," he says. "Back when we got married, I had a trade. I'm a machinist. Then they bring in the efficiency experts with their clipboards, timing every move I make. They turn me from a machinist into a machine. I say, what the hell, it's still good money. Then they take away the money. What a mug I was to think we were on Easy Street. What have I got left?"

"You've got a wife and kids wearing cardboard in the bottoms of their shoes," she says.

"Take in a show," he says.

People think you get away from the Depression in the movies, but Hollywood knows there's hard times and unrest, and they don't just show it in the newsreels.

When Mickey Mouse first came along in "Steamboat Willie" he was a mean little pest, and now Walt Disney is making him the common man, a hero like the common man in the murals the government artists paint in post offices. The little guy as hero. That's a change, all right.

In the "Thin Man" movies, they make William Powell a pal with every working stiff in the city—he stops to gas with the iceman, the news butcher, the local pickpocket before he goes off to drink martinis someplace with white telephones and Myrna Loy sliding around in a bathrobe suitable for a coronation. Witty as hell. You walk out of the theater wanting to not give a damn like that.

She says: "I read you were shot five times in the tabloids."

He says: "It's not true. He didn't come near my tabloids."

Here's the power of the movies: You read that John Dillinger and his gang pretend to be a movie company on location in front of a bank in Sioux Falls, S.D. The whole city gawks while inside, the pretend actors clean out the bank.

The FBI guns Dillinger down outside a movie theater in Chicago. You hear the coroner sent part of his anatomy to the Smithsonian Institution in Washington, it was that big.

YOU HEAR A LOT OF STORIES: YOU HEAR ABOUT A smart guy, out of work. He starts an employment agency and takes the first job he was supposed to fill.

The stories about stockbrokers jumping out windows on Black Tuesday, Oct. 29, 1929: the suicide rate was higher right before the Crash than after it, but nobody wants to hear it.

Everybody's brother-in-law knows a banker who works as a caddie at his old country club.

In 1931, Cameroon, in West Africa, sent New York City a check for $3.77 to help the starving. Immigrants are going back to Europe by the shipload. Makes you feel bad.

When Roosevelt closed all the banks in 1933, you hear about one lucky woman who overdrew her account the day before.

In Deming, N.M., the Southern Pacific yard dicks drive so many hobos off the trains, the town has to hire a constable to drive them back on. On the Grand Concourse in the Bronx they have a poorhouse for the rich, the Andrew Freedman home, a mansion, so when the rich lose their money they don't have to live like the poor.

Eleanor Roosevelt is out visiting the poor and she sees a boy hiding a pet rabbit. His sister says: "He thinks we are not going to eat it. But we are."

Babies go hungry while farmers in Iowa dump their milk trying to get the price up to where they can keep producing milk so babies won't go hungry.

Herbert Hoover himself believes that "many persons left their jobs for the more profitable one of selling apples."

The apple story is enough to make you think the Reds are right.

In 1930, right after the Crash, Washington State has a bumper crop of apples. Too many to sell. So instead of dumping them, they give them to vendors on credit.

Next thing, men are lined up in Wall Street, wearing homburgs and selling apples, 5 cents apiece. There are so many of them they start cutting prices on each other. At the same time, the growers get greedy—raise the prices and don't cull the rotten ones. Pretty soon, you can't make any money in the apple business, and it's all over.

The feeling is: damned if you do, damned if you don't. Like playing the Irish Sweepstakes. Lots of gambling now: bingo, punchboards, slot machines, the numbers.

SOME PEOPLE SAY COMMUNISM WILL SAVE US. GUYS in black hats and leather jackets at the union meetings. They know how to organize, they know what they think, but you wonder if they could sell apples any better than anybody else. People are scared of the Reds. A witness tells the House Un-American Activities Committee that out in Hollywood, Shirley Temple is "a stooge of the Reds" for sending money to the Spanish Loyalists. A little girl!

They say J. Edgar Hoover and the FBI will save us from the Reds, the Nazi spies, the gangsters. The kids love him, running around in their Junior G-Man badges.

They say Roosevelt will save us. He comes on the radio in the Fireside Chats, not like Father Coughlin yelling about Reds and Jews. Just talking. "My friends," he says. Like he knows you know he knows how you feel. He doesn't have it all figured out like the Reds or Huey Long. He'll try anything until the Supreme Court knocks it down. The problem is, things don't get much better. He said in 1932:

"The only thing we have to fear is fear itself." He's still right.

And science will save us. You go to the world's fairs in Chicago and New York and learn how technocrats will build things out of plastic and beryllium bronze, the World of Tomorrow. Diesel trains. Television.

No class struggle because science solved all the problems. You never have to sweat out a toothache. Modern management. All you need is brains, not courage. You wonder, though: Is that the American way?

What you know for sure is, whoever's running things right now, it isn't you.

First it was the trusts and the railroads that took control of your life, then Wall Street and advertising, and now it's Roosevelt's Brain Trust and the alphabet agencies—NRA, PWA, WPA, CCC, CWA. They prove everything with numbers and polls; 37 percent of housewives spend 22 percent more hours blah blah…

Everything's scientific. You don't just get married, you go to college and take a course in "modern marriage." Half the babies in the country are born in hospitals. A mother isn't supposed to feed her baby with her own milk. It doesn't have enough of the vitamins they've discovered now. Science turns into a fashion. White tile and stainless steel, waitresses wearing white uniforms. Progress.

ONE DAY THE OUT-OF-WORK SALESMAN AND HIS wife down the block are gone. Not a word of goodbye.

The machinist gets a job in an airplane factory, making bombers.

When your nephew comes to the breakfast table, he swings his leg over the back of the chair, like Clark Gable in "It Happened One Night." Or Mickey Rooney in the Andy Hardy movies with Judy Garland.

Men don't wear tops on their bathing suits anymore.

Girls wear saddle shoes and apron dresses. They drink Cokes in drugstores. The soda jerk thinks they all have a crush on him, his white paper hat cocked to one side.

If you want to show your social consciousness, you don't have a "cleaning woman" anymore, you have a "cleaning lady."

How is vaudeville going to stand up to movies and radio? What will Milton Berle do for a living?

Modern furniture gets crazier. You see a picture of a bedroom in Hollywood with these reading chairs only Ming the Merciless could be comfortable in, and a laminated wood bed you could put on a Mayan funeral barge, everything tapered—table legs, lamps, vases.

You hear stories that Roosevelt, the British and the Jews are trying to get us into a war.

Huey Long gets shot dead in Baton Rouge.

There's a feeling you hardly notice after a while—a shabby feeling, dust and phone wires, a cold spring wind, things exposed…

From the *Washington Post National Weekly Edition,* October 25, 1999, pp. 10–11. © 1999 by The Washington Post. Reprinted by permission.

A Promise DENIED

The Bonus Expeditionary Force

In 1932 World War I veterans seeking a bonus promised by Congress were attacked and driven out of Washington, D.C., by troops of the U.S. Army under the command of Douglas MacArthur, Dwight D. Eisenhower and George Patton.

Wyatt Kingseed

ARMY CHIEF OF STAFF and Major General Douglas MacArthur watched a brigade of steel-helmeted soldiers precisely align themselves in a straight four-column phalanx, bayonets affixed to rifles. He nodded his head in satisfaction. Discipline was wonderful. Up ahead, Major George Patton kicked his heels against his mount, and the big horse reared forward to signal a line of cavalry. The riders drew their sabers, and the animals stepped out in unison, hoofs smacking loudly on the street. Five Renault tanks lurched behind. Seven-ton relics from World War I and presumably just for show, the old machines nonetheless left little doubt as to the seriousness of the moment. On cue, at about 4:30 p.m. on July 28, 1932, the infantry began a slow, steady march forward. Completing the surreal atmosphere, a machine gun unit unlimbered, and its crew busily set up.

This was no parade, although hundreds of curious office workers had interrupted their daily routines to crowd the sidewalk or hang out of windows along Pennsylvania Avenue between the White House and the Capitol to see what would happen. Up ahead, a group of weary civilians, many dressed in rags and ill-fitting, faded uniforms, waited in anticipation amid their sorry camp of tents and structures made from clapboard and sheets of tin covered in tar paper. Some loitered in the street. They had heard something was afoot—expected it after what happened earlier. Now, a murmur rose from the camp crowd. Upon seeing the Army's menacing approach, they were momentarily stunned, disbelieving.

Recovering their senses, a few of the men cursed and sent bottles and bricks flying toward the troops—ineffective weapons against so formidable a force. The missiles shattered on impact on the hard pavement or bounced off the flanks of horses and soldiers. Undaunted, the roughly 600 troops maintained their discipline with tight-lipped determination. The extra training MacArthur had recently ordered was paying off.

Some of the camp inhabitants had already begun running from the oncoming soldiery, but angry packs held their ground, defiantly wielding clubs and iron bars, yelling profanities. An officer signaled, and the infantry halted to don masks and toss gas grenades. Forming into two assault waves, they continued their push. Clouds of stinging, gray fumes wafted through the air, forcing most of the remaining unarmed veterans to flee in panic. One particularly pesky truckload continued to throw debris, prompting a quick response from Patton: "Two of us charged at a gallop and [striking with the flat of our swords] had some nice work at close range with the occupants of the truck, most of whom could not sit down for some days."

As cavalry dispersed a group of outnumbered veterans waving a U.S. flag, a shocked bystander, his face streaked with tears from the gas, accosted MacArthur as he rode along in a staff car. "The American flag means nothing to me after this," the man yelled. The general quieted him with a stern rebuke, "Put that man under arrest if he opens his mouth again." The energetic officer was in his element.

One reporter observed, "General MacArthur, his chest glittering with medals, strode up and down Pennsylvania Avenue, flipping a riding crop against his neatly pressed breeches."

MacArthur could not help being euphoric. If the tactics were not textbook, the results were everything he hoped for—a complete rout. The troops had exercised perfect restraint in completely clearing the downtown area without firing a shot. Within hours it was all over. Troopers set the abandoned camp ablaze as the former inhabitants retreated, demoralized and beaten, across the Third Street bridge. MacArthur called a halt to allow his troops to rest and eat while he considered his next move.

AS MANY AS 20,000 former soldiers and their families had converged on Washington in the summer of 1932, the height of the Great Depression, to support Texas Congressman Wright Patman's bill to advance the bonus payment promised to World War I veterans. Congress had authorized the plan in 1924, intending to compensate the veterans for wages lost while serving in the military during the war. But payment was to be deferred until 1945. Just one year earlier, in 1931, Congress overrode a presidential veto on a bill to provide, as loans, half the amount due to the men. When the nation's economy worsened, the half-bonus loans were not enough, and the unemployed veterans now sought the balance in cash. Known as Bonus Marchers, they came in desperation from all across the nation, hopping freight trains, driving dilapidated jalopies or hitchhiking, intent on pressuring Congress to pass the legislation. The administration vehemently opposed the measure, believing it inflationary and impractical given the $2 billion annual budget deficit.

At first the march was a trickle, led by Walter Waters, a 34-year-old former sergeant from Portland, Ore. It soon became a tidal wave, drawing national press attention. The first contingent reached the nation's capital in May 1932. They occupied parks and a row of condemned buildings along Pennsylvania Avenue, between the White House and the Capitol. When new arrivals overflowed that site, they erected a shanty-town on the flood plain of the Anacostia River, southeast of Capitol Hill. Theirs was a miserable lot, alleviated somewhat by the beneficence of the city's superintendent of police, Pelham Glassford, himself a war veteran.

Glassford pitied the beleaguered itinerants and solicited private aid to secure medical assistance, clothing, food and supplies. During a May 26 veterans meeting, Glassford suggested they officially call themselves the Bonus Expeditionary Force. Adopting the name—which was commonly shortened to Bonus Army—they asked him, and he agreed, to serve as secretary-treasurer of the group. Working together, Waters and Glassford managed to maintain enough discipline and order in the ranks to ward off eviction. Glassford likely hoped that the horde would eventually lose interest and return home, but Waters had other ideas. "We'll stay here until the bonus bill is passed," Waters told anyone who would listen, "till 1945, if necessary." He staged daily demonstrations before the Capitol and led peaceful marches past the White House. President Herbert Hoover refused to give him an audience.

In June the House of Representatives narrowly passed the Patman bill, but the Senate defeated the measure with a lopsided vote of 62 to 18. Congress was scheduled to adjourn in mid-July, and about one-quarter of the veterans accepted the government's offer of free transportation home. Hoover had apparently won. Perhaps now he could concentrate on an economic recovery plan and the upcoming reelection campaign. But many of the marchers felt betrayed and disillusioned. With nowhere else to go, they decided to stay. Ominously, their disappointment festered in Washington's muggy summer heat. To complicate matters, at this point the American Communist Party saw an opportunity to cause trouble, and sent forth John Pace as the catalyst with instructions to incite riot. The degree of his success is uncertain and will be forever a matter of debate, but his presence alarmed the Washington power structure.

'General MacArthur, his chest glittering with medals, strode up and down Pennsylvania Avenue, flipping a riding crop against his neatly pressed breeches.'

Historian Kenneth S. Davis theorizes that Pace may have had a hand in escalating the tensions, goading the angry veterans to become more aggressive. A more plausible explanation for rising tension may simply be that frustrations finally reached a boiling point. In any case, Secretary of War Patrick Hurley had had enough. On July 28 he ordered Glassford to immediately evacuate the occupied buildings, which were scheduled for demolition to make way for new government offices. The veterans stubbornly refused to budge. For whatever reason, Glassford and his police officers became the target of bricks and stones, and one officer suffered a fractured skull. As the melee got out of hand, an angry veteran, apparently feeling that Glassford had betrayed the Bonus Marchers, tore off the chief's gold police badge. Fearing for their safety, police opened fire, killing one veteran and mortally wounding another.

The officers retreated while Glassford sought the advice of his Board of Commissioners. Quick to pass on the responsibility, and perhaps overreacting, the commissioners called the president to deploy the Army from nearby Fort Myer to restore order. Describing the attack on police as a "serious riot," the commissioners asserted, "It will be impossible for the Police Department to maintain law and order except by the free use of firearms." They went on to argue that only the presence of federal troops could resolve the crisis.

Hoover, upset by the continued presence of the Bonus Marchers, now had the excuse he was looking for to expel them from the capital. He directed Secretary Hurley to unleash MacArthur, who received the following instruction: "You will have United States troops proceed immediately to the scene of the disorder. Surround the affected area and clear it without delay. Any women and children should be accorded every consideration and kindness. Use all humanity consistent with the execution of this order."

Not surprisingly, MacArthur now executed his orders in a manner seemingly designed to maximize media attention. In a highly unusual but characteristic decision—one purportedly against the advice of his aide, 42-year-old Major Dwight Eisenhower—he chose to oversee the operations in the field with the troops. Military protocol called for a commanding officer to remain at headquarters. This was especially true for MacArthur, whose post was administrative rather than operational. So while he charged General Perry Miles with carrying out the eviction, MacArthur assumed the real responsibility. Although no other situation offers an exact comparison, MacArthur's action was as if General Maxwell Taylor, the head of the Joint Chiefs of Staff in 1963, had led National Guard troops to the University of Alabama to confront Alabama Governor George Wallace.

Having driven the veterans from the downtown area, MacArthur had fulfilled his mission. But whether his blood was up, or he merely sensed a need to inflict a coup de grâce against the purported Communist element—an enemy he considered more insidious than disgruntled veterans—MacArthur did not rest on his laurels. He ordered his troops to advance upon the 11th Street bridge leading to Anacostia Flats. Someone, waving a white shirt as a flag of truce, came racing across to plea for time to evacuate the women and children. MacArthur granted an hour's reprieve.

THOUGH ACCOUNTS DIFFER, the president now seemed suddenly to exhibit an untimely case of nerves. Fearing repercussions, he twice sent word that the Army was not to cross the bridge. MacArthur refused to listen, saying he hadn't time to be bothered by people coming down and pretending to bring orders. He sent the troops across against explicit instructions. Using more gas, the soldiers moved into Bonus City. Its occupants fled in terror, refugees rousted from their pitiful camp.

"One of the soldiers threw a bomb," said one woman hiding in a nearby house with her family. "…[W]e all began to cry. We got wet towels and put them over the faces of the children. About half an hour later my baby began to vomit. I took her outside in the air and she vomited again. Next day she began to turn black and blue and we took her to the hospital." Either veterans or soldiers torched the entire area—no one knows for sure. In the confusion, one baby was left behind, dead from gas inhalation.

Endeavoring to eliminate any doubt as to his motives, MacArthur next conducted an impromptu press conference—a job more appropriately left to civilian authorities. The conference allowed the general to expound on the claim that Reds had concocted the riot, the president's safety was at stake, and the government was threatened with insurrection. Describing the mob, MacArthur said: "It was animated by the essence of revolution. They had come to the conclusion, beyond a shadow of a doubt, that they were about to take over in some arbitrary way either the direct control of the government or else to control it by indirect methods. It is my opinion that had the president let it go on another week the institutions of our government would have been very severely threatened." It was a masterful performance. In praising the president and war secretary, MacArthur nearly absolved himself of responsibility—perhaps a calculated move.

Hoover watched the red glow of the bonfire at Anacostia Flats from a White House window. If he had second thoughts, he didn't include them in his record of the event; and in any case, it was too late. MacArthur's boldness had boxed him into a corner. The president's best option now was to vigorously support the general.

"A challenge to the authority of the United States Government has been met, swiftly and firmly," Hoover said in a statement the next morning. "The Department of Justice is pressing its investigation into the violence which forced the call of army detachments, and it is my sincere hope that those agitators may be brought speedily to trial in the civil courts."

Hysteria colored much of Washington's official view of the Bonus Army. In defense of both men, MacArthur and Hoover seem to have genuinely believed that Communists controlled the organization, with Walter Waters merely serving as the Bonus Army's titular head. Hoover believed that veterans made up no more than 50 percent of Bonus Army members, while MacArthur set an even lower number—10 percent. Waters said that was a "damned lie." While Communist operatives certainly tried to infiltrate the ranks of the Bonus Army and instigate trouble, evidence indicates they had little real influence. The president and Army chief of staff's estimates were badly overstated. A postevent study conducted by the Veterans Administration revealed that 94 percent of the marchers had Army or Navy service records. Nevertheless, the Communist Party was happy to take credit for what was billed as an uprising.

EVENTS ELSEWHERE HELP explain Hoover and MacArthur's state of mind. Students loudly interrupted the general's commencement address at the University of Pittsburgh that summer as he spoke against demonstrators protesting the government. More alarming, a union-inspired hunger march at a Detroit auto plant that spring had turned ugly. Police killed four civilians while trying to maintain control, injuring 60 others. Communist Party leaders retaliated, organizing a 6,000-man funeral procession, waving red banners and marching in cadence to the party's anthem, the "Internationale." Fearing a similar or worse result in Washington, Hoover and MacArthur acted with dispatch when confronted by a large group of disgruntled citizens. Throughout their lives, both officials clung stubbornly to the claim that subversive elements bent on destroying capitalism were behind the veterans. Neither man ever accepted the Bonus Army as primarily a group of destitute, desperate, hungry men trying to support their families.

The day's toll was three dead, 54 injured and 135 arrests. In the rush to point fingers, in addition to the Communist element, Congressman Patman and colleagues received their share of the blame. The *Chicago Tribune* editorialized that responsibility for the incident "lies chiefly at the door of men in public life who have encouraged the making of unreasonable demands by ex-service men and inflamed their mistaken sense of judgment." But Alabama Senator and future Supreme Court Justice Hugo Black directed his venom at a different target.

Arguing that Hoover had overreacted to the situation, Black said, "As one citizen, I want to make my public protest against this militaristic way of handling a condition which has been brought about by wide-spread unemployment and hunger." *The New York Times* hinted that other senators felt the same. Indeed, it was a common charge hurled by the opposition party during that fall's presidential election. Senator Hiram Johnson, speaking in Chicago a few days before the presidential vote, dubbed the incident "one of the blackest pages in our history." Hoping to evoke feelings of sympathy and patriotism, he continued, noting that the displaced veterans had been hailed as heroes and saviors only a decade earlier: "The president sent against these men, emaciated from hunger, scantily clad, unarmed, the troops of the United States army. Tanks, tear-bombs, all of the weapons of modern warfare were directed against those who had borne the arms of the republic."

The public soon followed Black's lead. Frustrated by Depression-era economics and in tune with Franklin D. Roosevelt's comparatively more aggressive assistance programs after he assumed the presidency, the public increasingly questioned the government's response to the plight of the Bonus Army. Many came to see it as callous and heavy-handed. Theater audiences reacted to Bonus Army newsreel footage with choruses of boos.

Ever conscious of his own place in history, MacArthur blinked. At least publicly the general would voice a more sympathetic view of the marchers he once routed. At first he had called them a "bad mob," but gradually time, or concern over public opinion, softened his expressed view. In his memoirs, MacArthur took credit for supplying the marchers with tents and rolling kitchens, and declared them a "vanguard of a starved band," remembering the whole affair as a "poignant episode."

If it was a purposeful attempt to improve his image, it failed. His reputation has remained forever scarred. MacArthur biographer William Manchester called his actions that day "flagrantly insubordinate" and "indefensible." An-

other historian, echoing Manchester's sentiment, said the general acted "with overzealous determination and reckless impulsiveness."

Likely influencing the judgment of historians was MacArthur's demonstrated knack for upsetting his superiors. Twenty years after the Bonus Army incident, President Harry Truman would relieve the general of his Korean command for perceived insubordination. In the end, the general's personality and ambition proved too great an obstacle for history to erase its view of his performance against the Bonus Army.

Along with MacArthur, two other soldiers who participated in the action would go on to write their names large in history—Eisenhower and Patton. Eisenhower would eventually undergo an even more dramatic transformation than his boss in describing the affair. Normally a frank diarist, Ike merely noted at the time that he "took part in Bonus Incident of July 28," and went on to say, "A lot of furor has been stirred up but mostly to make political capital." By the time he published *At Ease* 30 years later, Ike portrayed himself as a frustrated hero of sorts, claiming that he tried to dissuade MacArthur from personally leading the charge. He advised him that Communists held no sway over the marchers, and he reiterated the old claim that his boss ignored White House orders to halt operations. Interestingly, Ike waited until after MacArthur's death in 1964 to present this version. If it distorted history, MacArthur was not around to contest it.

It was a messy affair for everyone. Patton, a man who revered duty, had mixed emotions, calling it a "most distasteful form of service." Within months he criticized the Army's tactics, believing they violated every precept of how to handle civil unrest. Still, he commended both sides: "It speaks volumes for the high character of the men that not a shot was fired. In justice to the marchers, it should be pointed out that had they really wanted to start something, they had a great chance here, but refrained." And while Patton was disgusted that "Bolsheviks" were in the mix, he considered most of the Bonus Army "poor, ignorant men, without hope, and without really evil intent." To his dismay, the routed marchers included Joseph Angelo, who 14 years earlier had saved the wounded Patton's life by pulling him to safety from a foxhole.

THE EPISODE WOULD DOG President Hoover in his attempt to win a second term of office in the fall of 1932. Presidents had called out federal troops before to suppress civil unrest, but this was the first time they had moved against veterans. It left a bad taste in the mouths of voters. A letter to the *Washington Daily News* expressed the sentiments of many. "I voted for Herbert Hoover in 1928," one disgusted woman wrote. "God forgive me and keep me alive at least till the polls open next November!"

Hoover's Democratic challenger in that fall's presidential election, Franklin D. Roosevelt, understood the political significance of the president's use of force. Like his opponent, the New York governor did not support payment of the bonus, but he found Hoover's tactics appalling. "He should have invited a delegation into the White House for coffee and sandwiches," Roosevelt told one aide as he perused the morning papers. Already confident of success, Roosevelt now felt victory was certain. This was a black eye no one could overcome. Roosevelt won decisively, capturing 42 states with 472 electoral votes compared to just 59 for his Republican rival.

Hoover had no illusions, but he could not help but feel bitter. Stopping just short of calling Roosevelt a liar, the former president later wrote of the campaign: "This whole Democratic performance was far below the level of any previous campaign in modern times. My defeat would no doubt have taken place anyway. But it might have taken place without such defilement of American life." The vision of Regular Army troops marching on veterans would provide propaganda for the Left for years to come.

Long before that, the remnants of the Bonus Army drifted home, stopping for a brief period in Johnson, Pa., until that community too urged them on. The government buried the two Bonus Army veterans slain by police at Arlington National Cemetery with full military honors. One year later, another contingent of veterans came to Washington to press the issue of the bonus payment. The new president was no more receptive than the last, but instead of the Army he sent his wife, Eleanor, to speak with the former servicemen. More important, he created the Civilian Conservation Corps, which offered the men employment. And three years later, Congress passed legislation over FDR's veto to complete the bonus payment, resolving one of the more disturbing issues in American politics.

A Monumental Man

FDR's chiseled features defined an American epoch

By Gerald Parshall

Franklin Roosevelt made no small plans—except for his own commemoration. The first Roosevelt memorial, now all but forgotten, was installed outside the National Archives building in 1965. A marble slab about the size of Roosevelt's desk, it was scaled to its subject's wishes. The new Roosevelt memorial now being completed in Washington is scaled to its subject's significance: Some 4,500 tons of granite went into it. Designer Lawrence Halprin laid out a wall that meanders over 7.5 acres, forming four outdoor rooms, each devoted to one of FDR's terms in the White House and each open on one side to a stunning vista of the Tidal Basin. Waterfalls, reflecting pools, and sculptures are set along what is likely to become one of the most popular walks in the nation's capital. The entry building contains a photograph of FDR in his wheelchair and a replica of the chair itself. The memorial's time line includes these words: "1921, STRICKEN WITH POLIOMYELITIS—HE NEVER AGAIN WALKED UNAIDED." But because no statue depicts him in his wheelchair, the dedication ceremony on May 2 faces a threatened protest by the disabled. Controversy often surrounded Roosevelt in life; his spirit should feel right at home.

THE POWER OF HIS SMILE

Today, we carry the face of Franklin Roosevelt in our pockets and purses—it is stamped on more than 18 billion dimes. From 1933 to 1945, Americans carried it in their hearts. It was stamped on their consciousness, looking out from every newspaper and newsreel, FDR's smile as bright as the headlight on a steam locomotive. Roosevelt's portrait hung in bus stations, in barber shops, in kitchens, in parlors, in Dust Bowl shacks—and in Winston Churchill's bedchamber in wartime London. It was the face of hope and freedom for the masses. Even among the "economic royalists," the haters of "that man in the White House," the portrait could stir emotion—as a dartboard.

In 1911, when the 28-year-old Roosevelt was newly elected to the New York Senate, the *New York Times* found him "a young man with the finely chiseled face of a Roman patrician" who "could make a fortune on the stage and set the matinee girl's heart throbbing with subtle and happy emotion." Tammany Hall Democrats, however, weren't swooning. They noted the freshman's habit of tossing his head back and peering down his nose (on which he wore pince-nez like Theodore Roosevelt, a fifth cousin) and read in it a squire's disdain for grubby city boys. The quirk persisted but acquired a new meaning decades later, when FDR wrestled with unprecedented domestic and foreign crises. His upturned chin and eyes, along with his cigarette holder, itself tilted toward the heavens, became symbols of indomitable determination to triumph over adversity—his own and the country's.

It was, indeed, the face of a great actor, a living sculpture continuously reshaped by the artist. The knowing twinkle. The arched eyebrow. The eloquent grimace. Roosevelt was a master of misdirection. He could lie without blinking, disarm enemies with infectious bonhomie, and make a bore feel like the most fascinating fellow on Earth. Officials with rival agendas often came away from the Oval Office equally sure that they alone had the president's ear. "Never let your left hand know what your right is doing," FDR once confided to a cabinet member. Idealism and duplicity fused behind his smile, buttressing one another like the two sides of a Roosevelt dime.

THE WARMTH OF HIS WORDS

He was one of the greatest orators of his time but suffered from stage fright. While he waited on the dais, Franklin Roosevelt fidgeted, shuffled the pages of his speech, chain-smoked, and doused the butterflies in his stomach with gulps of water. At last, they let him start—"My friends...." In a New York minute, his nervousness was gone and the audience under his spell. His voice—languid one moment, theatrical the next—dripped with Groton, Harvard, and centuries of blue blood. Yet no president has ever communicated better with ordinary people.

ATLANTA CHANCE—FRANKLIN D. ROOSEVELT LIBRARY
Revisionist. FDR rewrote his speeches until they sang.

A Roosevelt speech sounded spontaneous, straight from the heart, effortless—effects that took much effort to achieve. Some speeches went through a dozen drafts, with speech writers laboring at the big table in the Cabinet Room until 3 a.m. Roosevelt then revised mercilessly—shortening sentences, substituting words with fewer syllables, polishing similes—until his own muscular style emerged. Sometimes, he wrote a speech entirely by himself. He used a yellow legal pad to draft his first inaugural address, which rang with one of the most effective buck-up lines in history: "The only thing we have to fear is fear itself." He dictated to his secretary most of the Pearl Harbor message he delivered to Congress. He edited himself, changing "a date which will live in world history" to "a date which will live in infamy."

Roosevelt held two press conferences a week right in the Oval Office. Relaxed and jocular, he gently decreed what could and could not be printed. He talked to reporters, John Dos Passos remembered, in a fatherly voice "like the voice of a principal in a first-rate boy's school." Likewise, Roosevelt's "fireside chats" on the radio reverberated with paternal intimacy. He had a flair for homely analogies, such as equating Lend-Lease aid to Britian with loaning your neighbor a garden hose to put out a house fire. Who wouldn't do that? Speaking into the microphone, he gestured and smiled as if the audience would somehow sense what it could not see. Millions shushed the children and turned up the radio. They ached for leadership and "Doctor New Deal"—soon to become "Doctor Win the War"—was making a house call.

THE SPLENDOR OF HIS STRIDE

At the 1936 Democratic National Convention, Franklin Roosevelt fell down as he moved across the podium to address the delegates. He was quickly pulled up again, his withered legs bruised but unbroken. No newspaper stories or radio reports mentioned this incident—and for good reason. It hadn't happened. America was in denial. Prejudice against "cripples" was widespread. The nation wanted no reminders that it was following a man who could not walk.

From the earliest days of the polio that ravaged his legs in 1921, denial had been Roosevelt's way of coping. He spoke of his infirmity with no one, not even with members of his family. For seven years, almost every day, he took his crutches, tried—and failed—to reach the end of his Hyde Park driveway. He could not walk. But how he ran. Campaigning animatedly from open cars and the rear platform of trains, he was elected governor of New York twice and president of the United States four times. No crutches were seen and no wheelchair. His steel leg braces were painted black to blend with his socks; he wore extra long trousers. The Secret Service built ramps all over Washington, D.C., to give his limousine close access to his destinations. FDR jerkily "walked" the final distance by holding on to one of his sons with his left arm and supporting his right side with a cane. Newsreel cameras stopped; press photographers took a breather. If an amateur was spotted attempting to get a picture, the Secret Service swiftly closed in and exposed the film.

"FDR's splendid deception," historian Hugh Gallagher dubbed the little conspiracy in his book of that title. It worked so well that most Americans never knew of Roosevelt's disability, or they repressed what they did know. Such was the national amnesia, cartoonists even drew him jumping. FDR dropped the ruse for only one group. Military amputee wards were filled with men brooding about what fate had done to their futures. A high official sometimes came calling. The severely wounded GIs recognized the visitor immediately—no face was more famous—and his arrival brought an exhilarating revelation. Down the aisles came the nemesis of Hitler and Hirohito, his wheelchair in full view and looking like a royal chariot.

THE MAINSPRING OF HIS MIND

When the British monarch visited America in 1939, Franklin Roosevelt greeted him with unaccustomed familiarity. He served him hot dogs at a Hyde Park picnic and addressed him not as "your majesty" but as "George." "Why don't my ministers talk to me as the president did tonight?" an enchanted George VI remarked to a member of his entourage. "I felt exactly as though a father were giving me his most careful and wise advice." It was Roosevelt's genius to treat kings like commoners and commoners like kings. And both loved him for it.

His monumental self-assurance was bred in the bone. His mother, Sara, had reared him, her only child, to believe he had a fixed place in the center of the cosmos like other Roosevelts.

She—and the example set by cousin Theodore—imparted another formative lesson: Privileged people have a duty to do good. Noblesse oblige, Christianity, and the golden rule made up the moral core of the aristocrat who became both the Democrat of the century and the democrat of the century.

Critics called him a socialist and a "traitor to his class." History would call him the savior of capitalism, the pragmatist who saved free enterprise from very possibly disappearing into the abyss and taking democracy with it. It seemed evident to him that only government could curb or cushion the worst excesses of industrialism. But, at bottom, he was less a thinker than a doer. Luckily, like gardeners and governesses, intellectuals could be hired. Roosevelt hired a brain trust and pumped it for ideas to which he applied this test: Will it work? If one program belly-flopped, he cheerfully tried another. "A second-class intellect," Justice Oliver Wendell Holmes pegged him. "But a first-class temperament."

For all his amiability, FDR knew with Machiavelli that self-seekers abound this side of paradise. Navigating perilous domestic and foreign waters by dead reckoning, he often felt compelled to be a shameless schemer. He hid his intentions, manipulated people, set aides to contrary tasks—all to keep control of the game in trustworthy hands (his own). Charm and high purposes palliated the pure ether of his arrogance. Franklin Roosevelt was hip-deep in the muck of politics and power, but his eyes were always on the stars.

The Greatest Convention

In 1940, the contest was never closer, the stakes never higher.

Charles Peters

Political conventions have not always been so devoid of excitement that television networks cover them only grudgingly. Nominees have not always been determined months in advance of the proceedings whose original purpose was to choose them. But it has been a long time since. The last closely contested Republican convention was between Gerald Ford and Ronald Reagan in 1976. The Democrats have to look back another 20 years to find their last real nailbiter.

That was when Estes Kefauver barely defeated John Kennedy for the vice presidential nomination in 1956. The Republicans also saw a reasonably close fight between Dwight Eisenhower and Robert Taft in 1952, and the Democrats had another for the vice presidency between Henry Wallace and Harry Truman in 1944.

That brings us back to 1940, and the convention that had it all—the five days in Philadelphia during which the Republicans took six ballots to select a candidate. Not only was the convention exciting, but the stakes were also high: Would this country keep its head in the sands of isolationism, or would it face the menace of Adolf Hitler?

The 1940 race began with Tom Dewey, who had gained national attention as a crusading district attorney, comfortably in the lead for the Republican nomination, with over 50 percent in the Gallup poll, followed by Ohio senator Robert Taft and Michigan senator Arthur Vandenberg. Although Dewey and Vandenberg would later become internationalists—and Dewey may have been a closet one even then—all three men were campaigning as isolationists, determined to keep this country out of World War II, which had started the previous September. In this regard, they probably reflected the attitudes of most Americans and certainly those of the great majority of Republicans. The Nazi conquest of Poland had settled into "the phony war," with neither side doing much of anything. Most Americans disliked Hitler, but they felt little danger from him because the mighty British fleet appeared to control the seas, and on land, behind the supposedly impregnable Maginot Line, there was the

French army, widely considered to be the best in the world, standing ready to repel the Nazis.

One potential Republican presidential candidate was clearly more concerned about Hitler than the others. This was Wendell Willkie, the president of Commonwealth and Southern, a utility holding company in New York. Willkie had become a public figure because of his spirited defense of the private electric companies against the threat presented by New Deal public-power projects like the Tennessee Valley Authority.

Born in a small town in Indiana, Willkie still had his hair cut "country-style." He seemed to have stepped out of a Norman Rockwell painting. He was also handsome, vital, and warm, with immense personal appeal. To Republicans who liked Franklin Roosevelt's sympathy for the allies but had a low opinion of his economic policy, Willkie began to look like an interesting presidential possibility. This group was not large in early 1940, but it was highly influential. It included much of the staff of *The New York Herald Tribune*, the voice of the northeastern Republican establishment. Willkie had met that newspaper's publishers, Helen and Ogden Reid, through their friend and his mistress Irita Van Doren, the *Herald Tribune*'s book editor. Van Doren also introduced him to a wide range of journalists and writers, including the novelist Sinclair Lewis and his wife, the prominent columnist Dorothy Thompson.

At a conference in August 1939, Willkie met and was immediately befriended by Russell Davenport, the editor of *Fortune*. Through Davenport he met Henry Luce, the most powerful publisher in America. Luce, who strongly opposed Hitler, owned *Life*, the first and by far the most popular picture magazine whose impact at the time could only be compared to that of a combination of several of today's television networks. Luce also owned *Time*, the most popular of the magazines devoted to reporting current events. *Time* did not hesitate to propagandize for Luce's causes, molding the political thinking of much of the American middle class.

The great New York banks, led by Thomas Lamont of J.P. Morgan, and their Wall Street lawyers also tended to favor the allies. They had much more power and influence than they do today. Lawyers and bankers all over America were careful not to get on the bad side of the big boys from New York, who could cut them in on lucrative business.

Thus, Willkie was not without friends. But at the beginning of April their efforts had only resulted in his getting three percent in the Gallup poll, far behind Dewey, Taft and Vandenberg. But then on April 9, 1940, Hitler invaded and quickly conquered Norway and Denmark. People became more concerned about the threat from abroad, and interest in Willkie rapidly escalated. A young Wall Street lawyer named Oren Root launched a petition movement on Willkie's behalf that quickly took fire and led to the establishment of Willkie clubs throughout the country.

We want Willkie

On May 10, the Nazis invaded Belgium and France. Soon, the Belgians surrendered, the British were evacuated from Dunkirk, and the French army was reeling in retreat across the Seine. Willkie's warnings about Hitler now seemed prescient. A movement that had originally seemed composed exclusively of Harvard, Yale, and Princeton alumni—Alice Roosevelt Longworth said it sprang from the "grass roots of a thousand country clubs"—now expanded to include millions of average citizens. Tens of thousands of enthusiastic volunteers flocked to the Willkie clubs. Luce's propaganda machine churned out one pro-Willkie article after another. So did two of the nation's other most popular magazine, *Look*, and *The Saturday Evening Post*. And the *Herald Tribune*'s influential columnists Walter Lippmann and Dorothy Thompson, as well as its editorial writers, seemed to become more passionately committed to Willkie every day.

On June 22, France surrendered. A keystone of the isolationists' faith had crumbled—the French army had failed to hold off Hitler. Now only Britain stood between us and the Nazis, and, among Republicans, only Willkie favored all-out aid to Britain. Still, as the balloting at that week's convention began, Willkie had only 105 votes on the first ballot. This was enough to put him ahead of Vandenberg, who seemed to have lost his stomach for the fight, but Willkie still needed 501 to win. Dewey was well out in front with 360, and seemed within striking distance of victory. But at 38, the prosecutor's youth and inexperience worried delegates who were beginning to think that a more seasoned leader was needed to confront the grave world situation.

On the second ballot, Dewey lost 22 votes. Taft's total improved from 189 to 203. Willkie gained the most, going from 105 to 171. Willkie's volunteers had packed the gallery and kept chanting "we want Willkie." That morning, the latest Gallup poll of GOP voters around the country showed Willkie had moved ahead of all of the other candidates.

A liberal Democrat

Still, there were great obstacles to Willkie's candidacy. He simply was not a typical Republican. Not only did he not share their isolationism, but he was also in many ways a liberal Democrat—on race, for example, more liberal than Franklin Roosevelt. Indeed, he had only recently changed his party registration to Republican. Them was also a danger that Dewey and Taft would join forces against him. They had enough votes to control the convention. But they had to move fast. Willkie was continuing to gain.

On the third ballot, he jumped into second place ahead of Taft with 259 votes. Taft gained nine for a total of 212. Dewey was still in the lead but continued to lose votes and was now down to 315. Managers for the candidates raced around the floor trying to pry delegates away from their opponents, and to keep those already on their side from defecting.

On the fourth ballot, with chants of "We Want Willkie" ringing through Philadelphia's Convention Hall, Willkie moved ahead with 302 votes. Taft, with 254, also passed Dewey, whose total decreased to 250.

Dewey and Taft managers tried to make a deal. But each of their candidates wanted to be president, with the other settling for the vice presidency. Neither man would budge.

The fifth ballot saw the collapse of Dewey's candidacy. He got just 57 votes. The race was now between Willkie and Taft, who each added exactly the same number of votes, 123. Taft was "Mr. Republican" to most of the delegates, and probably their real preference. But Willkie had begun to have the smell of a winner; even to isolationist delegates, this meant he might be a better vote-getter than Taft, and that his presence at the head of the ticket might help lesser Republicans get elected.

The large delegation from Michigan, which had stuck with Vandenberg, and the even larger one from Pennsylvania, which had been voting for its favorite son, Gov. Arthur James, were now the targets of desperate pleas from the Willkie and Taft camps. On the sixth ballot, the race was still close when Michigan was recognized. The delegation's chairman announced that Sen. Vandenberg had released his delegates, and that Willkie would get 35 of its 38 votes. Pennsylvania then gave Willkie all of its 72 votes. He now had a total of 502, one more than a majority, which meant that the man who had stood at 3 percent in the polls less than three months earlier had become the nominee of the Republican Party. And Franklin Roosevelt had an opponent who would support his foreign policy. The significance for Britain, the United States, and the world was not inconsiderable.

Charles Peters, the *Washington Monthly*'s founding editor, is writing a book about the 1940 Republican convention and its consequences to be published by Public Affairs in 2005.

We Need to Reclaim the Second Bill of Rights

Cass R. Sunstein

On January 11, 1944, the United States was involved in its longest conflict since the Civil War. The effort was going well. In a remarkably short period, the tide had turned sharply in favor of the Allies. Ultimate victory was no longer in serious doubt. The real question was the nature of the peace.

At noon, America's optimistic, aging, self-assured, wheelchair-bound president, Franklin Delano Roosevelt, delivered his State of the Union address to Congress. His speech wasn't elegant. It was messy, sprawling, unruly, a bit of a pastiche, and not at all literary. But because of what it said, this address, proposing a Second Bill of Rights, has a strong claim to being the greatest speech of the 20th century.

In the last few years, there has been a lot of discussion of World War II and the Greatest Generation. We've heard much about D-Day, foreign occupations, and presidential leadership amid threats to national security. But the real legacy of the leader of the Greatest Generation and the nation's most extraordinary president has been utterly lost. His Second Bill of Rights is largely forgotten, although, ironically, it has helped shape countless constitutions throughout the world—including the interim Iraqi constitution. To some extent, it has guided our own deepest aspirations. And it helps us to straighten out some national confusions that were never more prominent, and more pernicious, than they are today.

It's past time to understand it.

Roosevelt began his speech by emphasizing that war was a shared endeavor in which the United States was simply one participant. Now that the war was in the process of being won, the main objective for the future could be "captured in one word: Security." Roosevelt argued that the term "means not only physical security which provides safety from attacks by aggressors," but also "economic security, social security,

moral security." He insisted that "essential to peace is a decent standard of living for all individual men and women and children in all nations. Freedom from fear is eternally linked with freedom from want."

The United States seems to have embraced a confused and pernicious form of individualism.

Moving to domestic affairs, Roosevelt emphasized the need to bring security to all American citizens. He argued for a "realistic tax law—which will tax all unreasonable profits, both individual and corporate, and reduce the ultimate cost of the war to our sons and daughters." We "cannot be content, no matter how high that general standard of living may be, if some fraction of our people—whether it be one-third or one-fifth or one-tenth—is ill-fed, ill-clothed, ill-housed, and insecure," he declared.

At that point, the speech became spectacularly ambitious. Roosevelt looked back, not entirely approvingly, to the framing of the Constitution. At its inception, the nation had protected "certain inalienable political rights—among them the right of free speech, free press, free worship, trial by jury, freedom from unreasonable searches and seizures," he noted. But over time, those rights had proved inadequate, as "we have come to a clear realization of the fact that true individual freedom cannot exist without economic security and independence."

"We have accepted, so to speak, a Second Bill of Rights under which a new basis of security and prosperity can be established for all—regardless of station, race, or creed."

Then he listed the relevant rights:

The right to a useful and remunerative job in the industries or shops or farms or mines of the Nation.

The right to earn enough to provide adequate food and clothing and recreation.

The right of every farmer to raise and sell his products at a return which will give him and his family a decent living.

The right of every businessman, large and small, to trade in an atmosphere of freedom from unfair competition and domination by monopolies at home or abroad.

The right of every family to a decent home.

The right to adequate medical care and the opportunity to achieve and enjoy good health.

The right to adequate protection from the economic fears of old age, sickness, accident, and unemployment.

The right to a good education.

Having cataloged these eight rights, Roosevelt again made clear that the Second Bill of Rights was a continuation of the war effort. "America's own rightful place in the world depends in large part upon how fully these and similar rights have been carried into practice for our citizens. For unless there is security here at home there cannot be lasting peace in the world." He concluded that government should promote security instead of paying heed "to the whining demands of selfish pressure groups who seek to feather their nests while young Americans are dying."

Roosevelt, dead 15 months after delivering his speech, was unable to take serious steps toward putting his Bill of Rights into effect. But his proposal, now largely unknown within the United States, has had an extraordinary influence internationally. It played a major role in the Universal Declaration of Human Rights, completed in 1948 under the leadership of Eleanor

Roosevelt and publicly endorsed by American officials at the time. The declaration proclaims that everyone has the "right to a standard of living adequate for the health and well-being of himself and of his family, including food, clothing, housing, and medical care and necessary social services, and the right to security in the event of unemployment, sickness, disability, widowhood, old age, or other lack of livelihood in circumstances beyond his control." The declaration also provides a right to education and social security. It proclaims that "everyone has the right to work, to free choice of employment, to just and favorable conditions of work and to protection against unemployment."

By virtue of its effect on the Universal Declaration, the Second Bill of Rights has influenced dozens of constitutions throughout the world. In one or another form, it can be found in countless political and legal documents. The current constitution of Finland guarantees everyone "the right to basic subsistence in the event of unemployment, illness, and disability and during old age as well as at the birth of a child or the loss of a provider." The constitution of Spain announces, "To citizens in old age, the public authorities shall guarantee economic sufficiency through adequate and periodically updated pensions." Similarly, the constitutions of Ukraine, Romania, Syria, Bulgaria, Hungary, Russia, and Peru recognize some or all of the social and economic rights cataloged by Franklin Roosevelt.

*W*e might even call the Second Bill of Rights a leading American export. As the most recent example, consider the interim Iraqi constitution, written with American help and celebrated by the Bush administration. In Article XIV it proclaims, "The individual has the right to security, education, health care, and social security"; it adds that the nation and its government "shall strive to provide prosperity and employment opportunities to the people."

In fact, the United States itself continues to live, at least some of the time, under Roosevelt's constitutional vision. A consensus supports several of the rights he listed, including the right to education, the right to social security, the right to be free from monopoly, possibly even the right to a job. In the 1950s and 1960s, the U.S. Supreme Court started to go much further, embarking on a process of giving constitutional recognition to some of the rights that Roosevelt had listed. The court suggested

that there might be some kind of right to an education; it ruled that people could not be deprived of welfare benefits without a hearing; it said that citizens from one state could not be subject to "waiting periods" that deprive them of financial and medical help in another state. In a 1970 decision, the court said: "Welfare, by meeting the basic demands of subsistence, can help bring within the reach of the poor the same opportunities that are available to others to participate meaningfully in the life of the community." Public assistance, the court added, "is not mere charity, but a means to 'promote the general Welfare, and secure the Blessings of Liberty to ourselves and our Posterity.'"

By the late 1960s, respected constitutional thinkers could conclude that the Supreme Court was on the verge of recognizing a right to be free from desperate conditions—a right that captures much of what Roosevelt had cataloged. But all that was undone by the election of Richard Nixon in 1968. President Nixon promptly appointed four justices—Warren E. Burger, William H. Rehnquist, Lewis F. Powell Jr., and Harry A. Blackmun—who showed no interest in the Second Bill of Rights. In a series of decisions, the new justices, joined by one or two others, rejected the claim that the existing Constitution protects the kind of rights that Roosevelt had named.

Roosevelt himself did not argue for constitutional change. He wanted the Second Bill of Rights to be part of the nation's deepest commitments, to be recognized and vindicated by the public, not by federal judges. He trusted democratic processes, not judicial ones. Having seen many of his reforms struck down by the Supreme Court, he feared that judges would be unwilling to protect rights of the sort he favored. He thought that his bill should be seen in the same way as the Declaration of Independence—as a statement of the fundamental aspirations of the United States. In fact, Roosevelt's speech echoed Thomas Jefferson's famous language with its own declaration: "In our day these economic truths have become accepted as self-evident."

But Roosevelt's hopes have not been realized. Much of the time, the United States seems to have embraced a confused and pernicious form of individualism, one that has no real foundations in our history. That approach endorses rights of private property and freedom of contract; it respects political liberty, but claims to distrust "government intervention" and to

insist that people must largely fend for themselves. Its form of so-called individualism is incoherent—a hopeless tangle of confusions. As Roosevelt well knew, no one is really against government intervention. The wealthy, at least as much as the poor, receive help from government and from the benefits that it bestows.

Roosevelt himself pointed to the essential problem as early as 1932. In a campaign address in San Francisco, he said that the exercise of "property rights might so interfere with the rights of the individual that the government, without whose assistance the property rights could not exist, must intervene, not to destroy individualism but to protect it." The key phrase here is "without whose assistance the property rights could not exist." Those of us who are doing well, and who have plenty of money and opportunities, owe a great deal to an active government that is willing and able to protect what we have. Once we can appreciate that point, we will find it impossible to complain about "government interference" as such or to urge, ludicrously, that our rights are best secured by getting government "off our backs." The same people who object to "government intervention" depend on it every day of every year.

*R*emarkably, the confusions that Roosevelt identified have had a rebirth since the early 1980s. Time and again, politicians argue that they oppose government intervention, even though property rights themselves cannot exist without such intervention. Time and again, American culture is said to be antagonistic to "positive rights," even though property rights themselves require "positive" action and even though the Second Bill of Rights helped to define our nation's political reforms for much of the 20th century. In recent years, we have been seeing the rise of a false and a historical picture of American culture and history, a picture that is increasingly prominent not just in America but also in Europe.

Unfortunately, that picture is far from innocuous. America's self-image—our sense of ourselves—has a significant impact on what we actually do. We should not look at ourselves through a distorted mirror.

Amid the war on terrorism, the problem goes even deeper. America should have taken the attacks of September 11, 2001, as the basis for a new recognition of human vulnerability and of our collective responsibilities to those who need help. Recall that threats from abroad led Roosevelt to a renewed emphasis on the importance of "security"—with an understanding that the term included not merely protection against bullets and bombs, but also against hunger, disease, illiteracy, and desperate poverty. Hence President Roosevelt supported a strongly progressive income tax aimed at "unreasonable profits" and offering help for those at the bottom. By contrast, President Bush has supported a tax cut giving disproportionate help to those at the top. President Roosevelt saw the relationship between freedom from fear and freedom from want. Most important, he saw external threats as a reason to broaden the class of rights enjoyed by those at home. To say the least, President Bush has utterly failed to do the same.

Roosevelt was right. Liberty and citizenship are rooted in security. In a sense, America lives under the Second Bill of Rights. But in another sense, we have lost sight of it. It should be reclaimed in its nation of origin.

Cass R. Sunstein *is a professor of political science at the University of Chicago and a professor of jurisprudence at the university's law school. His most recent book is* The Second Bill of Rights: FDR's Unfinished Revolution and Why We Need It More Than Ever, *to be published next month by Basic Books.*

What They Saw When They Landed

Everything about the day was epic in scale, but the best way to appreciate it is to hear the story one soldier at a time

DOUGLAS BRINKLEY

It was quite a sight. There was the oldest man in the D-day invasion, 56-year-old Brigadier General Theodore Roosevelt Jr. (son of the former President) barking orders at Utah Beach. Although he had a heart condition, Roosevelt insisted that his presence and leadership would help boost troop morale. With German artillery exploding all around him, he paraded up and down Utah Beach, ordering U.S. tanks to secure the flanks and U.S. engineers to breach eight 50-yd. lanes through beach obstacles. He refused to wear a helmet, preferring to don a knit wool hat. "We have landed in the wrong place," shouted Roosevelt, who would receive the Medal of Honor for his valor that day. "But we will start the war from here."

Everything about D-day was dramatic—the overarching strategy, the vast mobilization, the sheer number of troops. But it's the daring boldness and intrepid courage of the men that stand out. One can read biographies of Dwight Eisenhower or watch film footage shot by John Ford, but the only way to understand D-day, the largest invasion force ever assembled, is as a battle at its smallest: that is, one soldier and one reminiscence at a time.

The landing target of the D-day invaders was a 50-mile stretch of shoreline in the middle of the Cherbourg—Le Havre crescent in France. On the night of June 5, the operation began as Allied paratroopers boarded planes and gliders. "O.K., let's go" was Eisenhower's direct order. Just after midnight, June 6, they began landing behind enemy lines, with orders to attack and destroy German gun batteries. Meanwhile, an armada started making its way toward the designated beaches. Allied troops began landing at 6:30 a.m. Wading through the water onto French soil, they met vastly different fates. At Utah Beach, the farthest west, bombardments had decimated the German defenses. Moreover, an opportune navigational mistake had landed the troops at a practically unguarded stretch of the beach. The Americans who landed there sustained relatively few casualties. The British and Canadian forces who landed at Gold and Juno beaches fought their way ashore, according to plan, and were soon followed by tanks, the mere sight of which swept most of the German resistance away. The fighting was harder at Sword Beach, where German defenders stiffened against the specter of the Allies' capturing the nearby city of Caen. The hardest fighting of all raged throughout the day on the fifth beach, Omaha. It was a relatively narrow strand of shoreline overshadowed by 100-ft. cliffs. Troops trying to land there found themselves in a horrify-

ing position, vulnerable to machine-gun and mortar fire from above. The only route out lay through four ravines carved by the wind and water through the cliffs. American soldiers were bewildered, their officers were confused, and their comrades were lying dead all around, in the water and on the beach. In the chaos, there were not even any boats to evacuate the wounded, many of whom died on Omaha of injuries that would have been treatable on any other beach. By late morning, amid the crushing noise, violence and justifiable fear racing through the air, some troops managed to drag themselves up the cliffs in small fighting forces. By the end of the day, at a cost too high to be measured in mere statistics, they took the beach and carved out a piece of Free France 2 miles wide and 6 miles long.

Operation Overlord was not over on D-day. With astonishing speed, the stage managers of the operation moved tons of materials onto the Allied beachhead, building floating docks to receive thousands of tons more. Even Omaha Beach was a vast and busy port by June 9. D-day had made an Allied victory inevitable. To be more precise, the men of the invading force had made an Allied victory inevitable. Here are their patriotic voices, recalling the day they—and world history—will never forget.

"WE KNEW THAT SOMETHING ABSOLUTELY OVERWHELMING WAS GOING TO TAKE PLACE."

—John Robinson

A pilot with the 344th Bomb Group, Robinson, 24, flew two successful sorties over Normandy on June 6

WE FLEW MARTIN B-26 MARAUDERS, which were, without any doubt, the best bombers in the whole wide world. Several weeks prior to June 5, the squadron doctor had passed out a small pill to each crew member. He said the pills were intended to keep the crews awake in case we had to work around the clock. Everybody knew that this was in preparation for D-day. I don't know how they worked on anybody else, but they kept me awake for three nights and three days, completely unable to sleep.

It was our job to prepare the ground to enable the infantry to get ashore, to stay ashore and fight and win. We also hoped that they'd kill a whole bunch of those damned antiaircraft gunners for whom we had no love and no pity. A couple of hours after dinner on June 5, someone came into the hut and said quietly, "Get to bed early

tonight, fellows." We'd all seen the loading list on the bulletin board. From the size of the list, it looked like a maximum effort. I climbed into bed and went right to sleep. It was probably 2 a.m. when some guy who had the duty that night shook my shoulder and told me to get up, have breakfast and report for briefing. We got dressed, and as I was walking past the bunk of Hank Avner, who wasn't going that day, he raised up on one elbow and said, and I quote exactly, "Bite them on the ass for me, Johnny."

We rode our bicycles down to the mess hall, had breakfast and rode the bikes to the briefing room. It was dark, and it was raining, and the cloud cover was complete. We just sort of felt our way around. Inside the briefing room, the crowd was quiet. The big map at the end of the room was covered as usual with its drawstring curtains. Pretty soon, in came the colonel, and he went to one end of the curtains. A captain went to the other end and held the drawstrings. They looked at their watches—looked at each other. The colonel nodded his head to

the captain. The captain began to draw open the curtains, and Colonel Vance said in a quiet voice, "Gentlemen, this is it."

And, by George, there it was, all laid out with ribbons leading from our base to a point on the English coast. From there, the ribbons led to the French coast, then along the coast to the drop zone described as Utah Beach. Someone asked if we could expect much fighter opposition over the target. The colonel answered that one very simply by saying, "There will be approximately 3,500 Allied fighters over the beach this morning." That brought a big sigh of relief from the group.

We gave our personal things such as wallets and other identification to the guys in the security room, picked up our parachutes and steel helmets, got into the trucks and rode out to the planes. It was still raining and quite dark, and we knew there would be no delay on account of weather on this day. It had begun to sink in that we were involved in what was to be one of the greatest moments in history.

"THE PLANE IS BOUNCING LIKE SOMETHING GONE WILD."

—Dwayne T. Burns

A private with the 508th Parachute Infantry Regiment, Burns, 19, landed behind enemy lines, far from his drop zone

AT 22:30, ALL OVER ENGLAND, engines started. We were ready to go. Now here we sat, each man alone in the dark with his own thoughts and fears. "Lord," I prayed, "please let me do everything right. Don't let me get anybody killed, and don't let me get killed either. I really think I'm too young for this. I should be home having a good time. Who ever told me I was a fighter anyway?" We blacked our faces with burnt cork. Some of the guys cut their hair Mohawk style. Some shaved it all off. Each trooper was going into combat in whatever style that suited him best. I left mine in a crew cut.

Finally, the signal came down to us to get aboard. We shook hands and wished one another good luck, saying, "We'll see you on the ground." We chuted up and pulled the adjustment straps down good and tight

because we knew we were so loaded that we were going to get one hell of an opening shock. The two chutes, rifle, two bandoliers, cartridge belt, first-aid kit, shovel, canteen kit, jump knife, trench knife, bayonet, gas mask, land mine, rations, billfold, clean socks and underwear, toothbrush, New Testament and message book, plus other odds and ends—I must have weighed well over 300 lbs. Once we were chuted up, we had to stay on our feet because it would be impossible to get back up without help. We pushed and pulled one another up the steps just to get up the plane.

In the air, we start picking up flak, light at first. I know we have just crossed the coastline. Flak is getting heavy as we stand waiting for the green light. Now the plane's being hit from all sides. The noise is awesome. The roar of the engines, the flak hitting the wings and fuselage—and everyone is yelling, "Let's go!," but still the green light does not come on. The plane is bouncing like something gone wild. I can hear a ticking sound as machine-gun rounds walk across the wings. It's hard to stand up, and troopers are falling down and getting up; some are getting sick. Of all the training we

had, there was not anything that prepared us for this. Then the red light goes out, and the green snaps on. We shuffle out the door into the dark fresh air.

I'm amazed at how quiet it is outside. We were to jump at 600 ft., but it seems to be much higher than that. I hear the sound as the ship fades away. I seem to be far south of our drop zone. It looks like I'm on the outer edge of all the action. To the north, I see tracers arcing across the sky. And in spite of all of this going on, I think of how beautiful they appear.

I look down. I can just make out rows of trees. I think to myself, This is France, and now I'm in combat. This is for real. I landed in a long, narrow field with two antiglider poles in it, and I hit hard and roll over on my back, tangled in my shroud lines. I see one chute go down behind the trees on the other side of the field, so I know that I'm not completely alone. I've landed on good solid ground. I lie in the grass trying to get out of my harness. In my mind's eye, I can see Germans running with fixed bayonets to kill me, and I'm having trouble with the harness buckles. To say I'm scared is an understatement. I reach down to my right ankle and pull out my trench knife and stick it in the ground beside me. I think at least a knife is better than no weapon at all. Then I unsnap my harness, untangle myself, stand up and run to the hedgerow where I saw the chute go down.

"Flash" was our code word, and countersign was "Thunder." We also had been given a child's cricket snapper. One snap was to be answered by two snaps ... or was it the other way around? "Oh, hell," I mutter. "Just snap the damn thing a few times." In reply, I get, "Look out, I'm coming

over." He sounds good to me, and I say, "Come on."

The two of us went back across the field that I had landed in and found some troopers coming up the hedgerow. I didn't know who they were, but right now it didn't make any difference as long as I was with somebody. We moved north about 100 yds. and stopped. It was there I saw my first German. While we were stopped, I thought I'd have a look over the top of the hedgerow to see what was on the other side. I climbed up and slowly looked over,

and as I did, a German on the other side raised up and looked over. I couldn't see his features, just a square silhouette of his helmet. We stood there looking at each other, then slowly each one of us went back down. I sat there wondering what to do about him. I could throw a grenade over, but I might kill more troopers than Germans. While I sat there thinking, we started to move again, so I left him sitting on his side of the hedgerow wondering what to do about me.

"MY UPPER JAW WAS SHATTERED; THE LEFT CHEEK WAS BLOWN OPEN."

—Harold Baumgarten

Baumgarten, 19, a rifleman with the 116th Infantry, was wounded five times during the battle for Omaha Beach

HAVING MY COLLEGE EDUCATION AND a good background in American history and wartime battles, I realized that it was not going to be easy, and I did not expect to come back alive. I wrote such to my sister in New York City—to get the mail before my parents and break the news gently to them when she received the telegram that I was no longer alive.

We left the marshaling area with full battle equipment, about 100 lbs. per man, and went in trucks to the huge seaport of Weymouth, England. That night we boarded a liberty ship, *Empire Javelin*, which was to carry us across the Channel to Normandy. The harbor of Weymouth was crowded with ships of every size, shape and description, most of them flying the Stars and Stripes. We had the old battleships *Arkansas*, *Nevada* and *Texas* with us. On the evening of June 5, the harbor came alive. I could see one ship signaling to the other that this was it.

At 3:30 a.m., we left the *Javelin* on British LCAs [landing craft assault]. It was pitch black, and the Channel was rough. The huge bluish-black waves rose high over the sides of our little craft and batted the boat with unimaginable fury. [The waves] broke our front ramp, and the boat began to fill with icy Channel water. The water reached my waist, and things looked black for us as our little boat began to sink. But the lieutenant rammed his body against the inner door of the ship and said, "Well, what the hell are you waiting for? Take off your helmets and start bailing the water out." All

our equipment as well as ourselves were wet. Our TNT was floating around the boat. We were dead tired from pumping hand pumps and bailing out water with our helmets. Our feet were frozen blue.

At about 6:30 a.m., I saw the beach with its huge seawall at the foot of a massive bluff. An 88-mm shell landed right in the middle of the LCA [to] the side of us, and splinters of the boat, equipment and bodies were thrown into the air. Bullets were passing through the thin wooden sides of our vessel. The ramp was lowered, and the inner door was opened. A German machine gun trained on the opening took a heavy toll of lives. Many of my 30 buddies went down as they left the LCA.

I got a bullet through the top of my helmet first, and then as I waded through the deep water, a bullet aimed at my heart hit the receiver of my M-1 rifle. The water was being shot up all around me. Clarius Riggs, who left the assault boat in front of me, went under, shot to death. About 8 or 10 ft. to my right, as we reached the dry sand, I heard a hollow thud, and I saw Private Robert Dittmar hold his chest and heard him yell, "I'm hit! I'm hit!" I hit the ground and watched him as he continued to go forward about 10 more yards. He tripped over a tank obstacle, and as he fell, his body made a complete turn, and he lay sprawled on the damp sand with his head facing the Germans, his face looking skyward. He seemed to be suffering from shock and was yelling, "Mother, Mom," as he kept rolling around on the sand.

There were three or four others wounded and dying right near him. Sergeant Clarence Roberson, from my boat team, had a gaping wound on the left side of his forehead. He was walking crazily in the water, without his helmet. Then I saw him get down on his knees and start pray-

ing with his rosary beads. At this moment, the Germans cut him in half with their deadly cross fire. I saw the reflection from the helmet of one of the snipers and took aim, and later on, I found out, I got a bull's-eye on him. It was my only time that rifle fired—due to the bullet that hit my rifle. It must have shattered the wood, and the rifle broke in half, and I had to throw it away.

Shells were continually landing all about me in a definite pattern, and when I raised my head up to curse the Germans in the pillbox on our right flank who were continually shooting up the sand in front of me, one of the fragments from an 88-mm shell hit me in my left cheek. It felt like being hit with a baseball bat, only the results were much worse. My upper jaw was shattered; the left cheek was blown open. My upper lip was cut in half. I washed my face out in the cold, dirty Channel water and managed somehow not to pass out. I got rid of most of my equipment. Here I was happy that I did not wear the invasion jacket. I wore a regular Army zippered field jacket, with a Star of David drawn on the back and THE BRONX, NEW YORK written on it. Had I worn the invasion jacket, I probably would have drowned.

The water was rising about an inch a minute as the tide was coming in, so I had to get moving or drown. I had to reach a 15-ft. seawall, which appeared to be 200 yds. in front of me. Finally, I came to dry sand, and there was only another 100 yds. or maybe less to go, and I started across the sand, crawling very fast. The Germans in the pillbox on the right flank were shooting up the sand all about me. I expected a bullet to rip through me at any moment. I reached the stone wall without further injury. I was now safe from the flat-trajectory weapons of the enemy. All I had to fear now were enemy mines and artillery shells.

Things looked pretty black and one-sided until Brigadier General Norman D. Cota rallied us by capturing some men himself and running around the beach with a hand grenade and a pistol in his hand. [He] ran down the beach under fire and sent a call for reinforcements. Every man who could walk and fire a weapon charged up the hill later on in the day toward the enemy. I got hit in the left foot while crawling by a mine.

At the end of June 6, we were only in about half a mile. As the evening progressed, I felt like I was getting very weak,

and along the way, I got another bullet through the face again. I was starting to feel very weak from all that bleeding. As it got dark, I became very trigger happy, and anything that moved in front of me, I started to fire at.

About 3 a.m., I found myself lying near a road above the bluffs in the vicinity south of Vierville. I got an ambulance to stop by firing [in its direction], and it stopped, and two men came out and asked if I could sit up in the ambulance. [Later] they took me out and put me in a stretcher, and I saw a huge statue. I think later on, in retrospect,

it was a church near the beach, silhouetted in the darkness. The next morning I saw the German prisoners marching by me. The 175th Infantry Regiment apparently landed around that time, and German snipers opened up on the beach, including the wounded. I got shot in my right knee in the stretcher. I had received five individual wounds that day in Normandy. The 1st Battalion of the 116th Infantry was more or less sacrificed to achieve the landing and was completely wiped out. It was a total sacrifice.

"I SAW AN ARMADA LIKE A PLAGUE OF LOCUSTS. THE NUMBER OF SHIPS WAS UNCOUNTABLE."

—Anton Herr

The German officer, 24, commanded a dozen tanks in a company stationed near Falaise

IT WAS ACTUALLY A RELIEF for me when the invasion finally happened. I was having trouble keeping my crews in a state of readiness. I knew it was coming off when a young man from the chateau where we were staying brought me a tract to translate that had been dropped from an Allied plane. It ordered him and his family to get out of the chateau into the surrounding fields because they were going to start bombing it. I told him instead to take all the civilians to the deepest cellar, where they'd have a better chance of surviving.

That was good advice, since I learned later that they all survived.

We left at around 5 a.m. for Caen. The whole way up, we were never fired at. But when we got to Caen, the Allies were bombing the bridge over the River Orne. I noticed the cadence of the bombs, and I sent my tanks over one by one between the bombs and didn't lose any of them. We were the first of the tanks over that bridge, and we continued north. The town seemed completely untouched by war at that time.

None of the German tank companies were communicating with the others. We'd been told to keep radio silence so the Allies couldn't pick us up. We were like an orchestra without a conductor, and there I was playing flute. I continued all the way up to the coast, and when I got

there, I saw an armada like a plague of locusts. The number of ships was uncountable, and the Allies' superior firepower was obvious. But in war, what you lose first is reason. I wanted to attack. I wanted to vanquish them.

We were fired at, and one tank took a direct hit—I never knew whether from the enemy or our own tanks—and the whole crew was killed. After we took another hit, we found a little wood and dug in. The order to all tank units, maybe from the Führer, was not to yield a single meter. Before I slept that night under my tank, I wrote an angry letter home. As a young officer, I thought we could have broken the invasion if we'd been better led.

"I PULLED MY LEGS UP AS FAR AS I COULD TO GET AWAY FROM A STREAM OF TRACERS."

—Edward Jeziorski

A paratrooper with the 507th Parachute Infantry Regiment, Jeziorski, 23, was dropped into the inferno over Normandy

OUT THE DOOR WE WENT. JUST AS I peeled out, it seemed that the whole world lit up right underneath me. A tremendous ball of fire. And a bunch of black smoke mixed in with the red fire, just a great fireball. And I said to myself, The bastards are waiting for us. I tried to slip away from the thing, and tracers were coming up and through the silk. They were coming up just in strings. I can remember them being so close that I actually pulled my legs up as far

as I could, my knee into my stomach, to get away from a stream of tracers. I slammed into the ground, and I was immediately pinned down by machine-gun fire. There was no way to raise up. Every time I tried to turn, the machine gun would open up. Every time I tried to move, there would be a burst. Apparently the great big ball of fire was a C-47 that had been shot down, and I was silhouetted between this guy's gun and the ship, and I couldn't move. I finally was able to bring my right leg up close enough to where I could get my jump knife out of my boot. I cut the harness loose.

In the meantime, this guy is still shooting. When I cut loose, I rolled over in a little depression; fortunately, it was deep enough. I had my hand on my rifle, and I

was able to squeeze off a couple of rounds where the fire was coming from, and that eased it up real quick. He stopped. I'm sure I didn't hit him, but at any rate, by golly, it got his attention that I was now in a position to start working on him.

Just a little bit after that, there was a good deal of thrashing going on on the other side of the hedgerow. It [turned out to be] my assistant gunner, Grover Boyce. There were two of us together now. It seemed like a better world all of a sudden. [Soon] we located a parapack, and believe me, we were fortunate. One of the packs we opened had a machine gun. We really felt pretty good having that thing in our hands. We didn't know where we were, but we knew that we weren't anywhere near where we were supposed to be. We were getting ready to go ahead and set up some sort of a decent roadblock in both directions when somebody yelled, "Here come the Krauts!" A little stone fence or hedge was leading on into the end of the town. A squad of Germans was following the hedge toward us. Guys popped their rifles at them, and they fired back at us. By then I was ready with my light machine gun, and I turned loose a couple of bursts, and they gave it back with an MG42, and we just traded for a couple of bursts back and forth. I took the Jerry out of there. There wasn't any more noise from him. We moved on after that.

We backed off about 200 yds. and, son of a gun, here came another group of Germans. All of D-day, we just moved, moved, moved, and we never seemed to get away from activity by the Germans. It was one fire fight after another. Getting up into the afternoon, pretty late, we went back inland a couple of hundred yards. We picked out a pair of good and decent spots, and we were going to take a break. I remember lying down and lighting a cigarette, and that's all I recall until I felt something nudging me and a real soft voice, kind of a questioning voice, was saying, "*De lait, de lait, de lait.*" It was an old man who had just finished milking his

cow and was offering me some of the warm milk. I took it, against all regulations, by golly. By gosh, I drank it. Not since being a kid did anything taste so good as that did.

That's the way D-day went for us. I don't believe any group anywhere in Normandy tied up any more of the enemy, proportionately, than this little gang did. And not a scratch on anyone. But I lost my best buddy. We found him and cut him down where he had been shot in an apple tree where he had gotten entangled.

"AS OUR BOAT TOUCHED SAND AND THE RAMP WENT DOWN, I BECAME A VISITOR TO HELL."

—Harry Parley

Private Parley, 24, carried a flamethrower in the first wave on Omaha Beach with the 116th Infantry Regiment

THERE WAS SOME HUMOR TO BEING the flamethrower. While waiting to be loaded onto the ships at dockside, I would often light a cigarette using my weapon. Being experienced with it, I knew all the safety factors. I could, without triggering the propelling mechanism, light a cigarette by simply producing a small flame at the mouth of the gun. In doing so, it produced the same hissing sound as when the thrower was actually being fired. When my team would hear the terrifying sound, I would immediately be the only one on the dock.

The liquid used in the flamethrower [for training] had always been a pinkish-red in color and had a consistency similar to warm Jell-O. As we made ready for what we thought would be just another practice run, and as I filled my tanks, I saw that the liquid was not the usual Jell-O-like substance. What I was pumping was a mucus-like liquid both in color and consistency. I realized that morning that the invasion was on.

In the landing craft, I cowered with the others as we circled, waiting for our signal to approach. I remember looking back and seeing the Navy coxswain at the controls of our boat standing high above us completely exposed to enemy fire, doing his job as ordered. As our boat touched sand and the ramp went down, I became a visitor to hell. Some boats on either side of us

had been hit by artillery and heavy weapons. I was aware that some were burning and some were sinking. I shut everything out and concentrated on following the men in front of me down the ramp and into the water. I stepped off the ramp into a deep pocket in the sand, and went under completely. With no footing whatsoever, and with the weight of the 80-lb. flamethrower on my back, I was unable to come up. I knew I was drowning, and made a futile attempt to unbuckle the flamethrower harness. Inadvertently, I had raised the firing arm, which is about 3 ft. long, above my head. One of my team saw it, grabbed hold, and pulled me up out of the hole to solid sand. Then slowly, half-drowned, coughing water and dragging my feet, I began walking toward the chaos ahead.

During that walk (I was unable to run), I got my first experience with enemy fire. Machine-gun fire was hitting the beach, and as it hit the wet sand, it made a "sip sip" sound like someone sucking on their teeth. Ahead of me in the distance, I could see survivors of the landing already using the base of the bluffs as shelter. Due to my near drowning and exhaustion, I had fallen behind the advance. To this day, I don't know why I didn't dump the flamethrower and run like hell for shelter. But I didn't.

What I found when I finally reached the seawall at the foot of the bluffs is difficult to describe. Men were trying to dig or scrape trenches or foxholes for protection against incoming fire. Others were carrying or helping the wounded to areas of shelter. We had to crouch or crawl on all fours when moving about. Most of us were in no condition to carry on. All were trying

to stay alive for the moment. Behind us, other landing craft were attempting to unload their equipment and personnel in the incoming tide and were coming under enemy fire as well. I realized that we had landed in the wrong beach sector and that many of the people around me were from other units and were strangers to me. What's more, the terrain before us was not what I had been trained to encounter. We could see nothing above us to return fire to. We were the targets.

By now we were being urged by braver and more sensible noncoms and one or two surviving officers to get off the beach and up to higher ground. But it would be some time before enough courage returned for us to attempt it. One or two times I was able to control my fear enough to race across the sand to drag a helpless G.I. from drowning in the incoming tide. That was the extent of my bravery that morning.

By now, clear thinking was replacing some of our fear, and many of us accepted the fact that we had to get off the beach. Word was passed that a small draw providing access up the bluff had been found and that attempts were being made to blow up the barbed wire with bangalore torpedoes and find a way up through the mines. As I started up, I saw the white tape marking a safe path through the mines, and I also saw the price paid to mark that path for us. Several G.I.s had been blown to death, and another, still alive, was being attended to. As I passed, I could see that both his legs were gone, and tourniquets were being applied by a medic.

The rest of the day is a jumbled memory of running, fighting and hiding. We moved like a small band of outlaws, much of the time not knowing where we were, often meeting other groups like ours, joining and separating as situations arose. I remember one time, while moving along a road, suddenly coming under fire from some sort of artillery piece around the bend. I could also hear the clank of a track vehicle and realized that it was a tank or half-track of some kind. Terrified, I turned, ran like hell, and dove into a deep covered roadside ditch. Already there was a tough old sergeant from the 1st Division lying on his side as one would relax on a sofa. Knowing that the 1st Division was combat experienced, I screamed at him, "I think it's a tank—what the hell can we do now?" He stared calmly at me for a few seconds, poker-faced, and said, "Relax, kid, maybe it will go away." And sure enough, it did go away.

"IN A FIELD OPPOSITE, WE SAW THE MOST TERRIBLE CARNAGE. THERE WERE GLIDERS UPENDED ON THE POSTS AND DEAD MEN EVERYWHERE."

—John Kite

Kite, 23, a special-forces sergeant in the British army, took part in the assault on Juno Beach

OUR DESTINATION FIVE OR SIX MILES inland was Douvres-la-Délivrande; our primary objective was the radar station, then the school, which had to be cleared for an HQ. The night before, I handed the men cards to write out their last will and testament, and a little note that could be sent to their parents without being censored (we would be away by the time they got them). I also gave the men 40 francs each. We studied everything thoroughly, over and over again. I told them that if anyone was hit, you don't pick him up, there were others detailed to do that; the assault could not be held up. All told we carried a load of 78 lbs. on our backs. And we had a silly rubber ring—it was supposed to keep us afloat. We used it afterward as a pillow.

When we were due to land, we were told to get down in the hull of the ship. I had my last words with the men and said,

"Make peace with your Maker; good luck." I was so scared, all the bones in my body were shaking. I said to myself, Pull yourself together, you're in charge and supposed to show an example. When the ramp went down dead on 0600 [hours], I looked around, and there were pools of water by my men. It wasn't seawater. The Canadians revved the tanks up before we left the ship; the noise was huge, and it helped.

We went into the water and luckily were able to touch bottom. We could see an 8 ft. wall on which the engineers had put up wire mesh for us to climb. We waded through the water, avoiding mines, and my platoon eventually got to the beach. Jim, my other sergeant, took the men up the sand dunes and over the wall, whilst I reported to the beach master the number of troops I had brought ashore and my code number. He said thank you, get off this beach … quickly.

In a field opposite, we saw the most terrible carnage. There were gliders upended on the posts and tree stumps left for that purpose by the Germans. There were dead men, and dead cattle and horses every-

where. The men [in our unit] had shot a couple of Germans, and we rolled them off the road into a ditch so that they wouldn't be run over. We walked single file up the road, as the verges could have been mined. There was sniping. I gave instructions that the section leader should give a burst of fire at any thick foliage or any windows that were open. The windows soon shut. We stopped to have a cup of tea; we stayed in the ditch, and one of the men who could speak fluent French brought back a pail of boiling water.

At Douvres-la-Delivrande we checked out a school and ensured it was free of booby traps so it could be used as a brigade HQ. My next job was to go to the radar station—a concrete blockhouse, a huge hexagon with apertures all round. The Germans were inside, but the Royal Marine Commandos were outside. We went on to Hermanville, which was on the main road to Caen. When we arrived it was 5 p.m. We had been up since 3 a.m. We dug a trench at the corner of a field and slept.

"THE ENEMY WAS LEANING OVER AND THROWING DOWN HAND GRENADES BY THE BUSHEL BASKETFUL."

—James Eikner

Eikner, 30, was a communications officer with the 2nd Rangers Battalion, which scaled the cliffs at Pointe du Hoc to eliminate fortified German gun emplacements

POINTE DU HOC WAS EQUIDISTANT between Omaha Beach and Utah Beach. The six 155-mm guns had a 25,000-yd. range, and they could rain destruction down on either of the beaches and reach far out into the sea and cause tremendous damage to naval craft. So this installation was [considered] the most dangerous within the in-

vasion area. Toward the sea the cliffs dropped off about 100 ft. on the average, from vertical to near vertical to actually overhanging.

We put the landing craft into the water, and of course it was pitch black and nothing could be seen. The waves were headed right into us, and water began to leak in through the front ramp. Just as there was enough daylight to make out the headlands, things didn't look right. Our little three-company flotilla was two or three miles east of Pointe du Hoc. Colonel Rudder, who was leading the attack, convinced the British officer who was in charge of that craft that he was in error and made him

flank left, and then we had to parallel the coastline for a couple of miles. We landed at Pointe du Hoc some 40 minutes late.

We were on our own then. Some of the rockets we carried had grappling hooks that trailed ladders made of ropes, and we got into position a certain distance from shore so that the angle was proper. We would fire two at a time. Some of the ropes didn't make it to the cliff top because the ropes had become wet and heavy. Some of the others pulled out, and the enemy cut some, but we did have enough in order to get the job done.

Most of us had something in the way of equipment to take off the boat, and my responsibility was to take off a cloverleaf of 60-mm mortar shells. So I ran down the ramp and in the water up to my knees, and headed on across what I thought was the beach. But I stepped into a shell hole that was covered with water and went down over my head. Some of our people were getting hit, and I remember one young man who was hit three times on the landing craft and twice more on the beach. Believe it or not, that young man survived.

I laid my mortar shells down under the cliff, and there was a rope right in front of me. So I started up that cliff—there were two or three guys ahead of me—and the enemy was leaning over and shooting at us and throwing down hand grenades by the bushel basketful. Before we got to the top, about two-thirds of the way up, a tremen-

dous explosion occurred just above us. It brought down tons of rock and dirt, and of course we all went back down the cliff. I caught on a little ledge; I was covered up to my knees.

The enemy was still up there shooting and throwing down grenades. I got my tommy gun out, took aim at one of the characters up there, and—my gun wouldn't fire. So there I was in the grandest invasion in history with no weapon. I looked around and spied a youngster with a radio on his back down in a cave beneath Pointe du Hoc at water level. I scrambled down the cliff, went to him and asked if he had sent any messages yet, but he said that he hadn't. I had a number of priority messages to get out, and I sent the message, "Praise the

Lord." This was a code phrase that meant all the men were up the cliff.

As some of you may have read, the big guns were not in place. One patrol led by a sergeant from D Company ran upon the big guns about a mile inland. The enemy had moved them up there for better protection. So while a buddy of his was standing guard, the sergeant sneaked into the area where the guns were being camouflaged and put thermite grenades in the breech blocks to make them inoperable. There was a large stockpile of shells there all ready to go, and had we not been there, we felt quite sure that those guns would have been put into operation and it would have brought much death and destruction down on our men.

"WE CAUGHT UP WITH MY OWN COMPANY. I WAS WITH MY VERY CLOSE BUDDIES. THAT WAS A GOOD FEELING."

—Robert L. Williams

Williams, 21, a sergeant with the 101st Airborne Division, landed in 3 ft. of water in a flooded field behind Utah Beach

OUR PILOT HAD TO TAKE EVASIVE ACTION and fly very low, about 650 ft., so our paratroops ended up being widely scattered. I joined up with three other paratroopers, and we started walking north, directly toward a German machine-gun nest, as it turned out. There was a burst of gunfire, and I realized something had gone through my left pant-leg pocket. I crouched in shallow water, with just my nose and mouth exposed. I was unhurt, but two of the men I was with were killed. I kept moving, crouched in the water, until it was only a foot deep, and it started to get light.

At dawn that morning, I saw formations of B-26 bombers making their run along the beach, less than a mile away. I was exhausted, and the weight of my wet clothes and equipment was too much. I lay down across a big rosebush growing out of the water—I didn't care about the thorns. A few minutes later, I saw three men moving toward me with their rifles pointed in my direction. Luckily they were our guys. We could see a barn in the distance. We headed for it, but then we got pinned down by rifle fire. I was tired of the water and continued to head for the barn and dry ground. Fortunately the sniper was a lousy shot.

The next morning, we caught up with a group that consisted mostly of my own company. For the first time I was with my very close buddies. That was a good feeling. Midmorning we moved toward the village of Vierville and were ambushed in the center of town. The Germans had a ma-

chine gun in a church tower and a line of infantry entrenched parallel to the road. Sergeant Benjamin Stoney took a burst of machine-gun fire in the face as he peered around a stone wall to return fire, and was killed. He had jumped just ahead of me from plane No. 48. He was fourth; I was fifth. The battle lasted most of the afternoon around his body. We began to run low on ammunition.

We heard a tank approaching. It was one of ours. We pointed to the church tower, and with one shot the tank blew a big hole in the tower. Our platoon leader, Lieut. Baranowski, climbed on the tank and got the crew to mount the big .50-cal. machine gun on top. He manned that gun like a madman, killing Germans left and right as fast as he could shoot. We captured more Germans than we knew what to do with—125 prisoners, 125 dead. We had six wounded, one dead.

"FOR THE FIRST TIME IN MY LIFE, I TOUCHED A DEAD MAN."

—Elbert Legg

Legg, 19, a sergeant with the 603rd Quartermaster Graves Registration Company, flew into Normandy on a glider

OUR GLIDER CAME IN OVER A HEDGEROW of trees about 80 ft. high and nosed down into a level pasture. It was a hard,

pancake-type landing. The front strut came through the wooden floor of the glider and ripped toward the rear, barely missing the legs of some of the troops. We had landed a hundred yards from the personnel-assembly point at the crossroads of Les Forges. It was early evening, and we had about four hours before dark. After a quick check of the surrounding area, I selected a large field adjacent to the Les Forges crossroads as the first work site.

Four dead paratroopers already lay in the corner by the crossroads. As I examined the site, two jeeps with trailers loaded with bodies drove in and were directed to the corner of the field where the other bodies lay. The drivers made it clear they were delivering but not unloading. I sized up the situation and decided the time had come for me to act like the graves-registration representative that I was. For the first time in my life, I touched a dead man. I grabbed the leg of one of the bodies and rolled it off onto the ground. As I struggled, the drivers gave in and assisted me with the remainder of the bodies. There were now 14 dead lying in a row, and more loaded vehicles were driving into the field.

After studying the surrounding terrain, I went to one corner of the field and stuck my heel in the ground. This would be the upper left corner of the first grave. I found an empty K-ration carton and split it into wooden stakes. I paced off the graves in rows of 20 and marked them with the stakes. I had no transit, tape measure, shovels, picks or any other equipment needed to establish a properly laid-out cemetery.

Lieut. Fraim returned and said he had arranged for about 35 Frenchmen to start digging graves. The next morning, I could see them coming my way, carrying a mixture of picks, shovels and lunch pails. All the men were very old or crippled in some way. There was little conversation, since I spoke no French and they spoke no English. The long row of bodies and marking stakes made it apparent what was to be done.

I began the job of processing bodies. There were plenty of parachutes in the field, so nylon panels served as personal-effects bags and body bags. Each body was searched and all personal effects were secured, but no inventory was taken. A ruled tablet served as Graves Registration Form No. 1. Both identification tags were left with the body until it was ready to be placed into a grave. One tag stayed with the body after burial, and the other was attached to the stake that served as a grave marker. Today a small monument at the Les Forges crossroads marks the cemetery location and records that 6,000 Allied troops from the Normandy invasion were buried there. Later, the bodies were moved to permanent cemeteries in Normandy or sent back to the U.S. for burial.

Interviews for this story were drawn from the oral-history project at the Eisenhower Center for American Studies in New Orleans as well as reporting by Helen Gibson/London, James Graff/Paris and Barbara Maddux/New York

Douglas Brinkley *is the co-author, with Ronald J. Drez, of the new book* Voices of Valor: D-Day: June 6, 1944

The Biggest Decision: Why We Had to Drop the Atomic Bomb

Robert James Maddox

On the morning of August 6, 1945, the American B-29 Enola Gay dropped an atomic bomb on the Japanese city of Hiroshima. Three days later another B-29, *Bock's Car*, released one over Nagasaki. Both caused enormous casualties and physical destruction. These two cataclysmic events have preyed upon the American conscience ever since. The furor over the Smithsonian Institution's *Enola Gay* exhibit and over the mushroom-cloud postage stamp last autumn are merely the most obvious examples. Harry S. Truman and other officials claimed that the bombs caused Japan to surrender, thereby avoiding a bloody invasion. Critics have accused them of at best failing to explore alternatives, at worst of using the bombs primarily to make the Soviet Union "more manageable" rather than to defeat a Japan they knew already was on the verge of capitulation.

By any rational calculation Japan was a beaten nation by the summer of 1945. Conventional bombing had reduced many of its cities to rubble, blockade had strangled its importation of vitally needed materials, and its navy had sustained such heavy losses as to be powerless to interfere with the invasion everyone knew was coming. By late June advancing American forces had completed the conquest of Okinawa, which lay only 350 miles from the southernmost Japanese home island of Kyushu. They now stood poised for the final onslaught.

> *Okinawa provided a preview of what an invasion of the home islands would entail. Rational calculations did not determine Japan's position.*

Rational calculations did not determine Japan's position. Although a peace faction within the government wished to end the war—provided certain conditions were met—militants were prepared to fight on regardless of consequences. They claimed to welcome an invasion of the home islands, promising to inflict such hideous casualties that the United States would retreat from its announced policy of unconditional surrender. The militarists held effective power over the government and were capable of defying the emperor, as they had in the past, on the ground that his civilian advisers were misleading him.

Okinawa provided a preview of what invasion of the home islands would entail. Since April 1 the Japanese had fought with a ferocity that mocked any notion that their will to resist was eroding. They had inflicted nearly 50,000 casualties on the invaders, many resulting from the first large-scale use of kamikazes. They also had dispatched the superbattleship *Yamato* on a suicide mission to Okinawa, where, after attacking American ships offshore, it was to plunge ashore to become a huge, doomed steel fortress. *Yamato* was sunk shortly after leaving port, but its mission symbolized Japan's willingness to sacrifice everything in an apparently hopeless cause.

The Japanese could be expected to defend their sacred homeland with even greater fervor, and kamikazes flying at short range promised to be even more devastating than at Okinawa. The Japanese had more than 2,000,000 troops in the home islands, were training millions of irregulars, and for some time had been conserving aircraft that might have been used to protect Japanese cities against American bombers.

Reports from Tokyo indicated that Japan meant to fight the war to a finish. On June 8 an imperial conference adopted "The Fundamental Policy to Be Followed Henceforth in the Conduct of the

War," which pledged to "prosecute the war to the bitter end in order to uphold the national polity, protect the imperial land, and accomplish the objectives for which we went to war." Truman had no reason to believe that the proclamation meant anything other than what it said.

Against this background, while fighting on Okinawa still continued, the President had his naval chief of staff, Adm. William D. Leahy, notify the Joint Chiefs of Staff (JCS) and the Secretaries of War and Navy that a meeting would be held at the White House on June 18. The night before the conference Truman wrote in his diary that "I have to decide Japanese strategy—shall we invade Japan proper or shall we bomb and blockade? That is my hardest decision to date. But I'll make it when I have all the facts."

Truman met with the chiefs at three-thirty in the afternoon. Present were Army Chief of Staff Gen. George C. Marshall, Army Air Force's Gen. Ira C. Eaker (sitting in for the Army Air Force's chief of staff, Henry H. Arnold, who was on an inspection tour of installations in the Pacific), Navy Chief of Staff Adm. Ernest J. King, Leahy (also a member of the JCS), Secretary of the Navy James Forrestal, Secretary of War Henry L. Stimson, and Assistant Secretary of War John J. McCloy. Truman opened the meeting, then asked Marshall for his views. Marshall was the dominant figure on the JCS. He was Truman's most trusted military adviser, as he had been President Franklin D. Roosevelt's.

Marshall reported that the chiefs, supported by the Pacific commanders Gen. Douglas MacArthur and Adm. Chester W. Nimitz, agreed that an invasion of Kyushu "appears to be the least costly worthwhile operation following Okinawa." Lodgment in Kyushu, he said, was necessary to make blockade and bombardment more effective and to serve as a staging area for the invasion of Japan's main island of Honshu. The chiefs recommended a target date of November 1 for the first phase, code-named Olympic, because delay would give the Japanese more time to prepare and because bad weather might postpone the

invasion "and hence the end of the war" for up to six months. Marshall said that in his opinion, Olympic was "the only course to pursue." The chiefs also proposed that Operation Cornet be launched against Honshu on March 1, 1946.

Leahy's memorandum calling the meeting had asked for casualty projections which that invasion might be expected to produce. Marshall stated that campaigns in the Pacific had been so diverse "it is considered wrong" to make total estimates. All he would say was that casualties during the first thirty days on Kyushu should not exceed those sustained in taking Luzon in the Philippines—31,000 men killed, wounded, or missing in action. "It is a grim fact," Marshall said, "that there is not an easy, bloodless way to victory in war." Leahy estimated a higher casualty rate similar to Okinawa, and King guessed somewhere in between.

King and Eaker, speaking for the Navy and the Army Air Forces respectively, endorsed Marshall's proposals. King said that he had become convinced that Kyushu was "the key to the success of any siege operations." He recommended that "we should do Kyushu now" and begin preparations for invading Honshu. Eaker "agreed completely" with Marshall. He said he had just received a message from Arnold also expressing "complete agreement." Air Force plans called for the use of forty groups of heavy bombers, which "could not be deployed without the use of airfields on Kyushu." Stimson and Forrestal concurred.

Truman summed up. He considered "the Kyushu plan all right from the military standpoint" and directed the chiefs to "go ahead with it." He said he "had hoped that there was a possibility of preventing an Okinawa from one end of Japan to the other," but "he was clear on the situation now" and was "quite sure" the chiefs should proceed with the plan. Just before the meeting adjourned, McCloy raised the possibility of avoiding an invasion by warning the Japanese that the United States would employ atomic weapons if there were no surrender. The ensuing discussion was inconclusive be-

cause the first test was a month away and no one could be sure the weapons would work.

In his memoirs Truman claimed that using atomic bombs prevented an invasion that would have cost 500,000 American lives. Other officials mentioned the same or even higher figures. Critics have assailed such statements as gross exaggerations designed to forestall scrutiny of Truman's real motives. They have given wide publicity to a report prepared by the Joint War Plans Committee (JWPC) for the chiefs' meeting with Truman. The committee estimated that the invasion of Kyushu, followed by that of Honshu, as the chiefs proposed, would cost approximately 40,000 dead, 150,000 wounded, and 3,500 missing in action for a total of 193,500 casualties.

That those responsible for a decision should exaggerate the consequences of alternatives is commonplace. Some who cite the JWPC report profess to see more sinister motives, insisting that such "low" casualty projections call into question the very idea that atomic bombs were used to avoid heavy losses. By discrediting that justification as a cover-up, they seek to bolster their contention that the bombs really were used to permit the employment of "atomic diplomacy" against the Soviet Union.

> *Myth holds that several of Truman's top military advisers begged him not to use the bomb. In fact, there is no persuasive evidence that any of them did.*

The notion that 193,500 anticipated casualties were too insignificant to have caused Truman to resort to atomic bombs might seem bizarre to anyone other than an academic, but let it pass. Those who have cited the JWPC report in countless op-ed pieces in newspapers and in magazine articles have created a myth by omitting key considerations: First, the report itself is studded with qualifications that casualties "are not subject to accurate estimate" and that the projection "is admittedly only an educated guess." Second, the figures never were conveyed to Truman. They were excised at high military echelons, which is why Marshall cited only estimates for the first thirty days on Kyushu. And indeed, subsequent Japanese troop buildups on Kyushu rendered the JWPC estimates totally irrelevant by the time the first atomic bomb was dropped.

Another myth that has attained wide attention is that at least several of Truman's top military advisers later informed him that using atomic bombs against Japan would be militarily unnecessary or immoral, or both. There is no persuasive evidence that any of them did so. None of the Joint Chiefs ever made such a claim, although one inventive author has tried to make it appear that Leahy did by braiding together several unrelated passages from the admiral's memoirs. Actually, two days after Hiroshima, Truman told aides that Leahy had "said up to the last that it wouldn't go off."

Neither MacArthur nor Nimitz ever communicated to Truman any change of mind about the need for invasion or expressed reservations about using the bombs. When first informed about their imminent use only days before Hiroshima, MacArthur responded with a lecture on the future of atomic warfare and even after Hiroshima strongly recommended that the invasion go forward. Nimitz, from whose jurisdiction the atomic strikes would be launched, was notified in early 1945. "This sounds fine," he told the courier, "but this is only February. Can't we get one sooner?" Nimitz later would join Air Force generals Carl D. Spaatz, Nathan Twining, and Curtis LeMay in recommending that a third bomb be dropped on Tokyo.

Only Dwight D. Eisenhower later claimed to have remonstrated against the use of the bomb. In his *Crusade in Europe*, published in 1948, he wrote that when Secretary Stimson informed him during the Potsdam Conference of plans to use the bomb, he replied that he hoped "we would never have to use such a thing against any enemy," because he did not want the United States to be the first to use such a weapon. He added, "My

views were merely personal and immediate reactions; they were not based on any analysis of the subject."

Eisenhower's recollections grew more colorful as the years went on. A later account of his meeting with Stimson had it taking place at Ike's headquarters in Frankfurt on the very day news arrived of the successful atomic test in New Mexico. "We'd had a nice evening at headquarters in Germany," he remembered. Then, after dinner, "Stimson got this cable saying that the bomb had been perfected and was ready to be dropped. The cable was in code… 'the lamb is born' or some damn thing like that." In this version Eisenhower claimed to have protested vehemently that "the Japanese were ready to surrender and it wasn't necessary to hit them with that awful thing." "Well," Eisenhower concluded, "the old gentleman got furious."

The best that can be said about Eisenhower's memory is that it had become flawed by the passage of time. Stimson was in Potsdam and Eisenhower in Frankfurt on July 16, when word came of the successful test. Aside from a brief conversation at a flag-raising ceremony in Berlin on July 20, the only other time they met was at Ike's headquarters on July 27. By then orders already had been sent to the Pacific to use the bombs if Japan had not yet surrendered. Notes made by one of Stimson's aides indicate that there was a discussion of atomic bombs, but there is no mention of any protest on Eisenhower's part. Even if there had been, two factors must be kept in mind. Eisenhower had commanded Allied forces in Europe, and his opinion on how close Japan was to surrender would have carried no special weight. More important, Stimson left for home immediately after the meeting and could not have personally conveyed Ike's sentiments to the President, who did not return to Washington until after Hiroshima.

On July 8 the Combined Intelligence Committee submitted to the American and British Combined Chiefs of Staff a report entitled "Estimate of the Enemy Situation." The committee predicted that as Japan's position continued to deteriorate, it might "make a serious effort to

use the USSR [then a neutral] as a mediator in ending the war." Tokyo also would put out "intermittent peace feelers" to "weaken the determination of the United Nations to fight to the bitter end, or to create inter-allied dissension." While the Japanese people would be willing to make large concessions to end the war, "For a surrender to be acceptable to the Japanese army, it would be necessary for the military leaders to believe that it would not entail discrediting warrior tradition and that it would permit the ultimate resurgence of a military Japan."

Small wonder that American officials remained unimpressed when Japan proceeded to do exactly what the committee predicted. On July 12 Japanese Foreign Minister Shigenori Togo instructed Ambassador Naotaki Sato in Moscow to inform the Soviets that the emperor wished to send a personal envoy, Prince Fuminaro Konoye, in an attempt "to restore peace with all possible speed." Although he realized Konoye could not reach Moscow before the Soviet leader Joseph Stalin and Foreign Minister V. M. Molotov left to attend a Big Three meeting scheduled to begin in Potsdam on the fifteenth, Togo sought to have negotiations begin as soon as they returned.

American officials had long since been able to read Japanese diplomatic traffic through a process known as the MAGIC intercepts. Army intelligence (G-2) prepared for General Marshall its interpretation of Togo's message the next day. The report listed several possible constructions, the most probable being that the Japanese "governing clique" was making a coordinated effort to "stave off defeat" through Soviet intervention and an "appeal to war weariness in the United States." The report added that Undersecretary of State Joseph C. Grew, who had spent ten years in Japan as ambassador, "agrees with these conclusions."

Some have claimed that Togo's overture to the Soviet Union, together with attempts by some minor Japanese officials in Switzerland and other neutral countries to get peace talks started through the Office of Strategic Services (OSS), constituted clear evidence that the Japanese were near surrender. Their sole prerequisite was retention of their sacred emperor, whose unique cultural/religious status within the Japanese polity they would not compromise. If only the United States had extended assurances about the emperor, according to this view, much bloodshed and the atomic bombs would have been unnecessary.

A careful reading of the MAGIC intercepts of subsequent exchanges between Togo and Sato provides no evidence that retention of the emperor was the sole obstacle to peace. What they show instead is that the Japanese Foreign Office was trying to cut a deal through the Soviet Union that would have permitted Japan to retain its political system and its prewar empire intact. Even the most lenient American official could not have countenanced such a settlement.

Togo on July 17 informed Sato that "we are not asking the Russians' mediation in *anything like unconditional surrender* [emphasis added]." During the following weeks Sato pleaded with his superiors to abandon hope of Soviet intercession and to approach the United States directly to find out what peace terms would be offered. "There is… no alternative but immediate unconditional surrender," he cabled on July 31, and he bluntly informed Togo that "your way of looking at things and the actual situation in the Eastern Area may be seen to be absolutely contradictory." The Foreign Ministry ignored his pleas and continued to seek Soviet help even after Hiroshima.

"Peace feelers" by Japanese officials abroad seemed no more promising from the American point of view. Although several of the consular personnel and military attachés engaged in these activities claimed important connections at home, none produced verification. Had the Japanese government sought only an assurance about the emperor, all it had to do was grant one of these men authority to begin talks through the OSS. Its failure to do so led American officials to assume that those involved were either well-meaning individuals acting alone or that they were being orchestrated by Tokyo. Grew characterized such "peace feelers" as "familiar weapons of psychological warfare" designed to "divide the Allies."

Some American officials, such as Stimson and Grew, nonetheless wanted to signal the Japanese that they might retain the emperorship in the form of a constitutional monarchy. Such an assurance might remove the last stumbling block to surrender, if not when it was issued, then later. Only an imperial rescript would bring about an orderly surrender, they argued, without which Japanese forces would fight to the last man regardless of what the government in Tokyo did. Besides, the emperor could serve as a stabilizing factor during the transition to peacetime.

There were many arguments against an American initiative. Some opposed retaining such an undemocratic institution on principle and because they feared it might later serve as a rallying point for future militarism. Should that happen, as one assistant Secretary of State put it, "those lives already spent will have been sacrificed in vain, and lives will be lost again in the future." Japanese hard-liners were certain to exploit an overture as evidence that losses sustained at Okinawa had weakened American resolve and to argue that continued resistance would bring further concessions. Stalin, who earlier had told an American envoy that he favored abolishing the emperorship because the ineffectual Hirohito might be succeeded by "an energetic and vigorous figure who could cause trouble," was just as certain to interpret it as a treacherous effort to end the war before the Soviets could share in the spoils.

There were domestic considerations as well. Roosevelt had announced the unconditional surrender policy in early 1943, and it since had become a slogan of the war. He also had advocated that peoples everywhere should have the right to choose their own form of government, and Truman had publicly pledged to carry out his predecessor's legacies. For him to have formally *guaranteed* continuance of the emperorship, as opposed to merely accepting it on American terms pending free elections, as he later did, would have constituted a blatant repudiation of his own promises.

Nor was that all. Regardless of the emperor's actual role in Japanese aggression, which is still debated, much wartime propaganda had encouraged

Americans to regard Hirohito as no less a war criminal than Adolf Hitler or Benito Mussolini. Although Truman said on several occasions that he had no objection to retaining the emperor, he understandably refused to make the first move. The ultimatum he issued from Potsdam on July 26 did not refer specifically to the emperorship. All it said was that occupation forces would be removed after "a peaceful and responsible" government had been established according to the "freely expressed will of the Japanese people." When the Japanese rejected the ultimatum rather than at last inquire whether they might retain the emperor, Truman permitted the plans for using the bombs to go forward.

Reliance on MAGIC intercepts and the "peace feelers" to gauge how near Japan was to surrender is misleading in any case. The army, not the Foreign Office, controlled the situation. Intercepts of Japanese military communications, designated ULTRA, provided no reason to believe the army was even considering surrender. Japanese Imperial Headquarters had correctly guessed that the next operation after Okinawa would be Kyushu and was making every effort to bolster its defenses there.

General Marshall reported on July 24 that there were "approximately 500,000 troops in Kyushu" and that more were on the way. ULTRA identified new units arriving almost daily. MacArthur's G-2 reported on July 29 that "this threatening development, if not checked, may grow to a point where we attack on a ratio of one (1) to one (1) which is not the recipe for victory." By the time the first atomic bomb fell, ULTRA indicated that there were 560,000 troops in southern Kyushu (the actual figure was closer to 900,000), and projections for November 1 placed the number at 680,000. A report, for medical purposes, of July 31 estimated that total battle and non-battle casualties might run as high as 394,859 *for the Kyushu operation alone*. This figure did not include those men expected to be killed outright, for obviously they would require no medical attention. Marshall regarded Japanese defenses as so formidable that even after Hiroshima he asked MacArthur to consider alternate landing sites and began contemplating the use of atomic bombs as tactical weapons to support the invasion.

By late July the casualty projection of 31,000 that Marshall had given Truman at the June 18 strategy meeting had become meaningless.

The thirty-day casualty projection of 31,000 Marshall had given Truman at the June 18 strategy meeting had become meaningless. It had been based on the assumption that the Japanese had about 350,000 defenders in Kyushu and that naval and air interdiction would preclude significant reinforcement. But the Japanese buildup since that time meant that the defenders would have nearly twice the number of troops available by "X-day" than earlier assumed. The assertion that apprehensions about casualties are insufficient to explain Truman's use of the bombs, therefore, cannot be taken seriously. On the contrary, as Winston Churchill wrote after a conversation with him at Potsdam, Truman was tormented by "the terrible responsibilities that rested upon him in regard to the unlimited effusions of American blood."

Some historians have argued that while the first bomb *might* have been required to achieve Japanese surrender, dropping the second constituted a needless barbarism. The record shows otherwise. American officials believed more

than one bomb would be necessary because they assumed Japanese hard-liners would minimize the first explosion or attempt to explain it away as some sort of natural catastrophe, precisely what they did. The Japanese minister of war, for instance, at first refused even to admit that the Hiroshima bomb was atomic. A few hours after Nagasaki he told the cabinet that "the Americans appeared to have one hundred atomic bombs… they could drop three per day. The next target might well be Tokyo."

Even after both bombs had fallen and Russia entered the war, Japanese militants insisted on such lenient peace terms that moderates knew there was no sense even transmitting them to the United States. Hirohito had to intervene personally on two occasions during the next few days to induce hard-liners to abandon their conditions and to accept the American stipulation that the emperor's authority "shall be subject to the Supreme Commander of the Allied Powers." That the militarists would have accepted such a settlement before the bombs is farfetched, to say the least.

Some writers have argued that the cumulative effects of battlefield defeats, conventional bombing, and naval blockade already had defeated Japan. Even without extending assurances about the emperor, all the United States had to do was wait. The most frequently cited basis for this contention is the *United States Strategic Bombing Survey,* published in 1946, which stated that Japan would have surrendered by November 1 "even if the atomic bombs had not been dropped, even if Russia had not entered the war, and even if no invasion had been planned or contemplated." Recent schol-

arship by the historian Robert P. Newman and others has demonstrated that the survey was "cooked" by those who prepared it to arrive at such a conclusion. No matter. This or any other document based on information available only after the war ended is irrelevant with regard to what Truman could have known at the time.

What often goes unremarked is that when the bombs were dropped, fighting was still going on in the Philippines, China, and elsewhere. Every day that the war continued thousands of prisoners of war had to live and die in abysmal conditions, and there were rumors that the Japanese intended to slaughter them if the homeland was invaded. Truman was Commander in Chief of the American armed forces, and he had a duty to the men under his command not shared by those sitting in moral judgment decades later. Available evidence points to the conclusion that he acted for the reason he said he did: to end a bloody war that would have become far bloodier had invasion proved necessary. One can only imagine what would have happened if tens of thousands of American boys had died or been wounded on Japanese soil and then it had become known that Truman had chosen not to use weapons that might have ended the war months sooner.

Robert James Maddox teaches American history at Pennsylvania State University. His Weapons for Victory: Hiroshima Fifty Years Later *is published by the University of Missouri Press (1995).*

From *American Heritage*, May/June 1995, pp. 70-74, 76-77 © 1995 by Forbes, Inc. Reprinted by permission of *American Heritage* magazine, a division of Forbes, Inc.

UNIT 5

From the Cold War to 2006

Unit Selections

Key Points to Consider

- What was the Marshall Plan and why did US policymakers believe it was necessary? How and why did the United States permit France to use recovery funds to finance its war in Indochina?

- When the war ended and the men came home, "Rosie the Riveter" was supposed to exchange her working clothes for an apron. What was wrong with this scenario?

- What was "The Spirit of '68?" Does John Judis make a convincing case for his claims about the impact the 1960s had on American culture?

- Discuss the American involvement in Vietnam as a part of the decades-long Cold War. What vital interests, if any, did the United States have in Vietnam?

- Why did the Vietnam War cause such dislocation at home and call into question American goals abroad?

- Discuss Bill Clinton's presidency. What did he accomplish, which of his objectives eluded him? How did his personal failings destroy his presidency?

- President George W. Bush had on his team a number of self-styled national security experts. How could they have been so utterly clueless about 9/11? Was it simply faulty intelligence, or was it their preoccupation with other matters such as Iraq?

Student Website

www.mhcls.com/online

Internet References

Further information regarding these websites may be found in this book's preface or online.

Coldwar
  http://www.cnn.com/SPECIALS/cold.war

The American Experience: Vietnam Online
  http://www.pbs.org/wgbh/amex/vietnam/

The Federal Web Locator
  http://www.infoctr.edu/fwl

Federalism: Relationship between Local and National Governments
  http://www.infidels.org/~nap/index.federalism.html

The Gallup Organization
  http://www.gallup.com/

STAT-USA
  http://www.stat-usa.gov/stat-usa.html

U.S. Department of State
  http://www.state.gov/

P resident Franklin D. Roosevelt sought to build a working relationship with Soviet leader Josef Stalin throughout World War II. Roosevelt believed that the wartime collaboration had to continue if a lasting peace were to be achieved. At the Yalta Conference of February 1945, a series of agreements were made that FDR hoped would provide the basis for continued cooperation. Subsequent disputes over interpretation of these agreements, particularly with regard to Poland, raised doubts in Roosevelt's mind that Stalin was acting in good faith. Roosevelt died on April 12, 1945, and there is no doubt that he was moving toward a "tougher" position during the last weeks of his life.

His successor, Harry S. Truman, assumed the presidency with little knowledge of Roosevelt's thinking. Truman had not been part of the administration's inner circle and had to rely on discussions with the advisers he inherited and his own reading of messages passed between FDR and the Soviets. Aside from an ugly encounter with Soviet Foreign Minister V. M. Molotov at the White House only eleven days after Roosevelt's death, Truman attempted to carry out what he believed were Roosevelt's intentions: be firm with the Soviets, but continue to seek accommodation. He came to believe that Molotov was trying to sabotage US-Soviet relations and that the best way to reach agreements was to negotiate directly with Stalin. This he did at the Potsdam Conference during the summer of 1945, and left the talks believing that Stalin was a hard bargainer but one who could be trusted.

Events during the late summer and early autumn eroded Truman's hopes that the Soviets genuinely wanted to get along. Disputes over Poland and other Eastern European countries, the treatment of postwar Germany, and a host of other issues finally persuaded Truman that it was time to stop "babying" the Soviets. A militant public speech by Stalin, which one American referred to as the "declaration of World War III," appeared to confirm this view. Increasingly hostile relations led to what became known as the "Cold War," during which each side increasingly came to regard the other as an enemy rather than merely an adversary.

Meanwhile the United States had to cope with the problems of reconversion to a peacetime economy. Demobilization of the armed forces proved especially vexing as the public clamored to have service men and women, stationed virtually all over the world, brought home and discharged as quickly as possible. When the administration seemed to be moving too slowly, the threat "no boats, no votes" became popular. Race riots, labor strife, and inflation also marred the postwar period.

The war had devastated the economic and social fabric of Europe. An unusually severe winter in 1946/1947 brought further dislocation, causing American officials to fear some European states might collapse into chaos with possible takeovers by Communists. To stave off this possibility the United States inaugurated what became as the "Marshall Plan." European nations were invited to confer together, then to submit to the United States estimates of what it would take to get them back on their feet. The Marshall Plan was a success on the whole, but as pointed out in "The Tangled Web: America, France, and Indochina, 1947–1950," an unanticipated consequence was that France began spending the funds it received to finance its war in Indochina. This marked the beginning of the American involvement in Vietnam.

A series of events during the late 1940s escalated the Cold War into a global conflict. Soviet conduct in Eastern and Southern Europe, and its first test explosion of an atomic bomb heightened the sense of peril. Revelations of domestic spying for the "Reds," and the Chinese Communist victory over our ally Chiang Kai-Shek seemed to confirm the notion that "they" were everywhere. Then, in 1950, a scant five years after the end of World War II, the United States found itself at war again. The North Korean invasion of the South in June of that year appeared to American leaders as a Soviet-inspired probe to test Western resolve. Failure to halt aggression there, many believed, would embolden the Soviets to strike elsewhere just as Hitler had done in the 1930s.

Domestically, the 1950s offered a mixed bag. Social critics denounced the conformity of those who plodded up the corporate latter, purchased tract homes that all looked alike, or who had no greater ambition than to sit

in front of their television sets every night. "From Rosie the Riveter to the Global Assembly Line" shows that much of the discontent that burst to the surface in the 1960s had roots in the previous decade, particularly with regard to women. At the same time, anti-New Deal conservatism began to grow, fueled in part by fears that Communism was taking over the world. "The Rise of Conservatism Since World War II" describes how this movement eventually took over the Republican party. "The Split-Level Years" provides a sketch of the decade that witnessed the emergence to stardom of Marilyn Monroe, Howdy Doody, and James Dean.

The period from the mid-1960s to the early 1970s was a turbulent era. Blacks and their allies mounted increasing protests against the pervasive racism in this country. They used a variety of tactics such as sit-ins at lunch counters and in buses, and organizing marches in various cities. Opposition to the Vietnam War grew and often spilled over into violence, many young people denounced the beliefs of their elders, and drug use skyrocketed. John B. Judis, in "The Spirit of 68," claims that during the 1960s the United States changed from a culture based on work, sacrifice, and deferred gratification to one that emphasized "consumption, lifestyle, and quality of life." He sees this passage as the result of what he calls "consumer capitalism."

In 1975 the long divisive war in Vietnam came to an end when North Vietnamese tanks entered Saigon. George C. Herring's "The Cold War in Vietnam" places that conflict within the decades-old struggle against the Soviet Michael Barone's "The American Century" plays off a famous 1941 editorial of the same name written by publisher Henry Luce. Victory in World War II and American leadership in the Cold War appeared to validate this prophecy. Then, as the Vietnam War dragged on and domestic problems mounted, "the elites lost confidence in America and the American people lost confidence in the elites." The nation appeared to regain its confidence in the last third of the century.

The final three essays in this volume have to do with presidential conduct. "Soft Power: Reagan the Dove" analyzes Ronald Reagan's performance during the final years of the Cold War. Once dismissed as an amiable dunce by many, Reagan's stature has risen since he left office in part because of his search for peace with the Soviet Union. "The Tragedy of Bill Clinton" treats this extremely talented but deeply flawed president. Gary Wills believes that it would have been better for him and for his programs had he resigned from office. "The Pros From Dover" points out that President George W. Bush surrounded himself with what should have been a crack team of national security experts. "So What Went Wrong?" asks author John Prados with regard to 9/11. He suggests that the Bush group was preoccupied with other agendas such as the preparation for war against Iraq.

The Tangled Web

AMERICA, FRANCE AND INDOCHINA 1947-50

*Sami Abouzahr untangles US policy towards France at
the time of the Marshall Plan and the war in Indochina.*

Sami Abouzahn

AMERICAN INVOLVEMENT in Vietnam is well-charted territory. The emotional impact of the war on a generation of Americans and Europeans, its continued impact on American politics and the office of the President, and the lessons it yields to contemporary American policy have made it an attractive subject for historians. The interpretation of the causes of US involvement in the war is one of the fault lines that separates orthodox and post-revisionist Cold War observers from revisionist or radical ones. To many, the Vietnam War defines their view of the nature of US international policy.

Given the complexity of an issue such as the Indochinese Wars, it seems unlikely that a clear pattern of cause and effect can exist. However, approaching the early stages of American commitment to the region from a European perspective provides an interesting angle on US policy towards Indochina. European issues in the early postwar period were of vital importance to the subsequent involvement of America in Indochina, first through France's struggle to keep its colony, and later in the Vietnamese civil war itself.

In particular, the Marshall Plan, which provided Western European countries with aid and a framework for European co-operation during the years 1947-50, played a vital role in the development of US policy towards Indochina. Washington needed French co-operation in the reconstruction of Western Europe along US policy lines, and this requirement made it impossible for the US to condemn or attempt to alter French policy in Indochina.

By 1949 the US had become committed to keeping Communism out of Southeast Asia within its own Cold War strategy. This pushed the US to pour money and aid into the hopeless French attempt to keep its imperial possession. By the time the French abandoned the effort after the catastrophic defeat at Dien Bien Phu (1954), the US was financing 80 per cent of the French war effort, and had committed itself financially, politically and emotionally to preventing a Communist victory there.

In 1945–47, the Soviet presence in Eastern Europe, the strength of Communist movements in France and Italy, and disagreements among the allies over the future of Germany suggested that it was in Europe that the United States would have to resist Communism.

During the first half of 1947, the Truman administration began defining its policy priorities, and the best means of strengthening the non-Communist areas of the world against the USSR. The State Department's head of long-term planning, George Kennan, in his Long Telegram from Moscow, defined the threat. The State Department and Kennan's Policy Planning Staff identified the means of resistance, which Secretary of State George Marshall made public in a landmark speech on June 5th, 1947.

The means of resistance consisted of a programme of aid centred on Western Europe that would remove the economic conditions that fostered Communism, help create a liberalised system of global trade, and provide the necessary foundations for rearma-

ment should such a step prove necessary. The aim was to create a stable and productive Europe, whose economic and security needs would be tied together by market forces and liberalised trade, and guided by strong supra-national organisations.

At this stage, Indochina itself was of little importance to the US State Department; France, however, was vital to the European recovery effort. The Marshall Plan depended on the effective revitalisation of its industry and the maximisation of its material and human resources. France was also politically pivotal as, without its co-operation, Western Europe would not allow the industrial reconstruction of Germany.

The State Department believed Europe could not become a strong and stable economic force without full German rehabilitation, and that the Plan would make German reconstruction possible by absorbing it into a wider framework of Western European co-operation. But if France was key to Europe's acceptance of German rehabilitation and reconstruction, the war in Indochina was a major obstacle jeopardising the achievement of these goals.

France had ruled the Indochinese states of Laos, Cambodia and Vietnam since the late nineteenth century. The oppressive nature of French rule helped sow the seeds of rebellion. In August 1945, the most prominent independence movement, the Viet Minh, seized power and proclaimed Vietnamese independence. Fighting between Vietnamese rebels and French forces escalated into full-blown conflict in December 1946.

During the Second World War, President Roosevelt and Ho Chi Minh had been united in their desire to end French colonial rule. Ho was convinced that the US would support his fight for the freedom they had battled for in 'their own heroic struggle for independence'. Roosevelt had been determined not to let the French take back the colony they had lost to the Japanese. Like many Americans imbued with a strong sense of anti-colonialism, he disliked the 'poor colonizers' who had 'badly managed' Indochina, and felt that it was time for the US to accept the forces of nationalism in Asia, while preserving access to the region's wealth of raw materials.

Within the climate of the emerging Cold War, however, the importance of rebuilding Western Europe overshadowed America's concern for nationalist movements. In 1946 and 1947, American priorities in the developing world began to shift from anti-colonialism to anti-Communism. Historians still debate whether or not Ho was fundamentally a nationalist or a Communist, in an effort to condemn or justify American policy. Certainly, neither officials in Saigon nor the Secretary of State himself could find links between Ho and the Kremlin. By 1949, however, the State Department had decided that the issue was irrelevant: 'all Stalinists in colonial areas are nationalists'. With their nationalist aims achieved, their objective 'necessarily becomes subordination of state to Commie [sic] purposes.'

The Indochinese war threatened the success of the Marshall Plan by damaging the French economy, and weakening the position of the government. The drain on France's resources inhibited the reconstruction effort and channelled funds out of the country. The effect on France's political stability threatened the continuation of the Marshall Plan, and the achievement of American aims with regard to Germany and Western Europe as a whole.

By 1949, the Indochinese war was the greatest financial burden on the French economy. By autumn of 1952 the war had cost the French one trillion French francs, twice the amount of Marshall Aid to France during the same period. Adding to this was the loss of Indochina as one of France's most profitable colonies from trade in rubber and pepper.

Franco-American co-operation required political stability and a strong, centrist government in Paris. This was a difficult requirement. The Fourth Republic was unstable, changing government twenty-seven times between 1946 and 1958. French politics was torn between so-

cialist and Communist groups on one side, and the supporters of Charles de Gaulle on the other. Both had strong public support and used the war in Indochina to attack the government. Public opinion was divided between its desire to maintain the glory associated with empire, and concern that the conflict in Indochina was unjustified and could not be won.

In the immediate postwar years, however, the empire seemed indispensable to French prestige. Imperial power was the link to France's more glorious past, and the key to moving beyond the humiliation of German occupation and Vichy collaboration. As France's most valuable colony, Indochina became representative of France's quest to regain world status. It also became representative of France's position on the rest of its colonies. As the Governor General in Algeria warned: negotiation with Ho Chi Minh meant negotiation in Madagascar and Algeria.

To France, the war therefore became a campaign of national status, and failure could send the country into turmoil. The US wanted France to seek a solution in Indochina that would cater to non-Communist nationalists and allow France to curb the drain on its economy. But Washington could not conceive 'setbacks to long-range interests of France which would not also be setbacks to our own'. And as the British reminded the Americans, it was not worth the risk, 'in winning Vietnam … to lose France'. Despite the United States' desire for France to seek a political solution in Indochina, Washington could not oppose French actions as long as Western European recovery remained its priority.

The importance of Indochina to French political stability was clear to Dean Acheson, when he became Secretary of State in 1949:

We have an immediate interest in maintaining in power a friendly French government to assist in the furtherance of our aims in Europe. This immediate and vital interest has in consequence taken precedence over active steps looking towards the realisation of our aims in Indochina.

The US did not provide direct assistance to the French in Indochina through the Marshall Plan, although aid was extended to a number of European dependencies, and to French colonies in North Africa. The exclusion of Indochina in this way reflected the uncertainty of America's position on the is-

sue, and Washington's reluctance to appear as a sponsor of colonialism.

To French prime minister Bidault, Marshall Aid was nevertheless a blessing that would allow him to 'avoid the abandonment of French positions'. European Recovery Program (ERP) appropriations let France finance the war in Indochina at the expense of domestic reconstruction projects favoured by the European Cooperation Administration, the body in charge of administering Marshall Aid. As George Kennan noted:

As we do not contribute ERP aid directly to Indochina, the charges are being passed on to us in Europe.

The lack of historical research on the direct or indirect use of ERP funds by France to pursue its policy in Indochina makes it difficult to assess Washington's attitude to the issue. Some historians of America's involvement in Vietnam believe that Washington was 'willing and happy to look the other way while France used Marshall Aid to fight a colonial war'. Their analysis coloured by subsequent events, they seem to imply that Washington made a decision to use Marshall Aid as a means of supporting France in Indochina without official commitment to French policy. There does not seem, however, to be sufficient evidence of such a decision in Washington.

It was clear, though, that it would have been difficult for France to accept the burden of war without the Marshall Plan. The billions of dollars France received from the US, therefore, indirectly helped finance the campaign in Indochina, while constituting a significant drain on the Marshall Plan. Resources that should have gone to projects stimulating the French economy were used to finance the war.

The emergence of hostility between the United States and the Soviet Union had brought with it profound changes to the way the US prioritised its foreign policy. Movements of national self-determination were now viewed through the prism of anti-Soviet concerns; Southeast Asian problems could no longer be evaluated without European issues. The Cold War shaped American policy into a global web of economic and security issues, tied together by fear of Communism and the urgency of securing access to markets and strategic commodities. Between 1947 and 1949, the State Department struggled to make sense of the contradictions posed by this view of the world. Indochina was particularly difficult.

Washington acknowledged the importance of the colony to France, and therefore to the ERP; it also accepted the danger of Communist power spreading through Southeast Asia. But most American policy-makers agreed that French attempts to regain Indochina by force were neither realistic nor a solution to the problem. The US favoured a solution whereby France would commit enough resources to the establishment of a viable Vietnamese state, able to maintain its own defences, while at the same time granting Vietnam the autonomy necessary to attract popular support away from Ho Chi Minh.

The 'Bao Dai solution' was France's attempt to satisfy American calls for Indochinese independence under French patronage. Under the March 8th, 1949, agreements, the ex-emperor Bao Dai headed the latest in a string of Vietnamese governments that were theoretically autonomous within the framework of the French Union. Under the agreements, Bao Dai would be given little real control over the country's foreign affairs, and other key areas of government. In the long run, however, Washington hoped the Bao Dai solution would provide the first step towards the creation of a non-communist, independent Vietnam.

American policy was contradictory, as the influential commentator Walter Lippmann explained in April 1950. The Bao Dai experiment could only succeed if the French promised future independence to Vietnam. But how could the French be persuaded to maintain their current expenditure and presence in Indochina if they were fighting to regain a colony they had promised to give away? It seemed clear to Lippmann that the French would withdraw if they had to accept such a compromise. America could not allow France to withdraw from Indochina, but nor could it sponsor a colonial war against a struggle for national independence. Lippmann could only conclude that 'we have as yet no adequate policy in Southeast Asia'.

This dilemma was the focus of a debate within the State Department, between those who favoured the prioritisation of European issues at the expense of a strong Southeast Asian policy, and those who felt that America's actions in Indochina could define America's status and position in the region for good or bad. The Southeast Asian Office felt that support for France was undermining US credibility in the region and that French action was doomed to failure. They wanted France to be given an ultimatum to grant sovereignty to Indochina or lose a portion of their aid appropriations. The European department, meanwhile, emphasised the priority of Western European recovery, and France's pivotal role in the ERP and rearmament programmes.

According to David Bruce, US Ambassador to France, aid to Indochina provided an opportunity for the US to resist Communist expansion into a vital strategic area, while at the same time helping to maintain the political stability in France necessary for the European recovery effort. Bruce's advice was taken and the Southeast Asian desk accused him of smothering repeated warnings to France to face up to its responsibilities by granting genuine autonomy to the Vietnamese government. As they saw it, the US was now faced with the choice of accepting Communism in Indochina or 'pouring treasure into a hopeless cause'. Kennan agreed: the United States was supporting the French in an undertaking that 'neither they, nor we, nor both of us together can win'.

Many historians have emphasised the importance to America of open markets around the world, both to counter Communist expansion, and to support the domestic economy. With this idea came the theory of 'capitalistbloc multilateralism' whereby Germany and Japan would be reconstructed into major industrial powers, linked to regional economic spheres of influence, and fuelled by Middle Eastern oil. The regional sphere of economic influence in Japan's case was Southeast Asia, the Far East's main source of petroleum, tin, quinine, copra, hard fibre and rubber.

While other historians have questioned the theory that economic considerations were the primary driving force in US policy, it remains clear that American interests lay, to some extent, in the creation of an open, multilateral trading system, and that the reconstruction of Japan and Germany was crucial.

Japanese economic health had always depended on its relationship to the Asian periphery. In 1947, this would have meant primary emphasis on a non-Communist China. When this ceased to be a possibility in 1949, Kennan became concerned about 'the terrific problem of how the Japanese are going to get along [without Chinese trade] unless they again reopen some sort of empire towards the south … clearly we have got … to achieve opening up of trade possibilities … for Japan'.

Keeping an open access to Southeast Asia would allow the region to support the Western European and Japanese economies with commodities and raw materials, and provide a market for processed goods. Southeast Asia thus became economically as well as politically significant to the Marshall Plan. By 1949 production levels in Western Europe were above prewar levels, and dollar imbalances between Western Europe and America had become the main concern of the Marshall planners. With appropriations set to end in 1952, the United States and the Marshall Plan participants searched for ways to overcome Western Europe's balance of trade deficit with the dollar area.

The Communist victory in China and worsening crises in Indochina, Burma and Malaya highlighted the urgency of strengthening the region against Communism. During the summer of 1950, the Korean War and China's intervention against the American-led UN troops, seemed to highlight the Far East as the major Cold War battleground, with Southeast Asia the key to victory.

Southeast Asia was now seen as a vital crossroads of communications linking the non-Communist areas of India, Japan and Australia. According to the National Security Council, Indochina was the region's 'most strategically important' country, whose fall would inevitably lead to the fall of the rest of Southeast Asia. This would shift the frontline of the free world back to the Philippines, destabilise Japan's economy, and threaten the security of Southern Asia and even Australia. The loss of Southeast Asia would jeopardise American stockpiling projects. Communist control of the region would allow China to alleviate its food shortages, and help Soviet importing of key raw materials. As this early expression of the domino theory showed, France could not be allowed to withdraw from Indochina.

By 1950, State Department officials had accepted the role of Ho Chi Minh as a Communist pawn. Washington officials endeavoured to convince Congress of the urgency of the situation, and the role of the Soviets in guiding the Viet Minh leader to defeat the forces of the free world. In the words of Dean Rusk, Assistant Secretary of State for Far Eastern Affairs, this was not an 'ordinary civil war, against colonialism', it was:

> A civil war which has been in effect captured by the Politburo and, beside, has been turned into a tool of the Politburo …. It is part of an international war and … I don't think we can look at it in simple terms of liberal democratic revolution.

With no alternative to France's Bao Dai solution, the United States appeared to be faced with the choice of Communism in Indochina, or some form of neo-colonialism, and it preferred the latter. In February 1950, the US State Department made public its decision to send a 'special mission' to Southeast Asia to review the possibilities of extending aid to countries in the region. Indochina was given primary importance among the Southeast Asian countries because of its geostrategic position, and the instability of conditions in Vietnam. The mission's recommendations in June assigned $23.5 million to Indochina, with Indonesia receiving the next highest amount of aid, with $14.5 million. The Foreign Assistance Act of June 1950 formed the basis of the aid programme to Southeast Asia.

According to American propaganda, the economic programme aimed to show the people of Indochina 'in village terms, that freedom's ways are the best answer'. In this way, the local governments could combat the Communists who had 'assumed the familiar but effective pose of nationalists fighting for freedom and for economic well-being'.

The outbreak of the Korean War had a significant impact on American attitudes, and reinforced Washington's decision to send aid to the French in Indochina. To President Truman, the 'Russian feeler in Korea is an exact imitation of Japan in Manchuria; Hitler in the Rhineland and Mussolini in Ethiopia'. As the President told prime minister Attlee, 'the problem we were facing was part of a pattern. After Korea, it would be Indochina, then Hong Kong, then Malaya'. For policy-makers who were 'wondering whether this is the beginning of World War III', the North Korean invasion seemed to forecast the emergence of the Far East as the Cold War battleground. On June 27th, two days after the North Koreans moved across the 38th Parallel, Truman called for the protection of the Taiwan straits from Communist invasion, and directed an acceleration of aid to Indochina.

Events in Korea brought the Marshall Plan to a premature conclusion, and heralded a shift from economic to military assistance. The transition from reconstruction to rearmament increased the importance of French cooperation on German reintegration into the military and economic framework of Western Europe. The Korean War and the issue of rearmament tied Western Europe even more closely to US security priorities, and further broke down American distinctions of nationalism and Communism in Indochina.

American attitudes towards Indochina centred on the State Department's inability to reconcile diverging priorities in its foreign policy. On the one hand, Washington sought to encourage non-Communist Asian nationalism within a global framework of economic multilateralism and security that would allow the region to support the core economies of the Far East and Western Europe. At the same time, however, America needed French co-operation to reconstruct a secure, integrated Western Europe that would encompass German recovery and participate in America's conception of the global economy. Washington had to recognise that France's empire was vital to its self-perceived status as a world power, and the achievement of US aims in Western Europe required the acceptance and support of French policy.

With the development of the Marshall Plan, Indochinese policy was evaluated by its relationship with Western European recovery. The importance of Indochina to France precluded any attempt by Washington to press for an alternative solution to Vietnamese nationalism. As an unintended consequence of the Marshall Plan, therefore, France was able to fight a hopeless war in Indochina, and enlist American support and eventual commitment to French victory.

Sami Abouzahr is an international manager with HSBC. This article is based on his undergraduate dissertation, which was joint winner of the Royal Historical Society/History Today Undergraduate Dissertation of the Year, 2004.

From Rosie the Riveter to the Global Assembly Line

American Women on the World Stage

Leila J. Rupp

In 1939, shortly after the outbreak of war in Europe, American pacifist and feminist Emily Greene Balch wrote from Geneva to colleagues in the Women's International League for Peace and Freedom (WILPF) about their plight. "Ringed around by a wall of violence, we draw closer together" (1). It was a hopeful statement about organizational and gender solidarity in the face of impending doom, but it can perhaps also serve as a foreshadowing of the ways that, in the more than half century since the end of World War II, women across the continents have at times been able to make connections across national differences to confront common problems, including gendered violence. From a twenty-first century vantage point, we can look back over the decades and see how intimately connected the changes in American women's lives have been with events unfolding on the world stage and how little of what happens to women in the United States is unconnected to larger global forces.

The magnitude of the worldwide conflict that ended in 1945 with the surrender of Germany and Japan, the liberation of the concentration camps, and the unleashing of the atomic bomb had brought American women, like women elsewhere, into areas of the labor force previously reserved for men. Like Rosie the Riveter, the symbol of American women patriotically taking up factory jobs previously reserved for men, women in all of the combatant countries went to work as men left to fight. Women even made inroads into the armed forces, although not, in the United States, as combatants. Spared the devastation of bombed-out cities and the massive losses suffered by the peoples of Europe and Asia, Americans set about reestablishing "normal life," although in a vastly reconfigured global context. Men returning home sought both their jobs and the comforts of a wife at home, if they could afford it. Although many women who had moved from poorly paid service jobs into more financially rewarding factory jobs preferred to remain, employers moved to restore the prewar sexual division of labor. In fact, even as increasing numbers of white middle-class women were entering the paid labor force in the postwar years, the goal of returning women to the home became a hallmark of American life, in contrast to the Soviet-bloc countries, where women were encouraged to combine paid work and motherhood. Equally striking was the fact that the American occupation authorities in both Germany and Japan, assuming that women could serve as the foundation of democratic governments, insisted that those countries' new constitutions grant women equal rights, while the Equal Rights Amendment at home languished in congressional committees.

In the context of the Cold War that followed closely on the heels of the end of hostilities, differences between the Soviet employment of women, especially in factory labor, and American domesticity took on political and diplomatic importance. Symbolic of this cultural clash was the famous "kitchen debate" between U.S. vice president Richard Nixon and Soviet premier Nikita Khrushchev in 1959 at the opening of the American National Exhibition in Moscow. Nixon praised capitalism for providing U.S. housewives with an array of consumer goods and the choice of brands of appliances while Khrushchev, although also touting domesticity, boasted about the productivity of Soviet women workers. It was a debate that laid bare the ideological and economic differences between the two systems as they competed for dominance in the world system.

One way that rivalry played out was in competition for the hearts and minds of what carne to be known as the "Third World." Just as the two superpowers raced to try to make over in their own image countries newly inde-

Image courtesy of the National Archives and Records Administration.

During World War II, women, like "Rosie the Riveter," could do a man's work while maintaining their femininity.

threatened by Soviet expansion and Chinese revolution without and Communist subversion within, Americans, according to the conventional story, clung to home and family life. White men, taking advantage when they could of mortgages and college educations made possible by the G.I. Bill, became "organization men" loyal to their corporate employers and took up "do-it-yourself" projects in their suburban homes on the weekends. White women stayed home in the expanding suburbs, giving birth to more children and drinking coffee with their neighbors. Such prosperity depended on U.S. domination of the world economy in the aftermath of the war. Suburban mothers chastised children reluctant to clean their plates to "think of the starving children in Europe;" with European economic recovery, the line shifted to the starving children in Africa. When Michael Harrington published *The Other America* in 1962, the fact that poverty existed at home came as something of a shock to those not experiencing deprivation themselves. A decade later, the revelation of the "feminization of poverty" both in the United States and globally called attention to the economic impact of discrimination against women, the sexual division of labor, the wage gap between women and men, and women's responsibility for rearing children.

Just as the reality of poverty underlay American prosperity in the 1950s, so too the domesticity and tranquility of the 1950s was far more apparent than real. In the burgeoning civil rights movement, African American women and men organized their communities and launched determined protests against segregation and discrimination, taking heart from national liberation movements in Africa and elsewhere. From the group of mostly mothers whose challenge to the segregated school system of Topeka, Kansas, contributed to the Supreme Court decision declaring segregation inherently unequal in *Brown* v. *Board of Education* (1954) to Rosa Parks, who refused to move to the back of the bus in 1955 and helped launch the Montgomery bus boycott, black women played critical roles in calling the attention of the country and the world to the second-class status of African Americans. In the West, Mexican American working-class women and men also took up civic activism on the local level, like African Americans inspired by nationalist movements in the Third World. Within the beleaguered union movement, in the peace movement, in the remnants of the women's movement, in the vilified Communist Party, in the homophile movement that sought acceptance for lesbian and gay Americans, women fought for social change despite the proclaimed contentment of the era.

The recognition that a great deal was going on beneath the surface calm of the 1950s goes a long way toward helping us understand the origins of the explosive decade of the 1960s. The social protest movements of the 1960s had their roots in the tensions and contradictions of the 1950s. But they also occurred in a global context, as national liberation movements increasingly freed former colonies from the grip of imperialism. Transnational con-

pendent of colonial rule so, too, transnational women's organizations from each bloc sought to bring developing countries into their fold. The new Women's International Democratic Federation (WIDF), launched out of the Communist-led resistance movements of World War II and dominated by the Soviet Union, challenged the traditiona] transnational women's organizations such as the International Council of Women, the International Alliance of Women, and the WILPF and competed with them at the United Nations over who really represented the world's women. The older organizations, dedicated to women's rights and peace, had long sought to make their membership "truly global" but remained dominated in terms of membership and leadership by women from western and northern Europe and the United States. The WIDF, in contrast, although founded in Paris and supported from the Soviet Union, won adherents throughout the Third World through its commitment to "win and defend national independence and democratic freedoms, eliminate apartheid, racial discrimination and fascism" (2). In the United States, organizations associated with the WIDF found themselves accused of Communist affiliations in the postwar crackdown.

The decade of the 1950s has indeed gone down in American history as Nixon depicted it to Khrushchev—a period of prosperity, conformity, domesticity, and suburbanization. Retreating from the disruptions of war and nections can be glimpsed in Martin Luther King Jr.'s embrace of Gandhian nonviolence, while Gandhi himself used tactics in the Indian struggle for independence inspired by militant British women fighting for the right to vote. Or in the anthem of the civil rights movement, "We Shall Overcome," with origins in the "sorrow songs" of slaves brought from. Africa, then sung by striking tobacco workers in the 1940s, and then sung in Arabic by Palestinians, in Spanish by members of the United Farmworkers, and, in a sense going home, in the South African antiapartheid movement.

Social upheavals occurring across the globe made the year 1968 synonymous with struggles for social justice. It was in 1968, when French students threw up barricades in the Left Bank quarter and protesting Mexican students were gunned down by the government, that a group of feminists gathered in Atlantic City to protest the objectification of women in the Miss America Pageant. In what has become a legend in the history of the resurgence of feminism—and what gave rise to the mistaken notion that feminists burned their bras—feminists dumped bras, corsets, and hair rollers into a "freedom trash can" and crowned a sheep Miss America.

The turmoil of the 1960s sparked renewed activism by women all around the globe, although feminist movements almost everywhere had roots reaching back to earlier struggles by women for education, civil and political rights, employment opportunities, and other legal and social changes. Sometimes, as in the United States, women in male-dominated social justice movements began to adapt class or national or racial/ethnic critiques to their own situation as women, particularly if they found themselves pushed aside or relegated to second-class citizenship after fighting alongside men for freedom and justice. Although women's movements took on different shapes in various parts of the world—liberal feminism calling for the extension of the rights of men to women, socialist feminism advocating revolutionary change, radical feminism challenging the devaluing of women and the exploitation of women's sexuality and reproductive capacity—feminist movements growing from indigenous roots and influenced as well by a transnational exchange of ideas and strategies flourished. Feminism as a world view emphasizing the equal worth of women and men, a recognition of male privilege, an understanding of the ways that gender intersects with race, class, ethnicity, sexuality, ability, and other forms of difference, and a commitment to work for social justice found footholds everywhere. In different contexts, women organized and fought for access to education and employment, for control of their bodies, and against various forms of violence against women, including in wartime.

In the United States, African American, Latina, Asian American, and Arab American women, often angered by the white, middle-class assumptions of women's movement groups, connected their struggles to those of women in the Third World, taking on the term "Third World women" to describe themselves. Under the auspices of the United Nations, which included the principle of equality between women and men in its charter from its founding, women from across the globe came together in a series of conferences. A meeting in celebration of International Women's Year in Mexico City in 1975 gave rise to the UN's "Decade for Women," marked by a gathering in Copenhagen in 1980, and Nairobi in 1985, followed up by a fourth international conference in Beijing in 1995. From the beginning, conflicts erupted among women. In Mexico City, Domitila Barrios de Chungara, representing an organization of Bolivian tin miners' wives, expressed shock at discussions of such issues as prostitution, lesbianism, and male abuse of women, arguing that women in her group sought to work with men to change the system so that both women and men would have the right to live, work, and organize. In these meetings, the diverse lives of women came to light and made clear the need to broaden the definition of what counted as a "women's issue."

These international meetings brought together not only official government representatives but, more productively, auxiliary forums of nongovernmental organizations. There debates about the impact of development policies, poverty, welfare systems, population policies, imperialism, and national liberation movements on women raised consciousness among women in the United States and other industrialized nations. Women from the global South voiced criticism of the narrowly defined interpretation of gender interests often articulated by women from the affluent North in a way that resonated with the critiques of women of color in the United States. What difference does the "glass ceiling" that keeps U.S. women from reaching the top rungs of their professions make to women who have no right to land and cannot feed their families? And perhaps more troubling, who is making the clothing worn by professional women in the industrialized countries, who is cleaning their houses and caring for their children, and under what conditions? The United Nations nongovernmental gatherings helped to articulate the multiple ways that the experiences of women of different nations were intertwined, from Asian and Latin American women producing clothing and electronic products on the global assembly line for purchase by U.S. women to the international sex trade that makes prostitution and the "entertainment industry" a major employer of women in a number of Asian countries, to the immigration of women from the Philippines, Mexico, and Latin America to work in U.S. and European homes as maids and nannies while forced to leave behind their own children.

As the twentieth century drew to a close and the Cold War ended, the world had come a long way from the "kitchen debate" of 1959. By the dawn of the new millennium, the divisions between the global North and South had superceded the old political rivalries, and the question of globalization's impact on women came to the fore. What happens to women's traditional work in agriculture or trade when international lending agencies require a country to gear its economy for the world market? Where does "surplus" female labor go? Connecting such questions to the employment of women in sweatshops, as domestics, and in the sex tourism industry makes clear the impact of large-scale forces on women's lives and the ties that bind women in developing countries to those in wealthy industrialized ones like the United States. The pressing questions for women all around the world are what kinds of work they do, how much they are paid, what kinds of opportunities are open to them, who does the housework and takes care of the children, how much control they have over their sexuality and reproductive capacity, who makes decisions for the family and nation. These are the questions with which transnational feminism grapples. All point to the interconnections of gender, class, race, ethnicity, sexuality, ability, and nation. In a world in which we are still, as Emily Greene Balch lamented, "ringed around by a wall of violence," hope lies in the connections American women can make with each other and with women around the globe.

Endnotes

1. Emily Greene Balch to International Executive Meeting, November 21, 1939, WILPF papers, reel 4.
2. WIDF Constitution, quoted in Cheryl Johnson-Odim and Nina Emma Mba, *For Women and the Nation: Funmilayo Ransome-Kuti of Nigeria* (Urbana, IL: University of Illinois Press, 1997), 137.

Sources

Dublin, Thomas and Kathryn Kish Sklar. "Women and Social Movements in the United States, 1775–2000."< http://www.womhist.binghamton.edu.> Website on the history of women's involvement in a variety of forms of activism throughout U.S. history.

Evans, Sara M. *Tidal Wave: How Women Changed America at Century's End*. New York: Free Press, 2003. An examination of the U.S. women's movement that emphasizes the diversity of participants, the geographical spread of activism, and the continuity of struggle.

Ferree, Myra Marx and Beth B. Hess. *Controversy and Coalition: The New Feminist Movement Across Four Decades of Change*. 3rd edition. New York: Routledge, 2000. A comprehensive sociological survey of the U.S. women's movement, tracing its development over time and its changing structure and strategies.

Freedman, Estelle B. *No Turning Back: The History of Feminism and the Future of Women*. New York: Ballantine Books, 2002. An analysis of the women's movement in global perspective, surveying the emergence of feminist movements, their varied approaches to work, family, sexuality, politics, and creativity, and the diversity of views and participants that ensures the continuation of feminist struggle.

Jayawardena, Kumari. *Feminism and Nationalism in the Third World*. London: Zed, 1986. A classic work on the history of women's political struggles in Asia and the Middle East since the late nineteenth century, arguing that feminism has indigenous roots throughout the Third World.

Johnson-Odim, Cheryl and Nina Emma Mba. *For Women and the Nation: Funmilayo Ransome-Kuti of Nigeria*. Urbana, IL: University of Illinois Press, 1997. A biography of a Nigerian activist involved with women's issues in her own country and transnationally through the Women's International Democratic Federation.

May, Elaine Tyler. *Homeward Bound: American Families in the Cold War Era*. New York: Basic Books, 1988. An analysis of the ways that the Cold War affected all aspects of American women's lives in the 1950s, from sexuality and reproduction to consumerism and family life.

Meyerowitz, Joanne, ed. *Not June Cleaver: Women and Gender in Postwar America, 1945–1960*. Philadelphia: Temple University Press, 1994. A collection of essays on diverse women's activities in the United States in the 1950s that explodes the myth of domesticity and contentment.

Miller, Francesca. *Latin American Women and the Search for Social Justice*. Hanover, NH: University Press of New England, 1991. A history of women's organizing in Latin America that includes Latin American women's involvement in international women's movements.

Naples, Nancy A. and Manisha Desai, eds. *Women's Activism and Globalization: Linking Local Struggles and Transnational Politics*. New York: Routlege, 2002. A collection of essays dealing with contemporary women's activism in opposition to the consequences of globalization.

Richardson, Laurel, Verta Taylor, and Nancy Whittier, eds. *Feminist Frontiers*. 6th ed. New York: McGraw-Hill, 2004. A women's studies text that includes articles detailing diverse women's experiences with appearance, socialization, work, family life, sexuality, reproduction, violence, politics, and the women's movement.

Rosen, Ruth. *The World Split Open: How the Modern Women's Movement Changed America*. New York: Viking, 2000. A comprehensive study, based on oral histories and archival research, of the women's movement and its impact on American society.

Rupp, Leila J. *Worlds of Women: The Making of an International Women's Movement*. Princeton, NJ: Princeton University Press, 1997. A history of the first wave of transnational organizing among women from the 1880s to 1945, focusing on the International Council of Women, the International Alliance of Women, and the Women's International League for Peace and Freedom.

Smith, Bonnie G., ed. *Global Feminisms Since 1945*. London: Routledge, 2000. A collection of essays focusing on women's movements in different parts of the world.

United Nations Division for the Advancement of Women. *Women Go Global: The United Nations and the International Women's Movement, 1945–2000*. CD-ROM. United Nations, 2000. An interactive CD-ROM on the events that have been shaping the international agenda for women's equality since the founding of the UN.

Leila J. Rupp is a professor and chair of Women's Studies at the University of California, Santa Barbara. A historian by training, her teaching and research focus on sexuality and women's movements. She is coauthor with Vena Taylor of *Drag Queens at the 801 Cabaret* (2003) and *Survival in the Doldrums: The American Women's Rights Movement, 1945 to the 1960s* (1987) and author of *A Desired Past: A Short History of Same-Sex Sexuality in America* (1999), *Worlds of Women: The Making of an International Women's Movement* (1997), and *Mobilizing Women for War: German and American Propaganda, 1939–1945* (1978). She is also completing an eight-year term as editor of *The Journal of Women's History*.

The Split-Level Years

1950–1960: Elvis, Howdy Doody time, McDonald's and the rumblings of rebellion

By Henry Allen
Washington Post Staff Writer

Smell it, smell it all, smell the sour cities you leave behind in bosomy cars that smell of dusty sunlight and thump over Eisenhower's concrete interstate highways whose joints ooze tar that smells like industrial licorice till you arrive in a suburb smelling of insecticide and freshly cut grass outside identical houses full of the scents of postwar America: baked air hovering over the TV set; the mucilage on stickers for your art-appreciation course—"Mona Lisa," "American Gothic"...; the cozy stink of cigarette smoke freshened by Air-Wick deodorizer amid sweet pine paneling whose knots watch over you like the loving eyes of Disney forest creatures.

How sweet and new it all is, this incense of mid-century, this strange sense of coziness and infinite possibility at the same time.

Don't worry, Ike seems to say as he smiles and hits another tee shot. You light another Camel, knowing that "It's a psychological fact: pleasure helps your disposition: For more pure pleasure— have a CAMEL."

There's a cartoon fullness to things. Everybody is somebody. Everything is possible. Hence a cushiony give in the national psyche, a pleasant ache that feels like nostalgia dispensed by a spray can. You believe in the future, be it a perfect marriage, racial integration, commuting via your personal autogiro, Formica countertops, or a day coming soon when everybody will be sincere and

mature. ("Sincerity" and "maturity" are major virtues.)

Ignore the viruses of dread that float through family rooms: the hydrogen bomb erupting from the South Pacific like a cancerous jellyfish the size of God; or the evil Sen. Joseph McCarthy and the evil Commies he never catches one of, not one, though he does manage to strew the land with damaged lives and the liberal tic of anti-anti-communism; or Sputnik, the first satellite, built by Russian slave labor, no doubt, while our top scientists were developing the Princess phone, 3-D movies and boomerang-shaped coffee tables.

Ignore Marilyn Monroe saying: What good is it being Marilyn Monroe? Why can't I just be an ordinary woman?... Oh, why do things have to work out so rotten? And ignore the Korean War, which is nothing but ugly except for the embroidered silk dragon jackets the soldiers bring back. Ignore the newspaper pictures of racists with faces like wet-combed hand-grenades, screaming at Martin Luther King's boycotters and schoolchildren who will overcome... people whose isolation and invisibility in this white society are incalculable....

Progress will take care of everything.

Amid the Ford Country Squire station wagons and slate roofs, wealthier homeowners boast that neighborhood covenants still keep out Jews and Negroes. They offer you highballs and cigarettes. They show you black-and-white photo-

graphs of themselves waving from the rail of the Queen Elizabeth. They turn on lights till their houses blaze like cruise ships. What lonely darkness are they keeping off? Do they know their time has gone?

Meanwhile, amid the tract housing and developments, the genius of William Levitt and Henry Kaiser creates the loneliness of growing up in your own bedroom, in your own house where the green grass grows all around. It takes some getting used to, but do you really want to go back to the apartment with three kids to a bedroom and Nana mumbling over the cabbage? You know your future is here. You wish you knew what it held.

"Children, your father's home!" Mom yells.

A father's Florsheim Imperials are heard. A Dobbs center-dent fedora is seen, with a jaunty trout-fly feather on the grosgrain band. Dad exudes the tired authority of cigarette smoke and Arrid underarm deodorant cream. His knuckles whiten on a Christmas-present attaché case.

"Can't you kids get up off your duffs and do something instead of sitting there watching..."

"Hey, Dad's home."

"...'Howdy Doody,' a little children's show?"

"There's nothing else on, Dad."

Dad shouts over his shoulder: "Doris! You have any chores for these kids?"

"No, hon, everything's hunky-dory. You hungry?"

"Hell, yes, I'm hungry."

"Be dinner soon's I do the limas."

Sighing as if he has made a huge decision, Dad walks into the kitchen. He cracks ice for a drink. "The kids," he says. "It's like I'm not even here."

"Well, it's like I always am," she says. "They're scared of you, but they take me for granted."

"Make you a drink?"

"Not too big, now."

His face struggles toward some home truth, but doesn't find it. "Aw, Doris," he says. "Turn off the stove and let's go to the Roma for veal scaloppine. Please. Just the two of us."

"I have to drop Tommy at Boy Scouts, and then Kitty Kennard is doing her slide show at L'Esprit Francais. Forgive me?"

Doris and Tom Sr. are only trying to live by what their parents taught them—manliness, graciousness, a day's work, good posture—and pass it on to their children. The problem is, they don't quite believe it themselves, anymore, but they have to teach their kids something.

Should they really confess their emptiness and bad faith instead? Should the children feel betrayed by parents who are only trying to do the best they know how?

H OW SQUALID. LETS LEAVE ALL this behind. It's a symptom, not a cause, a failure where success is what you see on "Ozzie & Harriet" and all the other shows about breakfast-nook families where no one is taken for granted and everyone says hello.

Hi, Rick. Hi, Pop. Hi, Dave. Good morning, Mom.

Dad's a bit of a bumbler, and what won't those darn kids think of next! Nevertheless, perfection is attainable. How smug one feels to know this. How inadequate one feels to know one hasn't attained it yet, oneself, but one can put on a long-playing record of the perfect Ella Fitzgerald singing the Jerome Kern songbook perfectly.

Some of the young folks seem to have a hard time adjusting.

If I could have just one day when I wasn't all confused.... If I felt I belonged someplace.

—James Dean as the anguished son in "Rebel Without a Cause"

Be part of progress like everybody else—the everybody you see on television and in Life magazine. Here's the equation: If you're just like everybody, then you're somebody.

The way to be somebody is to buy something that makes you like everybody else who's bought the same thing—Ford owners reading their Ford Times, Parliament smokers joined in aromatic sophistication. Remember: Consumption is a moral good. Madison Avenue admen are cultural heroes, with cool slang like 'Let's run it up the flagpole and see who salutes.'

Look at all the college kids stuffing themselves into phone booths and Volkswagens. And a lovely girl whose picture appears in Life next to the comment: "She has forgotten all about emancipation and equality. To belong is her happiness." And Mary Ann Cuff, a regular among the teen dancers who appear on Dick Clark's "American Bandstand": "What it is we all want is to get married and live on the same street in new houses. We'll call it Bandstand Avenue."

Ignore the hipsters and intellectuals sneering at Bandstand Avenue, and at the triumphalism of tailfins, Time magazine and pointy bras whose tips sort of crinkle under sweaters. Fun can be made of bomb shelters stocked with Franco-American canned spaghetti and Reader's Digest Condensed Books.

J.D. Salinger can appeal to adolescent self-righteousness by railing against phonies in "The Catcher in the Rye." Scorn can be heaped on Ray Kroc, who runs those new McDonald's drive-ins; he writes a memo: "We cannot trust some people who are non-conformist. The organization cannot trust the individual, the individual must trust the organization."

And certainly critics can make a living by attacking the men in the gray flannel suits, the organization men, the lonely crowd of ulcer-proud hidden persuaders bringing us ads where women in crinoline-fluffed shirtwaists invite us to

buy into the carefree new patio-perfect world of hyper-power Torqueflite Cyclamatic Teletouch Whatever that gives you more pleasure. (Repeat thru fade-out: MORE PLEASURE! MORE PLEASURE! MORE PLEASURE!)

W HICH DOES NOT MEAN SEX, boys and girls. Sex is for Europeans, people in movies (off-screen) and juvenile delinquents. White people believe that colored people have sex lives of unimaginable ecstasy and variety. Italian kids drive surly Mercurys to the Jersey Shore, spread blankets and neck in Acecombed 1953 look-at-me majesty beneath the outraged stares of moms in bathing suits with little skirts… prefiguring the erotic insolence of Elvis, Marilyn, James Dean, and the secret subtext of Annette on "The Mickey Mouse Club."

Otherwise, sex, the lonely vandal, is safe in the stewardship of middle-class women who manage the courtship rituals of dating, going steady, pinning and engagement, and aren't very interested in sex anyway, according to the Kinsey Report on Women. Life magazine sums it up: "Woman is the placid gender, the female guppy swimming all unconcerned and wishing she could get a few minutes off to herself, while the male guppy pursues her with his unrelenting courtship.... Half or more of all women… seldom dream or daydream about sex; they consider the human body to be, if anything, rather repulsive."

Maybe men make cracks about women's driving and spending, and they want dinner served on time, but Life has learned that the unrelenting guppy is becoming "the new American domesticated male" who is "baby tender, dishwasher, cook, repairman.... Some even go to baby-care classes, learn to wrap a neat diaper and to bubble Junior deftly. With father available as sitter, wives can have their hair done, shop, go to club meetings." Lawn mowing gives him "a sense of power and a gadget to tinker with."

What happened to the red-blooded, can-do, all-American male? And female?

Well, sexed women and powerful men are a threat. We don't need them now. Passion has been replaced by love, adventure by fun. If you want sex, watch Elvis Presley on "The Ed Sullivan Show," even if Ed refuses to show the King below the waist. Or go to a movie with Marilyn Monroe or Ava Gardner. If you want male brooding and rage, go see Marlon Brando or Montgomery Clift, the prince of loneliness. The great thing about the '50s is that rebels can fling their grenades of anger and irony into the cafes of the conformists, safe in the knowledge that they can't really change anything. The '50s are an irresistible force still in search of an immovable object.

So pay no attention to that slouching bohemian with sunglasses black as telephones and a tremor induced by his benzedrine inhaler. He says he wants to get back to Europe, "where they really know how to live, where they don't have these hang-ups."

"Europe?" asks the astonished corporate executive who helped liberate Europe from the Nazis only a decade or so ago. "You can't even drink the water in Europe."

"You drink wine, man," says the bohemian. "You drink wine."

Don't worry about snooty intellectuals, either. For a moment, a Columbia University professor named Charles Van Doren is a national celebrity on a big-money TV quiz show called "Twenty-One." He appears on the cover of Time. He seems to be the answer to the old American question: "If you're so smart, why aren't you rich?"

Then it turns out the producers are slipping him the answers to keep him on the show. Van Doren is disgraced, treated like a traitor for lying on television. Well, intellectuals. It just goes to show you. They're all homos or Commies anyway.

And don't worry about the alienation of the modern jazz that lures college boys to the big city for a taste of hip, and the self-loathing notion that "white cats don't swing."

Don't worry about rock-and-roll, which sounds like a national anthem for the republic of vandalism and anarchy, which it is. Rock may drive the young folk to drugs and groin-thrusting madness, it may cause riots in the streets and insurrection in the schools, which it does—but it can't last, it's just a fad.

Ignore the sly joke of Frankie Lymon and the Teenagers singing "No, no, no, no, no, I'm not a juvenile delinquent" to suburban kids who actually think JDs are cool in their rumbles fought with bicycle chains and switchblade knives. So cool that Leonard Bernstein, Mr. Music Appreciation Class himself, will write "West Side Story," a musical that puts romantic love and gang wars together in a climactic switchblade duel.

Forget about civil rights workers heading south, where they're known as "Northern agitators." And the revival of pinko folk singers like Pete Seeger and the Weavers. And marijuana in Harvard Square. And Hugh Hefner proposing in Playboy magazine that we should think of sex as fun, like a game of picnic badminton where nobody tries too hard to win.

"There's a place for us," the cast sings at the end of "West Side Story," to reassure us that, despite the tragedy of Tony and Maria, the promise of progress is intact. "Someday, somewhere, we'll find a new way of living."

There are no VA mortgages for veterans of gang wars, but America will find a way to get them into little Cape Cod starter homes sooner than you think. Haircuts, briefcases, Peter Pan blouses, Formica, Bisquick and pole lamps while the whole family sits in front of the television to sing along with Mitch:

I'm looking over a four-leaf clover...
How could it be otherwise?

From the *Washington Post National Weekly Edition*, November 8, 1999, pp. 9–10. © 1999 by The Washington Post. Reprinted by permission.

The Rise of Conservatism Since World War II

Dan T. Carter

In the 1964 presidential election, Republican presidential nominee Barry Goldwater suffered a decisive defeat at the hands of Lyndon Johnson. Goldwater, the dream candidate of his party's conservative wing, had offered a "choice not an echo" in his campaign and the American people seemed to have little doubt about *their* choice. Goldwater carried only his home state of Arizona and five Deep South states where opposition to the Civil Rights movement was at high tide. Johnson took the rest with sixty-one percent of the popular vote and his coattails increased the Democratic majority by thirty-eight House members and two new senators. By all the traditional measurements of American politics, the election of 1964 was a disaster for American conservatism. Not only was their choice decisively rebuffed by the voters, but the overwhelming Democratic victory gave Johnson the opportunity to enact his "Great Society" programs, collectively the most far-reaching liberal legislation since Franklin Roosevelt's New Deal.

If 1964 was a decisive political defeat for Barry Goldwater, it was only a temporary setback in the steady growth of a conservative movement which would reach new heights in the election of Ronald Reagan in 1980 and the creation of a Republican majority in both houses of Congress in 1994. The complex story of that conservative resurgence—centered politically in the Republican Party but extending throughout American society—is one of the most critical developments in the last half of the twentieth century.

The rise of this conservative movement had its roots in the three decades before the Goldwater campaign, drawing upon two powerful and interrelated impulses. The first was an unambiguous defense of laissez-faire capitalism. Such conservative ideas ran deep in American history, but they had been badly discredited during the 1930s by the fact that most Americans attributed the Depression to the excesses of the capitalist system in general and the rapacious greed of corporate and business interests specifically. During the 1930s, most Americans seemed to accept the argument that the federal government had an obligation to protect the American people against those whom Franklin Roosevelt described as "malefactors of great wealth" by regulating and controlling these financial interests. At the same time, the establishment of a limited national welfare system—symbolized most concretely by the Social Security Act of 1935—represented a new and expanded role for the national state.

Despite the popularity of these measures, a vocal and articulate minority of Americans maintained their hostility to the national government (1). Apart from their complaint that the welfare state led to idleness and undermined the work ethic of its recipients, they argued that the heavy hand of government thwarted the wealth-producing force of individual entrepreneurs with its stifling red tape and burdensome taxes.

The second conservative impulse came from the linking of the "welfare state" (and the Democratic Party that created it) with fears of international communism. Since the Bolshevik Revolution, American conservatives warned of the threat of international communism, but in the aftermath of World War II, their arguments fell upon particularly receptive ears. Joseph Stalin's ruthless suppression of democratic governments in eastern Europe after World War II and their absorption behind the Iron Curtain, the Soviet Union's emergence as a nuclear power in 1949, and the victory of Mao Tse Tung's Communist forces China that same year stunned and alarmed Americans. At the same time, the disclosure that a number of Americans had spied and passed on nuclear and other defense secrets, launched the great Red Scare of the late 1940s and 1950s. Anticommunism—most dramatically reflected in the emergence of Senator Joseph McCarthy—was undoubtedly inflamed by politics. Although there were spies and homegrown subversives operating within the United States, the heated political context of the Cold War vastly exaggerated their numbers. By charging that the "liberal" administrations of Franklin Roosevelt and Harry Truman sheltered traitors and thus strengthened America's Cold War adversaries, conservatives could strike a blow at their political enemies.

But these arguments were more than simply crude political tools. In the decade from 1943 to 1953, conservative intellectuals—led by the Austrian born economist and social philosopher Frederick Hayek—argued that the flaws of "Rooseveltian" liberalism went far deeper than the question of spies or internal subversion. There was, argued Hayek, a *philosophical* affinity between any "collectivist" political movement (like the New Deal) and the forces of totalitarianism. Communism and

German National Socialism were simply the mature results of all forms of "collectivism." As he argued in his brief but influential 1944 book, *The Road to Serfdom*, any attempt to control the economic freedom of individuals inevitably led (as his title suggested) to serfdom and barbarism (2). Hayek's book was one of several works that would prove to be critical in the thinking of a new generation of conservative intellectuals (3).

Even more important in creating an intellectual foundation for the new conservatism was the creation of the *National Review* magazine under the editorial leadership of William F. Buckley Jr. Founded in 1964 and bankrolled by wealthy business conservatives, the new magazine soon became the crossroads through which most intellectual and political conservatives passed. In the years that followed, there would be other magazines and other conservative institutions created, but the *National Review* remained, in many ways, the "Mother Church" of this new movement.

Still, the arguments of intellectuals did not create an electoral majority anymore than either businessmen's distaste for government bureaucrats or the angry passions of McCarthyism. While Republicans won the presidency in 1952 and again in 1956, it was not with their longtime conservative standard-bearer, Robert Taft of Ohio, but with the soothing and distinctly moderate war hero, Dwight Eisenhower. To the despair (and disgust) of the conservative faithful, Eisenhower made little effort to challenge the basic contours of the national state created during the Roosevelt and Truman years. While Richard Nixon, the unsuccessful 1960 Republican nominee, was more strident in his anticommunist rhetoric, he also expressed little interest in rolling back the changes of the previous three decades.

If the foundation for a conservative resurgence was being laid for the future (even as the national political movement suffered repeated political setbacks through the 1950s), conservatives usually captured the attention of the media and academics only in its most bizarre and extreme forms. There were the dozens of fanatical anticommunist ideologues, many combining religious enthusiasm with their hatred of the "Red Menace." At the violent fringe could be found Robert Pugh's Minutemen, with their storehouses of automatic weapons and their plans for guerilla war once the communists who controlled the United States government had removed the mask of liberalism and shown their true face. And there were the marginally more respectable spokesmen for the new Right and their organizations: the Rev. Carl McIntire's Twentieth Century Reformation, Dr. Fred Schwarz's Christian Anti-Communism Crusade, the Rev. Billy James Hargis's Christian Crusade, Edgar Bundy's League of America, Dean Clarence Manion's American Forum, Texas oilman H.L Hunt's nationwide radio "Life Line" broadcasts and, of course, Robert Welch's John Birch Society. The title of three of the most influential works of this period give some sense of the perspective of what we might call "establishment" attitudes: *The Radical Right*, edited by Daniel Bell; Arnold Forster and Benjamin Epstein's *Danger on the Right*; and Richard Hofstadter's *The Paranoid Style in American Politics* (4).

These groups were, however, the extreme right of a far broader movement that was often unnoticed or, in many instances, simply described, indiscriminately as "extremist." One critical building block for that new conservative movement was laid in the burgeoning suburban development of postwar America. In her study of Orange County, California, historian Lisa McGirr has given us a portrait of this emerging constituency—the "Suburban Warriors" of the new conservatism. Mainline political pundits of the 1950s had often described these new political activists as "antimodern." While it is true that they often rebelled against what they saw as the excesses of change, they were in fact products of suburban prosperity, "winners" for the most part who had benefitted from the Cold War prosperity of the 1950s and 1960s. In the case of McGirr's subjects, many, in fact, worked in the burgeoning defense industries of southern California.

The new suburban communities that surrounded declining inner cities offered a safe and relatively secure launching pad of privatized civic culture to attack the secular humanists and liberal social engineers who demanded much, notably higher taxes, and offered little: the charmless attraction of unruly public spaces and expensive public programs for what these new conservatives called the "undeserving poor." In these new communities, there was little space for or interest in a "public sphere." Instead, conservative churches and a fierce political activism created a different kind of community of political and cultural activists dedicated to protecting the status quo.

The ideology of this New Right centered around the traditional conservative demands of the 1950s: rolling back communism abroad, rooting out "Reds" at home, and shrinking the welfare state. But there was also a distinctly religious and "traditionalist" aspect to these new "suburban warriors." The 1950s were a period of astounding religious resurgence; by one estimate, the number of Americans who described themselves as regular churchgoers increased more than seventy percent during the decade. Most of that growth could be attributed to evangelical and culturally conservative churchgoers, like Southern Baptists, who were profoundly unsettled over the social "liberalization" of society (5).

In part, the reason for the invisibility of this movement lay in the fact that much of it took place at the community level. Suburbia became the setting for new forms of community mobilization as middle- and upper-middle-class conservatives organized neighborhood meetings, showed "anticommunist" movies, launched petition drives to block sex education in the local schools, elected school board members who would guarantee the adoption of "proAmerican" texts, and, in the case of Los Angeles, selected a school board superintendent who barred discussion of the United Nations in the classroom.

The opening that allowed the dramatic growth of American conservatism came in the 1960s. In part it was an almost inevitable response to the ambitious liberalism of Lyndon Johnson's Great Society programs. Although liberals would deride the timidity and limited nature of the Johnson agenda, it did mark a substantial step in the expansion of the New Deal welfare state. Even before the Johnson landslide of 1964, he had persuaded Congress to enact the Economic Opportunity Act of 1964, the first measure of what he called an "unconditional war on poverty." In 1965 and 1966, he was even more successful in pushing through dozens of measures ranging from expanded public housing to the creation of the National Endowments for the Arts and the Humanities, as well as education subsidies, consumer protection, and environmental preservation measures. The capstone of this sweeping legislative agenda was the creation of Medicare and Medicaid.

As one might expect, conservatives attacked the Great Society on both fiscal and philosophical grounds. It was too expensive, they charged, and it discouraged initiative by giving the poor "handouts" rather than forcing them to find work on their own. But Johnson's program was more than simply an expansion of traditional social welfare programs, it also plunged into the thicket of racial politics. The New Deal had seen a shift in the allegiance of African Americans. Traditionally stalwarts of the party of Abraham Lincoln, black voters had turned to Roosevelt and then in even greater numbers to Harry Truman after he backed a strong civil rights plank in the 1948 Democratic Party platform. While the support of black voters in key northern industrial states proved critical to Truman's reelection, it also led to the creation of the third party "Dixiecrat Movement" and laid the foundation for the future defection of white Democratic voters in the South who had often backed their party's "liberal" economic agenda, but were adamantly opposed to the efforts of northern liberals to end segregation.

Nor had that racial backlash been confined to white southern Democrats. As a growing number of African Americans migrated to northern industrial cities, white urban working class and white-collar voters often reacted with growing hostility to what they perceived as "threats" to their neighborhoods and to their jobs. Urban historians who have studied such cities have found a growing disaffection among these traditional white Democratic working-class and middle-class voters well before the 1960s (6).

But it was during the 1960s that this white backlash proved critical in the conservative movement. During the early 1960s, "respectable" conservatives made a conscious decision to distance themselves from the more extremist elements in the movement, an action symbolized by William F. Buckley Jr.'s decision to condemn John Birch Society founder Robert Welch for his claim that Dwight Eisenhower had been a "dedicated, conscious agent of the Communist conspiracy. ..." (7)

If leading conservatives also sought to distance themselves from the cruder forms of racism, there was broad opposition to the Civil Rights movement as it emerged in the 1950s and 1960s. The more "extremist" conservative organizations such as the John Birch Society, and most of the prominent "anticommunist" leaders constantly linked movement leaders such as Martin Luther King Jr. with the international Communist movement, but more respectable mainline conservative groups were equally hostile to any attempts to use the power of government to protect the civil rights of African Americans. In an unsigned editorial in the *National Review* in 1957, Buckley told his readers that whites in the Deep South were the "advanced race" and thus entitled to take "such measures [as] are necessary to prevail, politically and culturally. ..." Besides, he added, the "great majority of the Negroes of the South who do not vote do not care to vote and would not know for what to vote if they could (8)." When Barry Goldwater announced his opposition to the Civil Rights Act of 1964, it was

the logical culmination of a decade of fairly consistent conservative opposition to any federal action designed to protect the rights of African Americans (9).

Traditional antistatism, muscular anticommunism, a vague uneasiness over accelerating social change, and a hostility to federally supported civil rights may have furnished the foundations for the growth of conservatism, but it was the tumultuous and unsettling events of the 1960s that made millions of Americans more responsive to conservative arguments.

First, in the long hot summers of the mid-1960s, angry African American civil rights activists retreated into a militant "black power" movement and race riots erupted in dozens of American cities across the Northeast, Midwest, and West. Large scale upheavals in such cities as Newark, the Watts district of Los Angeles, Washington, and Detroit left dozens dead and thousands of shops and buildings burned and looted. At the same time, American involvement in the Vietnam War accelerated from peaceful "teach-ins" in the nation's college classrooms to angry street demonstrations and confrontations with police.

As the signs of public disorder accelerated, conservatives bitterly attacked the Johnson administration for failing to quell "lawlessness" in American cities at home or to crush the North Vietnamese and Vietcong guerrillas abroad. These public manifestations of disorder increasingly reflected (in the minds of conservatives) a general social decay. Rising crime rates, the legalization of abortion, the rise of "out-of-wedlock" pregnancies, the increase in divorce rates, and the proliferation of "obscene" literature and films undermined traditional cultural symbols of conservatism and unnerved millions of Americans, an uneasiness reinforced by the new medium of television. For most Americans, their own community, their own neighborhood, might be relatively calm, but through the "immediacy of television," they became angered and felt menaced. Who were these disrespectful and unpatriotic drug-crazed hippies angrily burning the American flag night after night on the flickering screen while American soldiers died in Vietnam for their country? Who were these armed black men in combat fatigues and dark sunglasses, exultantly brandishing their semi-automatic weapons as they marched out of college classrooms? Who were these brazen women, flaunting their sexuality, burning their bras and challenging traditional "family values." In another time, these threatening events, these threatening individuals, would have remained remote, even abstract. Now they came directly into America's living room in living color (10).

The general political impact could be felt in a growing anti-Washington rhetoric, for the federal government now seemed complicit in these assaults on traditional American values. Conservatives charged that the United States Justice Department proposed that northern schools be integrated and that the federal courts "pandered" to criminals and banned state-sponsored prayer from the schools even as it opened the nation's bookstores to "filth and pornography." Spurred by fire-eating politicians and a powerful new communication network of right-wing talk show hosts, federal bureaucrats from Internal Revenue Service agents to forest rangers to Occupational Safety and Health Administration inspectors to Environmental Protection Agency enforcement officers to Bureau of Alcohol, Tobacco, and Firearms agents were increasingly depicted as power hungry, arrogant, jackbooted thugs intent on harassing honest taxpaying citizens with mindless and unnecessary red tape while diverting their hard-earned dollars to shiftless and lazy undeserving poor and predominantly black people.

Barry Goldwater's 1964 campaign marked the first major effort of post-New Deal conservatives to take the political highground. The boisterously crude 1968 campaign of Alabama Governor George Wallace reflected the tumult of the politics of the 1960s. Wallace had begun his national political career in 1964 on one issue: opposition to the Civil Rights Act of that year. When he launched his 1968 "American Independent" Party candidacy, Wallace couched his anti-civil rights message in a political rhetoric that avoided explicit racism, but his angry attacks on "bussing," "welfare abuse," and "civil rights professional agitators" skillfully exploited the growing hostility of many white Americans to what they saw as the excesses of the Civil Rights movement. At the same time, Wallace married his racial message to the "social" issues of the 1960s, calling for the curbing of constitutional rights for "street hoodlums" and dramatic reductions in welfare expenditures. From race to religion (Wallace was the first national politician to call for a constitutional amendment restoring school classroom prayers), Wallace articulated the new conservative agenda. Six weeks before the November election, more than twenty-one percent of America's voters told pollsters that Wallace was their choice for president. Although his final vote faded to fourteen percent, he came within an eyelash of throwing the election of 1968 into the House of Representatives (11).

Richard Nixon had cautiously sought to exploit this growing conservative movement while depicting himself as a "centrist" candidate; he learned from his narrow escape. Between 1968 and 1972, guided by the advice of such advisers as Harry Dent of South Carolina and voter analyst Kevin Philips, Nixon worked to make certain that those voters who had supported Wallace moved from his third party candidacy into the Republican Party. He did so by taking conservative views on a number of issues, particularly such controversial questions as bussing. Nixon's "Southern Strategy" was a critical factor in the electoral shift away from Democratic (and liberal) dominance. But his role in this process was cut short by the Watergate scandal, allowing the election of Jimmy Carter in 1976.

The last building block of the conservative movement fell into place during the Carter administration. By the 1970s, conservative evangelicals built a powerful group of educational, publishing, and broadcasting institutions. During the 1960s, they became alarmed over what they saw as an increasing drift toward a liberal secularism that undermined "traditional" values in American society. The Supreme Court's decisions in 1962 and 1963 outlawing official school prayers were a key complaint, but the Carter administration's demand that church schools (because they were tax exempt) undertake affirmative efforts to secure minority students pushed many evangelicals into politics. After 1978, under the leadership of evangelical activists like Marion "Pat" Robertson and Jerry Falwell, religious conservatives mobilized around such hot-button issues as abortion, school prayer and the teaching of evolution, becoming crit-

ical partners in a new coalition of social, cultural and economic conservatives. Conservative Christians had become Christian conservatives.

In 1980, conservatives finally achieved the victory they had lost in 1964 as Ronald Reagan swept into the White House, decisively defeating incumbent Jimmy Carter by promising dramatic tax cuts, a rollback of the federal government, a dramatic rebuilding of American military might, and a return to "traditional" American values. The eight years of the Reagan presidency left many of the staunchest conservatives dissatisfied. As one prominent spokesman of the New Right concluded, he had given little but symbolism to religious and social conservatives who wanted a return to "traditional" American values; he had done even less to slow the growth of government. Domestically, his only accomplishment was to dramatically cut taxes primarily for the well-off, thus creating such an enormous public debt that liberals in the future would be stymied in proposing any new additional government initiatives. Paul Weyrich's gloomy assessment was correct in many respects, but he underestimated the extent to which Reagan—notoriously uninformed on specific issues—had managed to create an "aura" of confidence. By the end of the Reagan years, conservatives had created a powerful and well-financed national constituency of small businessmen, suburbanites hostile to increasing taxes, religiously conservative evangelicals and traditional Catholics, gun owners passionately opposed to any control over firearms, and white blue-collar workers angry at affirmative action. Conservatives had also moved from the fringe to parity in the television media and dominance in the influential world of talk radio.

The decade of the 1990s saw both victories and defeats for conservatives. The victory of Democrat Bill Clinton in 1992 and his ability to survive eight years in the White House was a source of deep disappointment to movement leaders. But the 1994 strong showing of Republican conservatives under the leadership of Newt Gingrich reflected the shift that had taken place in American politics. The failure of the Equal Rights Amendment, the defeat of welfare entitlement while the Democratic Clinton was in the White House, the gradual erosion of Affirmative Action and, in general, the increasing conservatism of the United States Supreme Court showed that the framework for shaping public policy had shifted further to the right through the 1980s and 1990s.

Still, it is not, at all clear that there is a clear conservative hegemony. George W. Bush won the 2000 presidential election not by promising ultraconservative values, but by appealing to the American voters in a distinctly moderate tone. And yet he still did not capture a majority of the votes cast. In fact, by a popular margin of fifty-two to forty-eight percent, Americans supported a more liberal Albert Gore and a decidedly more left-wing Ralph Nader. Conservatives today are united in their opposition to what they see as the excesses of American liberalism, but they remain divided between those who would emphasize libertarian approach to personal as well as economic behavior and those who believe it is the duty of the state to enforce strict standards of public morality and public order.

Finally, the conservative movement ultimately will be judged by the extent to which it creates a just as well as a free society. But the gap between rich and poor has grown steadily with the rise of American conservatism in the last quarter of the twentieth century. According to the statistics compiled by the Congressional Budget Office, the income of the poorest one-fifth of Americans fell twelve percent between the late 1970s and the end of the 1990s; the top twenty percent saw its income rise by nearly forty percent and the top one percent of Americans saw their after-tax income grow by one hundred twenty percent. (The income of Americans between the fortieth and eightieth percentiles changed very little). By the beginning of the twenty-first century, the United States had become the most unequal society in the industrialized West. Although that growing inequality has been fed by many sources, it has clearly been reinforced by conservative priorities that have emphasized reducing the progressive nature of the federal income tax while holding the line or cutting back public services for the poor (12).

Not surprisingly, those who have benefitted from these policies and priorities have responded by opening their pocketbooks and by voting early and often. By one estimate, voters in the top twenty percent of the electorate cast as much as thirty percent of the votes in general elections and even more in local and off-year elections. Conservatives have traditionally accepted economic inequality as the price that must be paid for encouraging competition and economic productivity. But implicit in this postwar movement was the promise that conservatives would create a just as well as a moral and free society. Conservatives will ultimately succeed only if they move beyond their contempt for American liberalism and, in the words of a historian of the movement, "offer a model of political freedom that would protect the citizen against blind, impersonal economic forces, in which one man's freedom would not be another's subjection" (13).

Endnotes

1. Gary Wills describes, from a critical perspective, this deep-seated antigovernment tradition in American culture in *A Necessary Evil: A History of American Distrust of Government* (New York: Simon & Schuster, 1999).

2. Frederick Hayek, *The Road to Serfdom* (Chicago: University of Chicago Press, 1944).

3. While any list would be somewhat arbitrary, most historians of American conservatism would probably add Ayn Rand's best selling novel *The Fountainhead* (Indianapolis, IN: The Bobbs Merrill Company, 1943); Richard Weaver, *Ideas Have Consequences* (Chicago: University of Chicago Press, 1948); and Russell Kirk, *The Conservative Mind, from Burke to Santayana* (Chicago: H. Regnery Co., 1953). For an overview of the role played by these and other writers and intellectuals see George H. Nash, *The Conservative Intellectual Movement in America Since 1945* (New York: Basic Books, 1976).

Forster and Epstein, *Danger on the Right* (New York: Random House, 1964); and Hofstadter, *The Paranoid Style in Ameri-*

can *Politics and Other Essays* (New York: Alfred A. Knopf, 1965). Hofstadter's essay, originally delivered as a lecture at Oxford University in the fall of 1963, was clearly triggered by the Goldwater movement.

4. Daniel Bell, ed., *The New American Right* (New York: Criterion Books, 1955).

5. This religious resurgence was not limited to evangelicals. One measure of the growth of the new piety may be gauged by the fact that the number of individuals entering the priesthood dramatically increased in the post-World War II era. See Winthrop S. Hudson, *Religion in America* (New York: Charles Scribner's Sons, 1965), 396; Phillip E. Hammond, *Religion and Personal Autonomy: The Third Disestablishment in America*, (Columbia, SC: University of South Carolina Press, 1992), 114; Barry A. Kosmin and Seymour P. Lachman, *One Nation Under God: Religion in Contemporary American Society*, (New York: Harmony Books, 1993), 4–7, 298–99.

6. Thomas J. Sugrue, "Crabgrass-Roots Politics: Race, Rights, and the Reaction against Liberalism in the Urban North, 1940–1964," *Journal of American History*, 82 (1995): 551–78.

7. While Buckley and most other mainstream conservatives disavowed Welch's assertion that Eisenhower was a communist agent, they did not attack the John Birch Society or other far-right groups. See Jonathan Schoenwald, *A Time for Choosing: The Rise of Modern American Conservatism* (New York: Oxford University Press, 2001), 71–73.

8. *National Review,* 24 August 1957.

9. See, for example, the articles of November 1964 in the *National Review* on race and the election.

10. Dan T. Carter, *The Politics of Rage: George Wallace, the Origins of the New Conservatism and the Transformation of American Politics*, (New York: Simon & Schuster, 1995), 375–77.

11. Dan T. Carter, *From George Wallace to Newt Gingrich: Race in the Conservative Counterrevolution, 1963–1994* (Baton Rouge: Louisiana State University Press, 1996), 19, 23, 35.

12. *New York Times*, 5 September 1999, 14; see also Frank Levy's *The New Dollars and Dreams: Americans Incomes and Economic Change* (New York: Russell Sage Foundation, 1998).

13. Godfrey Hodgson, *The World Turned Right Side Up: A History of the Conservative Ascendancy in America* (Boston: Houghton Mifflin, 1996), 315.

Dan T. Carter is the Educational Foundation Professor of History at the University of South Carolina, where he teaches twentieth-century United States and Southern regional history. He is the author of *The Politics of Rage: George Wallace, the Origins of New Conservatism, and the Transformation of American Politics,* and *From George Wallace to Newt Gingrich: Race in the Conservative Counterrevolution.* He also won an Emmy in 2001 for Outstanding Individual Achievement in a Craft as a researcher for the PBS American Experience documentary based on his 1995 biography of Wallace, "George Wallace, Settin' the Wood on Fire."

The Spirit of '68

What really caused the Sixties.

By John B. Judis

This year Bob Dylan's album *Time Out of Mind* won the Grammy for best popular record, and teenagers in my local video store were waiting in line to rent *Don't Look Back*, D.A. Pennebaker's 1967 documentary about the irreverent Dylan. The National Organization for Women, the Consumer Federation of America, the Environmental Defense Fund, and other organizations from the Sixties are still influential in American politics. On the other hand, a host of grumpy social critics and cultural commissars, from Robert Bork and William Bennett to John Leo and Hilton Kramer, have continued to make a career out of denouncing that climactic period of American politics and culture. According to these critics, the 'Vietnam syndrome" ruined our foreign policy, and the spirit of permissiveness and "anything goes" corrupted our schools and youth and destroyed the nuclear family. "The revolt was against the entire American culture," Bork declared recently.

Why all the fuss? As a political era—one characterized by utopian social experiments, political upheaval, and dramatic reform—the Sixties ended sometime during Richard Nixon's presidency. But the era left an indelible mark on the decades that followed. It vastly expanded the scope of what citizens expect from their government—from clean air and water to safe workplaces, reliable products, and medical coverage in their old age. It also signaled a change in what Americans wanted out of their lives. During the Sixties, Americans began to worry about

the "quality of life" and about their "lifestyle" rather than simply about "making a living." The Sixties unleashed conflicts within these new areas of concern—over affirmative action, abortion, homosexuality, drugs, rock lyrics, air pollution, endangered species, toxic waste dumps, and automobile safety. And the era raised questions about the purpose of America and its foreign policy that are still being debated. The Sixties have preoccupied late-twentieth-century America almost as much as the Civil War preoccupied late-nineteenth- century America.

The difficulty in understanding the Sixties lies partly in the sheer diversity of people, events, and institutions that defined it—from John Kennedy's New Frontier to the Weatherman "Days of Rage," from the Black Panther Party to the Ford Foundation, from Betty Friedan and Ralph Nader to Barry Goldwater and George Wallace. Many of the books and articles that purport to be about the Sixties focus on one aspect of the era to the exclusion of the others. Todd Gitlin's excellent book, for instance, has only a passing reference to Nader and to the Sierra Club's David Brower but multiple references to Carl Oglesby, Huey Newton, and Staughton Lynd.

The nature of the Sixties has also been clouded by conservative jeremiads. Much of what disturbs the critics of the Sixties—from the spread of pornography to the denigration of the work ethic—was not the product of radical agitators but of tectonic shifts in American capitalism.

Many of those who complain most vociferously about the Sixties' counterculture, such as House Speaker Newt Gingrich, are themselves products of the period. They no longer carry signs, as Gingrich once did, proclaiming the right of campus magazines to publish nude pictures, but, even as they denounce the Sixties, they echo the decade's themes and vocabulary in articulating their own political objectives. Unable to come to terms with their own past, they sow confusion about one of the most important periods in our history.

Like most periods described by the name of a decade, the Sixties don't strictly conform to their allotted time span. You could make a good case that the Sixties began in December 1955, when Rosa Parks refused to give up her seat in a segregated Montgomery, Alabama, bus, and only ended in 1973 or 1974, when the New Left lost its fervor. You could also make a case for dividing the Sixties into two periods. The first period—running from 1955 to 1965—spans the rise of the Southern civil rights movement and of Martin Luther King, the founding of Students for a Democratic Society (SDS) in 1960, the passage of the civil rights bills and Medicare, and the initiation of the War on Poverty. The second period begins with the escalation of the war and the ghetto riots and goes through the rise of the black power and militant antiwar movements, the growth of the counterculture, the rapid development of environmental, consumer, and women's movements, and the major legislative achievements of Nixon's first term.

On the most visible level—the level at which most books about the period have dwelled—there is a pronounced shift in mood during the escalation of the war and the onset of the riots in the mid-'60s. The antiwar and black movements became violent and apocalyptic, and the country itself seemed on the verge of disintegration. But the sharp difference in tone between the two periods obscures important continuities. Most of the major movements that began in the Sixties—the consumer and environmental movements, the modern women's movement—started in the early years of the decade. And the roots of the counterculture go back well into the 1950s, if not before. These movements, as well as the counterculture, took root in Europe, too. In the United States, the simultaneous presence of massive antiwar demonstrations, riots, and demands for black power merely lent those movements and the counterculture a frenzy and an urgency that they might otherwise not have possessed.

The first period of the Sixties looks exactly like a belated continuation of the Progressive era and the New Deal. Just as in earlier periods of reform, political change was precipitated by an economic downturn. Successive recessions in 1958 and 1960 helped Democrats increase their margin in Congress and helped put Kennedy in the White House. In 1964, Johnson, benefiting from a buoyant economy and an impolitic opponent, Barry Goldwater, identified with Southern segregationists and with a trigger-happy foreign policy, won a landslide victory, and liberal Democrats gained control of Congress for the first time since 1936.

Just as before, reform was aided by an alliance of popular movements, elite organizations, and pragmatic business leaders. By the early '60s, the Southern civil rights movement enjoyed enormous support in the North, financial backing from the Ford Foundation and the Rockefeller Brothers Fund, and editorial support from the major media. Business leaders, encouraged by prosperity after having endured four recessions in a decade, accepted Johnson and the administration's major legislative initiatives with equanimity. They didn't oppose Medicare (only the American Medical Association lobbied against it), and they actively backed the Great Society and War on Poverty programs, which they saw, correctly, as creating demand for new private investment. When Johnson appointed a National Commission on Technology, Automation, and Economic Progress, the nation's most powerful businessmen joined labor and civil rights leaders in recommending a guaranteed annual income and a massive job-training program.

The spirit of the early '60s—epitomized in Johnson's vision of the Great Society—was one of heady, liberal optimism. Many of the key leaders of the period, including Martin Luther King Jr., George McGovern, Hubert Humphrey, and Walter Mondale, were raised on the Protestant Social Gospel's millennial faith in the creation of a Kingdom of God in America. The political-economic premise of this optimism, enunciated in Galbraith's *The Affluent Society* and in Michael Harrington's *The Other America*, was that American industry, which was becoming highly automated, was capable of producing great abundance, but archaic political and economic arrangements were preventing many Americans from enjoying its fruits. The goal of such programs as Medicare and the War on Poverty was to allow the poor, the aged, and the disadvantaged to share in this abundance.

This first phase of the Sixties was also marked by signs of a looming redefinition of politics that would differentiate it from early reform epochs. During the Progressive era and the New Deal, politics pivoted primarily on conflicts among different sectors of business and between business and labor. The great battles of the first five decades of the twentieth century had been over the trusts, the tariff, the banking system, the abolition of child labor, and government regulation of collective bargaining. No legislative struggle attracted so many lobbyists, was fought as fiercely, and had as much impact on presidential politics as the Taft-Hartley labor bill in 1947.

In the early '60s, new issues that didn't fit easily within this pattern began to emerge. Americans became concerned not merely with obtaining lower prices for goods but with government overseeing the safety, reliability, and quality of goods. President Kennedy announced a consumer bill of rights in 1962. That same year, over the strong objection of the clothing industry, Congress passed landmark legislation requiring flame-resistant fabrics in children's clothing. In 1964, Assistant Secretary of Labor Daniel P. Moynihan hired a young Harvard Law graduate, Ralph Nader, to research auto safety. Two years later, amidst the furor created by Nader's work, Congress passed the National Traffic and Motor Vehicle Safety Act.

In the early '60s, Americans also became concerned about the environment—not merely as a source of renewable resources or as a wildlife preserve but as the natural setting for human life. In 1962, Rachel Carson's *Silent Spring* became a best-seller. Congress passed its first Clean Air Act in 1963 and its first Clean Water Act in 1965. During the early '60s, American women also began to stir as a political force in their own right. In 1963, Betty Friedan published *The Feminine Mystique*, and, three years later, she and other feminists formed the National Organization for Women. While the older women's movement had focused on suffrage, the new movement reached into the workplace and the home and even into the private lives of men and women.

The new concerns about work, consumption, and personal life were part of a fundamental change in American culture that began to manifest itself clearly in the early '60s. During the nineteenth and early twentieth centuries, Americans had still adhered to the Protestant work ethic introduced by seventeenth-century English emigrants to America and memorialized in Benjamin Franklin's *Autobiography*. They viewed idleness and leisure as sinful and saw life and work as unpleasant prerequisites to a heavenly reward. By the early '60s, Americans had begun to abandon this harsh view for an ethic of the good life. They wanted to discover a "lifestyle" that suited them.

They worried about the "quality of life," including the kinds of foods they ate, the clothes they wore, and the cars they drove.

This change was not the work of sinful agitators but reflected deep-seated changes that had taken place in American capitalism over the century. In the nineteenth century and early twentieth century, economic growth, and the growth of the working class itself, was driven by the expansion of steel, railroads, machine tools, and other "capital goods" industries. Workers' consumption was held down in order to free up funds that could be used to invest in these new capital goods. To prevent recurrent economic crises, American industrialists were always on the lookout—in China, among other places—for new outlets for investment in railroads and other capital goods. But, as the historian Martin J. Sklar has demonstrated, sometime around the 1920s, the dynamic of economic growth changed. The growth of capital goods industries became, ironically, a threat to prosperity.

It happened because American industry, like American agriculture, became too successful for its own good. The introduction of electricity and the assembly line made the modern factory so productive that it could now increase its output without increasing its overall number of employees. During the '20s, manufacturing output grew 64 percent, but the number of workers in capital goods industries fell by twelve percent. Expanding the production of capital goods no longer required the sacrifice of workers' consumption. By the same token, it imperiled prosperity by encouraging the production of more goods than those producing them—the workers—could purchase and consume.

During the '20s, Edward Filene and other far-seeing businessmen understood that the fulcrum of the economy had shifted from production to consumption and that, to avoid depressions, employers would have to pay higher wages and induce their workers, through advertising, to spend money on consumer goods. Filene advocated a different kind of "industrial democracy" centered on workers' freedom to consume. After World War II, businesses adopted Filene's ethic

and his strategy. They paid higher wages and devoted growing parts of their budgets to advertising, which was aimed at convincing Americans to spend rather than to save. Advertising budgets doubled between 1951 and 1962. Businesses and banks also introduced the installment plan and consumer loans and, later, credit cards as inducements to buy rather than to save.

In search of profit, businesses also invaded the family and home. They sold leisure and entertainment on a massive scale; they produced not merely clothes but fashion; they processed exotic foods and established fast-food chains; they sold physical and psychological health; they filled the home with appliances and gadgets. They convinced Americans that they should care about more than just having food on the table, a house to live in, and clothes on their backs. They encouraged the idea that Americans could remake themselves—that they could create their own "look," their own personality. They encouraged the idea that sex was not merely a means to procreate but a source of pleasure and visual excitement.

The origins of the counterculture lay at the interstices of this new American culture of leisure and consumption that business helped to promote. The counterculture was a product of the new culture at the same time as it represented a critique of and a counter to it. It rejected Filene's suggestion that workers seek their freedom entirely in consumption rather than work. It held out for meaningful work, but not as defined by the nineteenth or early twentieth centuries. In 1960, when Paul Goodman, writing in *Growing' Up Absurd*, complained that "there are not enough worthy jobs in our economy for average boys and adolescents to grow up toward," he was not complaining about the lack of jobs at General Motors or on Wall Street.

The counterculture also rejected TV dinners and cars with tail fins that the advertisers urged Americans to buy, but it did so on behalf of more discriminating standards of its own. The critique of consumerism—articulated in the '50s by Vance Packard's *The Waste Makers* and

The Hidden Persuaders—led directly to the formation of the modern consumer and environmental movements. And the rejection of sex symbols and stereotypes did not lead to a celebration of abstinence but to a wider exploration into sexual pleasure and to a reevaluation of homosexuality and heterosexuality. In the early '60s, all these concerns became the subjects not merely of books and small artistic cults, but of political manifestos and platforms and embryonic social movements.

The movements initially took root among college students and recent college graduates. Students who entered college in 1960 had been born after the Depression—they had been, in the words of SDS's Port Huron Statement, "bred in at least modest comfort." Living in a time of unprecedented prosperity, they could afford not to worry about whether they would be able to get a job. They were raised to think about the "quality of life" rather than the iron law of wages, even to scorn some elements of what was then called "materialism." By 1960, they had become a major social group, capable on their own of disrupting society and upsetting its politics.

The New Left movements of the early '60s attacked the new economy, but they, too, implicitly used the new standards and ideals it had fostered. SDS's Port Huron Statement condemned the "idolatrous worship of things" but called for "finding a meaning in life that is personally authentic"—a formulation that would have made no sense to an industrial worker in 1909. In Berkeley, the Free Speech Movement of 1964—aimed at reclaiming the rights of students to distribute political literature on campus—gave way the next year to the Filthy Speech Movement, aimed at defending students against literary and sexual censorship. Over the next decade, these two movements—political and cultural—would develop in tandem.

The second period of the Sixties began with the Watts riot and Lyndon Johnson's escalation of the Vietnam War in 1965. These events signified and helped to precipitate a darker, more frenzied and violent period of protest. By escalating the war, Johnson broke a campaign promise not to send "our American boys to do the fighting for Asian boys." The war's escalation also threw into question the purpose of American foreign policy. Students who entered college in the Sixties had been imbued with the idea that America's mission was to create a democratic world after its own image. But, in Vietnam, the United States was backing a corrupt dictatorship, which, at our urging, had ignored the 1954 Geneva agreements to hold elections in Vietnam. The seeming contradiction between U.S. intervention and American ideals, Johnson's dishonesty and betrayal, and the rising list of casualties on both sides of the war inspired a growing rage against Johnson and the government. The antiwar movement split into a moderate wing that sought a negotiated withdrawal and a violent pro-North Vietnamese wing that threatened to bring the war home." As the conviction grew that U.S. intervention was not an unfortunate blunder but reflected the priorities of American capitalism and its power elite, antiwar militants began to see the United States itself as the enemy. SDS, the leading student organization, imagined itself by 1969 to be the vanguard of a violent revolution *against* the United States.

The first ghetto riots took place in the summer of 1964 and then grew in size and strength over the next three summers. In the Watts riot of 1965, 1,072 people were injured, 34 were killed, 977 buildings were damaged, and 4,000 people were arrested. In July 1967, there were 103 disorders, including five full-scale riots. In Detroit, 43 people were killed, and 7,200 were arrested. 700 buildings were burned, and 412 were totally destroyed. The riots were spontaneous, but they were invariably triggered by black perceptions of unequal treatment, particularly at the hands of white police officers.

At the same time that the riots began, Martin Luther King Jr. attempted to take the civil rights movement northward to Chicago. Contrary to the fantasies of his current conservative admirers, King never saw political and civil equality as ends in themselves but as part of a longer struggle for full social and economic equality. King wanted to desegregate housing in the North (which was the key to de facto school segregation), improve city services for blacks, and gain higher wages and better jobs for blacks. He failed abysmally in Chicago. The combination of the ghetto riots and King's failure contributed to the radicalization of the black movement. By 1968, when King was assassinated in Memphis while trying to support striking black garbagemen, many in the black movement had turned toward insurrectionary violence. It saw the Northern ghettos as Third World colonies that had to be liberated from their white imperialist oppressors.

Both the radical antiwar and the black power movements espoused what they called "revolutionary politics." They saw themselves in the tradition of Marx, Lenin, Mao, Fanon, Castro, and even Stalin, but, by the late '60s, they had become unwitting participants in a much older American tradition of Protestant millennialism. As historian William G. McLoughlin argued in *Revivals, Awakenings and Reform*, the Sixties were part of a religious revival comparable to the great awakenings of the mid-eighteenth and early nineteenth centuries. At such times, the seeming discord between ideal and reality has inspired intense self-examination, the proliferation of new sects and schisms, and alternating visions of doom and salvation. While the first phase of the Sixties saw the revival of the post-millennial Protestant Social Gospel—the view that the world would end after the millennium—the second phase saw "pre-millennial" visions of the apocalypse and Armageddon occurring before the millennium.

The emergence of this pre-millennial vision was provoked by the war's escalation and the combination of rage and guilt (guilt at complicity in the slaughter of seeming innocents) that it inspired; the repeated visions of violence and destruction in Vietnam and in American cities, which reinforced an image of change as conflagration; the assassinations of John and Robert Kennedy and of Martin Luther King, Jr., and Malcolm X; the Republican advances in 1966 and Nixon's election in November 1968, which discouraged New Left activists who had believed they could achieve majority support for their revolutionary aspirations; and the apparent success of the North Vietnamese in the war and the onset of China's Cultural Revolution, which suggested that revolution in the United States would occur only after a global revolution against American imperialism had succeeded.

The New Left of the late '60s dreamed not of America's salvation but of its destruction. If socialism or the "good life" were to come to the United States, it would be only after Armageddon—after a victorious armed struggle that would lay waste to the United States. The Panthers referred to the United States as "Babylon." When the Weatherman group took over SDS in 1969, it changed the name of SDS's newspaper, *New Left Notes*, to *Fire*. The new revolutionaries steeled themselves for a life of sacrifice and eventually death in the service of world revolution. Huey Newton, the cofounder of the Panther Party, described its program as "revolutionary suicide." Hal Jacobs, a Weatherman sympathizer, wrote in the movement magazine *Leviathan:* "Perhaps the best we can hope for is that in the course of the struggle we can develop human social relations among ourselves, while being engulfed by death and destruction."

The vision of Weatherman or the Panthers perfectly matched that of the Millerites—the precursors of today's Seventh Day Adventists. They were preparing themselves to be saved in the face of an imminent Armageddon. Even their organization resembled that of earlier Christian sects. The Weatherman group abandoned any pretense of building a mass movement. Instead, it sought to establish "revolutionary Marxist-Leninist-Maoist collective formations" that, through "criticism—self-criticism," would convert its members to true revolutionaries. Under Weatherman leadership, SDS, which at one point boasted 100,000 members, dwindled to several hundred aspiring visible saints.

During the late '60s, many of the people in the New Left, myself included, got caught up in the debate over class struggle, imperialism, racism, and revolution as if it were a genuine discussion based on reasonable, if debatable, assessments of world conditions. But others sensed that something was deeply wrong. In his 1968 campaign as the Democratic anti-war candidate, Eugene McCarthy continually frustrated his own followers by counseling calm and "reasoned judgment." Said McCarthy, "It is not a time for storming the walls, but for beginning a long march." Paul Goodman, whose writings had inspired the New Left, realized by 1969 that the political movement had turned unworldly even while it pretended to speak of world revolution:

If we start from the premise that the young are in a religious crisis, that they doubt there is really a nature of things and they are sure there is no world for themselves, many details of their present behavior become clearer. Alienation is a powerful motivation, of unrest, fantasy and feckless action. It can lead… to religious innovation, new sacraments to give life meaning. But it is a poor basis for politics, including revolutionary politics.

At the time, however, these voices were largely ignored. The question wasn't whether it made any sense at all to talk of revolution, but when the revolution would come and who would be on what side of the barricades.

This turn toward violence and revolutionary fantasy alienated many Americans and led to the rise of Ronald Reagan in California and George Wallace's surprising showing in the 1968 presidential election. That year, Richard Nixon ran a subtle "law and order" campaign to exploit the unpopularity of the antiwar and black protesters. Yet these movements still wielded enormous influence over the nation's political and legislative agenda. By the early '70s, they had helped force the Nixon administration to withdraw from Vietnam and had provoked Congress and the administration into pouring money into cities and adopting a strategy of affirmative action in hiring and federal contracts. During Nixon's first term, spending on Johnson's Great Society programs and on welfare and Food Stamps dramatically increased, while spending on the military went down.

There were two reasons for the movements' remarkable success. First, the movements were large and unruly enough to pose a constant threat of disruption. The major riots stopped by 1969, but the threat of riots persisted—both in actual fact and in the rhetoric and behavior of the black activists. In the summer of 1970 alone, city officials reported that black and Chicano militants made over 500 attacks on police, resulting in the deaths of 20 policemen. The antiwar movement also became increasingly violent. During the fall semester in 1970, 140 bombings occurred; at Rutgers, classes had to be vacated 175 times because of bomb threats.

Second, these movements had either the support or sympathy of policy elites. Some members of the foreign policy elite, acting partly out of conviction and partly out of fear of further disruption, favored immediate negotiation with the North Vietnamese and later unilateral withdrawal from Vietnam. By 1968, these included *The New York Times* editorial board and prominent members of the Council on Foreign Relations. Foundations and policy groups responded to the antiwar movement and to the riots and the black power movement the same way elite organizations in the early 1900s had responded to the threat of socialist revolution. They sought to tame the militants by helping them achieve their more reasonable objectives.

The Ford Foundation, the wealthiest and most powerful of all the foundations, with assets four times that of the Rockefeller Foundation, was particularly important. In 1966, Henry Ford and foundation board chairman John McCloy desirous that the foundation play a more active role in national affairs, brought in former Kennedy national security adviser McGeorge Bundy as the new president. Bundy threw the foundation into the struggle for racial equality. He helped new groups get off the ground, including La Raza and the Mexican-American Legal Defense Fund. But he also embroiled the foundation in controversy. Money that Ford gave to the Congress of Racial Equality in Cleveland went to funding a voter registration drive that helped elect Democrat Carl Stokes as Cleveland's first black mayor—in seeming violation of the foundation's nonpartisan status. In New York, Bundy sold New York City Mayor John Lindsay on a plan for community control of schools that put local blacks in charge of their own schools, which ended up pitting the city's blacks against the predominantly Jewish teachers' union.

While the late '60s are remembered mainly for the violent antiwar and black power movements, their most enduring legacy was the establishment of the environmental, consumer, and women's movements. By the early '70s, the National Organization for Women had 200 local chapters and had been joined in effort by the National Women's Political Caucus, the National Association for the Repeal of Abortion Laws, and hundreds of small local and national women's organizations. The movement enjoyed remarkable success. In 1972, the year Ms. magazine was founded, Congress approved the Equal Rights Amendment to the Constitution, strengthened and broadened the scope of the Equal Employment Opportunity Commission, and included a provision in the new Higher Education Act ensuring equal treatment of men and women.

The consumer and environmental movements enjoyed equally spectacular success. Organizations like the Sierra Club, Wilderness Society, and the Audubon Society expanded their purview and quadrupled their membership from 1960 to 1969. They were also joined by new groups, including Environmental Action, the Environmental Defense Fund, and Friends of the Earth. The Consumer Federation of America, a coalition of 140 state and local groups, was founded in 1967, and Consumers Union, which had published a magazine since 1936, moved its office to Washington in 1969. These groups got the Nixon administration and Congress to adopt a raft of reforms from establishing the Environmental Protection Agency and the Consumer Product Safety Commission to major amendments to the Clean Air and Clean Water acts.

The key individual behind these movements was Nader. He used his fame and income from *Unsafe at Any Speed*—his best-selling book about auto safety—and his successful battle with General Motors to help build a consumer movement. Nader started hiring young lawyers called "Nader's Raiders" in 1968 and founded his first campus-based Public Interest Research Group in 1970. By the mid-'70s, he had founded eight new organizations, including the Center for Responsive Law, Congress Watch, and the Health Research Group, which played an important role in getting Congress to pass a mass of new legislation, including the Wholesome Poultry Products Act, the Natural Gas Pipeline Safety Act, and the Occupational Safety and Health Act.

If Nader was the key individual, the key institution was once more the Ford Foundation. The foundation stepped in when the Audubon Society, worried about its own contributors, balked at funding the Environmental Defense Fund, the first public interest law firm designed to force business and government to comply with the new environmental laws. Ford also gave generous grants to the Sierra Club Legal Defense Fund and to the Los Angeles-based Center for Law in the Public Interest. By 1972, Ford was providing 86 percent of the grants to groups practicing consumer and environmental public interest law.

Unlike the later antiwar and civil rights movements, the environmental and consumer movements enjoyed enormous popular support. Republican and Democratic politicians vied to sponsor environmental and consumer legislation. In 1970, Nixon and Edmund Muskie, who was planning to run for president in 1972, got into a bidding war for the movements support, with each championing successively tougher revisions to the Clean Air Act. Businesses might have fought environmental and consumer legislation, but, in these years, they were restrained by a combination of complacency and defensiveness. From February 1961 to September 1969, the United States enjoyed the longest consecutive boom on record. The economy grew by 4.5 percent a year, compared to 3.2 percent in the '50s. Secure in their standing, only 50 corporations had registered lobbyists stationed in Washington in the early '60s.

In the mid-'60s, as the country's mood darkened, the public's opinion of business began to fall precipitously, but, as David Vogel recounts in *Fluctuating Fortunes*, business's initial response was to stress corporate social responsibility and to accommodate the demands of the consumer and environmental movements. While the auto and tobacco companies took umbrage at regulations targeted at them, business as a whole thought it could adapt the new environmental and consumer legislation to its own ends just as it had done earlier with the Interstate Commerce Commission and the Federal Trade Commission. A *Fortune* survey in February 1970 found 53 percent of Fortune 500 executives in favor of a national regulatory agency and 57 percent believing that the federal government should "step up regulatory activities." In a spirit of social responsibility, 85 percent of the executives thought that the environment should be protected even if that meant "reducing profits."

In the second phase of the Sixties, the counterculture spread from Berkeley, Madison, Ann Arbor, and Cambridge to almost every high school and college in America. Teenagers from pampered suburban homes who had never read Allen Ginsberg or Nelson Algren nevertheless denounced the "rat race" and the "neon wilderness." In extensive polls and interviews conducted from 1968 to 1974, Daniel Yankelovich saw steadily growing "acceptance of sexual freedom," rejection of "materialism," opposition to the laws against marijuana, and questioning of "such traditional American views as putting duty before pleasure [and] saving money regularly."

Like the other movements of the Sixties, the counterculture had its theorists, and its own millennial vision, which propounded a utopian version of consumer capitalism. Sociologist Theodore Roszak, ecologist Murray Bookchin, Yale Law School professor Charles Reich, and other post-millennialists foresaw a transformation in human nature and human arrangements that would subordinate work to play and science to art. The instrument of change would not be a political movement but the change

in consciousness that had already begun among college students. Reich saw the essence of change in the new "freedom of choosing a lifestyle." Work would become an "erotic experience, or a play experience."

Reich attributed the new counterculture to capitalism—what he called the "machine." As capitalism became capable of producing more goods than it could sell, it was forced to devise ways to expand people's needs and wants. It had to transform people themselves, moving them from the work ethic of "Consciousness II" to the lifestyle ethic of "Consciousness III," where a human being could "develop the aesthetic and spiritual side of his nature."

Reich, Roszak, and other spokesmen for the counterculture did not exalt idleness but artistic expression. They didn't promote pornography but eroticism. Most of what their current critics like Bork and Kramer lay at their door was attributable to consumer capitalism rather than the counterculture. And, while much of their vision of the future appears daffy, they—in contrast to their latter-day critics—realized that America had turned a corner. What they didn't understand was exactly where it was headed.

As a political era, the Sixties came to a close around 1973. In January 1973, Nixon signed a peace accord with North Vietnam, which not only put an end to the antiwar movement but, in doing so, removed a major source of political mobilization and energy. In 1969, the booming war economy also began a six-year slowdown. This slowdown, aggravated by the energy crisis of 1973, put a damper on the counterculture. Students became focused on preparing for jobs and careers rather than discovering the meaning of life.

The downturn of the early '70s, combined with a wave of strikes that began in 1969 and with growing competition from Japan and Western Europe, made American business leaders lose their tolerance for new government intervention. They began to push hard to limit new consumer and environmental regulations. They began hiring lobbyists and establishing corporate offices in Washington and funding policy groups and think tanks, and by the mid-'70s, many business leaders were beginning to look fondly upon Republican conservatives who combined their opposition to the social movements of the Sixties with support for business's agenda of "deregulation." By 1978, these two groups were setting the nation's political and legislative agenda, even with Democrats in control of the White House and Congress.

What, then, is the legacy of the Sixties? It endures, for one thing, in Bill Clinton's passionate commitment to racial reconciliation and in Al Gore's ardent environmentalism. It also could be found in Clinton's mistaken belief after November 1992 that he could fashion a "new beginning," including a wildly ambitious health care plan. But the era also endures ironically in its most bitter opponents—Gingrich, Dick Armey, Phil Gramm, and many of the leaders of the religious right. Gingrich and Armey's fantastic belief that they had led a "revolution" in November 1994 was straight out of the late '60s. So, too, is Gingrich's futurism and his insistence that Americans should have the highest "range of choices of lifestyle." Within the religious right, Weatherman has been reincarnated as Operation Rescue, and the commu-

nards of the Sixties have become the home-schoolers of the 1990s.

The Sixties clearly bequeathed political conflicts that continue to seethe but also made lasting contributions that cannot easily be undone. Medicare and the environmental and consumer legislation of Nixon's first term have withstood furious attacks from conservatives and business. While the issues of urban poverty and decay that King addressed in the last years of his life remain unsettled, the premises of the Civil Rights Act of 1964 and the Voting Rights Act of 1965 are no longer open to question.

The Sixties enlarged the scope of politics by adding new issues and constituencies to the traditional mix created by business and labor, and they changed the way politics was conducted. A proliferation of new movements, interests, and interest groups—some of them funded door-to-door and others through the mail—shifted the struggle to change the country from the halls of Congress to the media and even to time streets. By the 1980s, business lobbyists were employing "grassroots" techniques developed by shaggy protesters from the Sixties.

Perhaps most important of all, America passed irreversibly during the Sixties

from a culture of toil, sacrifice, saving, and abstinence to a culture of consumption, lifestyle, and quality of life The agent of this change was not the counterculture but consumer capitalism, to which the counterculture, like the religious right, is a reaction. This new stage of capitalism has opened to the average American possibilities of education, leisure, and personal fulfillment that had been reserved in the past for the upper classes. It has also, of course, exalted consumption over production, razed redwoods, turned shorelines into boardwalks, flooded cyberspace with spam, used sex to sell detergents, and helped to transform many American teenagers into television zombies. If our cultural commissars would understand this distinction between the culture of capitalism and the counterculture, perhaps they would waste less of our time blaming the radicals of the Sixties for all of today's problems and turn their attention to the real causes.

This article draws from JOHN B. JUDIS's book on twentieth-century American politics, *The Paradox of American Democracy* (Pantheon Books, 2000).

The Cold War and Vietnam

George C. Herring

The cold war and the American war in Vietnam cannot be disentangled. Had it not been for the cold war, the U.S., China, and the Soviet Union would not have intervened in what would likely have remained a localized anticolonial struggle in French Indochina. The cold war shaped the way the Vietnam War was fought and significantly affected its outcome. The war in Vietnam in turn influenced the direction taken by the cold war after 1975.

The conflict in Vietnam stemmed from the interaction of two major phenomena of the post-World War II era, decolonization—the dissolution of colonial empires—and the cold war. The rise of nationalism in the colonial areas and the weakness of the European powers after the Second World War combined to destroy a colonial system that had been an established feature of world politics for centuries. A change of this magnitude did not occur smoothly, and in Vietnam it led to war. When France fell to Germany in 1940, Japan imposed a protectorate upon the French colony in Vietnam, and in March 1945 the Japanese overthrew the French puppet government. In August 1945, Vietnamese nationalists led by the charismatic patriot Ho Chi Minh seized the opportunity presented by Japan's surrender to proclaim the independence of their country. Determined to recover their empire, the French set out to regain control of Vietnam. After more than a year of ultimately futile negotiations, a war began in November 1946 that would not end until Saigon fell in April 1975.

At the very time Vietnamese nationalists were engaged in a bloody anticolonial war with France, the cold war between the U.S. and the Soviet Union was evolving into an ideological and power struggle with global dimensions. The conjunction of these historical trends explains the internationalization of the war in Vietnam.

What was unique about decolonization in Vietnam—and from the American standpoint most significant—was that the nationalist movement, the Viet Minh, was led by Communists, and this would have enormous implications, transforming what began as a struggle against French colonialism into an international conflict of dangerous proportions. At least from 1949 on, U.S. officials viewed the struggle in Indochina in terms of the cold war. Ho Chi Minh had been a Communist operative for many years. Although Americans could find no evidence of Soviet support for the Viet Minh, they viewed the revolutionary movement suspiciously. When Mao Tse-tung's Communists seized power in China in August 1949, they offered sanctuary and military assistance to the Viet Minh, heightening U.S. concerns. Recognition of the Viet Minh by China and the Soviet Union in early 1950 settled the matter for American officials, revealing Ho Chi Minh, in Secretary of State Dean Acheson's words, in his "true colors as the mortal enemy of native independence in Indochina" (1). Unable to accept the essentially nationalist origins of the Vietnamese revolution, Americans were certain that Ho and the Viet Minh were part of a monolithic Communist bloc controlled by the Kremlin.

U.S. officials also concluded that the fall of Vietnam to communism would threaten their nation's vital interests. NSC 68, a key 1950 statement of cold war policies, posited that the Soviet Union, "animated by a new fanatical faith," sought "to impose its absolute authority on the rest of the world." It had already gained control of Eastern Europe and China. In the frantic milieu of 1949–1950, Americans concluded that "any substantial further extension of the area under the control of the Kremlin would raise the possibility that no coalition adequate to confront the Kremlin with greater strength could be assembled" (2). In this context of a world divided into two hostile power blocs, a fragile balance of power, a zero-sum game in which any gain for Communism was automatically a loss for the "free world," previously unimportant areas such as Vietnam suddenly took on huge significance. The North Korean invasion of South Korea in June 1950 seemed to confirm American fears of Communist expansion and to heighten the significance of Vietnam.

There were other reasons related to the cold war why Americans attached great significance to Vietnam. The so-called domino theory held that the fall of Vietnam to Communism would cause the loss of all Indochina and then the rest of Southeast Asia, with economic and geopolitical repercussions spreading west to neutral India and east to key allies such as Japan and the Philippines. Lessons drawn from recent history, the so-called Manchuria/Munich analogy, stressed that the failure of the western democracies to stand firm against Japanese and German aggression in the 1930s had encouraged further aggression until World War II was the result. The "lesson" was that to avoid a larger, possibly even a nuclear war, it was essential to stand firmly against Communist aggression at the outset. The alleged "loss" of China to the Communists set off a political bloodletting in the U.S., called McCarthyism after one of its most unscrupulous practitioners, Republican Senator Joseph McCarthy of Wisconsin. The result was a militant anti-Communism that seemed to require political leaders, especially Democrats, to prevent the loss of additional real estate to the Soviet bloc.

Policymakers from Harry S. Truman to Lyndon Baines Johnson acted upon these cold war imperatives in Vietnam, gradually escalating U.S. involvement to full-scale war. In 1950, the U.S. began to assist France against the Viet Minh, eventually absorbing much of the cost of the war. When France faltered in 1954, accepting a settlement at the Geneva Conference that temporarily divided Vietnam at the seventeenth parallel, the U.S. moved to block further Communist expansion in Southeast Asia by creating an independent, non-Communist government in southern Vietnam. When the elections called for by Geneva to unify the country were not held, former Viet Minh in South Vietnam launched an insurgency against the U.S.-backed regime of Ngo Dinh Diem and Communist North Vietnam supported it by infiltrating men and supplies into South Vietnam. The U.S. responded by significantly expanding its assistance to the Diem government. That government fell in 1963, and when the National Liberation Front insurgency, backed by growing support from North Vietnam, seemed likely to topple its fragile successors, Johnson began bombing North Vietnam in early 1965 and dispatched major increments of combat troops to the South. By this time the Sino-Soviet "bloc" was torn by bitter ideological and geopolitical disputes, but the president still felt compelled to uphold cold war commitments. "[E]verything I knew about history," LBJ later observed, "told me that if I got out of Vietnam and let Ho Chi Minh run through the streets of Saigon, then I'd be doing exactly what Chamberlain did in World War II. I'd be giving a big fat reward to aggression ... once we showed how weak we were, Moscow and Peking would move in a flash to exploit our weakness.... And so would begin World War III" (3).

Just as the cold war influenced Johnson to intervene in Vietnam, so it also shaped the way he fought the war. The primary U.S. goals were to deter Communist, especially Chinese, expansion and to maintain the credibility of U.S. cold war commitments by preserving an independent. non-Communist South Vietnam. The U.S. never set out to win the war in the traditional sense. It did not seek the defeat of North Vietnam. On the contrary, vivid memories of Chinese intervention in the Korean War in 1950 and the more recent Cuban missile crisis of 1962 led the administration to wage a limited war.

The U.S. fought in "cold blood." Fearing that full mobilization might trigger alliances among the Communist nations and provoke a larger war, perhaps even the nuclear Armageddon the Vietnam commitment was designed to deter in the first place, the president did not seek a declaration of war from Congress. He refused to mobilize the reserves. No Office of War Information was created, as in World War II, and no dramatic programs were undertaken to rally popular support for the war. In a nuclear world, Secretary of State Dean Rusk later explained, "it is just too dangerous for an entire people to get too angry and we deliberately ... tried to do in cold blood what perhaps can only be done in hot

blood" (4). It proved very difficult to maintain public support in a protracted war fought under these conditions.

The Johnson administration went to great lengths to keep the war limited. It escalated the commitment gradually and quietly to minimize the danger of confrontation with the major Communist powers. Administration officials repeatedly assured the Soviet Union and China that their goals were limited. They scrupulously avoided the sort of rash military moves that might provoke a Soviet or Chinese response. Johnson refused to permit the military to pursue North Vietnamese and National Liberation Front units into their sanctuaries in Laos, Cambodia, and across the demilitarized zone separating the two Vietnams. He tightly restricted the bombing near the Chinese border and around Haiphong harbor. He lived in mortal terror, by some accounts, that an American pilot—from his hometown of Johnson City. Texas, in his most graphic nightmares—would drop a bomb down the smokestack of a Soviet freighter, thus starting World War III.

Johnson's caution appears warranted—there is ample evidence that a serious threat to destroy North Vietnam would have brought the Soviet Union and China into the war—but it complicated achievement of his war aims. Gradual escalation gave Hanoi time to adapt to the bombing, shield its most precious resources, and develop one of the most deadly air defense systems ever employed in warfare, all of which increased its capacity to resist American military pressures. Deeply committed to securing a unified Vietnam, North Vietnamese leaders countered America's limited war with all-out war, producing an asymmetrical conflict that helped neutralize America's vastly superior military power. At the same time, as each escalation failed to produce the desired results, the U.S. moved to the next level, resulting in what one official called an "all-out limited war," a massive, elephantine effort that inflicted vast destruction on North and South Vietnam, earning for the administration widespread and often merited criticism at home and abroad. LBT's limited war thus produced the worst of both worlds.

The cold war worked to North Vietnam's advantage in other ways. Up to 1964, both of the major Communist powers had been consummate pragmatists, neither hindering nor in any major way assisting North Vietnam's efforts to "liberate" the South, but U.S. escalation forced them to make hard choices. Bitter rivals and now vigorously competing for leadership of world communism, each felt compelled to assist an embattled ally, and Hanoi skillfully exploited their rivalry by extracting maximum assistance from each while scrupulously controlling its own destiny. The Soviets provided the modern fighter planes and surface-to-air missiles (SAMs) to fend off the American bombing, and Soviet technicians manned antiaircraft batteries and SAM sites. The Chinese provided huge quantities of small arms, vehicles, and food. More than 300,000 Chinese troops helped maintain the vital supply route from China. Total Soviet and Chinese aid has been estimated at more than $2 billion. It helped neutralize U.S. air attacks, replace equipment lost in the bombing, and free North Vietnam to send more troops to the South. "The fact that the Soviets and Chinese supply almost all war material to Hanoi ... [has] enabled the North Vietnamese to carry on despite all our operations," a National Security Council document concluded in 1969 (5). Johnson could do nothing to stop such aid short of the provocative measures he feared would dangerously escalate the war.

After 1968, the cold war and the war in Vietnam remained intimately connected, but in more subtle and complex ways. By 1969, the Soviet Union and China were engaged in fighting along their long common border. Johnson's successor Richard M. Nixon sought to capitalize on the rivalry by reshaping relations with each cold war enemy and gaining an edge over both. Eager to end the Vietnam War, which he considered a distraction from more important foreign policy priorities, Nixon and his top adviser Henry A. Kissinger sought to use the leverage gained from improved relations with the Soviet Union and China to end the Vietnam War in a way that would secure the "peace with honor" they deemed necessary to maintain America's world position.

Nixon and Kissinger succeeded for the short-term in effecting major changes in the cold war. In one of the most dramatic events of his presidency, the one-time red-baiter par excellence traveled to Beijing in early 1972 to begin normalizing relations with a nation once America's most bitter enemy. Shortly after, in Moscow, he and Soviet leader Leonid Brezhnev reached agreements on expanded trade and nuclear arms limitations. Nixon's diplomacy did not end the cold war, but it dramatically altered the contours of the conflict.

Nixon did not enjoy similar success with Vietnam. China and the Soviet Union played a double game, seeking improved relations with the U.S. and urging North Vietnam to compromise at the same time they provided Hanoi with the military hardware to launch large-scale conventional offensives against South Vietnam in 1972 and again in 1974–75. Following the failure of their 1972 Easter Offensive, the North Vietnamese had to retreat from their longstanding demand for dismantling the South Vietnamese government. Confronting a tired and divided nation and facing an election, Nixon also had to compromise, however, agreeing to permit some 150,000 North Vietnamese troops to remain in the South and to withdraw U.S. military forces by March 31, 1973 in exchange for the return of American prisoners of war. The war in Vietnam would continue without the direct military participation of the U.S.

After the summer of 1973, Nixon was in no position to influence events in Vietnam. Ironically, the abuses of power he authorized to curtail mounting domestic opposition to his Vietnam War policies and facilitate his reelection led to the Watergate scandals that paralyzed his presidency and eventually forced his resignation. His successor Gerald Ford could therefore do little when the North Vietnamese invaded South Vietnam in 1974–1975. Ford and Kissinger again resorted to traditional cold war warnings that to do nothing while an ally of twenty-five years fell to the Communists would cripple America's world position. Ironically, however, the process of detente with the Soviet Union and rapprochement with China weakened the power of cold war appeals among a war-weary and financially strapped people. Congress rejected Ford's calls for additional aid to South Vietnam. On April 30, 1975 North Vietnamese tanks crashed the gates of Saigon's presidential palace, signifying the end of America's longest war.

The Vietnam War had consequences for the cold war far different than Americans had foreseen. The domino theory worked in former French Indochina, with Laos and Cambodia also falling to Communist rebels in the spring of 1975. But instead of a unified Communist bloc threatening the rest of Southeast Asia, old nationalist rivalries provoked the various Communist governments to fight each other. The brutal Khmer Rouge regime in Cambodia established close relations with China, causing Vietnam to invade Cambodia, establish a puppet government, and plunge into a debilitating quagmire of its own. China had spent substantial blood and treasure supporting. Vietnam against the U.S., but their shaky alliance rekindled ancient fears and suspicions. In 1979, China sent troops across its southern border to "teach Vietnam a lesson," setting off a short and inconclusive war that did anything but (6). The Vietnam War did not have major consequences for Soviet-American relations. The Soviet Union seemed to come away the winner, exploiting U.S. preoccupation with Vietnam to achieve nuclear parity and assisting its client to defeat its most formidable cold war rival. Over the long haul, however, Vietnam proved a drain on Moscow's limited resources. While the U.S. nursed its so-called "Vietnam syndrome" by turning inward, the Soviet Union dabbled in the Horn of Africa and Central America. Most significantly, it invaded Mghanistan in 1978. Historically as hostile to foreign invaders as Vietnam, Afghanistan became the Soviet Union's Vietnam, exhausting its money and manpower and eventually contributing to its collapse. The Vietnam War may thus have contributed indirectly to Soviet defeat in the cold war, but hardly in the way U.S. policymakers had intended.

Endnotes

1. *Department of State Bulletin*, February 13, 1950, 244.
2. NSC-68, April 14, 1950, printed in *Naval War College Review* 61 (May-June 1975): 51–108.
3. Doris Kearns Goodwin, *Lyndon Johnson and the American Dream*, (New York: Harper and Row, 1976), 252.
4. Michael Charlton and Anthony Moncrief, *Many Reasons Why: The American Involvement in Vietnam*, reprint (New York: Hill and Wang, 1989), 115.
5. National Security Study Memorandum No. 1, January 21, 1969, in Robert J. McMahon, *Major Problems in the History of the Vietnam War*, 3 ed. (New York: DC Heath, 2003), 393. The complex involvement of the Soviet Union and China in the war is skillfully analyzed in Ilya V. Gaiduk, *The Soviet Union and the Vietnam War* (Chicago: Ivan R. Dee Inc., 1996), and Qiang Zhai, *China and the Vietnam Wars*, 1950-1975 (Chapel Hill, NC: University of North Carolina Press, 2000).
6. Zhai, *China and the Vietnam Wars*, 214.

George Herring is Alumni Professor of History at the University of Kentucky. Much of his research and writing has focused on the Vietnam War, and he is the author of *America's Longest War: The United States and Vietnam, 1950–1975*, 4th ed. (2001).

Soft Power

Reagan the dove.

VLADISLAV M. ZUBOK

Death, NOT SURPRISINGLY, has secured Ronald Reagan's place in history. In recent days, policy veterans, journalists, and scholars have placed him among the top ranks of twentieth-century presidents. In a *New York Times* op-ed written shortly after Reagan's death, Mikhail Gorbachev, the former Soviet leader, acknowledged Reagan's role in bringing about the end of the cold war. Reagan's conservative admirers go even further. They proclaim him the architect of "victory" against the USSR, citing his support of the anti-communist mujahedin in Afghanistan, of the anti-Soviet Solidarity movement in Poland, and, above all, his Strategic Defense Initiative (SDI). Former White House Chief of Staff Donald Regan told CNN seven years ago that Gorbachev's failure to convince President Reagan to give up SDI at the Reykjavik summit in 1986 meant it was "all over for the Soviet Union." A memorial plaque in the court of the Ronald Reagan Presidential Library in Simi Valley, California, flatly states that Reagan's SDI brought down Soviet communism.

Newly released Soviet documents reveal that Reagan indeed played a role in ending the cold war. Yet, it was not so much because of SDI or the support of anti-Soviet forces around the world. Rather, it was the sudden emergence of another Reagan, a peacemaker and supporter of nuclear disarmament—whom conservatives opposed—that rapidly produced a new U.S.-Soviet détente. This détenté facilitated Gorbachev's radical overhaul of Soviet domestic and foreign policy—changes that brought the USSR crashing down and that would have been impossible had Reagan remained the hawk conservatives now celebrate.

In RETROSPECT, IT's hard to see SDI as anything but a bit player in the final act of the cold war. In 1983, the year Reagan announced the program to stop Soviet missiles in space (immediately dubbed "star wars"), the Soviet leadership convened a panel of prominent scientists to assess whether SDI posed a long-term security threat. The panel's report remains classified, but various leaks point to the main finding (one that mirrored the assessment of independent U.S. scientists): In the next decade or even beyond, SDI would not work. The rumor circulating in politburo circles was that "two containers of nails hurled into space" would be enough to confuse and overwhelm U.S. anti-missile defenses. In a compromise decision between Kremlin leaders and military commanders reached by 1985, a number of R&D labs received limited funds to look into possible countermeasures to SDI. The budget of the Soviet "anti-SDI" program, a fraction of the huge allocations to the Soviet military-industrial complex, remained at the same modest level through the rest of the '80s.

Gorbachev feared SDI less for the military threat it posed to the USSR than for the practical threat it posed to his political agenda. The young general secretary belonged to a generation shaped by the denunciations of Stalinist crimes, the cultural liberalization of the 1960s, and East-West déetente; this generation wanted to reform the Soviet Union and end the confrontation with the United States. But the reformists remained a minority and operated in a milieu of anti-American paranoia. As a result, Gorbachev was frustrated by the Reagan administration's hawkish actions—such as increased military assistance to Afghanistan, provocative naval exercises near Soviet coasts, and the CIA's unrelenting "spy war" against the KGB.

The Soviets interpreted SDI as an outgrowth of this renewed American aggressiveness, which made it harder for Gorbachev to push his reforms. As Boris Ponomarev, a Communist apparatchik, grumbled in early 1986, "Let the Americans change their thinking instead.... Are you against military strength, which is the only language that imperialism understands?" Gorbachev admitted in his memoirs that he was initially too cautious to resist this pressure. At the politburo, he adopted hard-line language, describing the American president as a "troglodyte" in November 1985.

Still, the early interactions between Gorbachev and Reagan revealed that there might be enough common ground between the two leaders to allow Gorbachev to press ahead: As it happened, both men were closet nuclear abolitionists. For all his outward toughness, Reagan connected nuclear threats to the prophecy of Armageddon and, under the influence of his wife, Nancy, who saw ending the cold war as an opportunity to save the president's legacy from the taint of Iran-Contra, wanted to be remembered as a peacemaker. Gorbachev, likewise, saw eliminating the danger of nuclear confrontation between the superpowers as his top priority. When Gorbachev participated in a strategic game simulating the Soviet response to a nuclear attack shortly after coming to power, he allegedly refused to press the nuclear button "even for training purposes."

Though the continuing U.S.-Soviet confrontation obscured the common anti-nuclear agenda for much of the '80s, the shared goal surfaced suddenly in a dramatic exchange at the Reykjavik summit in October 1986. Gorbachev proposed eliminating all ballistic missiles. When Reagan demurred, Gorbachev raised the ante. Both leaders then began proposing that more and more categories of weapons be abolished until they had agreed upon total disarmament. But Gorbachev refused to cut anything if SDI remained, prompting the frustrated Reagan to interject: "What the hell use will anti-ballistic missiles or anything else be if we eliminate nuclear weapons?" The Soviet leader held firm, at which point the summit collapsed and Reagan returned home feeling angry and cheated.

Though conservatives lauded Reagan for courageously avoiding what they saw as a Soviet trap, administration insiders were furious at the president for even broaching the idea of a nuclear-free world. They were right to be concerned. By the end of 1987, Reagan had begun to distance himself from the extreme hawks who opposed any negotiations (the most prominent of them, Secretary of Defense Caspar Weinberger, left the administration in 1987) and was relying increasingly on the pragmatic advice of Secretary of State George Shultz. In December 1987, the president and Gorbachev met in Washington to sign a treaty eliminating intermediate-range missiles. And, by June 1988, Reagan was kissing Russian babies in Red Square and had nonchalantly dropped the "evil empire" label he had affixed to the Soviet Union in 1983.

For his part, Gorbachev used the increasingly warm encounters with Reagan as capital for domestic reforms. Soviet journalists, as well as the entire international media, covered the summits, transforming Gorbachev into a TV star. Back home, millions of Soviets felt proud of their leader for the first time in years. Reykjavik, in particular, increased Gorbachev's domestic standing; the Soviet audience appreciated his tough talk with Reagan, but not as much as his "struggle for peace." This enhanced stature allowed Gorbachev to make a series of crucial changes in the aftermath of various U.S.-Soviet summits: the release of the Nobel Laureate and political prisoner Andrei Sakharov in December 1986 and the introduction of glasnost came on the heels of Reykjavik; the withdrawal of troops from Afghanistan in January 1988 came just after the Washington summit the previous December; the liberalization of the communist political system began with the announcement of parliamentary elections during the summer of 1988, just after Reagan's visit to Moscow.

I⊤ WAS PERHAPS inevitable that some of Reagan's former advisers would begin to rewrite his legacy using their hard-line script. Back in the '80s, however, this script produced nothing but new cold war crises, an accelerated arms race, and a huge budget deficit. With the notable exception of the support of Polish Solidarity, U.S. measures to "bleed" the Soviet Union only bred mutual fears of war. The most notorious symbol of U.S. "victory" in the cold war, SDI, still remains an unfulfilled promise 20 years later.

It is not clear how much vision regarding the end of Soviet communism Ronald Reagan had. What Reagan certainly had in abundance was luck and instinct. He was lucky that a new reformist leadership came to power in Moscow looking for a partner to end the cold war. He sensed a historic opportunity in his relationsisp with Gorbachev and finally seized on it. It was Reagan the peacemaker, not the cold warrior, who made the greatest contribution to history. One only wishes more Americans were aware of this paradox as they pay homage to their fortieth president.

Vladislav M. Zubok, *a professor of history at Temple University, is the author of the forthcoming book* THE ENEMY THAT WENT HOME (*University of North Carolina Press*).

The Tragedy of Bill Clinton

Garry Wills

So far, most readers of President Clinton's book seem to like the opening pages best, and no wonder. Scenes of childhood glow from many memoirs—by Jean-Jacques Rousseau, Henry Adams, John Ruskin, John Henry Newman, and others. It is hard to dislike people when they are still vulnerable, before they have put on the armor of whatever career or catastrophe lies before them as adults. In fact, Gilbert Chesterton advised those who would love their enemies to imagine them as children. The soundness of this tactic is proved by its reverse, when people become irate at attempts to imagine the childhood or the youth of Hitler—as in protests at the Menna Meyjez film *Max*. So it is hard, even for his foes, to find Clinton objectionable as a child. Yet the roots of the trouble he later had lie there, in the very appeal of his youth.

Another reason we respond to narratives of childhood is that first sensations are widely shared by everyone—the ways we became aware of the world around us, of family, of school, of early friends. One might expect Clinton's pineywood world to be remote from people who did not grow up in the South. But since he experienced neither grinding poverty nor notable privilege, there is an everyman quality to what he is writing about. His relatives were not blue-collar laborers but service providers—as nurse (mother and grandmother), heavy equipment salesman (father), car dealer (first stepfather), hairdresser (second stepfather), food broker (third stepfather). This was no Dogpatch, as one can tell from the number of Clinton's childhood friends who went on to distinguished careers. (The daughters of one of his ministers became, respectively, the president of Wellesley and the ombudsman of *The Washington Post*.)

Admittedly, Clinton's family was notably fissiparous, with a litter of half-relatives filling the landscape—but even that is familiar to us in this time of frequent divorce and divided custodies. It may seem out of the ordinary for Clinton's father to have been married four times by the age of twenty-six, his first stepfather to have been married three times (twice to Clinton's mother), his second stepfather to have been married twice (with twenty-nine months in jail for fraud bridging the two). His mother, because of the mortality rate of her husbands, was married five times (though two of the times were to the same man). Clinton, who has had the gift of empathy throughout his life, remained astonishingly close to all the smashed elements of this marital kaleidoscope—even to his stepfather, whose abuse of his mother Clinton had to stop with physical interventions and calls to the police. He took time from college to give his stepfather loving care at the end of his life. The most recurrent refrain in this book is "I liked him," and it began at home.

Clinton usually looked at the bright side. What the jumble of marriages gave him as a boy was just more relatives to charm and be cosseted by. Later the same people would be a political asset. The first time he ran for office, "I had relatives in five of the district's twenty-one counties." Later still, he could rely on "a big vote in south Arkansas, where I had lots of relatives." One might think he was already preparing for a political career when he got along so well with all his scattered families. But he was, even then, a natural charmer, with an immediate gratification in being liked, not looking (yet) for remoter returns from politics. Clinton won others' affection for a reason Aristotle famously gave—we enjoy doing things that we do well.[1]

Clinton claims that his sunny adaptability as a child was a front, that he lived a secret "parallel life" imposed on a "fat band boy" by his father's violence and alcoholism. He is preparing his explanation of the Monica Lewinsky affair as a product of this secret life. It is true that we all have a public self and several private ones. It is also true that childhood and adolescence prompt dark or lonely moments in most people. But the India-rubber-man resiliency of Clinton makes it hard to believe his explanation-excuse for later aberrations. "Slick Willie," the nickname he says he dislikes most, was always an unlikely brooder. The thing that would impress others about Clinton's later philandering, which long preceded the Monica stuff, was its lack of secrecy, its flamboyant risk-taking.

His attempt at a Dickensian shoe-black-factory childhood is therefore unconvincing. One of the afflictions he says he had to bear in silence was going to church in shoes his mother bought him; "pink and black Hush Puppies, and a matching pink suede belt." But since he shared his mother's idolatry of Elvis, his S-C (sartorially correct) attitude is probably retrospective. In fact, the "fat band boy" was very popular, with a wide circle of friends who stayed true to him (and he to them) ever after. His ability to enthrall others would become legendary, and one of the pleasures of his book is watching him get around obstacles by force of personality and cleverness:

—As a Yale law student organizing New Haven for the nascent McGovern campaign, Clinton goes to the city's Democratic boss, Arthur Barbieri, who tells him he has the money and organization to crush the McGovern insurgency:

> I replied that I didn't have much money, but I did have eight hundred volunteers who would knock on the doors of every house in his stronghold, telling all the Italian mothers that Arthur Barbieri wanted to keep sending their sons to fight and die in Vietnam. "You don't need that grief," I said. "Why do you care who wins the nomination? Endorse McGovern. He was a war hero in World War II. He can make peace and you can keep control of New Haven."

Barbieri is struck by this law student—he and Matty Troy of New York are the only old-line bosses to endorse McGovern in the primary.

—Wanting to take Hillary Rodham to a special exhibit in the Yale art gallery for their first date, he finds the gallery locked, but talks his way in by telling the custodian that he will clean up the litter in the gallery courtyard if he lets them go through the exhibit.

—Fresh from law school, Clinton hears his application for a teaching job is turned down by the dean of the University of Arkansas Law School because he is too young and inexperienced, and he says those qualities are actually a recommendation:

> I'd be good for him, because I'd work hard and teach any courses he wanted. Besides, I wouldn't have tenure, so he could fire me at any time. He chuckled and invited me to Fayetteville for an interview.

He gets the job.

—After doing the whole Lamaze course to assist his wife when their first child is born; he learns that she must have a Caesarean section because the baby is "in breech." No one is allowed in the operating room during surgery. He pleads that Hillary has never been in a hospital before and she needs him. He is allowed to hold her hand during the delivery. Can no one say no to this man?

Persuasiveness on Clinton's scale can be a temptation. The ability to retrieve good will can make a person careless about taking vulnerable steps. Indeed, a certain type will fling himself over a cliff just to prove he can always catch a branch and crawl back up to the top. There is nothing, he begins to feel, for which he cannot win forgiveness. This kind of recklessness followed by self-retrieval is what led Clinton to think of himself as "the comeback kid" (the use of the word "kid" is probably more indicative than he intended). Famous charmers are fun to be around, but they are not people to depend on.

Washington

David Broder at his sniffiest declared that Clinton was a social usurper in Washington: "He came in here and he trashed the place, and it's not his place."[2] Clinton was simply "not one of us." But unlike Broder he had gone to school there. From the time he saw Washington as a high school member of Boys Nation and shook President. Kennedy's hand, Clinton wanted to get back there. His college placement counselor, Edith Irons, told me she urged him to apply to several colleges, not just one. But he filled out forms only for Georgetown—not because it was a Jesuit school, or a good school. Because it was in Washington. And so ingratiating was this Southern Baptist in a cosmopolitan Catholic school that he quickly became class president as a freshman and sophomore. He did not run for the office in his third year because by then he was an intern in Arkansas senator William Fulbright's office. He had to be given security clearance because he ran classified documents from place to place on Capitol Hill. Already he was a Washington insider.

Some of the freshest pages in the book register Clinton's impressions of the senators he observed. These were models against which he was measuring his future career, and the images were printed deep in him. He saw Carl Hayden of Arizona, whom a friend called "the only ninety-year-old man in the world who looks twice his age." The senior senator from his own state, John McClellan, had sorrows "drowned in enough whiskey to float the Capitol down the Potomac River." Clinton was especially interested in Senator Robert Kennedy, brother to his own fallen hero:

> He radiated raw energy. He's the only man I ever saw who could walk stoop-shouldered, with his head down, and still look like a coiled spring about to release into the air. He wasn't a great speaker by conventional standards, but he spoke with such intensity and passion it could be mesmerizing. And if he didn't get everyone's attention with his name, countenance, and speech, he had Brumus, a large, shaggy Newfoundland, the biggest dog I ever saw. Brumus often came to work with Senator Kennedy. When Bobby walked from his office in the New Senate Building to the Capitol to vote, Brumus would walk by his side, bounding up the Capitol steps to the revolving door on the rotunda level, then sitting patiently outside until his master returned for the walk back. Anyone who could command the respect of that dog had mine too.

One of Clinton's housemates at Georgetown worked in Robert Kennedy's office, and another was in Henry "Scoop" Jackson's office. A Georgetown girl he was dating hated Kennedy because she was working for his rival, Eugene McCarthy, whose lassitude Clinton compared unfavorably with Kennedy's energy. He especially admired his own boss, Senator Fulbright:

> I'll never forget one night in 1967 or '68. I was walking alone in Georgetown when I saw the Senator and Mrs. Fulbright leaving one of the fashionable homes after a dinner party. When they reached the street, apparently with no one around to see, he took her in his arms and danced a few steps. Standing in the shadows, I saw what a light she was in his life.

Oxford

Clinton not only worked for Fulbright in Washington but drove him around Arkansas. He sincerely admired his opposition to the Vietnam War—among other things it gave him an excuse for avoiding the war. The flap over Clinton's "draft dodging" looks quaint in retrospect. He first tried to do what George W. Bush did, join the National Guard, but he did not have the contacts to be accepted. The differences are that he, unlike Bush, did not support the war, and he is honest in saying that he was trying to avoid combat. He was in his first term as a Rhodes Scholar at Oxford, and a friend and housemate of his (Frank Aller) was defying the draft as a conscientious objector. Aller said Clinton should risk the draft in order to have a political career, though he could not do that himself.

A man much admired by his Oxford contemporaries but tortured by his scruples, Aller later committed suicide. Robert McNamara, who came to know of Aller's anguish, wrote Clinton when he was elected president:

> By their votes, the American people, at long last, recognized that the Allers and the Clintons, when they questioned the wisdom and morality of their government's decisions relating to Vietnam, were no less patriotic than those who served in uniform.

After Clinton failed to get into the National Guard, his uncle tried to get him into a navy program (which would involve less danger, and a delay in enlistment). Clinton's third try was as an ROTC law student at the University of Arkansas in Fayetteville, which would have given him three to four years' delay in actual service—but would have kept him from continuing at Oxford. Only when he drew a low number in the draft did he take his chances on staying in England rather than going to Fayetteville. The famous letter he wrote to explain why he was not going to show up for the ROTC spot was a typical act of ingratiation with the man who had admitted him into the program, Colonel Eugene Holmes. He said that he would "accept" the draft (he did not say he had been given a low number) only "to maintain my political viability within the [political] system." The ingratiation worked, at first. Colonel Holmes, when asked about Clinton's relations with ROTC, said for years that there was nothing abnormal about them. Only in the 1992 campaign did he write a letter denouncing Clinton as a draft dodger. Clinton suggests that Holmes may have had "help" with his memory from his daughter, a Republican activist in the Arkansas Bush campaign. Clinton's best biographer, David Maraniss, goes much further, and says that national officials of the Bush campaign "reviewed the letter before it was made public."[3]

Clinton's time in Oxford led to many silly charges against him. He was said to have been a protester in Arkansas, at a time when he was in England—an accusation that came up in his campaigns for state office. Much was made of his confession that he tried marijuana but "did not inhale." *Could* not inhale would have been more truthful—his allergies had kept him from smoking any kind of cigarette, and the respected British journalist Martin Walker, who was with Clinton at the time, confirmed that he and others tried to teach Clinton to inhale, but he could not—he would end up "leaning his head out an open window gasping for fresh air." The problem with a reputation for being "slick" is that even the simple truth can look like a ploy.

Clinton's asthma and allergies stood in his way during his first political campaign, but charm overcame the problem when two local figures he wanted to campaign for him in Arkansas took him out from town in a truck, pulled out a pack of Red Man chewing tobacco, and said, "If you're

man enough to chew this tobacco, we'll be for you. If not, we'll kick you out and let you walk back to town." Clinton hesitated a moment, then said: "Open the damn door." The two men laughed and became his campaigners for many years.

A more serious charge arising from his two years at Oxford came from his trip to Russia, which would later be called treasonous—a charge that the senior Bush's campaign tried to verify by breaking its own rules on passport and embassy reports. Clinton's interest in Russia came from the fact that his housemate and fellow Rhodes Scholar, Strobe Talbot, was already such an expert on the Russian language and history that he was translating the memoirs of Khrushchev, smuggled out to him by Jerry Schecter, the Moscow correspondent for *Time*. Clinton learned more about America than about either England or Russia during his time at Oxford, where his fellow Rhodes Scholars talked endlessly about their country and the war. Clinton gave up a third year and a degree in England to get back to the Yale Law School and antiwar activities, first in Joseph Duffey's failed Connecticut campaign for senator and then in McGovern's campaign for the presidency. In the latter cause, he had an ally in Hillary Rodham.

Yale

Clinton refers to various women he dated or traveled with in Europe, and he drops some indirect references to his reputation as a ladies' man —as inoculation, I suppose. He says he "had lived a far from perfect life," and carried "more baggage than an ocean liner." "The lies hurt, and the occasional truth hurt more." He even admits that when he proposed to Hillary, "nothing in my background indicated I knew what a stable marriage was all about." With women before Hillary, he was the one not seeking a commitment; but he pursued Hillary relentlessly. As law students, after they began living together, they traveled to Europe and the American West. He first proposed to her in England's Lake Country, but she said no. When she spent the summer of 1968 as an intern for a law firm in Oakland, California, he turned down an offer to organize the McGovern campaign in Miami and went with her to California for the whole summer. He was afraid he would lose her. What their marriage proves is that even a lecherous man can have the one great love affair of his life.

Lechery

In this book Clinton misleads not by equivocation but by omission. He gives a long account of his decision not to run for president in July of 1988—how he summoned friends with wide experience to Little Rock and weighed all the options. He admits that Gary Hart had withdrawn from the race two months earlier, and that "after the Hart affair, those of us who had not led perfect lives had no way of knowing what the press's standards of disclosure were." Clinton had to be paying close attention to the Hart campaign that year. He had worked closely with Hart on the McGovern team—in fact, Hart had rebuked him for paying too much attention to his "girl friend" (Hillary) during the campaign.[4] What Clinton leaves out of the account of his decision in 1988 is the brutal candor of the advice given him by his longtime aide, Betsey Wright. According to David Maraniss,

> Wright met with Clinton at her home on Hill Street. The time had come, she felt, for Clinton to get past what she considered his self-denial tendencies and face the issue squarely. For years, she told friends later, she had been covering up for him. She was convinced that some state troopers were soliciting women for him, and he for them, she said. Sometimes when Clinton was on the road, Wright would call his room in the middle of the night and no one would answer. She hated that part of him, but felt that the other sides of him overshadowed his personal weaknesses.
>
> …She started listing the names of women he had allegedly had affairs with and the places where they were said to have occurred. "Now," she concluded, "I want you to tell me the truth about every one." She went over the list twice with Clinton, according to her later account, the second time trying to determine whether any of the women might tell their stories to the press. At the end of the process, she suggested that he should not get into the race. He owed it to Hillary and Chelsea not to.[5]

No one who has seen Clinton with his daughter can doubt that he loves her deeply, and he does say that concern for her kept him out of the 1988 race, when she was eight years old. "Carl Wagner, who was also the father of an only daughter, told me I'd have to reconcile myself to being away from Chelsea for most of the next sixteen months." The same problem would arise, of course, four years later, when Chelsea would be twelve—yet he would run then. Wagner's advice is given a much different sense in his account to Maraniss. Wagner, who was a friend of Betsey Wright and had been given a job by her when he arrived in Little Rock, knew about her concerns, and shared them. After the conference with advisers, he stayed while the others left, to tell Clinton:

> When you reach the top of the steps, walk into your daughter's bedroom, look at her, and understand that if you do this, your relationship with her will never be the same. I'm not sure if it will be worse or better, but it will never be the same." [6]

Wagner was not worried about Clinton's absence from Chelsea, but about the presence of shadowy women in her young mind.

When Clinton ran in 1992, he admits that he anticipated trouble. A man in George H. W. Bush's White House, Roger Porter—with whom Clinton had worked on the President's "education initiative"—called him to say that "if I ran, they would have to destroy me personally."

> He went on to say the press were elitists who would believe any tales they were told about backwater Arkansas. "We'll spend whatever we have to spend to get whoever we have to get to say whatever they have to say to take you out. And we'll do it early."

Of course, this is Clinton's version of the phone call; it has the ring of a Lee Atwater campaign, although it can even be interpreted as kindly meant. Clinton was being forewarned that he could not expect to get a free pass on his background. Clinton presents his decision to run despite this warning as a brave refusal to be blackmailed: "Ever since I was a little boy I have hated to be threatened."

On Gennifer Flowers, Clinton did resort to equivocation. In the famous post—Super Bowl interview on *60 Minutes*, Steve Kroft asked about "what she calls a twelve-year affair with you." Clinton said, "That allegation is false" (referring to the twelve-year aspect). So, said Kroft, "you're categorically denying that you ever had an affair with Gennifer Flowers?" Clinton answered, "I've said that before, and so has she." Both answers were technically correct, though six years later he would admit that they were "misleading"—he did have an affair. Most people forget that Clinton's trouble with women taping their phone calls did not begin with Monica Lewinsky. In 1992

Flowers was taping him, at a time when she was publicly denying claims of their affair. When he called her after defeating Sheffield Nelson for governor, Clinton mocked Nelson for denying that he had charged Clinton with infidelity: "I knew he lied. I just wanted to make his asshole pucker. But I covered you," Clinton said on a tape that became public.[7]

The Lewinskiad

Clinton claims that he does not offer excuses for his past life in this book. But he now says that he lied because he was confused, fatigued, and angry at being surrounded by bloodhound prosecutors, a hostile Congress, and a barking press: "And if there had been no Kenneth Star —if we had different kind of people, I would have just said, 'Here are the facts. I'm sorry. Deal with it however you please.' " Here all the contrived contrition is forgotten—it was Ken Starr who made him lie. But what was he lying about? For that he has another excuse, his "parallel life" in which he kept embarrassing things secret. Well, we all do that. But why did he do the reckless things with Lewinsky that he had to keep secret? With both Dan Rather and Charlie Rose he said: "I think I did something for the worst possible reason, just because I could. I think that's the most—just about the most morally indefensible reason that anybody could have for doing anything, when you do something just because you could." Here he is applying to himself what Newt Gingrich said to him when Clinton asked why the Republicans shut down the government in 1995. The answer: "Because we could." Later Clinton says the prosecutors hunted him "because they could."

As applied to him, the answer is nonsense. First of all, he *couldn't* do it, if that meant doing it with impunity—as he found out. Moreover, that is not the worst possible reason for doing anything. There are far worse reasons—hatred, revenge, religious fanaticism, sadism. He avoids saying that he did it because he wanted to, but that is the only honest answer. He did it from lechery. And the absurdity of it, the risk, just spiced the matter with danger. He was not withdrawing into a secret self but throwing himself outward in flamboyant bravado. Clinton, like his mother, is a gambler. He does not, as she did, play the ponies. He dares the lightning. He knew he had numerous hunters and trackers circling him about. He knew that he already had to cope with Gennifer Flowers, Paula Jones,

and Kathleen Willey. The young woman he was adding to the list was not likely to be discreet—she boasted of earning her presidential kneepads, and wangled thirty-seven entrances to the White House, and snapped her thong, and preserved the candied semen. (DNA technology is still a comparatively young discipline, but it is not likely for some time to get a stranger exercise than testing the effluvia of presidential fellation.)

Flirting with ever greater peril, he repeatedly telephoned Lewinsky. He sent her presents (*Leaves of Grass* as Seducer's Assistant). He wore her present. He lied in risky forums. He put in jeopardy political efforts he cared about, as well as the respect and love of his wife and daughter. It was such a crazy thing to do that many of us could not, for a long time, believe he had done it. But Betsey Wright, from her long experience of the man, knew at once: "I was miserably furious with him, and completely unable to communicate with him from the time the Lewinsky stuff was unfolded on the national scene. This was a guy I had given thirteen years of my life to."[8]

Starr

Though Clinton's conduct was inexcusable, it does pale next to the deep and vast abuses of power that Kenneth Starr sponsored and protected. He is a deceptively sweet-looking fellow, a dimpled, flutily warbling Pillsbury Doughboy. But he lent himself to the schemes of people with an almost total disregard for the law. A man of honor would not have accepted his appointment by a right-wing judge to replace Robert Fiske, a Republican general counsel who was a distinguished prosecutor. Not only did Starr have no prosecutorial experience; he had already lent support to Paula Jones's suit against the President. He continued private practice for right-wing causes with right-wing funding. Five former presidents of the American Bar Association said that he had conflicts of interest for which he should recuse himself. At one point in his investigation, a *New York Times* editorial said he should resign. His own chosen ethics adviser, Sam Dash, left him in protest at his tactics. The American Civil Liberties Union had to bring an end to the "barbaric" conditions he imposed on the imprisoned Susan McDougal.[9]

Starr raised again the suspicion that Vince Foster was murdered, after his predecessor had disposed of that claim. This was a favorite cause of the man funding much of the right-wing pursuit of Clinton, Richard Mellon Scaife, who is a principal donor to Pepperdine College, where Starr now holds a chair. The list of Starr's offenses is long and dark. Congressman Barney Frank questioned him about the fact that he released his damning "sex report" on Clinton before the 1998 elections though he held findings that cleared Clinton of other charges—findings reached months earlier—until after the election. After Starr made several attempts at evading the question, Frank said, "In other words, you don't have anything to say [before an election] unless you have something bad to say."[10]

Starr prolonged his investigations as charge after charge was lengthily discredited, until the right-wing Rutherford Institute's lawyers, representing Paula Jones, could trap Clinton in a confession of his contacts with Monica Lewinsky, to which Starr then devoted his frenzied attention. The wonder is that Starr got away with all his offenses. For that he needed a complicit press, which disgraced itself in this period, gobbling up the illegal leaks that flowed from his office. The sniffy Washingtonians went so berserk over the fact that Clinton was Not One of Us that they bestowed on Starr an honorary Oneness with Usness. Sally Quinn wrote in *The Washington Post* that "Beltway Insiders" were humiliated by Clinton, and that "Starr is a Washington insider, too."[11]

Starr was one thing that made some people stay with Clinton, who says Starr's unfairness helped bring Hillary back to his side. Paul Begala admitted he was disgusted by what Clinton had done, but determined that he would not let Starr accomplish a "coup d'etat." That does not describe what a Starr success would have meant. Conviction on impeachment charges would not have brought in a Republican administration. Succession would have gone to Vice President Al Gore in Clinton's own administration. But Clinton agrees with Begala. He presents his fight with Starr as a defense of all the things the right wing disliked about him—his championship of blacks, and gays, and the poor. He works himself up to such a righteous pitch that he says his impeachment trial was a "badge of honor."

Honor

Actually, the honorable thing for Clinton would have been to resign. I argued for that in a *Time* magazine article as soon as he re-

vealed that he had lied to the nation.[12] I knew, of course, that he wouldn't. He had thrown himself off the highest cliff ever, and he had to prove he could catch a last-inute branch and pull himself, improbably, back up. And damned if he didn't. He ended his time as president with high poll numbers and some new accomplishments, the greatest of the Kid's comebacks—so great that I have been asked if I still feel he should have resigned. Well, I do. Why? Partly because what Ross Perot said in 1996 was partly true—that Clinton would be "totally occupied for the next two years in staying out of jail." That meant he would probably go on lying. He tried for as long as possible to "mislead" the nation on Gennifer Flowers. He still claims that Paula Jones and Kathleen Willey made false charges. Perhaps they did, but he became unbelievable about personal behavior after lying about Flowers and Lewinsky. I at first disbelieved the story Paula Jones told because it seemed too bizarre; but the cigar-dildo described by Monica Lewinsky considerably extended the vistas of the bizarre.

Though Clinton accomplished things in his second term, he did so in a constant struggle to survive. Unlike the current president, his administration found in Sudan the presence of a weapon of mass destruction (the nerve gas precursor Empta) and bombed the place where it had existed—but many, including Senator Arlen Specter and the journalist Seymour Hersh, said that Clinton was just bombing another country to distract people from his scandal.[13] "That reaction," according to Richard Clarke, "made it more difficult to get approval for follow-up attacks on al Quaeda."[14] Even when Clinton was doing things, the appearance of his vulnerability made people doubt it. It was said in the Pentagon that he was afraid to seize terrorists because of his troubles; but Clarke rebuts those claims—he says that every proposal to seize a terrorist leader; whether it came from the CIA or the Pentagon, was approved by Clinton "during my tenure as CSG [Counterterrorism Security Group] chairman, from 1992 to 2001."

We shall never know what was not done, or not successfully done, because of Clinton's being politically crippled. He has been criticized for his insufficient response to the ethnic cleansing in Kosovo. Michael Walzer said of the bombing raids Clinton finally authorized that "our faith in airpower is ... a kind of idolatry."[15] But Clinton was limited in what he could do by the fact that the House of Representatives passed a resolution exactly the opposite of

the war authorization that would be given George W. Bush—it voted to deny the President the power to commit troops. Walzer says that Clinton should have prodded the UN to take action; but a Republican Congress was not going to follow a man it distrusted when he called on an institution it distrusted.

At the very end of Clinton's regime, did Arafat feel he was not strong enough in his own country to pressure him into the reasonable agreement Clinton had worked out and Ehud Barak had accepted? Clinton suggests as much when he says that Arafat called him a great man, and he had to reply: "I am not a great man. I am a failure, and you have made me one."

Clinton had a wise foreign policy. But in an Oval Office interview, shortly before he admitted lying to the nation, he admitted that he had not been able to make it clear to the American people. His vision had so little hold upon the public that Bush was able to discard it instantly when he came in. Clinton summed up the difference between his and Bush's approach for Charlie Rose by saying that the latter thinks we should "do what we want whenever we can, and then we cooperate when we have to," whereas his policy was that "we were cooperating whenever we could and we acted alone only when we had to." The Bush people are learning the difference between the two policies as their preemptive unilateralism fails.

Clinton claims that he was not hampered in his political activity by scandals. He even said, to Charlie Rose, that "I probably was more attentive to my work for several months just because I didn't want to tend to anything else." That is improbable a priori and it conflicts with what he told Dan Rather about the atmosphere caused by the scandal: "The moment was so crazy. It was a zoo. It was an unr—it was—it was like living in a madhouse." Even if he were not distracted, the press and the nation were. His staff was demoralized. The Democrats on the Hill were defensive, doubtful, absorbed in either defending Clinton or deflecting criticism from themselves. His freedom to make policy was hobbled.

Clinton likes to talk now of his "legacy." That legacy should include partial responsibility for the disabling of the Democratic Party. There were things to be said against the Democratic Leadership Council (Mario Cuomo said them well) and the "triangulation" scheme of Dick Morris, by which

Clinton would take positions to the right of most congressional Democrats and to the left of the Republican Party. But Clinton, as a Southerner, knew that the party had to expand its base back into sources of support eroded by the New Right. This was a defensible (in fact a shrewd) strategy as Clinton originally shaped it. He could have made it a tactical adjunct to important strategic goals. But after the scandals, all his maneuvering looked desperate—a swerving away from blows, a flurried scrambling to find solid footing. His very success made Democrats think their only path to success was to concede, cajole, and pander. Al Gore began his 2000 campaign unhappy about his association with Clinton but trying to outpander him when he opposed the return of the Cuban boy Elian Gonzalez to his father. There is a kind of rude justice to the fact that the election was stolen from Gore in the state where he truckled to the Cubans.

Clinton bequeathed to his party not a clear call to high goals but an omnidirectional proneness to pusillanimity and collapse. This was signaled at the very outset of the new presidency. The Democrats, still in control of the Senate, facing a president not even strong enough to win the popular vote, a man brought into office by linked chicaneries and chance (Kathleen Harris, Ralph Nader, Antonin Scalia), nonetheless helped to confirm John Ashcroft as attorney general. The senators knew Ashcroft well; they were surely not impressed by his acumen or wisdom.

A whole series of capitulations followed. While still holding a majority in the Senate, the Democrats did not use subpoenas and investigative powers to challenge Dick Cheney's secret drafting of energy policy with Enron and other companies. A portion of the Democrats would support the welfare-to-billionaires tax cut. They fairly stampeded to support the Patriot Act and the presidential war authorization—with John Kerry, John Edwards, and Hillary Clinton at the front of the pack. The party had become so neutered that Al From and others from the Democratic Leadership Council called Howard Dean an extremist for daring to say what everyone is now saying about the war with Iraq—that it was precipitate, overhyped, and underprepared, more likely to separate us from the friends needed to fight terrorists than to end terrorism.

What would have happened had Clinton resigned? Gore would have been given a "honeymoon" in which he could have played with a stronger hand all the initiatives Clinton had begun, unashamed of them and able to bring them fresh energy. That is what happened when Lyndon Johnson succeeded John Kennedy. Clinton himself may have reaped a redeeming admiration for what he had sacrificed to recover his honor. Before him would have lain all the opportunities he has now, and more. Hillary Clinton's support of him in this act of real contrition would have looked nobler. Clinton's followers were claiming that it was all and only about sex. Clinton could have said, "Since that is what it is about, I'll step aside so more important things can be addressed." All the other phony issues Starr had raised would have fallen of their own insubstantiality.

Of course, this is just one of many what-ifs about the Clinton presidency. By chance I saw a revival of Leonard Bernstein's musical *Wonderful Town*, just before getting my copy of the Clinton book. All through the 957 pages of it, a song from the show kept running through my head: "What a waste! What a waste!"

Notes

1. Aristotle, *Nichomachean Ethics* 1097–1098.

2. Sally Quinn, "Not in Their Backyard: In Washington, That Let Down Feeling," *The Washington Post*, November 2, 1998.

3. David Maraniss, *First in His Class: A Biography of Bill Clinton* (Simon and Schuster, 1995), p. 205.

4. Garry Wills, "Lightning Rod," *The New York Review*, August 14, 2003.

5. Maraniss, *First in His Class*, pp. 440–441.

6. Maraniss, *First in His Class*, p. 441.

7. Maraniss, *First in His Class*, p. 457.

8. Interview in the Harry Thomason and Nicholas Perry film *The Hunting of the President* (Regent Entertainment, 2004).

9. The despicable treatment of Susan McDougal is movingly presented in *The Hunting of the President*, a film that has many trivializing touches (like intercut clips of old Hollywood melodramas). McDougal's story is backed up by a very impressive woman, Claudia Riley, the wife of Bob Riley, the former Arkansas governor and college president, who stayed with McDougal through her ordeal and describes the bullying tactics she witnessed.

10. Sidney Blumenthal, *The Clinton Wars* (Farrar, Straus and Giroux, 2003), p. 512.

11. Quinn, "Not in Their Backyard: In Washington, That Let Down Feeling."

12. Garry Wills, "Leading by Leaving," *Time*, August 31, 1998.

13. See the important work by two former National Security Council antiterrorist directors, Daniel Benjamin and Steven Simon, *The Age of Sacred Terror: Radical Islam's War Against America* (Random House, 2002), pp. 352–360. See also Richard Clarke, *Against All Enemies: Inside America's War on Terror* (Free Press, 2004), pp. 146–147.

14. Clarke, *Against All Enemies*, p. 189.

15. Michael Walzer, *Arguing About War* (Yale University Press, 2004), p. 99.

The pros from Dover

By John Prados

President Bush surrounded himself with what should have been a crack team of national security experts. So what went wrong? Did their system just not work, or did they have the wrong agenda?

There is a hilarious scene in the movie *M*A*S*H* where two young doctors from a field hospital at the front in the Korean War travel to Japan and proceed to have their way with local commanders and the military bureaucracy. Arriving to carry out the heart operation for which they have been summoned, the doctors call themselves the "pros from Dover."

In the way life has of imitating art, the national security process of the Bush administration has been the province of its own fresh set of professionals. The result has not been hilarity but something else. With the Bush people having gotten the United States enmeshed in situations of grave concern throughout the globe, it is important to ask whether the American government is up to handling the job, not in terms of capabilities but of policy process.

In the American system of government, the top executive authority, the president, is assisted in areas of foreign affairs and military matters by the National Security Council (NSC). The council consists of the president, vice president, secretary of state, and defense secretary. The national security adviser to the president does not have a statutory role but is typically made a senior member of the council. The director of central intelligence and chairman of the Joint Chiefs of Staff sit as advisers to the group. The president is the king of policy hill, of course, and may arrange the NSC and its work at his whim, organizing and reorganizing whenever it suits him. NSC staff members under the na-

tional security adviser directly serve the president by coordinating the issues and providing the chief executive with their understanding of the options, pros, and cons.

Three years into the Bush administration, in spite of a host of developments in the national security realm, there has yet to be any serious inquiry into its methods of policymaking and their impact on American security. That inquiry is overdue.

The players

George W. Bush has certainly benefited from a dream team of senior advisers on his National Security Council. Bush chose carefully among people of conservative cast of mind to match his own, and while one may deplore the ideology of the crew, the president's right to be served by the officials he wants is unquestioned. Ideology notwithstanding, the Bush people have the right stuff—the credentials to actually be the pros from Dover—from the top people on the NSC to the second tier at the agencies and staff. On January 21, 2001, an observer could have said this administration was primed for success.

In terms of organization of the policy process, the Bush administration also started out on familiar ground. Presidents create their own policy machinery, and different presidents have approached the national security process in a variety of ways.[1]

The Carter administration designed a two-committee structure that has become almost the standard NSC organization for subsequent presidencies, including that of George W. Bush. In the current scheme, the president meeting with his senior advisers constitutes the National Security Council. Without the president, the rump NSC meets as the Principals Committee, chaired by the vice president or national security adviser. These groups focus on decisions. Below them is the Deputies Committee, a group chaired by the deputy national security adviser, which concentrates on implementing the president's decisions. Staff assistants attend as required. Teleconferencing and secure video links between various U.S. government centers have enabled greater flexibility in participation, but the essence of the system remains the same.

The most remarkable aspect of Bush's national security organization is the role of the vice president. Historically, vice presidents have had a relatively minor impact on national security decision making. Walter Mondale and Al Gore were more active under presidents Carter and Clinton, and Bush's father, George H. W. Bush, had an enhanced role under Ronald Reagan. In the current administration, however, Dick Cheney is of critical importance in virtually all aspects of national security policy. From the first moments of George W. Bush's presidency, Cheney functioned as the power behind the throne, privately advocating policies, then coming out in public with discourse designed to build constituencies for those same policies. He also became the official whom Bush tapped for the tough jobs—and the president's hatchet man. Cheney emerged as an assistant with an agenda more ample than that of his master. His role encouraging Bush to make war on Iraq has been so widely remarked it has virtually eclipsed his work early in the administration heading a presidential commission on energy policy, his views on military transformation, and the task force on federal-local antiterrorism cooperation that Bush appointed him to chair four months before the 9/11 attacks.

To match his policy role, the vice president has crafted a sort of mini-NSC staff among his White House retinue. Where Al Gore as vice president employed Leon Fuerth as his national security adviser (plus a couple of staff aides), and Bush's father, as vice president under Reagan, had a security staff of two professionals (plus aides), Cheney employs a national security staff of 15. The importance Cheney gives that staff is indicated by the fact that his own overall chief of staff, I. Lewis ("Scooter") Libby, serves simultaneously as the vice president's national security adviser. Early last year, at a key moment in the run-up to the Iraq war, Cheney's deputy national security adviser Eric Edelman was appointed U.S. ambassador to Turkey, another indication of the standing of the Cheney national security staff. Edelman was succeeded by Aaron Friedberg, a China expert and former director of policy planning on the Cheney staff. That the staff even had a policy-planning component demonstrates the quantum advance of the Cheney operation over the staff resources available to previous vice presidents.

Cheney himself is no stranger to national security issues, or to government for that matter. In his current incarnation he is mostly known for his role as chief executive of the Halliburton Corporation during the 1990s, but less noted is the extent to which Halliburton worked with and for the U.S. military. More to the point, Cheney was defense secretary—the job Donald Rumsfeld now has—during the first Bush administration, including the first Gulf War. Before that, Cheney served as White House chief of staff to President Gerald R. Ford from 1975 to early 1977 and deputy chief of staff 1974-1975. At the time, he was deputy to Donald Rumsfeld, whom President Ford subsequently sent to the Pentagon. In the Ford White House, Cheney worked on a number of national security issues, most notably advising Ford on how to handle the intelligence scandals of 1975. Cheney was an architect of the presidential commission on intelligence (the Rockefeller Commission) created by Ford in an effort to head off what became the Church and Pike Committee investigations. While the attempt proved unsuccessful, Cheney gained experience he put to work later as a member of Congress and then in his own Pentagon job.

Next to the vice president, the person closest to the Oval Office is the national security adviser. For George Bush this is Condoleezza Rice. Like Cheney—like a number of the pros from Dover—Rice is no stranger to the issues, or even to the national security staff. Retired Air Force Gen. Brent Scowcroft (who held the post of national security adviser for Gerald Ford, alongside Cheney and Rumsfeld) discovered Rice during the 1980s at the Aspen Institute. She was then a recently minted academic with a doctorate in international relations from the University of Denver. Her dissertation was on Soviet political control of the Czechoslovak armed forces. She taught at Stanford University. When Scowcroft did a second tour as national security adviser in the administration of President George H. W. Bush, he brought in "Condi," as she is familiarly known, as director for Soviet affairs. Rice was active on the NSC staff during the passing of the Cold War, when the Soviet Union collapsed, Germany reunified, and the old Yugoslavia disintegrated, leaving in its wake the Bosnian civil war.

Among the stories told about Rice that show her willingness to do whatever was necessary is one from the beginning of the first Gulf War, when the NSC staff person responsible for the Iraq-Kuwait region was Richard Haass. When the first President Bush needed a set of talking points for his initial public comment on the Iraqi invasion of Kuwait, Haass could not respond quickly enough because, unfamiliar with computers, he had to hunt and peck at the keyboard. Rice took over and typed out the paper even though Middle East matters were far from her own bailiwick. In 1991 Rice returned to Stanford as a teacher—but not for long. A month after receiving tenure in 1993 she was appointed provost of the university and held that key management position during difficult years. She quickly rallied to the presidential campaign of George W. Bush, however, and was its foreign policy director from early 1999. Rice not only coordinated Bush's issues papers but kept in line the "Vulcans"—the brain trust of national security experts who periodically assembled to give Bush the benefit of their accumulated wisdom. All the Vulcans (Richard Armitage, Robert Blackwill, Stephen J. Hadley, Richard Perle, Paul Wolfowitz, Dov Zakheim, Robert Zoellick) went on to important jobs or advisory posts in the Bush administration, and it was hardly surprising that Rice landed as national security adviser.

Stephen J. Hadley became Rice's deputy. The only other of the Vulcans to make the leap to work directly within the president's official family, Hadley regarded himself as a detail man. He too had a national security past, having served as assistant secretary of defense for policy under Dick Cheney in the first Bush administration. For those who worried about the influence of Cheney in the White House, Hadley's presence suggested that the vice president, in addition to having his own mini-NSC staff, simultaneously had a front man who was deputy director of the Rice staff itself.

As for the seniors, the members of the actual council of the NSC, they were pros from Dover, too. Donald Rumsfeld has already been mentioned. He is the only person to serve twice as defense secretary—in two different administrations, separated by more than two decades. Colin Powell, retired four-star army general, had been chairman of the Joint Chiefs of Staff during the first Gulf War, a deputy national security adviser to Ronald Reagan, and military assistant to Defense Secretary Caspar Weinberger. CIA Director George Tenet was held over from the Clinton administration and had worked on the Hill, at the White House, or at the CIA since the late 1980s. Their seconds, people like Wolfowitz and Armitage, had similar credentials.

The system

President George W. Bush enhanced the role of his national security adviser by endowing her with cabinet rank. But formal organization of the system remained in limbo until mid-February 2001, when Bush issued his National Security Presidential Directive (NSPD) 1. That document ended speculation as to Vice President Cheney's role—a number of observers had anticipated that Cheney's deep interest in these matters would be reflected by his being made chairman of the Principals Committee.[2] This did not happen. Instead Rice, as national security adviser, would chair the group. What did happen was more significant: By avoiding the chairmanship of the Principals Committee, Cheney left himself free to be an advocate at national security meetings rather than having any responsibility to ensure that all views be aired.

The other significant thing about NSPD 1 was its lateness in the cycle. Most new administrations enter office determined to hit the ground running and typically put out their directives on NSC machinery their first day in office. Bush did not get around to this business for almost a month. By then there had already been two meetings of the Principals Committee. Even the appointments of Condi Rice and the top NSC staffers date from January 22, not the day after the inauguration. The implication is that, at least at the outset, Bush did not consider the national security agenda his top priority.

In terms of size and depth, the Rice NSC staff diminished from the standard under the Clinton administration, but this had more to do with notions of streamlining than with some idea of reducing the importance of national security. Rice cut the staff as a whole by about a third while reducing the number of professional staff from 70 to about 60. She eliminated the legislative affairs and communications offices, limited the staff to a single speechwriter and press spokesperson, and recast some functions. Most importantly, the Russian office merged into a single new desk that included all of Europe, the Balkans, and the former Soviet republics. The Asian affairs office reabsorbed Southeast Asia, which had been assigned to another regional unit in the Clinton White House. North Africa and the Middle East were combined as well. Africa and the Western Hemisphere completed the list of regional offices on the NSC staff. There were also functional specializations, including offices for defense policy and arms control and for intelligence.

Clinton had had an NSC staff unit to supervise nonproliferation and export controls. Under Rice this was reconceptualized as "Nonproliferation Strategy, Counterproliferation, and Homeland Defense." This is instructive for it served as a device to take the ballistic missile defense issue out of the defense policy basket and put it in the much more ideological framework of "homeland defense." That in turn became awkward after the September 11, 2001, attacks, when an Office of Homeland Defense was created at the White House as a parallel to the NSC staff, but in which "homeland defense" held a very different meaning.

The Clinton NSC staff also had a unit covering "transnational threats" and put terrorism at the top of that list. Clinton appointed Richard Clarke, a hard-headed advocate for proactive measures against those threats, to head the unit. Clarke stayed over into the Bush presidency even though, as a press account put it several weeks into the new era, what to do with the transnational threats office was "still up in the air."[3] It is here that the real story begins.

Bush and terrorism

Bill Clinton's last national security adviser, Samuel ("Sandy") Berger, held a number of briefings for Condoleezza Rice and the incoming national security staff as part of the transition from the Clinton to Bush presidencies. Every NSC staff office had been directed to compile a report and present its view of America's strengths and weaknesses to the new crowd. According to an account that has been disputed, the only one of these sessions Sandy Berger personally attended was that which concerned terrorism (Rice has said through a spokesperson that she recalls no briefing at which Berger was present).[4] Berger had left by the time Richard Clarke made the main presentation, but there can be no doubt that the briefing highlighted the need to act on terrorism.

Berger clearly had terrorism on his plate. The question is, did Rice? Berger would tell the joint House-Senate committee investigating the September 11, 2001, attacks that he had convened the Principals Committee every day for a month in an effort to stave off terrorist attacks timed around the millennium celebrations.[5] He quoted himself as telling Rice, "You're going to spend more time during your four years on terrorism generally and Al Qaeda specifically than any [other] issue."[6] For her part, Rice had numerous questions for Clarke, who was asked to prepare a paper on steps against Al Qaeda. Clarke not only had the paper on Stephen J. Hadley's desk within days of the inauguration, he saw the opportunity to get the new president to sign on to an action plan against terrorism, and his paper amounted to an outline. So far, so good. But Clarke's plan then sat gathering dust for weeks.

In speeches, articles, and conversations during the 2000 campaign, Rice had written and spoken of the need in national security to separate the marginal issues from what was truly important.

What Rice and the Bush team made centrally important in the weeks and months after entering office was not terrorism but changing the U.S.-European relationship. The troubles with "Old Europe" that seem so intractable in the wake of the Iraqi war did not just happen coincidentally in 2002-2003. They were prefigured in the very stuff of the NSC staff reorganization, when the Russian and Western European offices were consolidated. Publicly the Bush administration sought to end any notion of a special relationship with Russia, the former Soviet Union, cutting back funding for special cooperative programs designed to help secure Russian nuclear weapons and expertise, abrogating the Anti-Ballistic Missile (ABM) Treaty, and in a variety of other ways. The move on the ABM Treaty also came as a shock to Old Europe, as did Bush's rejection of the Kyoto protocols on environmental action, and the equally sudden U.S. coyness on formation of an international criminal court. When President Bush made his first visit to Europe in June 2001, these issues were the main stuff of American diplomacy.

On the overarching front of defense policy, the maneuver on the ABM Treaty is itself indicative of the Bush administration's goals. Defense Secretary Rumsfeld used the word "transformation" so many times that it became enshrined as the descriptive term for Bush defense policy. Ballistic missile defenses were a key component, and indeed President Bush chose to deploy a technically immature defense system just to ensure that the United States had committed itself to this program. Rumsfeld's talk about space platforms,

his predilection for air force programs, and his fight with the army over its future were the stuff of the transformation.

While circumstances dictated that an action plan on terrorism needed to move to the top of policy hill, the government was preoccupied with anything but that issue. It was only after Bush intervened that anything happened at all. One spring morning, following the departure of CIA briefers who had just given him news in the President's Daily Brief (PDB) of a manhunt for one particular terrorist, Bush complained to Rice: "I'm tired of swatting at flies. . . . I want to play offense, I want to take the fight to the terrorists," Bush said.[7] Rice took the implication that President Bush wanted a plan to attack the terrorists. When she asked the NSC staff how they could put something together, Richard Clarke had his original plan ready.

By late April 2001 the NSC was ready for a policy review on terrorism. After, we are told, six weeks of preliminary sessions, the Deputies Committee met on April 30 to consider an outline plan that Clarke presented. Stephen J. Hadley chaired the meeting, which included Scooter Libby (for Cheney), Richard Armitage (for Powell), Paul Wolfowitz (for Rumsfeld), and John McLaughlin (for Tenet). Here was a case in which the State Department favored going ahead but the CIA proved more cautious. Rather than initiating action, the Deputies Committee called for not one but three policy reviews, one on Al Qaeda, a second on Pakistani internal politics, and a third on the India-Pakistan problem.[8] According to Deputy National Security Adviser Hadley, "the goal was to move beyond the policy of containment, criminal prosecution, and limited retaliation for specific attacks, toward attempting to 'roll back' Al Qaeda."[9] The device of adding extra policy reviews inevitably slowed action, however. As Hadley noted in his response to 9/11 congressional investigators quoted above, between May and July there would be four successive meetings of the NSC Deputies Committee "directly related to the regional issues that had to be resolved in order to adopt a more aggressive strategy."[10] The last one of these sessions discussed the text of a draft presidential directive on July 16.

Meanwhile, on May 8 President Bush created a new unit to focus on terrorism within the Federal Emergency Management Agency, and a new interagency board to consider terrorism issues. He put Cheney in charge of that operation. This was the only actual action President Bush took before September 11, 2001, and it was not about rollback. Cheney's mandate was merely to study preparedness for homeland defense and make recommendations by October.

A second group, the Counterterrorism Security Group (CSG), part of the NSC interagency machinery, was chaired by Richard Clarke. It would be the CSG, not the vice president, that acted, or more properly, reacted. Beginning in March, U.S. intelligence and military sources received a series of reports indicating possible terrorist attacks. First came a report that Al Qaeda operatives in Canada might attack the United States in April.

In April, one source made a rather suggestive speculation that Osama bin Laden was interested in commercial aircraft pilots as terrorists for "spectacular and traumatic" attacks. In May came a report that Al Qaeda supporters were planning to enter the United States to carry out some operation using high explosives. There was also a Pentagon report that seven key suspected terrorists had begun moving toward Canada, the United States, and Britain. Between May and July, the National Security Agency intercepted no fewer than 33 communications suggesting an attack, including one evaluated at the time as an order to execute the plan. In June, the CIA Counterterrorism Center received information that key operatives were disappearing from view. At the end of June, Clarke convened the CSG, and by July 5 there were sufficient alarms to warrant a meeting among Rice, Clarke, and presidential chief of staff Andrew Card.

By then the intelligence scene had shifted and threats seemed centered on the American embassies in Rome, Paris, or Ankara. The CSG met again on July 6, and from then through the end of August, Clarke kept up meetings two or three times a week.[11]

In short, numerous disturbing intelligence reports came in over a period of months *after* President Bush had declared he wanted to go after terrorists, a period of time during which nothing happened with the U.S. government's planning for a rollback of Al Qaeda. Such Bush administration actions that occurred consisted entirely of putting certain selected military forces on precautionary (and defensive) alerts, or issuing warnings to the airlines.

Bush left for Crawford, Texas, and summer vacation on August 4. Two days later, he was given a fresh intelligence report—the PDB again mentioned terrorist attack. As characterized by national security adviser Rice, this PDB "was an analytic report that talked about [Osama bin Laden's] methods of operation, talked about what he had done historically in 1997, in 1998. It mentioned hijacking, but hijacking in the traditional sense, and in a sense said that the most important and most likely thing was that he would take over an airliner holding passengers [and then make demands]."[12]

Much has been speculated about what Bush knew about the Al Qaeda terrorist threat, especially after the leak of the existence of the August 6, 2001 PDB and the report that it had mentioned aircraft hijacking. But the most important thing about the intelligence reports is something we already know: Neither the August 6 PDB, any of the other reports, nor the daily flurry of NSC staff activity on terrorist warnings moved Bush to demand the action plan he had supposedly called for in the spring, to ask that its preparation be accelerated, or to take any other action whatsoever. There is also no indication that Rice, whose job it was to be aware of these alarming reports, made any move to remind the president of his interest in the matter.

Absent presidential initiative, in fact, the plan to roll back Al Qaeda sat dormant six full weeks after mid-July 2001. The draft National Security Presidential Directive was finally considered by the NSC Principals Committee on September 4, and the group recommended that President Bush approve it. When Rice, or others, claim that an approved directive was on Bush's desk on 9/11, they exaggerate. The president had approved nothing. He had received a recommendation to sign a directive that had finally worked its way up through the bureaucracy.

The response of the Bush administration after 9/11 was rather different. When investigators raised questions regarding what Bush had done about intelligence he had received before the attacks, Vice President Cheney mounted a frontal assault on the 9/11 investigators, alleging they were responsible for the appearance in the press of reports of National Security Agency intercepts regarding the attacks, intercepts that White House spokesmen had themselves mentioned in press briefings in the days immediately after 9/11. Cheney demanded and got an FBI investigation of the investigators.

Ever since the 9/11 attacks the Bush White House has taken pains to avoid the revelation of any of the intelligence material provided to the president. The White House denied this material to the joint congressional committee investigating 9/11. It has also stonewalled the national commission inquiring into the attacks. The official rationale has been that no one should ever see the reports provided to a president.

That is not a legitimate declassification policy. A number of PDBs have been declassified and are in the public domain, including ones sent to President John F. Kennedy during the Cuban Missile Crisis and to President Lyndon Johnson during the Vietnam war. Excerpts of PDBs have been leaked on other occasions, not only the one to Bush for August 6, 2001, but one to his father before the Gulf War of 1990-1991. Our democracy has not been shaken by these revelations. And declassification is an ultimate step; the issue here is whether official inquiries operating under full security safeguards are entitled to view documents that are material to their investigations. The real reason to shield them is political: They would reveal the extent of warnings to George W. Bush in the face of which he stood immobile.

The November 2003 Bush compromise with the National Commission on Terrorist Attacks Upon the United States is designed to protect the president while appearing to cooperate. Under the arrangement, the White House will provide edited texts of some PDBs to a team of four (out of ten) commissioners, who will be permitted to take notes that can then be edited by the White House. Two commissioners will be permitted to review all the PDBs and ask that the White House make available additional ones. This formula will be cumbersome in practice and will not ensure public confidence in the 9/11 investigation.

Fast forward

The truth about 9/11 is one of two things. Either Rice's NSC machinery did not work, or else it worked perfectly to ensure that what Bush and his cohorts considered a marginal issue like terrorism did not clutter up the schedule of a president intent on another agenda—transforming America's relationships with traditional allies and former enemies. Either of these conclusions is disturbing. Once the Iraq war is factored into the equation the outlook is even more troubling. Again the NSC machinery operated in a fashion to prevent important objections or alternative policies from coming to the fore. U.S. policy going into the Iraq war was indifferent to alliance politics, to failures to attain needed U.N. approval, to U.S. military objections that the war plan was inadequate, to intelligence warnings that war would be succeeded by guerrilla resistance, to global public opinion, to international disarmament monitors who failed to turn up evidence supporting the Bush rationale for war, and more.[13] Dick Cheney served as an important driver of the policy that would be implemented. Condoleezza Rice became one of its most prominent public advocates; indeed Rice has served far more frequently as a public proponent than any of her national security adviser predecessors. Even Stephen J. Hadley, in the infamous manipulation of speech texts now encapsulated as the "Sixteen Words" controversy, made key contributions to a course of action that became an international and domestic political disaster.

The gang who produced all this were pros from Dover, using a tried and tested organizational structure for national security machinery. How could it be? Hubris, wishful thinking, incorrect assessment of the major issue facing the United States, wrongheaded notions of imposing change on the world—each played a role. Yet no heads have rolled. President George W. Bush promised to bring a new standard of accountability to Washington. In *that* he has succeeded. The picture is not a pretty one.

1. An overview of presidents' practices is in John Prados, *Keepers of the Keys: A History of the National Security Council from Truman to Bush* (New York: William Morrow, 1991). The Bush in the title is, however, George H. W. Bush, the current president's father. There is no good study of the NSC during the Clinton years.
2. Jane Perlez, "Directive Says Rice, Bush Aide, Won't Be Upstaged by Cheney," *New York Times,* Feb. 16, 2001, p. A10.
3. Karen DeYoung and Steven Mufson, "A Leaner and Less Visible NSC," *Washington Post,* Feb. 10, 2001, p. A6.
4. Massimo Calabresi et al., "They Had a Plan: Special Report: The Secret History," *Time,* August 12, 2002, p. 30.
5. Samuel R. Berger, "Joint Intelligence Committee Testimony," prepared text (copy in author's possession), September 19, 2002, pp. 4-5.
6. Daniel Benjamin and Steven Simon, *The Age of Sacred Terror,* p. 328.
7. Barton Gellman, "A Strategy's Cautious Evolution: Before September 11 the Bush Anti-Terror Effort Was Mostly Ambition," *Washington Post,* Jan. 20, 2002, p. A1.
8. The main sources for this account are the Barton Gellman story cited in note 7 and the study by a large team of *Time* correspondents cited in note 4.
9. United States Congress (107th Congress, 2nd Session). Senate Select Committee on Intelligence and House Permanent Select Committee on Intelligence, *Report: Joint Inquiry Into Intelligence Community Activities Before and After the Terrorist Attacks of September 11, 2001,* hereafter cited as 9/11 Congressional Report (Washington: Government Printing Office, 2003), p. 235. White House sources deny that Richard Clarke's original January memorandum had featured an actual "plan," Calabresi et al. (cited in footnote 4) note that Slide 14 of Clarke's presidential transition briefing on dealing with Al Qaeda included the words "rollback" and "breakup." Although dated December 2002, disputes with the Bush White House over secrecy of material on some of the very subjects under discussion here delayed the actual appearance of this report for many months, into the fall of 2003.
10. Ibid.
11. The data on intelligence indications is from the 9/11 Congressional Report, pp. 201-205; the material on Counterterrorism Security Group activities is from Condoleezza Rice at her news conference of May 16, 2002 as cited in "Excerpt From National Security Adviser's Statement," *New York Times,* May 17, 2002, p. A22.
12. Rice news conference, May 16, 2002.
13. This subject cannot be treated at length here, but see John Prados, *Hoodwinked* (forthcoming).

The reference note about Clinton-era NSC staffer Daniel Benjamin, who worked with Richard Clarke in the transnational threats office, confirms both the briefing session itself and the presence of Berger. See Daniel Benjamin and Steven Simon, *The Age of Sacred Terror* (New York: Random House, 2002), p. 328.

John Prados is an analyst with the National Security Archive in Washington, D.C. His current books are *Hoodwinked* (forthcoming), on America headed into the Iraq war, and *White House Tapes* (2003), a selection of recordings that show American presidents at work on key issues of their times.

UNIT 6

New Directions for American History

Unit Selections

Key Points to Consider

- Is global warming a genuine threat, or merely a case of crying wolf? If it is a threat, what should we be doing about it?

- Even though the Cold War is over, an enormous number of nuclear missiles still exist that might be fired accidentally or by design. What can be done about this situation?

- American treatment of real or suspected terrorists has become extremely controversial. Photos of prisoners being degraded or tortured have intensified Anti-US feelings throughout the world. Were the individuals who perpetrated these atrocities simply a few bad apples, or did they believe they were following their superiors' wishes?

- President Bush's foreign policies to a great extent have been unilateral, while only lip service has been paid to the notion of collective security. Will this be, as author George Soros claims, counterproductive in the long run?

- Genetic engineering raises the apparently attractive prospect of being able to help determine the kind of children we have. What are the dangers involved?

Student Website
www.mhcls.com/online

Internet References
Further information regarding these websites may be found in this book's preface or online.

American Studies Web
http://www.georgetown.edu/crossroads/asw/
National Center for Policy Analysis
http://www.public-policy.org/web.public-policy.org/index.php
The National Network for Immigrant and Refugee Rights (NNIRR)
http://www.nnirr.org/
STANDARDS: An International Journal of Multicultural Studies
http://www.colorado.edu/journals/standards
Supreme Court/Legal Information Institute
http://supct.law.cornell.edu/supct/index.html

The breakup of the Soviet Union and the end of the Cold War could only be welcomed by those who feared a great power confrontation might mean all-out nuclear conflict. One scholar proclaimed that the collapse of Communism as a viable way of organizing society (only a few small Communist states remain and China is Communist in name only) in effect signaled "the end of history." By that he meant that liberal democracy has remained as the only political system with universal appeal. Not so, argued another scholar. He predicted that the "clash of cultures" would engender ongoing struggles in the post-Cold War era. At the time of this writing, the United States is enmeshed in a war against Iraq, the ostensible goals of which are to bring democracy to that unfortunate nation and to counter terrorism.

George Soros, in "The Bubble of American Supremacy" charges that President George W. Bush's response to September 11 marks a "discontinuity" in American foreign policy. Soros argues that the United States should pursue its interests within the framework of collective security rather than to act unilaterally. "Pssst...Nobody Loves a Torturer" claims that revelations

of torture at Abu Ghraib and elsewhere did more than anything else to turn the people of Iraq against the United States. Meanwhile, as Douglas Mahern points out in "Ending the Fools Game: Saving Civilization," the greatest threat to the world remains the possibility of nuclear annihilation whether through accident or design.

Environmentalists have long warned that, in addition to other degradations, global warming presents a clear and potentially disastrous threat to the planet. Others have criticized these people as doomsayers who wildly exaggerate the danger. "Breaking the Global-Warming Gridlock" argues that the debate over this issue has focused on the wrong issues and distracts our attention from what needs to be done. Its authors propose that instead of merely continuing the argument, we focus on the political and social conditions that cause people "to behave in environmentally disruptive ways."

Three essays focus on domestic matters. The death of Rosa Parks in 2005 elicited an outpouring of testimonials to her courage in resisting segregation in the 1950s. Unfortunately, Ellis

Cose argues in "A Legend's Soul is Rested," today's "softer" forms of segregation are more difficult to fight. He points out the alarming fact that segregation in our schools actually is increasing and "remains a fundamental American reality." The next article in this unit, "The Case Against Perfection" examines the issue of genetic engineering. Though the prospects appear dazzling, Michael J. Sandel warns of genetic arms races to produce what he calls "designer children" and "bionic athletes." Young adults today differ in many respects from their parents and grandparents with regard to their allegiance to political parties, their concept of "patriotism, and a host of other matters. "A Politics for Generation X" examines these differences, and speculates on whether their attitudes and goals will prevail in the future.

Breaking the
Global-Warming
GRIDLOCK

Both sides on the issue of greenhouse gases frame their arguments in terms of science, but each new scientific finding only raises new questions—dooming the debate to be a pointless spiral. It's time, the authors argue, for a radically new approach: if we took practical steps to reduce our vulnerability to today's weather, we would go a long way toward solving the problem of tomorrow's climate

by
DANIEL SAREWITZ
and ROGER PIELKE JR.

IN THE LAST WEEK OF OCTOBER, 1998, hurricane Mitch stalled over Central America, dumping between three and six feet of rain within forty-eight hours, killing more than 10,000 people in landslides and floods, triggering a cholera epidemic, and virtually wiping out the economies of Honduras and Nicaragua. Several days later some 1,500 delegates, accompanied by thousands of advocates and media representatives, met in Buenos Aires at the fourth Conference of the Parties to the United Nations Framework Convention on Climate Change. Many at the conference pointed to Hurricane Mitch as a harbinger of the catastrophes that await us if we do not act immediately to reduce emissions of carbon dioxide and other so-called greenhouse gases. The delegates passed a resolution of "solidarity with Central America" in which they expressed concern "that global warming may be contributing to the worsening of weather"

and urged "governments,… and society in general, to continue their efforts to find permanent solutions to the factors which cause or may cause climate events." Children wandering bereft in the streets of Tegucigalpa became unwitting symbols of global warming.

But if Hurricane Mitch was a public-relations gift to environmentalists, it was also a stark demonstration of the failure of our current approach to protecting the environment. Disasters like Mitch are a present and historical reality, and they will become more common and more deadly regardless of global warming. Underlying the havoc in Central America were poverty, poor land-use practices, a degraded local environment, and inadequate emergency preparedness—conditions that will not be alleviated by reducing greenhouse-gas emissions.

At the heart of this dispiriting state of affairs is a vitriolic debate between those who advocate action to reduce global

warming and those who oppose it. The controversy is informed by strong scientific evidence that the earth's surface has warmed over the past century. But the controversy, and the science, focus on the wrong issues, and distract attention from what needs to be done. The enormous scientific, political, and financial resources now aimed at the problem of global warming create the perfect conditions for international and domestic political gridlock, but they can have little effect on the root causes of global environmental degradation, or on the human suffering that so often accompanies it. Our goal is to move beyond the gridlock and stake out some common ground for political dialogue and effective action.

FRAMING THE ISSUE

In politics everything depends on how an issue is framed: the terms of debate, the allocation of power and resources, the potential courses of action. The issue of global warming has been framed by a single question: Does the carbon dioxide emitted by industrialized societies threaten the earth's climate? On one side are the doomsayers, who foretell environmental disaster unless carbon-dioxide emissions are immediately reduced. On the other side are the cornucopians, who blindly insist that society can continue to pump billions of tons of greenhouse gases into the atmosphere with no ill effect, and that any effort to reduce emissions will stall the engines of industrialism that protect us from a Hobbesian wilderness. From our perspective, each group is operating within a frame that has little to do with the practical problem of how to protect the global environment in a world of six billion people (and counting). To understand why global-warming policy is a comprehensive and dangerous failure, therefore, we must begin with a look at how the issue came to be framed in this way. Two converging trends are implicated: the evolution of scientific research on the earth's climate, and the maturation of the modern environmental movement.

Since the beginning of the Industrial Revolution the combustion of fossil fuels—coal, oil, natural gas—has powered economic growth and also emitted great quantities of carbon dioxide and other greenhouse gases. More than a century ago the Swedish chemist Svante Arrhenius and the American geologist T. C. Chamberlin independently recognized that industrialization could lead to rising levels of carbon dioxide in the atmosphere, which might in turn raise the atmosphere's temperature by trapping solar radiation that would otherwise be reflected back into space—a "greenhouse effect" gone out of control. In the late 1950s the geophysicist Roger Revelle, arguing that the world was making itself the subject of a giant "geophysical experiment," worked to establish permanent stations for monitoring carbon-dioxide levels in the atmosphere. Monitoring documented what theory had predicted: atmospheric carbon dioxide was increasing.

In the United States the first high-level government mention of global warming was buried deep within a 1965 White House report on the nation's environmental problems. Throughout the 1960s and 1970s global warming—at that time typically referred to as "inadvertent modification of the atmosphere," and today embraced by the term "climate change"—remained an intriguing hypothesis that caught the attention of a few scientists but generated little concern among the public or environmentalists. Indeed, some climate researchers saw evidence for global cooling and a future ice age. In any case, the threat of nuclear war was sufficiently urgent, plausible, and horrific to crowd global warming off the catastrophe agenda.

Continued research, however, fortified the theory that fossil-fuel combustion could contribute to global warming. In 1977 the nonpartisan National Academy of Sciences issued a study called *Energy and Climate*, which carefully suggested that the possibility of global warming "should lead neither to panic nor to complacency." Rather, the study continued, it should "engender a lively sense of urgency in getting on with the work of illuminating the issues that have been identified and resolving the scientific uncertainties that remain." As is typical with National Academy studies, the primary recommendation was for more research.

In the early 1980s the carbon-dioxide problem received its first sustained attention in Congress, in the form of hearings organized by Representative Al Gore, who had become concerned about global warming when he took a college course with Roger Revelle, twelve years earlier. In 1983 the Environmental Protection Agency released a report detailing some of the possible threats posed by the anthropogenic, or human-caused, emission of carbon dioxide, but the Reagan Administration decisively downplayed the document. Two years later a prestigious international scientific conference in Villach, Austria, concluded that climate change deserved the attention of policymakers worldwide. The following year, at a Senate fact-finding hearing stimulated by the conference, Robert Watson, a climate scientist at NASA, testified, "Global warming is inevitable. It is only a question of the magnitude and the timing."

At that point global warming was only beginning to insinuate itself into the public consciousness. The defining event came in June of 1988, when another NASA climate scientist, James Hansen, told Congress with "ninety-nine percent confidence" that "the greenhouse effect has been detected, and it is changing our climate now." Hansen's proclamation made the front pages of major newspapers, ignited a firestorm of public debate, and elevated the carbon-dioxide problem to pre-eminence on the environmental agenda, where it remains to this day. Nothing had so galvanized the environmental community since the original Earth Day, eighteen years before.

Historically, the conservation and environmental movements have been rooted in values that celebrate the intrinsic worth of unspoiled landscape and propagate the idea that the human spirit is sustained through communion with nature. More than fifty years ago Aldo Leopold, perhaps the most important environmental voice of the twentieth century, wrote, "We face the question whether a still higher 'standard of living' is worth its cost in things natural, wild, and free. For us of the minority,... the chance to find a pasque-flower is a right as inalienable as free speech." But when global warming appeared, environmentalists thought they had found a justification better than inalienable rights—they had found facts and rationality, and they fell head over heels in love with science.

Of course, modern environmentalists were already in the habit of calling on science to help advance their agenda. In 1967, for example, the Environmental Defense Fund was founded with the aim of using science to support environmental protection through litigation. But global warming was, and is, different. It exists as an environmental issue only because of science. People can't directly sense global warming, the way they can see a clear-cut forest or feel the sting of urban smog in their throats. It is not a discrete event, like an oil spill or a nuclear accident. Global warming is so abstract that scientists argue over how they would know if they actually observed it. Scientists go to great lengths to measure and derive something called the "global average temperature" at the earth's surface, and the total rise in this temperature over the past century—an increase of about six tenths of a degree Celsius as of 1998—does suggest warming. But people and ecosystems experience local and regional temperatures, not the global average. Furthermore, most of the possible effects of global warming are not apparent in the present; rather, scientists predict that they will occur decades or even centuries hence. Nor is it likely that scientists will ever be able to attribute any isolated event—a hurricane, a heat wave—to global warming.

A central tenet of environmentalism is that less human interference in nature is better than more. The imagination of the environmental community was ignited not by the observation that greenhouse-gas concentrations were increasing but by the scientific conclusion that the increase was caused by human beings. The Environmental Defense Fund, perhaps because of its explicitly scientific bent, was one of the first advocacy groups to make this connection. As early as 1984 its senior scientist, Michael Oppenheimer, wrote on the op-ed page of *The New York Times*,

> With unusual unanimity, scientists testified at a recent Senate hearing that using the atmosphere as a garbage dump is about to catch up with us on a global scale.... Carbon dioxide emissions from fossil fuel combustion and other "greenhouse" gases are throwing a blanket over the Earth.... The sea level will rise as land ice melts and the ocean expands. Beaches will erode while wetlands will largely disappear.... Imagine life in a sweltering, smoggy New York without Long Island's beaches and you have glimpsed the world left to future generations.

Preserving tropical jungles and wetlands, protecting air and water quality, slowing global population growth—goals that had all been justified for independent reasons, often by independent organizations—could now be linked to a single fact, anthropogenic carbon-dioxide emissions, and advanced along a single political front, the effort to reduce

those emissions. Protecting forests, for example, could help fight global warming because forests act as "sinks" that absorb carbon dioxide. Air pollution could be addressed in part by promoting the same clean-energy sources that would reduce carbon-dioxide emissions. Population growth needed to be controlled in order to reduce demand for fossil-fuel combustion. And the environmental community could reinvigorate its energy-conservation agenda, which had flagged since the early 1980s, when the effects of the second Arab oil shock wore off. Senator Timothy Wirth, of Colorado, spelled out the strategy in 1988: "What we've got to do in energy conservation is try to ride the global warming issue. Even if the theory of global warming is wrong, to have approached global warming as if it is real means energy conservation, so we will be doing the right thing anyway in terms of economic policy and environmental policy." A broad array of environmental groups and think tanks, including the Environmental Defense Fund, the Sierra Club, Greenpeace, the World Resources Institute, and the Union of Concerned Scientists, made reductions in carbon-dioxide emissions central to their agendas.

The moral problem seemed clear: human beings were causing the increase of carbon dioxide in the atmosphere. But the moral problem existed only because of a scientific fact—a fact that not only provided justification for doing many of the things that environmentalists wanted to do anyway but also dictated the overriding course of action: reduce carbon-dioxide emissions. Thus science was used to rationalize the moral imperative, unify the environmental agenda, and determine the political solution.

RESEARCH AS POLICY

THE summer of 1988 was stultifyingly hot even by Washington, D.C., standards, and the Mississippi River basin was suffering a catastrophic drought. Hansen's proclamation that the greenhouse effect was "changing our climate now" generated a level of public concern sufficient to catch the attention of many politicians. George Bush, who promised to be "the environmental President" and

to counter "the greenhouse effect with the White House effect," was elected that November. Despite his campaign rhetoric, the new President was unprepared to offer policies that would curtail fossil-fuel production and consumption or impose economic costs for uncertain political gains. Bush's advisers recognized that support for scientific research offered the best solution politically, because it would give the appearance of action with minimal political risk.

With little debate the Republican Administration and the Democratic Congress in 1990 created the U.S. Global Change Research Program. The program's annual budget reached $1 billion in 1991 and $1.8 billion in 1995, making it one of the largest science initiatives ever undertaken by the U.S. government. Its goal, according to Bush Administration documents, was "to establish the scientific basis for national and international policymaking related to natural and human-induced changes in the global Earth system." A central scientific objective was to "support national and international policymaking by developing the ability to predict the nature and consequences of changes in the Earth system, particularly climate change." A decade and more than $16 billion later, scientific research remains the principal U.S. policy response to climate change.

Meanwhile, the marriage of environmentalism and science gave forth issue: diplomatic efforts to craft a global strategy to reduce carbon-dioxide emissions. Scientists, environmentalists, and government officials, in an attempt to replicate the apparently successful international response to stratospheric-ozone depletion that was mounted in the mid-1980s, created an institutional structure aimed at formalizing the connection between science and political action. The Intergovernmental Panel on Climate Change was established through the United Nations, to provide snapshots of the evolving state of scientific understanding. The IPCC issued major assessments in 1990 and 1996; a third is due early next year. These assessments provide the basis for action under a complementary mechanism, the United Nations Framework Convention on Climate Change. Signed by 154 nations at the

1992 "Earth Summit" in Rio de Janeiro, the convention calls for voluntary reductions in carbon-dioxide emissions. It came into force as an international treaty in March of 1994, and has been ratified by 181 nations. Signatories continue to meet in periodic Conferences of the Parties, of which the most significant to date occurred in Kyoto in 1997, when binding emissions reductions for industrialized countries were proposed under an agreement called the Kyoto Protocol.

The IPCC defines climate change as any sort of change in the earth's climate, no matter what the cause. But the Framework Convention restricts its definition to changes that result from the anthropogenic emission of greenhouse gases. This restriction has profound implications for the framing of the issue. It makes all action under the convention hostage to the ability of scientists not just to document global warming but to attribute it to human causes. An apparently simple question, Are we causing global warming or aren't we?, has become the obsessional focus of science—and of policy.

Finally, if the reduction of carbon-dioxide emissions is an organizing principle for environmentalists, scientists, and environmental-policy makers, it is also an organizing principle for all those whose interests might be threatened by such a reduction. It's easy to be glib about who they might be—greedy oil and coal companies, the rapacious logging industry, recalcitrant automobile manufacturers, corrupt foreign dictatorships—and easy as well to document the excesses and absurdities propagated by some representatives of these groups. Consider, for example, the Greening Earth Society, which "promotes the optimistic scientific view that CO_2 is beneficial to humankind and all of nature," and happens to be funded by a coalition of coal-burning utility companies. One of the society's 1999 press releases reported that "there will only be sufficient food for the world's projected population in 2050 if atmospheric concentrations of carbon dioxide are permitted to increase, unchecked." Of course, neither side of the debate has a lock on excess or distortion. The point is simply that the climate-change problem has been framed in a way that catalyzes a determined and powerful opposition.

THE PROBLEM WITH PREDICTIONS

WHEN anthropogenic carbon-dioxide emissions became the defining fact for global environmentalism, scientific uncertainty about the causes and consequences of global warming emerged as the apparent central obstacle to action. As we have seen, the Bush Administration justified its huge climate-research initiative explicitly in terms of the need to reduce uncertainty before taking action. Al Gore, by then a senator, agreed, explaining that "more research and better research and better targeted research is absolutely essential if we are going to eliminate the remaining areas of uncertainty and build the broader and stronger political consensus necessary for the unprecedented actions required to address this problem." Thus did a Republican Administration and a Democratic Congress—one side looking for reasons to do nothing, the other seeking justification for action—converge on the need for more research.

How certain do we need to be before we take action? The answer depends, of course, on where our interests lie. Environmentalists can tolerate a good deal more uncertainty on this issue than can, say, the executives of utility or automobile companies. Science is unlikely to overcome such a divergence in interests. After all, science is not a fact or even a set of facts; rather, it is a process of inquiry that generates more questions than answers. The rise in anthropogenic greenhouse-gas emissions, once it was scientifically established, simply pointed to other questions. How rapidly might carbon-dioxide levels rise in the future? How might climate respond to this rise? What might be the effects of that response? Such questions are inestimably complex, their answers infinitely contestable and always uncertain, their implications for human action highly dependent on values and interests.

Having wedded themselves to science, environmentalists must now cleave to it through thick and thin. When research results do not support their cause, or are simply uncertain, they cannot resort to values-based arguments, because their political opponents can portray such arguments as an opportunistic abandonment of rationality. Environmentalists have tried to get out of this bind by invoking the "precautionary principle"—a dandified version of "better safe than sorry"—to advance the idea that action in the presence of uncertainty is justified if potential harm is great. Thus uncertainty itself becomes an argument for action. But nothing is gained by this tactic either, because just as attitudes toward uncertainty are rooted in individual values and interests, so are attitudes toward potential harm.

Charged by the Framework Convention to search for proof of harm, scientists have turned to computer models of the atmosphere and the oceans, called general circulation models, or GCMs. Carbon-dioxide levels and atmospheric temperatures are measures of the physical state of the atmosphere. GCMs, in contrast, are mathematical representations that scientists use to try to understand past climate conditions and predict future ones. With GCMs scientists seek to explore how climate might respond under different influences—for example, different rates of carbon-dioxide increase. GCMs have calculated global average temperatures for the past century that closely match actual surface-temperature records; this gives climate modelers some confidence that they understand how climate behaves.

Computer models are a bit like Aladdin's lamp—what comes out is very seductive, but few are privy to what goes on inside. Even the most complex models, however, have one crucial quality that non-experts can easily understand: their accuracy can be fully evaluated only after seeing what happens in the real world over time. In other words, predictions of how climate will behave in the future cannot be proved accurate today. There are other fundamental problems with relying on GCMs. The ability of many models to reproduce temperature records may in part reflect the fact that the scientists who designed them already "knew the answer." As John Firor, a former director of the National Center for Atmospheric Research, has observed, climate models "are made by humans who tend to shape or use their models in ways that mirror their own notion of what a desirable outcome would be." Although various models can reproduce past temperature records, and yield similar predictions of future temperatures, they are unable to replicate other observed aspects of climate, such as cloud behavior and atmospheric temperature, and they diverge widely in predicting specific regional climate phenomena, such as precipitation and the frequency of extreme weather events. Moreover, it is simply not possible to know far in advance if the models agree on future temperature because they are similarly right or similarly wrong.

In spite of such pitfalls, a fundamental assumption of both U.S. climate policy and the UN Framework Convention is that increasingly sophisticated models, run on faster computers and supported by more data, will yield predictions that can resolve political disputes and guide action. The promise of better predictions is irresistible to champions of carbon-dioxide reduction, who, after all, must base their advocacy on the claim that anthropogenic greenhouse-gas emissions will be harmful in the future. But regardless of the sophistication of such predictions, new findings will almost inevitably be accompanied by new uncertainties—that's the nature of science—and may therefore act to fuel, rather than to quench, political debate. Our own prediction is that increasingly complex mathematical models that delve ever more deeply into the intricacies and the uncertainties of climate will only hinder political action.

An example of how more scientific research fuels political debate came in 1998, when a group of prominent researchers released the results of a model analyzing carbon-dioxide absorption in North America. Their controversial findings, published in the prestigious journal *Science*, suggested that the amount of carbon dioxide absorbed by U.S. forests might be greater than the amount emitted by the nation's fossil-fuel combustion. This conclusion has two astonishing implications. First, the United States—the world's most profligate energy consumer—may not be directly contributing

to rising atmospheric levels of carbon dioxide. Second, the atmosphere seems to be benefiting from young forests in the eastern United States that are particularly efficient at absorbing carbon dioxide. But these young forests exist only because old-growth forests were clearcut in the eighteenth and nineteenth centuries to make way for farms that were later abandoned in favor of larger, more efficient midwestern farms. In other words, the possibility that the United States is a net carbon-dioxide sink does not reflect efforts to protect the environment; on the contrary, it reflects a history of deforestation and development.

Needless to say, these results quickly made their way into the political arena. At a hearing of the House Resources Committee, Representative John E. Peterson, of Pennsylvania, a Republican, asserted, "There are recent studies that show that in the Northeast, where we have continued to cut timber, and have a regenerating, younger forest, that the greenhouse gases are less when they leave the forest.... So a young, growing, vibrant forest is a whole lot better for clean air than an old dying forest." George Frampton, the director of the White House Council on Environmental Quality, countered, "The science on this needs a lot of work... we need more money for scientific research to undergird that point of view." How quickly the tables can turn: here was a conservative politician wielding (albeit with limited coherence) the latest scientific results to justify logging old-growth forests in the name of battling global warming, while a Clinton Administration official backpedaled in the manner more typically adopted by opponents of action on climate change—invoking the need for more research.

That's a problem with science—it can turn around and bite you. An even more surprising result has recently emerged from the study of Antarctic glaciers. A strong argument in favor of carbon-dioxide reduction has been the possibility that if temperatures rise owing to greenhouse-gas emissions, glaciers will melt, the sea level will rise, and populous coastal zones all over the world will be inundated. The West Antarctic Ice Sheet has been a subject of particular concern,

both because of evidence that it is now retreating and because of geologic studies showing that it underwent catastrophic collapse at least once in the past million years or so. "Behind the reasoned scientific estimates," Greenpeace warns, "lies the possibility of... the potential catastrophe of a six metre rise in sea level." But recent research from Antarctica shows that this ice sheet has been melting for thousands of years. Sea-level rise is a problem, but anthropogenic global warming is not the only culprit, and reducing emissions cannot be the only solution.

To make matters more difficult, some phenomena, especially those involving human behavior, are intrinsically unpredictable. Any calculation of future anthropogenic global warming must include an estimate of rates of fossil-fuel combustion in the coming decades. This means that scientists must be able to predict not only the amounts of coal, oil, and natural gas that will be consumed but also changes in the mixture of fossil fuels and other energy sources, such as nuclear, hydro-electric, and solar. These predictions rest on interdependent factors that include energy policies and prices, rates of economic growth, patterns of industrialization and technological innovation, changes in population, and even wars and other geopolitical events. Scientists have no history of being able to predict any of these things. For example, their inability to issue accurate population projections is "one of the best-kept secrets of demography," according to Joel Cohen, the director of the Laboratory of Populations at Rockefeller University. "Most professional demographers no longer believe they can predict precisely the future growth rate, size, composition and spatial distribution of populations," Cohen has observed.

Predicting the human influence on climate also requires an understanding of how climate behaved "normally," before there was any such influence. But what are normal climate patterns? In the absence of human influence, how stationary is climate? To answer such questions, researchers must document and explain the behavior of the pre-industrial climate, and they must also determine how the climate would have behaved over the past two centuries had human beings not been changing the composition of the atmosphere. However, despite the billions spent so far on climate research, Kevin Trenberth, a senior scientist at the National Center for Atmospheric Research, told the *Chicago Tribune* last year, "This may be a shock to many people who assume that we do know adequately what's going on with the climate, but we don't." The National Academy of Sciences reported last year that "deficiencies in the accuracy, quality, and continuity of the [climate] records… place serious limitations on the confidence" of research results.

If the normal climate is non-stationary, then the task of identifying the human fingerprint in global climate change becomes immeasurably more difficult. And the idea of a naturally stationary climate may well be chimerical. Climate has changed often and dramatically in the recent past. In the 1940s and 1950s, for example, the East Coast was hammered by a spate of powerful hurricanes, whereas in the 1970s and 1980s hurricanes were much less common. What may appear to be "abnormal" hurricane activity in recent years is abnormal only in relation to this previous quiet period. As far as the ancient climate goes, paleoclimatologists have found evidence of rapid change, even over periods as short as several years. Numerous influences could account for these changes. Ash spewed high into the atmosphere by large volcanoes can reflect solar radiation back into space and result in short-term cooling, as occurred after the 1991 eruption of Mount Pinatubo. Variations in the energy emitted by the sun also affect climate, in ways that are not yet fully understood. Global ocean currents, which move huge volumes of warm and cold water around the world and have a profound influence on climate, can speed up, slow down, and maybe even die out over very short periods of time—perhaps less than a decade. Were the Gulf Stream to shut down, the climate of Great Britain could come to resemble that of Labrador.

Finally, human beings have been changing the surface of the earth for millennia. Scientists increasingly realize that deforestation, agriculture, irrigation, urbanization, and other human activities can lead to major changes in climate on a regional or perhaps even a global scale. Thomas Stohlgren, of the U.S. Geological Survey, has written, "The effects of land use practices on regional climate may overshadow larger-scale temperature changes commonly associated with observed increases in carbon dioxide." The idea that climate may constantly be changing for a variety of reasons does not itself undercut the possibility that anthropogenic carbon dioxide could seriously affect the global climate, but it does confound scientific efforts to predict the consequences of carbon-dioxide emissions.

THE OTHER 80 PERCENT

IF predicting how climate will change is difficult and uncertain, predicting how society will be affected by a changing climate—especially at the local, regional, and national levels, where decision-making takes place—is immeasurably more so. And predicting the impact on climate of reducing carbon-dioxide emissions is so uncertain as to be meaningless. What we do know about climate change suggests that there will be winners and losers, with some areas and nations potentially benefiting from, say, longer growing seasons or more rain, and others suffering from more flooding or drought. But politicians have no way to accurately calibrate the effects—human and economic—of global warming, or the benefits of reducing carbon-dioxide emissions.

Imagine yourself a leading policymaker in a poor, overpopulated, undernourished nation with severe environmental problems. What would it take to get you worried about global warming? You would need to know not just that global warming would make the conditions in your country worse but also that any of the scarce resources you applied to reducing carbon-dioxide emissions would lead to more benefits than if they were applied in another area, such as industrial development or housing construction. Such knowledge is simply unavailable. But you do know that investing in industrial development or better housing would lead to concrete political, economic, and social benefits.

More specifically, suppose that many people in your country live in shacks on a river's floodplain. Floodplains are created and sustained by repeated flooding, so floods are certain to occur in the future, regardless of global warming. Given a choice between building new houses away from the floodplain and converting power plants from cheap local coal to costlier imported fuels, what would you do? New houses would ensure that lives and homes would be saved; a new power plant would reduce carbon-dioxide emissions but leave people vulnerable to floods. In the developing world the carbon-dioxide problem pales alongside immediate environmental and developmental problems. The *China Daily* reported during the 1997 Kyoto Conference:

> The United States… and other nations made the irresponsible demand…. that the developing countries should make commitments to limiting greenhouse gas emissions…. As a developing country, China has 60 million poverty-stricken people and China's per capita gas emissions are only one-seventh of the average amount of more developed countries. Ending poverty and developing the economy must still top the agenda of [the] Chinese government.

For the most part, the perspectives of those in the developing world—about 80 percent of the planet's population—have been left outside the frame of the climate-change discussion. This is hardly surprising, considering that the frame was defined mainly by environmentalists and scientists in affluent nations. Developing nations, meanwhile, have quite reasonably refused to agree to the targets for carbon-dioxide reduction set under the Kyoto Protocol. The result may feel like a moral victory to some environmentalists, who reason that industrialized countries, which caused the problem to begin with, should shoulder the primary responsibility for solving it. But the victory is hollow, because most future emissions increases will come from the developing world. In affluent nations almost everyone already owns a full complement of energy-consuming devices. Beyond a certain point increases in income do not result in proportional increases in energy consumption; people simply trade in the old model for a new and perhaps more efficient one. If present trends continue, emissions from the developing world are likely to exceed those from the industrialized nations within the next decade or so.

Twelve years after carbon dioxide became the central obsession of global environmental science and politics, we face the following two realities:

First, atmospheric carbon-dioxide levels will continue to increase. The Kyoto Protocol, which represents the world's best attempt to confront the issue, calls for industrialized nations to reduce their emissions below 1990 levels by the end of this decade. Political and technical realities suggest that not even this modest goal will be achieved. To date, although eighty-four nations have signed the Kyoto Protocol, only twenty-two nations—half of them islands, and none of them major carbon-dioxide emitters—have ratified it. The United States Senate, by a vote of 95-0 in July of 1997, indicated that it would not ratify any climate treaty that lacked provisions requiring developing nations to reduce their emissions. The only nations likely to achieve the emissions commitments set under Kyoto are those, like Russia and Ukraine, whose economies are in ruins. And even successful implementation of the treaty would not halt the progressive increase in global carbon-dioxide emissions.

Second, even if greenhouse-gas emissions could somehow be rolled back to pre-industrial levels, the impacts of climate on society and the environment would continue to increase. Climate affects the world not just through phenomena such as hurricanes and droughts but also because of societal and environmental vulnerability to such phenomena. The horrific toll of Hurricane Mitch reflected not an unprecedented climatic event but a level of exposure typical in developing countries where dense and rapidly increasing populations live in environmentally degraded conditions. Similar conditions underlay more-recent disasters in Venezuela and Mozambique.

If these observations are correct, and we believe they are essentially indisputable, then framing the problem of global warming in terms of carbon-dioxide reduction is a political, environmental, and social dead end. We are not suggesting that humanity can with impunity emit billions of tons of carbon dioxide into the atmosphere each year, or that reducing those emissions is not a good idea. Nor are we making the nihilistic point that since climate undergoes changes for a variety of reasons, there is no need to worry about additional changes imposed by human beings. Rather, we are arguing that environmentalists and scientists, in focusing their own, increasingly congruent interests on carbon-dioxide emissions, have framed the problem of global environmental protection in a way that can offer no realistic prospect of a solution.

REDRAWING THE FRAME

LOCAL weather is the day-to-day manifestation of global climate. Weather is what we experience, and lately there has been plenty to experience. In recent decades human, economic, and environmental losses from disasters related to weather have increased dramatically. Insurance-industry data show that insured losses from weather have been rising steadily. A 1999 study by the German firm Munich Reinsurance Company compared the 1960s with the 1990s and concluded that "the number of great natural catastrophes increased by a factor of three, with economic losses—taking into account the effects of inflation—increasing by a factor of more than eight and insured losses by a factor of no less than sixteen." And yet scientists have been unable to observe a global increase in the number or the severity of extreme weather events. In 1996 the IPCC concluded, "There is no evidence that extreme weather events, or climate variability, has increased, in a global sense, through the 20th century, although data and analyses are poor and not comprehensive."

What has unequivocally increased is society's vulnerability to weather. At the beginning of the twentieth century the earth's population was about 1.6 billion people; today it is about six billion peo-

ple. Almost four times as many people are exposed to weather today as were a century ago. And this increase has, of course, been accompanied by enormous increases in economic activity, development, infrastructure, and interdependence. In the past fifty years, for example, Florida's population rose fivefold; 80 percent of this burgeoning population lives within twenty miles of the coast. The great Miami hurricane of 1926 made landfall over a small, relatively poor community and caused about $76 million worth of damage (in inflation-adjusted dollars). Today a storm of similar magnitude would strike a sprawling, affluent metropolitan area of two million people, and could cause more than $80 billion worth of damage. The increase in vulnerability is far more dramatic in the developing world, where in an average year tens of thousands of people die in weather-related disasters. According to the *World Disasters Report 1999*, 80 million people were made homeless by weather-related disasters from 1988 to 1997. As the population and vulnerability of the developing world continue to rise, such numbers will continue to rise as well, with or without global warming.

Environmental vulnerability is also on the rise. The connections between weather impacts and environmental quality are immediate and obvious—much more so than the connections between global warming and environmental quality. Deforestation, the destruction of wetlands, and the development of fragile coastlines can greatly magnify flooding; floods, in turn, can mobilize toxic chemicals in soil and storage facilities and cause devastating pollution of water sources and harm to wildlife. Poor agricultural, forest-management, and grazing practices can exacerbate the effects of drought, amplify soil erosion, and promote the spread of wildfires. Damage to the environment due to deforestation directly contributed to the devastation wrought by Hurricane Mitch, as denuded hillsides washed away in catastrophic landslides, and excessive development along unmanaged floodplains put large numbers of people in harm's way.

Our view of climate and the environment draws on people's direct experience and speaks to widely shared values. It therefore has an emotional and moral impact that can translate into action. This view is framed by four precepts. First, the impacts of weather and climate are a serious threat to human welfare in the present and are likely to get worse in the future. Second, the only way to reduce these impacts is to reduce societal vulnerability to them. Third, reducing vulnerability can be achieved most effectively by encouraging democracy, raising standards of living, and improving environmental quality in the developing world. Fourth, such changes offer the best prospects not only for adapting to a capricious climate but also for reducing carbon-dioxide emissions.

The implicit moral imperative is not to prevent human disruption of the environment but to ameliorate the social and political conditions that lead people to behave in environmentally disruptive ways. This is a critical distinction—and one that environmentalists and scientists embroiled in the global-warming debate have so far failed to make.

To begin with, any global effort to reduce vulnerability to weather and climate must address the environmental conditions in developing nations. Poor land-use and natural-resource-management practices are, of course, a reflection of poverty, but they are also caused by government policies, particularly those that encourage unsustainable environmental activities. William Ascher, a political scientist at Duke University, has observed that such policies typically do not arise out of ignorance or lack of options but reflect conscious tradeoffs made by government officials faced with many competing priorities and political pressures. Nations, even poor ones, have choices. It was not inevitable, for example, that Indonesia would promote the disastrous exploitation of its forests by granting subsidized logging concessions to military and business leaders. This was the policy of an autocratic government seeking to manipulate powerful sectors of society. In the absence of open, democratically responsive institutions, Indonesian leaders were not accountable for the costs that the public might bear, such as increased vulnerability to floods, landslides, soil erosion,

drought, and fire. Promoting democratic institutions in developing nations could be the most important item on an agenda aimed at protecting the global environment and reducing vulnerability to climate. Environmental groups concerned about the consequences of climate change ought to consider reorienting their priorities accordingly.

Such long-term efforts must be accompanied by activities with a shorter-term payoff. An obvious first step would be to correct some of the imbalances created by the obsession with carbon dioxide. For example, the U.S. Agency for International Development has allocated $1 billion over five years to help developing nations quantify, monitor, and reduce greenhouse-gas emissions, but is spending less than a tenth of that amount on programs to prepare for and prevent disasters. These priorities should be rearranged. Similarly, the United Nations' International Strategy for Disaster Reduction is a relatively low-level effort that should be elevated to a status comparable to that of the Framework Convention on Climate Change.

Intellectual and financial resources are also poorly allocated in the realm of science, with research focused disproportionately on understanding and predicting basic climatic processes. Such research has yielded much interesting information about the global climate system. But little priority is given to generating and disseminating knowledge that people and communities can use to reduce their vulnerability to climate and extreme weather events. For example, researchers have made impressive strides in anticipating the impacts of some relatively short-term climatic phenomena, notably El Niño and La Niña. If these advances were accompanied by progress in monitoring weather, identifying vulnerable regions and populations, and communicating useful information, we would begin to reduce the toll exacted by weather and climate all over the world.

A powerful international mechanism for moving forward already exists in the Framework Convention on Climate Change. The language of the treaty offers sufficient flexibility for new priorities. The text states that signatory nations

have an obligation to "cooperate in preparing for adaptation to the impacts of climate change [and to] develop and elaborate appropriate and integrated plans for coastal zone management, water resources and agriculture, and for the protection and rehabilitation of areas… affected by drought and desertification, as well as floods."

The idea of improving our adaptation to weather and climate has been taboo in many circles, including the realms of international negotiation and political debate. "Do we have so much faith in our own adaptability that we will risk destroying the integrity of the entire global ecological system?" Vice President Gore asked in his book *Earth in the Balance* (1992). "Believing that we can adapt to just about anything is ultimately a kind of laziness, an arrogant faith in our ability to react in time to save our skin." For environmentalists, adaptation represents a capitulation to the momentum of human interference in nature. For their opponents, putting adaptation on the table would mean acknowledging the reality of global warming. And for scientists, focusing on adaptation would call into question the billions of tax dollars devoted to research and technology centered on climate processes, models, and predictions.

Yet there is a huge potential constituency for efforts focused on adaptation: everyone who is in any way subject to the effects of weather. Reframing the climate problem could mobilize this constituency and revitalize the Framework Convention. The revitalization could concentrate on coordinating disaster relief, debt relief, and development assistance, and on generating and providing information on climate that participating countries could use in order to reduce their vulnerability.

An opportunity to advance the cause of adaptation is on the horizon. The U.S. Global Change Research Program is now finishing its report on the National Assessment of the Potential Consequences of Climate Variability and Change. The draft includes examples from around the United States of why a greater focus on adaptation to climate makes sense. But it remains to be seen if the report will redefine the terms of the climate debate, or if it will simply become fodder in the battle over carbon-dioxide emissions.

Finally, efforts to reduce carbon-dioxide emissions need not be abandoned. The Framework Convention and its offshoots also offer a promising mechanism for promoting the diffusion of energy-efficient technologies that would reduce emissions. Both the convention and the Kyoto Protocol call on industrialized nations to share new energy technologies with the developing world. But because these provisions are coupled to carbon-dioxide-reduction mandates, they are trapped in the political gridlock. They should be liberated, promoted independently on the basis of their intrinsic environmental and economic benefits, and advanced through innovative funding mechanisms. For example, as the United Nations Development Programme has suggested, research into renewable-energy technologies for poor countries could be supported in part by a modest levy on patents registered under the World Intellectual Property Organization. Such ideas should be far less divisive than energy policies advanced on the back of the global-warming agenda.

As an organizing principle for political action, vulnerability to weather and climate offers everything that global warming does not: a clear, uncontroversial story rooted in concrete human experience, observable in the present, and definable in terms of unambiguous and widely shared human values, such as the fundamental rights to a secure shelter, a safe community, and a sustainable environment. In this light, efforts to blame global warming for extreme weather events seem maddeningly perverse—as if to say that those who died in Hurricane Mitch were symbols of the profligacy of industrialized society, rather than victims of poverty and the vulnerability it creates.

Such perversity shows just how morally and politically dangerous it can be to elevate science above human values. In the global-warming debate the logic behind public discourse and political action has been precisely backwards. Environmental prospects for the coming century depend far less on our strategies for reducing carbon-dioxide emissions than on our determination and ability to reduce human vulnerability to weather and climate.

Daniel Sarewitz is a research scholar at Columbia University's Center for Science, Policy and Outcomes. Roger Pielke Jr. is a scientist with the Environmental and Societal Impacts Group at the National Center for Atmospheric Research. They are the editors, with Radford Byerly Jr., of *Prediction: Science, Decision Making, and the Future of Nature* (2000).

A Legend's Soul Is Rested

ROSA PARKS, 1913–2005

Ellis Cose

FOR MOST OF AMERICA, SHE WAS NOT QUITE REAL—MORE an icon than a full-fledged human being. And Rosa Parks understood that better than anyone. "I understand I am a symbol," Parks wrote in 1992. She died last Monday at the age of 92; but she ascended to the realm of legend long ago. A weary seamstress on a bus in Montgomery, Ala., in 1955 refused to stand so a white man could sit, ushering in the age of equality. So goes the "children's version of the civil-rights movement," in the words of author Diane McWhorter. The complete story is considerably less child friendly. It would include at least a reference to Thomas Edward Brooks, a 21-year-old black soldier who got on a Montgomery bus in 1950. Brooks made the mistake of entering through the front door instead of the back. For that, as authors Donnie Williams and Wayne Greenhaw relate in "The Thunder of Angels," a policeman bashed him on the head with a billy club and shot him dead. At least two other black men were similarly killed in the years leading up to Parks's act of civil disobedience. Parks's quiet protest coincided with the NAACP's search for the perfect test case. Her courage led to the creation of the Montgomery Improvement Association, headed by Martin Luther King Jr., chosen in part because he was an outsider and thereby less subject to reprisals. The Montgomery Bus Boycott made history—and heroes out of both King and Parks. But the fame did not lead to fortune.

She and her husband lost their jobs and moved to Detroit, where they struggled financially. "I always thought it was a mistake for them [the black leadership] to let her leave Montgomery. I always thought Rosa Parks should have left this earth from the city she loved most and helped to make sacred," said the Rev. Fred Shuttlesworth, another civil-rights icon.

In 1964, Parks endorsed a young Detroit lawyer for Congress. And after John Conyers won, he hired her as a receptionist and assistant. "I didn't do it out of sympathy for her," said Conyers. She was a living connection to the civil-rights movement who happened to add a bit of celebrity cachet to the place. "People came to my office to see her," Conyers recalled, and they invariably left impressed with her humility and grace. "She was one of the most approachable heroes you could ever encounter," said Betty DeRamus, a columnist for The Detroit

News. Parks retired in 1988 and stayed largely out of the public eye until 1994, when she was attacked in her home and robbed by a crack user. Following that assault, fellow Detroiters saw to it that she was moved to a high rise on the Detroit River.

In the twilight of her life, Parks struggled with a range of woes, including poor health and dementia. She never ceased being a symbol of the epic battle for human rights; and she never claimed victory in the larger war. "I try to keep hope alive, but that's not always the easiest thing to do," she wrote in 1992. As The Detroit News observed after her death, her adopted home "is today the most segregated metropolitan area in the nation." And segregation remains a fundamental American reality.

In the newly published "The Shame of the Nation," Jonathan Kozol sheds a book's length of tears over segregation in schools. He cites research that shows segregation is worsening and notes that three fourths of black and Latino children attend schools with no or relatively few whites. It is a daunting task to convince poor, minority kids they can learn "when they are cordoned off by a society that isn't sure they really can," writes Kozol.

'I try to keep hope alive, but that's not always the easiest thing to do,' Parks wrote.

In their study of the Montgomery boycott, authors Williams and Greenhaw quote a white woman who, as a 13-year-old, witnessed the murder of the black soldier on the bus. The world has forgotten, she said, "about the white children who grew up in that society. They forgot that we suffered, too. I had nightmares for years, and I still can't get it off my mind sometimes."

It's easy looking back some 50 years to see the insanity of the old Southern system. It is much more difficult to see (or become outraged about) the harm in today's softer form of segregation. For despite the damage it may do psychologically, economically, and to the social fabric of our collective community, it doesn't generally leave dead bodies sprawled on the ground. But it's far from the brotherhood Rosa Parks dreamed of and spent her life trying to create.

Ending the Fool's Game;

Saving Civilization

Douglas Mattern

"**A** fool's game" is how retired General George Lee Butler, former head of the U.S. Strategic Command, refers to nuclear weapons. He says that these weapons offer no security and their complete elimination is "the only defensible goal."

A fool's game, indeed—and the United States is the biggest fool for allowing the power elite to maintain a stockpile of over thirty thousand nuclear weapons more than a decade after the end of the Cold War.

The ultimate absurdity is that thousands of U.S. and Russian nuclear warheads remain on hair-trigger alert and could be launched on a few minutes' notice, potentially destroying both countries in less than an hour. As Bruce Blair, head of the Center for Defense Information (CDI) and a former Minuteman Missile Launch officer states, "Both sides are cocked on hair-triggers … and both sides can retarget a missile in seconds—just a few strokes on a keyboard."

The result is that the United States continues to be under the daily threat of nuclear incineration whether initiated by an accidental missile launch, miscalculation, or design. Regarding miscalculation, the United States and Soviet Union had come frighteningly close to nuclear war over the years, with mere luck playing a major role in averting disaster.

Robert McNamara, secretary of defense in the Kennedy and Johnson administrations, acknowledges that during the Cuban missile crisis "we came within a hairbreadth of nuclear war without realizing it." He said, "It's no credit to us that we missed nuclear war—at least we had to be lucky as well as wise."

It can only be guessed how many other close calls there have been over the years but here are a few documented examples:

1979: A CNN Cold War program reported that a technician at the North American Air Defense Command mistakenly placed a training tape into the main systems at NORAD's Cheyenne Mountain Complex in Colorado. The tape caused NORAD's early-warning system computer to respond that the United States was undergoing a massive Soviet missile attack. NORAD officials were alerted but within minutes the error was discovered, ending the threat of launching U.S. missiles in retaliation. This incident was one of five missile warning system failures that occurred over an eight-month period.

1980: In the August 14, 1983, issue of *Parade*, Jack Anderson reports that on November 19, 1980, two Air Force missile officers were conducting a drill of a simulated missile launch of their Titan missile at McConnell Air Force Base near Wichita, Kansas. When Captain Henry Winsett and First Lieutenant David Mosley turned the keys for the simulated launch, something went wrong. They received a message of "Launch Sequence Go," which means the real missile launch sequence is underway. Fortunately, Winsett had the good sense to shut the missile down before it could be launched. Mosley said it couldn't be determined whether the missile's guidance system would have steered the missile to a target in Russia, which would assuredly have resulted in Soviet retaliation. But, he said, it would have gone somewhere "north." This close call still gives him tremors.

1984: As reported on the CNN Cold War program, in August 1984 a low-ranking officer at Soviet Pacific fleet headquarters in Vladivostok broadcast a war alert to Soviet forces at sea. For thirty minutes, until it was determined that the alert was false, Soviet ship commanders sent back urgent inquiries about the alert as they prepared for combat. In the meantime, U.S. and Japanese forces also went to a higher alert status.

1995: The Center for Defense Information (CDI) and several other reliable sources report that in 1995 the monitors of the Russian Strategic Rocket Force at the Olengrosk early-warning radar site registered the launch of a U.S.-Norwegian research missile probe of the upper atmosphere. To the Russians, the missile's trajectory looked like a U.S. Trident missile, which carries multiple nuclear warheads. This set off alarms at the Russian nuclear weapons command, which notified President Boris Yeltsin, who reportedly activated his "nuclear briefcase." For a few minutes perhaps the fate of the United States—and Western civilization—hung on Yeltsin's judgment.

> The story of Stanislav Petrov is perhaps the most dramatic of all the reported close calls, other than the Cuban Missile Crisis.

All of these incidents constituted alarmingly close calls. Blair believes that the closest the Americans and Soviets ever came to accidental nuclear war, however, was the 1983 incident involving Soviet Lieutenant Colonel Stanislav Petrov. His story has been reported by the BBC, on *NBC Dateline* and *NOVA*, and in the *London Daily Mail* and other sources and is perhaps the most dramatic of all the reported close calls, other than the Cuban Missile Crisis. This story could rightly be called "A Forgotten Hero of Our Time."

On September 26, 1983, Petrov was in charge of two hundred men, mostly officers, operating the Russian early-warning bunker just south of Moscow. Petrov's job that fateful night was to lead a staff monitoring incoming signals from satellites. He reported directly to the Russian early-warning system headquarters which reported directly to the Soviet leader on the possibility of launching a retaliatory attack.

It's important to note that this was a period of very high tension between the United States and the Soviet Union. U.S. President Ronald Reagan was continually referring to the Soviets as "the evil empire." The Soviet military had shot down a Korean passenger jet just three weeks prior to this incident and the United States and North Atlantic Treaty Organization were organizing a military exercise that centered on using tactical nuclear weapons in Europe. Some Soviet leaders were worried the West was planning a nuclear attack.

In an interview with the *Daily Mail*, Petrov recalled that night, when computer screens were showing an attack launched by the United States. He said, "I felt as if I'd been punched in my nervous system. There was a huge map of the States with a U.S. base lit up, showing that the missiles had been launched."

For several minutes Petrov held a phone in one hand and an intercom in the other as alarms blared, red lights blinked, and computers reported that U.S. missiles were on their way. In the midst of this horrific chaos and terror— the prospect of the end of civilization itself—Petrov made a historic decision not to alert higher authorities, somehow believing that, contrary to what all the sophisticated equipment was reporting, the alarm was an error.

"I didn't want to make a mistake," Petrov said. "I made a decision and that was it." As the *Daily Mail* states, "Had Petrov cracked and triggered a response, Soviet missiles would have rained down on U.S. cities. In turn, that would have brought a devastating response from the Pentagon."

As agonizing minutes passed, Petrov's decision proved correct. A computer error had falsely signaled the U.S. attack. In the *Daily Mail* interview, Petrov said, "After it was over, I drank half a liter of vodka as if it were only a glass and slept for 28 hours." He commented, "In principle, a nuclear war could have broken out. The whole world could have been destroyed."

In increasingly superficial modern societies that praise celebrities and all manner of fools as role models, many legitimate heroes go unnoticed and without reward. In the case of Petrov, he was dismissed from the army on a pension that in succeeding years would prove nearly worthless. Petrov's superiors were reprimanded for the computer error and all in the group were subjected to the same treatment.

The *Daily Mirror* report found Petrov's health destroyed by the enormous stress of the incident. His wife died of cancer and he lives alone in a second-floor flat in a small town about thirty miles from Moscow. "Once I would have liked to have been given some credit for what I did," said Petrov. "But it is too long ago and today everything is emotionally burned out inside me. I still have a bitter feeling inside my soul as I remember the way I was treated."

In a November 12, 2000, interview with Petrov, *Dateline* reporter Dennis Murphy said, "I know you don't regard yourself as a hero, Colonel, but, belatedly, on behalf of the people in Washington, New York, Philadelphia, Chicago, thank you for being on duty that night."

The twentieth anniversary of this incident revealed, once again, how little has changed with the thousands of nuclear warheads still on hair-trigger alert. The utter madness of this situation was demonstrated in a recent report by the BBC that some scientists and military people are worried that a small asteroid passing close to the Earth could accidentally trigger a nuclear war if mistaken for a missile strike.

> The greatest terrorism by far is that each day the people of the world continue to be under the threat of nuclear incineration whether by an accidental missile launch, a computer error, or design.

This dark scenario is exacerbated by President George W. Bush's nuclear weapons policy. Most ominous is National Security Presidential Directive 17, signed by Bush. This document declares that the United States reserves the right to respond with overwhelming force—including nuclear weapons—to the use of weapons of mass destruction against the United States, its forces abroad, friends, and allies. Military analyst William Arkin writes that the Bush administration's war planning "moves nuclear weapons out of their long-established special category and lumps them in with all the other military options."

The Bush team is also determined to build a new generation of tactical nuclear weapons designed to attack hardened underground bunkers. The United States has, for the first time in fourteen years, resumed production of plutonium parts for nuclear bombs. The Energy Department announced that plans are underway for a factory that could produce parts of hundreds of nuclear weapons a year. Congress gave the Bush team funding for this production—and just about everything it requested in the massive 2004 military budget of $401 billion. The CDI reports that U.S. military spending is equal to the military spending of the next twenty countries combined.

Blair reports that both the United States and Russia remain preoccupied with preparing to fight a large-scale nuclear war with each other. U.S. spy planes monitor the Russian coast and U.S. submarines still trail Russian submarines as soon as they leave port.

As the nuclear crisis escalates with scant reporting by the media, the words of General Douglas McArthur in a speech to the Congress of the Republic of the Philippines on July 5, 1961, seem appropriate:

> But this very triumph of scientific annihilation— this very success of invention—has destroyed the possibility of war's being a medium for the practical settlement of international differences. ... Global war has become a Frankenstein to destroy both sides. ... If you lose you are annihilated. If you win, you stand only to lose. No longer does it possess even the chance of the winner of a duel. It contains now only the germs of double suicide.

The nuclear policymakers have known the "double-suicide" consequences of nuclear weapons for decades. In the 1960s, McGeorge Bundy, assistant to President John F. Kennedy, said, "In the real world even one hydrogen bomb on one city would be a catastrophe; ten bombs on ten cities would be a disaster beyond history. A hundred, or even less, would be the end of civilization."

Today, in this fourth year of the new millennium, thirty thousand nuclear weapons remain stockpiled, while the nuclear club has expanded to include India, Israel, Pakistan, and possibly North Korea. And a recent International Atomic Energy Commission report states that up to forty other countries may be capable of building nuclear weapons.

Terrorism is a burning problem that the United States must counter. But the greatest terrorism by far is that each day the people of the world continue to be under the threat of nuclear incineration whether by an accidental missile launch, a computer error, or design.

An intelligent visitor from another world might conclude that Euripides was correct in saying, "Whom the gods would destroy they first make mad." Certainly the present nuclear condition is a madness created by those in power. It must be ended before it is too late, as Kennedy stated in his speech before the United Nations General Assembly on September 25, 1961:

> Every man, woman and child lives under a nuclear sword of Damocles, hanging by the slenderest of threads, capable of being cut at any moment by accident or miscalculation or madness. The weapons of war must be abolished before they abolish us.

We cannot count on a Petrov to always be on duty, or on the luck that has played a big role in averting nuclear war to this date. We can only count on ourselves to have the intelligence and the respect for humanity and life on this planet to mobilize with an unyielding determination to apply a constant pressure on world governments— particularly the United States as the leading culprit in the new escalation—until these weapons are abolished "before they abolish us."

The starting point is for all nuclear warheads to be removed from hair-trigger alert, placed in storage, and constantly inspected by representatives of the United States, Russia, and the United Nations. This would eliminate the possibility of a nuclear exchange starting by an accidental missile launch or computer error.

Beyond this first step, the goal that can never be compromised is the total elimination of nuclear weapons from the face of the Earth. Only then will humanity be liberated from the "fool's game" and the nuclear nightmare that began with the mushroom cloud over the obliterated city of Hiroshima, Japan, on August 6, 1945.

Douglas Mattern is president of the Association of World Citizens, a San Francisco-based international peace organization with branches in over thirty countries and nongovernmental organization status with the United Nations, including consultative status with the UN Economic and Social Council.

Pssst ... Nobody Loves a Torturer

Ask any American soldier in Iraq when the general population really turned against the United States and he will say, "Abu Ghraib."

Fareed Zakaria

As President Bush's approval ratings sink at home, the glee across the globe rises. He remains the most unpopular political figure in the world, and newspapers from Europe to Asia are delighting in his troubles. Last week's protests in Mar del Plata were happily replayed on televisions everywhere. So what is the leader of the free world to do? Well, I have a suggestion that might improve Bush's image abroad—and it doesn't require that Karen Hughes go anywhere. It would actually help Bush at home as well, and it has the additional virtue of being the right thing to do. It's simple: end the administration's disastrous experiment with officially sanctioned torture.

We now have plenty of documents and testimonials that make plain that the administration created an atmosphere in which the interrogation of prisoners could lapse into torture. After 9/11, high up in the administration—at the White House and the Pentagon—officials and lawyers were asked to find ways to bend and stretch the traditional rules of war. Donald Rumsfeld publicly declared that the Geneva Conventions did not apply to the war against Al Qaeda. Whether or not these legalisms were correct, their most important effect was the message they sent down the chain of command: "Push the envelope."

For example, when Rumsfeld read a report documenting some of the new interrogation procedures at Guantanamo in November 2002, including having detainees stand for four hours, he scribbled a note in the margin, "Why is standing limited to 4 hours? ... I stand for 8 hours a day." (Rumsfeld probably does not stand for eight hours, scarcely clad and barely fed, with bright lights, prison guards and attack dogs trained on him.) The signal Rumsfeld was sending was clear: "Get tougher." No one at the top was outlining what soldiers should not do, which lines they should not cross, which laws they should remember to adhere to strictly. The Pentagon's own report after investigating Abu Ghraib, by Gen. George Fay, speaks of "doctrinal confusion ... a lack of doctrine ... [and] systemic failures" as the causes for the incidents of torture. In a 2 million-person bureaucracy, such calculated ambiguities will inevitably lead to something like Abu Ghraib.

And the incidents clearly go well beyond Abu Ghraib. During the past few months, declassified documents and testimony from Army officers make abundantly clear that torture and abuse of prisoners is something that has become quite widespread since 9/11. The most recent evidence comes from autopsies of 44 prisoners who have died in Iraq and Afghanistan in U.S. custody. Most died under circumstances that suggest torture. The reports use words like "strangulation," "asphyxiation" and "blunt force injuries." Even the "natural" deaths were caused by "Arteriosclerotic Cardiovascular disease"—in other words, sudden heart attacks.

Sen. John McCain has proposed making absolutely clear in law that the United States does not permit the torture of prisoners—returning America to the position it had taken for five decades. McCain's amendment, endorsed by Colin Powell, passed the Senate last month by 90 to 9 in a stunning rebuke of administration policy. But Republicans in the House are trying to kill it. Vice President Cheney is making great exertions to gut it with loopholes. The White House has threatened to veto the entire defense budget, to which McCain's proposal was originally attached, unless his ban is removed. White House spokesmen don't answer questions about the bill plainly, and Cheney simply refuses to explain his views at all. (As the writer Andrew Sullivan has noted, someone needs to remind the vice president that he is an elected and accountable public servant, not a monarch.)

This is a case of more than just bad public relations. Ask any soldier in Iraq when the general population really turned against the United States and he will say, "Abu Ghraib." A few months before the scandal broke, Coalition Provisional Authority polls showed Iraqi support for the occupation at 63 percent. A month after Abu Ghraib, the number was 9 percent. Polls showed that 71 percent of Iraqis were surprised by the revelations. Most telling, 61 percent of Iraqis polled believed that no one would be punished for the torture at Abu Ghraib. Of the 29 percent who said they believed someone would be punished, 52 percent said that such punishment would extend only to "the little people."

America washes its dirty linen in public. When scandals such as this one hit, they do sully America's image in the world. But what usually also gets broadcast around the world is the vivid reality that the United States forces accountability and punishes wrongdoing, even at the highest levels. Initially, people the world over thought Americans were crazy during Watergate, but they came to respect a rule of law so strong that even a president could not break it. But today, what angers friends of America abroad is not that abuses like those at Abu Ghraib happened. Some lapses are probably an inevitable consequence of war, terrorism and insurgencies. What angers them is that no one beyond a few "little people" have been punished, the system has not been overhauled, and even now, after all that has happened, the White House is spending time, effort and precious political capital in a strange, stubborn and surely futile quest to preserve the option to torture.

The Bubble of American Supremacy

A prominent financier argues that the heedless assertion of American power in the world resembles a financial bubble—and the moment of truth may be here

By George Soros

It is generally agreed that September 11, 2001, changed the course of history. But we must ask ourselves why that should be so. How could a single event, even one involving 3,000 civilian casualties, have such a far-reaching effect? The answer lies not so much in the event itself as in the way the United States, under the leadership of President George W. Bush, responded to it.

Admittedly, the terrorist attack was historic in its own right. Hijacking fully fueled airliners and using them as suicide bombs was an audacious idea, and its execution could not have been more spectacular. The destruction of the Twin Towers of the World Trade Center made a symbolic statement that reverberated around the world, and the fact that people could watch the event on their television sets endowed it with an emotional impact that no terrorist act had ever achieved before. The aim of terrorism is to terrorize, and the attack of September 11 fully accomplished this objective.

Even so, September 11 could not have changed the course of history to the extent that it has if President Bush had not responded to it the way he did. He declared war on terrorism, and under that guise implemented a radical foreign-policy agenda whose underlying principles predated the tragedy. Those principles can be summed up as follows: International relations are relations of power, not law; power prevails and law legitimizes what prevails. The United States is unquestionably the dominant power in the post-Cold War world; it is therefore in a position to impose its views, interests, and values. The world would benefit from adopting those values, because the American model has demonstrated its superiority. The Clinton and first Bush Administrations failed to use the full potential of American

power. This must be corrected; the United States must find a way to assert its supremacy in the world.

This foreign policy is part of a comprehensive ideology customarily referred to as neoconservatism, though I prefer to describe it as a crude form of social Darwinism. I call it crude because it ignores the role of cooperation in the survival of the fittest, and puts all the emphasis on competition. In economic matters the competition is between firms; in international relations it is between states. In economic matters social Darwinism takes the form of market fundamentalism; in international relations it is now leading to the pursuit of American supremacy.

Not all the members of the Bush Administration subscribe to this ideology, but neoconservatives form an influential group within it. They publicly called for the invasion of Iraq as early as 1998. Their ideas originated in the Cold War and were further elaborated in the post-Cold War era. Before September 11 the ideologues were hindered in implementing their strategy by two considerations: George W. Bush did not have a clear mandate (he became President by virtue of a single vote in the Supreme Court), and America did not have a clearly defined enemy that would have justified a dramatic increase in military spending.

September 11 removed both obstacles. President Bush declared war on terrorism, and the nation lined up behind its President. Then the Bush Administration proceeded to exploit the terrorist attack for its own purposes. It fostered the fear that has gripped the country in order to keep the nation united behind the President, and it used the war on terrorism to execute an agenda of American supremacy. That is how September 11 changed the course of history.

Exploiting an event to further an agenda is not in itself reprehensible. It is the task of the President to provide leadership, and it is only natural for politicians to exploit or manipulate events so as to promote their policies. The cause for concern lies in the policies that Bush is promoting, and in the way he is going about imposing them on the United States and the world. He is leading us in a very dangerous direction.

The supremacist ideology of the Bush Administration stands in opposition to the principles of an open society, which recognize that people have different views and that nobody is in possession of the ultimate truth. The supremacist ideology postulates that just because we are stronger than others, we know better and have right on our side. The very first sentence of the September 2002 National Security Strategy (the President's annual laying out to Congress of the country's security objectives) reads, "The great struggles of the twentieth century between liberty and totalitarianism ended with a decisive victory for the forces of freedom— and a single sustainable model for national success: freedom, democracy, and free enterprise."

> ## September 11 introduced a discontinuity into American Foreign policy. The abnormal, the radical, and the extreme have been redefined as normal. The advocates of continuity have been pursuing a rearguard action ever since.

The assumptions behind this statement are false on two counts. First, there is no single sustainable model for national success. Second, the American model, which has indeed been successful, is not available to others, because our success depends greatly on our dominant position at the center of the global capitalist system, and we are not willing to yield it.

The Bush doctrine, first enunciated in a presidential speech at West Point in June of 2002, and incorporated into the National Security Strategy three months later, is built on two pillars: the United States will do everything in its power to maintain its unquestioned military supremacy; and the United States arrogates the right to pre-emptive action. In effect, the doctrine establishes two classes of sovereignty: the sovereignty of the United States, which takes precedence over international treaties and obligations; and the sovereignty of all other states, which is subject to the will of the United States. This is reminiscent of George Orwell's *Animal Farm*: all animals are equal, but some animals are more equal than others.

To be sure, the Bush doctrine is not stated so starkly; it is shrouded in doublespeak. The doublespeak is needed because of the contradiction between the Bush Administration's concept of freedom and democracy and the actual principles and requirements of freedom and democracy. Talk of spreading democracy looms large in the National Security Strategy. But when President Bush says, as he does frequently, that freedom will prevail, he means that America will prevail. In a free and open society, people are supposed to decide for themselves what they mean by freedom and democracy, and not simply follow America's lead. The contradiction is especially apparent in the case of Iraq, and the occupation of Iraq has brought the issue home. We came as liberators, bringing freedom and democracy, but that is not how we are perceived by a large part of the population.

It is ironic that the government of the most successful open society in the world should have fallen into the hands of people who ignore the first principles of open society. At home Attorney General John Ashcroft has used the war on terrorism to curtail civil liberties. Abroad the United States is trying to impose its views and interests through the use of military force. The invasion of Iraq was the first practical application of the Bush doctrine, and it has turned out to be counterproductive. A chasm has opened between America and the rest of the world.

The size of the chasm is impressive. On September 12, 2001, a special meeting of the North Atlantic Council invoked Article 5 of the NATO Treaty for the first time in the alliance's history, calling on all member states to treat the terrorist attack on the United States as an attack upon their own soil. The United Nations promptly endorsed punitive U.S. action against al-Qaeda in Afghanistan. A little more than a year later the United States could not secure a UN resolution to endorse the invasion of Iraq. Gerhard Schröder won re-election in Germany by refusing to cooperate with the United States. In South Korea an underdog candidate was elected to the presidency because he was considered the least friendly to the United States; many South Koreans regard the United States as a greater danger to their security than North Korea. A large majority throughout the world opposed the war on Iraq.

September 11 introduced a discontinuity into American foreign policy. Violations of American standards of behavior that would have been considered objectionable in ordinary times became accepted as appropriate to the circumstances. The abnormal, the radical, and the extreme have been redefined as normal. The advocates of continuity have been pursuing a rearguard action ever since.

To explain the significance of the transition, I should like to draw on my experience in the financial markets. Stock markets often give rise to a boom-bust process, or bubble. Bubbles do not grow out of thin air. They have a basis in reality—but reality as distorted by a misconception. Under normal conditions misconceptions are self-correcting, and the markets tend toward some kind of equilibrium. Occasionally, a misconception is reinforced by a trend prevailing in reality, and that is when a boom-bust process gets under way. Eventually the gap between reality and its false interpretation becomes unsustainable, and the bubble bursts.

Exactly when the boom-bust process enters far-from-equilibrium territory can be established only in retrospect. During the self-reinforcing phase participants are under the spell of the prevailing bias. Events seem to confirm their beliefs, strengthening their misconceptions. This widens the gap and sets the stage for a moment of truth and an eventual reversal. When that reversal comes, it is liable to have devastating consequences. This course of events seems to have an inexorable quality, but a boom-bust process can be aborted at any stage, and the adverse effects can be reduced or avoided altogether. Few bubbles reach the extremes of the information-technology boom that ended in 2000. The sooner the process is aborted, the better.

The quest for American supremacy qualifies as a bubble. The dominant position the United States occupies in the world is the element of reality that is being distorted. The proposition that the United States will be better off if it uses its position to impose its values and interests everywhere is the misconception. It is exactly by not abusing its power that America attained its current position.

Where are we in this boom-bust process? The deteriorating situation in Iraq is either the moment of truth or a test that, if it is successfully overcome, will only reinforce the trend.

Whatever the justification for removing Saddam Hussein, there can be no doubt that we invaded Iraq on false pretenses. Wittingly or unwittingly, President Bush deceived the American public and Congress and rode roughshod over the opinions of our allies. The gap between the Administration's expectations and the actual state of affairs could not be wider. It is difficult to think of a recent military operation that has gone so wrong. Our soldiers have been forced to do police duty in combat gear, and they continue to be killed. We have put at risk not only our soldiers' lives but the combat effectiveness of our armed forces. Their morale is impaired, and we are no longer in a position to properly project our power. Yet there are more places than ever before where we might have legitimate need to project that power. North Korea is openly building nuclear weapons, and Iran is clandestinely doing so. The Taliban is regrouping in Afghanistan. The costs of occupation and the prospect of permanent war are weighing heavily on our economy, and we are failing to address many festering problems—domestic and global. If we ever needed proof that the dream of American supremacy is misconceived, the occupation of Iraq has provided it. If we fail to heed the evidence, we will have to pay a heavier price in the future.

Meanwhile, largely as a result of our preoccupation with supremacy, something has gone fundamentally wrong with the war on terrorism. Indeed, war is a false metaphor in this context. Terrorists do pose a threat to our national and personal security, and we must protect ourselves.

Many of the measures we have taken are necessary and proper. It can even be argued that not enough has been done to prevent future attacks. But the war being waged has little to do with ending terrorism or enhancing homeland security; on the contrary, it endangers our security by engendering a vicious circle of escalating violence.

The terrorist attack on the United States could have been treated as a crime against humanity rather than an act of war. Treating it as a crime would have been more appropriate. Crimes require police work, not military action. Protection against terrorism requires precautionary measures, awareness, and intelligence gathering—all of which ultimately depend on the support of the populations among which the terrorists operate. Imagine for a moment that September 11 had been treated as a crime. We would not have invaded Iraq, and we would not have our military struggling to perform police work and getting shot at.

Declaring war on terrorism better suited the purposes of the Bush Administration, because it invoked military might; but this is the wrong way to deal with the problem. Military action requires an identifiable target, preferably a state. As a result the war on terrorism has been directed primarily against states harboring terrorists. Yet terrorists are by definition non-state actors, even if they are often sponsored by states.

The war on terrorism as pursued by the Bush Administration cannot be won. On the contrary, it may bring about a permanent state of war. Terrorists will never disappear. They will continue to provide a pretext for the pursuit of American supremacy. That pursuit, in turn, will continue to generate resistance. Further, by turning the hunt for terrorists into a war, we are bound to create innocent victims. The more innocent victims there are, the greater the resentment and the better the chances that some victims will turn into perpetrators.

> **If we ever needed proof that the dream of American supremacy is misconceived, the occupation of Iraq has provided it. If we fail to heed the evidence, we will have to pay a heavier price in the future.**

The terrorist threat must be seen in proper perspective. Terrorism is not new. It was an important factor in nineteenth-century Russia, and it had a great influence on the character of the czarist regime, enhancing the importance of secret police and justifying authoritarianism. More recently several European countries—Italy, Germany, Great Britain—had to contend with terrorist gangs, and it took those countries a decade or more to root them out. But those countries did not live under the spell of terrorism during all that time. Granted, using hijacked planes for suicide attacks is something new, and so is the prospect of terrorists with weapons of mass destruction. To come to terms with these threats will take some adjustment; but the threats cannot be allowed to dominate our existence. Exaggerating them will only make them worse. The most powerful country on earth cannot afford to be consumed by fear. To make the war on terrorism the centerpiece of our national strategy is an abdication of our responsibility as the leading nation in the world. Moreover, by allowing terrorism to become our principal preoccupation, we are playing into the terrorists' hands. *They* are setting our priorities.

A recent Council on Foreign Relations publication sketches out three alternative national-security strategies. The first calls for the pursuit of American supremacy through the Bush doctrine of pre-emptive military action. It is advocated by neoconservatives. The second seeks the continuation of our earlier policy of deterrence and containment. It is advocated by Colin Powell and other moderates, who may be associated with either political party. The third would have the United States lead a cooperative effort to improve the world by engaging in preventive actions of a constructive character. It is not advocated by any group of significance, although President Bush pays lip service to it. That is the policy I stand for.

The evidence shows the first option to be extremely dangerous, and I believe that the second is no longer practical. The Bush Administration has done too much damage to our standing in the world to permit a return to the status quo. Moreover, the policies pursued before September 11 were clearly inadequate for dealing with the problems of globalization. Those problems require collective action. The United States is uniquely positioned to lead the effort. We cannot just do anything we want, as the Iraqi situation demonstrates, but nothing much can be done in the way of international cooperation without the leadership—or at least the participation—of the United States.

Globalization has rendered the world increasingly interdependent, but international politics is still based on the sovereignty of states. What goes on within individual states can be of vital interest to the rest of the world, but the principle of sovereignty militates against interfering in their internal affairs. How to deal with failed states and oppressive, corrupt, and inept regimes? How to get rid of the likes of Saddam? There are too many such regimes to wage war against every one. This is the great unresolved problem confronting us today.

I propose replacing the Bush doctrine of pre-emptive military action with preventive action of a constructive and affirmative nature. Increased foreign aid or better and fairer trade rules, for example, would not violate the sovereignty of the recipients. Military action should remain a last resort. The United States is currently preoccupied with issues of security, and rightly so. But the framework within which to think about security is *collective* security. Neither nuclear proliferation nor international terrorism can be successfully addressed without international cooperation. The world is looking to us for leadership. We have provided it in the past; the main reason why anti-American feelings are so strong in the world today is that we are not providing it in the present.

GEORGE SOROS is the chairman of Soros Fund Management and the founder of a network of philanthropic organizations active in more than fifty countries. This essay is drawn from his book of the same name, to be published in January by Public Affairs.

The Case Against Perfection

What's wrong with designer children, bionic athletes, and genetic engineering?

By Michael J. Sandel

Breakthroughs in genetics present us with a promise and a predicament. The promise is that we may soon be able to treat and prevent a host of debilitating diseases. The predicament is that our newfound genetic knowledge may also enable us to manipulate our own nature—to enhance our muscles, memories, and moods; to choose the sex, height, and other genetic traits of our children; to make ourselves "better than well." When science moves faster than moral understanding, as it does today, men and women struggle to articulate their unease. In liberal societies they reach first for the language of autonomy, fairness, and individual rights. But this part of our moral vocabulary is ill equipped to address the hardest questions posed by genetic engineering. The genomic revolution has induced a kind of moral vertigo.

Consider cloning. The birth of Dolly the cloned sheep, in 1997, brought a torrent of concern about the prospect of cloned human beings. There are good medical reasons to worry. Most scientists agree that cloning is unsafe, likely to produce offspring with serious abnormalities. (Dolly recently died a premature death.) But suppose technology improved to the point where clones were at no greater risk than naturally conceived offspring. Would human cloning still be objectionable? Should our hesitation be moral as well as medical? What, exactly, is wrong with creating a child who is a genetic twin of one parent, or of an older sibling who has tragically died—or, for that matter, of an admired scientist, sports star, or celebrity?

Some say cloning is wrong because it violates the right to autonomy: by choosing a child's genetic makeup in advance, parents deny the child's right to an open future. A similar objection can be raised against any form of bioengineering that allows parents to select or reject genetic characteristics. According to this argument, genetic enhancements for musical talent, say, or athletic prowess, would point children toward particular choices, and so designer children would never be fully free.

At first glance the autonomy argument seems to capture what is troubling about human cloning and other forms of genetic engineering. It is not persuasive, for two reasons. First, it wrongly implies that absent a designing parent, children are free to choose their characteristics for themselves. But none of us chooses his genetic inheritance. The alternative to a cloned or genetically enhanced child is not one whose future is unbound by particular talents but one at the mercy of the genetic lottery.

Second, even if a concern for autonomy explains some of our worries about made-to-order children, it cannot explain our moral hesitation about people who seek genetic remedies or enhancements for themselves. Gene therapy on somatic (that is, nonreproductive) cells, such as muscle cells and brain cells, repairs or replaces defective genes. The moral quandary arises when people use such therapy not to cure a disease but to reach beyond health, to enhance their physical or cognitive capacities, to lift themselves above the norm.

Like cosmetic surgery, genetic enhancement employs medical means for nonmedical ends—ends unrelated to curing or preventing disease or repairing injury. But unlike cosmetic surgery, genetic enhancement is more than skin-deep. If we are ambivalent about surgery or Botox injections for sagging chins and furrowed brows, we are all the more troubled by genetic engineering for stronger bodies, sharper memories, greater intelligence, and happier moods. The question is whether we are right to be troubled, and if so, on what grounds.

In order to grapple with the ethics of enhancement, we need to confront questions largely lost from view—questions about the moral status of nature, and about the proper stance of human beings toward the given world. Since these questions verge on theology, modern philosophers and political theorists tend to shrink from them. But our new powers of biotechnology make them unavoidable. To see why this is so, consider four examples already on the horizon: muscle enhancement, memory enhancement, growth-hormone treatment, and reproductive technologies that enable parents to choose the sex and some genetic traits of their children. In each case what began as an attempt to treat a disease or prevent a genetic disorder now beckons as an instrument of improvement and consumer choice.

Muscles. Everyone would welcome a gene therapy to alleviate muscular dystrophy and to reverse the debilitating muscle loss that comes with old age. But what if the same therapy were used to improve athletic performance? Researchers have developed a synthetic gene that, when injected into the muscle cells of mice, prevents and even reverses natural muscle deterioration. The gene not only repairs wasted or injured muscles but also strengthens healthy ones. This success bodes well for human applications. H. Lee Sweeney, of the University of Pennsylvania, who leads the research, hopes his discovery will cure the immobility that afflicts the elderly. But Sweeney's bulked-up mice have already attracted the attention of athletes seeking a competitive edge. Although the therapy is not yet approved for human use, the prospect of genetically enhanced weight lifters, home-run sluggers, linebackers, and sprinters is easy to imagine. The widespread use of steroids and other performance-improving drugs in professional sports suggests that many athletes will be eager to avail themselves of genetic enhancement.

Suppose for the sake of argument that muscle-enhancing gene therapy, unlike steroids, turned out to be safe—or at least no riskier than a rigorous weight-training regimen. Would there be a reason to ban its use in sports? There is something unsettling about the image of genetically altered athletes lifting SUVs or hitting 650-foot home runs or running a three-minute mile. But what, exactly, is troubling about it? Is it simply that we find such superhuman spectacles too bizarre to contemplate? Or does our unease point to something of ethical significance?

It might be argued that a genetically enhanced athlete, like a drug-enhanced athlete, would have an unfair advantage over his unenhanced competitors. But the fairness argument against enhancement has a fatal flaw: it has always been the case that some athletes are better endowed genetically than others, and yet we do not consider this to undermine the fairness of competitive sports. From the standpoint of fairness, enhanced genetic differences would be no worse than natural ones, assuming they were safe and made available to all. If genetic enhancement in sports is morally objectionable, it must be for reasons other than fairness.

Memory. Genetic enhancement is possible for brains as well as brawn. In the mid-1990s scientists managed to manipulate a memory-linked gene in fruit flies, creating flies with photographic memories. More recently researchers have produced smart mice by inserting extra copies of a memory-related gene into mouse embryos. The altered mice learn more quickly and remember things longer than normal mice. The extra copies were programmed to remain active even in old age, and the improvement was passed on to offspring.

Human memory is more complicated, but biotech companies, including Memory Pharmaceuticals, are in hot pursuit of memory-enhancing drugs, or "cognition enhancers," for human beings. The obvious market for such drugs consists of those who suffer from Alzheimer's and other serious memory disorders. The companies also have their sights on a bigger market: the 81 million Americans over fifty, who are beginning to encounter the memory loss that comes naturally with age. A drug that reversed age-related memory loss would be a bonanza for the pharmaceutical industry: a Viagra for the brain. Such use would straddle the line between remedy and enhancement. Unlike a treatment for Alzheimer's, it would cure no disease; but insofar as it restored capacities a person once possessed, it would have a remedial aspect. It could also have purely nonmedical uses: for example, by a lawyer cramming to memorize facts for an upcoming trial, or by a business executive eager to learn Mandarin on the eve of his departure for Shanghai.

Some who worry about the ethics of cognitive enhancement point to the danger of creating two classes of human beings: those with access to enhancement technologies, and those who must make do with their natural capacities. And if the enhancements could be passed down the generations, the two classes might eventually become subspecies—the enhanced and the merely natural. But worry about access ignores the moral status of enhancement itself. Is the scenario troubling because the unenhanced poor would be denied the benefits of bioengineering, or because the enhanced affluent would somehow be dehumanized? As with muscles, so with memory: the fundamental question is not how to ensure equal access to enhancement but whether we should aspire to it in the first place.

Height. Pediatricians already struggle with the ethics of enhancement when confronted by parents who want to make their children taller. Since the 1980s human growth hormone has been approved for children with a hormone deficiency that makes them much shorter than average. But the treatment also increases the height of healthy children. Some parents of healthy children who are unhappy with their stature (typically boys) ask why it should make a difference whether a child is short because of a hormone deficiency or because his parents happen to be short. Whatever the cause, the social consequences are the same.

In the face of this argument some doctors began prescribing hormone treatments for children whose short stature was unrelated to any medical problem. By 1996 such "off-label" use accounted for 40 percent of human-growth-hormone prescriptions. Although it is legal to prescribe drugs for purposes not approved by the Food and Drug Administration, pharmaceutical companies cannot promote such use. Seeking to expand its market, Eli Lilly & Co. recently persuaded the FDA to approve its human growth hormone for healthy children whose projected adult height is in the bottom one percentile—under five feet three inches for boys and four feet eleven inches for girls. This concession raises a large question about the ethics of enhancement: If hormone treatments need not be limited to those with hormone deficiencies, why should they be available only to very short children? Why shouldn't all shorter-than-average children be able to seek treatment? And what about a child of average height who wants to be taller so that he can make the basketball team?

Some oppose height enhancement on the grounds that it is collectively self-defeating; as some become taller, others become shorter relative to the norm. Except in Lake Wobegon, not every child can be above average. As the unenhanced began to feel shorter, they, too, might seek treatment, leading to a hormonal arms race that left everyone worse off, especially those who couldn't afford to buy their way up from shortness.

But the arms-race objection is not decisive on its own. Like the fairness objection to bioengineered muscles and memory, it leaves unexamined the attitudes and dispositions that prompt the drive for enhancement. If we were bothered only by the injustice of adding shortness to the problems of the poor, we could remedy that unfairness by publicly subsidizing height enhancements. As for the relative height deprivation suffered by innocent bystanders, we could compensate them by taxing those who buy their way to greater height. The real question is whether we want to live in a society where parents feel compelled to spend a fortune to make perfectly healthy kids a few inches taller.

Sex selection. Perhaps the most inevitable nonmedical use of bioengineering is sex selection. For centuries parents have been trying to choose the sex of their children. Today biotech succeeds where folk remedies failed.

One technique for sex selection arose with prenatal tests using amniocentesis and ultrasound. These medical technologies were developed to detect genetic abnormalities such as spina bifida and Down syndrome. But they can also reveal the sex of the fetus—allowing for the abortion of a fetus of an undesired sex. Even among those who favor abortion rights, few advocate abortion simply because the parents do not want a girl. Nevertheless, in traditional societies with a powerful cultural preference for boys, this practice has become widespread.

Sex selection need not involve abortion, however. For couples undergoing *in vitro* fertilization (IVF), it is possible to choose the sex of the child before the fertilized egg is implanted in the womb. One method makes use of pre-implantation genetic diagnosis (PGD), a procedure developed to screen for genetic diseases. Several eggs are fertilized in a petri dish and grown to the eight-cell stage (about three days). At that point the embryos are tested to determine their sex. Those of the desired sex are implanted; the others are typically discarded. Although few couples are likely to undergo the difficulty and expense of IVF simply to choose the sex of their child, embryo screening is a highly reliable means of sex selection. And as our genetic knowledge increases, it may be possible to use PGD to cull embryos carrying undesired genes, such as those associated with obesity, height, and skin color. The science-fiction movie *Gattaca* depicts a future in which parents routinely screen embryos for sex, height, immunity to disease, and even IQ. There is something troubling about the *Gattaca* scenario, but it is not easy to identify what exactly is wrong with screening embryos to choose the sex of our children.

One line of objection draws on arguments familiar from the abortion debate. Those who believe that an embryo is a person reject embryo screening for the same reasons they reject abortion. If an eight-cell embryo growing in a petri dish is morally equivalent to a fully developed human being, then discarding it is no better than aborting a fetus, and both practices are equivalent to infanticide. Whatever its merits, however, this "pro-life" objection is not an argument against sex selection as such.

The latest technology poses the question of sex selection unclouded by the matter of an embryo's moral status. The Genetics & IVF Institute, a for-profit infertility clinic in Fairfax, Virginia, now offers a sperm-sorting technique that makes it possible to choose the sex of one's child before it is conceived. X-bearing sperm, which produce girls, carry more DNA than Y-bearing sperm, which produce boys; a device called a flow cytometer can separate them. The process, called MicroSort, has a high rate of success.

If sex selection by sperm sorting is objectionable, it must be for reasons that go beyond the debate about the moral status of the embryo. One such reason is that sex selection is an instrument of sex discrimination—typically against girls, as illustrated by the chilling sex ratios in India and China. Some speculate that societies with substantially more men than women will be less stable, more violent, and more prone to crime or war. These are legitimate worries—but the sperm-sorting company has a clever way of addressing them. It offers MicroSort only to couples who want to choose the sex of a child for purposes of "family balancing." Those with more sons than daughters may choose a girl, and vice versa. But customers may not use the technology to stock up on children of the same sex, or even to choose the sex of their firstborn child. (So far the majority of MicroSort clients have chosen girls.) Under restrictions of this kind, do any ethical issues remain that should give us pause?

The case of MicroSort helps us isolate the moral objections that would persist if muscle-enhancement, memory-enhancement, and height-enhancement technologies were safe and available to all.

It is commonly said that genetic enhancements undermine our humanity by threatening our capacity to act freely, to succeed by our own efforts, and to consider ourselves responsible—worthy of praise or blame—for the things we do and for the way we are. It is one thing to hit seventy home runs as the result of disciplined training and effort, and something else, something less, to hit them with the help of steroids or genetically enhanced muscles. Of course, the roles of effort and en-

hancement will be a matter of degree. But as the role of enhancement increases, our admiration for the achievement fades—or, rather, our admiration for the achievement shifts from the player to his pharmacist. This suggests that our moral response to enhancement is a response to the diminished agency of the person whose achievement is enhanced.

Though there is much to be said for this argument, I do not think the main problem with enhancement and genetic engineering is that they undermine effort and erode human agency. The deeper danger is that they represent a kind of hyper-agency—a Promethean aspiration to remake nature, including human nature, to serve our purposes and satisfy our desires. The problem is not the drift to mechanism but the drive to mastery. And what the drive to mastery misses and may even destroy is an appreciation of the gifted character of human powers and achievements.

To acknowledge the giftedness of life is to recognize that our talents and powers are not wholly our own doing, despite the effort we expend to develop and to exercise them. It is also to recognize that not everything in the world is open to whatever use we may desire or devise. Appreciating the gifted quality of life constrains the Promethean project and conduces to a certain humility. It is in part a religious sensibility. But its resonance reaches beyond religion.

It is difficult to account for what we admire about human activity and achievement without drawing upon some version of this idea. Consider two types of athletic achievement. We appreciate players like Pete Rose, who are not blessed with great natural gifts but who manage, through striving, grit, and determination, to excel in their sport. But we also admire players like Joe DiMaggio, who display natural gifts with grace and effortlessness. Now, suppose we learned that both players took performance-enhancing drugs. Whose turn to drugs would we find more deeply disillusioning? Which

aspect of the athletic ideal—effort or gift—would be more deeply offended?

Some might say effort: the problem with drugs is that they provide a shortcut, a way to win without striving. But striving is not the point of sports; excellence is. And excellence consists at least partly in the display of natural talents and gifts that are no doing of the athlete who possesses them. This is an uncomfortable fact for democratic societies. We want to believe that success, in sports and in life, is something we earn, not something we inherit. Natural gifts, and the admiration they inspire, embarrass the meritocratic faith; they cast doubt on the conviction that praise and rewards flow from effort alone. In the face of this embarrassment we inflate the moral significance of striving, and depreciate giftedness. This distortion can be seen, for example, in network-television coverage of the Olympics, which focuses less on the feats the athletes perform than on heartrending stories of the hardships they have overcome and the struggles they have waged to triumph over an injury or a difficult upbringing or political turmoil in their native land.

But effort isn't everything. No one believes that a mediocre basketball player who works and trains even harder than Michael Jordan deserves greater acclaim or a bigger contract. The real problem with genetically altered athletes is that they corrupt athletic competition as a human activity that honors the cultivation and display of natural talents. From this standpoint, enhancement can be seen as the ultimate expression of the ethic of effort and willfulness—a kind of high-tech striving. The ethic of willfulness and the biotechnological powers it now enlists are arrayed against the claims of giftedness.

The ethic of giftedness, under siege in sports, persists in the practice of parenting. But here, too, bioengineering and genetic enhancement threaten to dislodge it. To appreciate children as gifts is to accept them as they come, not as objects of our design or products of our will or instruments of our ambition. Parental love is not contingent on the talents and attributes a child happens to have. We choose our friends and spouses at least partly on the basis of qualities we find attractive. But we do not choose our children. Their qualities are unpredictable, and even the most conscientious parents cannot be held wholly responsible for the kind of children they have. That is why parenthood, more than other human relationships, teaches what the theologian William F. May calls an "openness to the unbidden."

May's resonant phrase helps us see that the deepest moral objection to enhancement lies less in the perfection it seeks than in the human disposition it expresses and promotes. The problem is not that parents usurp the autonomy of a child they design. The problem lies in the hubris of the designing parents, in their drive to master the mystery of birth. Even if this disposition did not make parents tyrants to their children, it would disfigure the relation between parent and child, and deprive the parent of the humility and enlarged human sympathies that an openness to the unbidden can cultivate.

To appreciate children as gifts or blessings is not, of course, to be passive in the face of illness or disease. Medical intervention to cure or prevent illness or restore the injured to health does not desecrate nature but honors it. Healing sickness or injury does not override a child's natural capacities but permits them to flourish.

Nor does the sense of life as a gift mean that parents must shrink from shaping and directing the development of their child. Just as athletes and artists have an obligation to cultivate their talents, so parents have an obligation to cultivate their children, to help them discover and develop their talents and gifts. As May points out, parents give their children two kinds of love: accepting love and transforming love. Accepting love affirms the being of the child, whereas transforming love seeks the well-being of the child. Each aspect corrects the excesses of the other, he writes: "Attachment becomes too quietistic if it slackens into mere acceptance of the child as he is." Parents have a duty to promote their children's excellence.

These days, however, overly ambitious parents are prone to get carried away with transforming love—promoting and demanding all manner of accomplishments from their children, seeking perfection. "Parents find it difficult to maintain an equilibrium between the two sides of love," May observes. "Accepting love, without transforming love, slides into indulgence and finally neglect. Transforming love, without accepting love, badgers and finally rejects." May finds in these competing impulses a parallel with modern science: it, too, engages us in beholding the given world, studying and savoring it, and also in molding the world, transforming and perfecting it.

The mandate to mold our children, to cultivate and improve them, complicates the case against enhancement. We usually admire parents who seek the best for their children, who spare no effort to help them achieve happiness and success. Some parents confer advantages on their children by enrolling them in expensive schools, hiring private tutors, sending them to tennis camp, providing them with piano lessons, ballet lessons, swimming lessons, SAT-prep courses, and so on. If it is permissible and even admirable for parents to help their children in these ways, why isn't it equally admirable for parents to use whatever genetic technologies may emerge (provided they are safe) to enhance their children's intelligence, musical ability, or athletic prowess?

The defenders of enhancement are right to this extent: improving children through genetic engineering is similar in spirit to the heavily managed, high-pressure child-rearing that is now common. But this similarity does not vindicate genetic enhancement. On the contrary, it highlights a problem with the trend toward hyperparenting. One conspicuous example of this trend is sports-crazed parents bent on making champions of their children. Another is the frenzied drive of overbearing parents to mold and manage their children's academic careers.

As the pressure for performance increases, so does the need to help distractible children concentrate on the task at hand. This may be why diagnoses of attention deficit and hyperactivity disorder have increased so sharply. Lawrence Diller, a pediatrician and the author of *Running on Ritalin*, estimates that five to six percent of American children under eighteen (a total of four to five million kids) are currently prescribed Ritalin, Adderall, and other stimulants, the treatment of choice for ADHD. (Stimulants counteract hyperactivity by making it easier to focus and sustain attention.) The number of Ritalin prescriptions for children and adolescents has tripled over the past decade, but not all users suffer from attention disorders or hyperactivity. High school and college students have learned that prescription stimulants improve concentration for those with normal attention spans, and some buy or borrow their classmates' drugs to enhance their performance on the SAT or other exams. Since stimulants work for both medical and nonmedical purposes, they raise the same moral questions posed by other technologies of enhancement.

However those questions are resolved, the debate reveals the cultural distance we have traveled since the debate over marijuana, LSD, and other drugs a generation ago. Unlike the drugs of the 1960s and 1970s, Ritalin and Adderall are not for checking out but for buckling down, not for beholding the world and taking it in but for molding the world and fitting in. We used to speak of nonmedical drug use as "recreational." That term no longer applies. The steroids and stimulants that figure in the enhancement debate are not a source of recreation but a bid for compliance—a way of answering a competitive society's demand to improve our performance and perfect our nature. This demand for performance and perfection animates the impulse to rail against the given. It is the deepest source of the moral trouble with enhancement.

Some see a clear line between genetic enhancement and other ways that people seek improvement in their children and themselves. Genetic manipulation seems somehow worse—more intrusive, more sinister—than other ways of enhancing performance and seeking success. But morally speaking, the difference is less significant than it seems. Bioengineering gives us reason to question the low-tech, high-pressure child-rearing practices we commonly accept. The hyperparenting familiar in our time represents an anxious excess of mastery and dominion that misses the sense of life as a gift. This draws it disturbingly close to eugenics.

The shadow of eugenics hangs over today's debates about genetic engineering and enhancement. Critics of genetic engineering argue that human cloning, enhancement, and the quest for designer children are nothing more than "privatized" or "free-market" eugenics. Defenders of enhancement reply that genetic choices freely made are not really eugenic—at least not in the pejorative sense. To remove the coercion, they argue, is to remove the very thing that makes eugenic policies repugnant.

Sorting out the lesson of eugenics is another way of wrestling with the ethics of enhancement. The Nazis gave eugenics a bad name. But what, precisely, was wrong with it? Was the old eugenics objectionable only insofar as it was coercive? Or is there something inherently wrong with the resolve to deliberately design our progeny's traits?

James Watson, the biologist who, with Francis Crick, discovered the structure of DNA, sees nothing wrong with genetic engineering and enhancement, provided they are freely chosen rather than state-imposed. And yet Watson's language contains more than a whiff of the old eugenic sensibility. "If you really are stupid, I would call that a disease," he recently told *The Times* of London. "The lower 10 percent who really have difficulty, even in elementary school, what's the cause of it? A lot of people would like to say, 'Well, poverty, things like that.' It probably isn't. So I'd like to get rid of that, to help the lower 10 percent." A few years ago Watson stirred controversy by saying that if a gene for homosexuality were discovered, a woman should be free to abort a fetus that carried it. When his remark provoked an uproar, he replied that he was not singling out gays but asserting a principle: women should be free to abort fetuses for any reason of genetic preference—for example, if the child would be dyslexic, or lacking musical talent, or too short to play basketball.

Watson's scenarios are clearly objectionable to those for whom all abortion is an unspeakable crime. But for those who do not subscribe to the pro-life position, these scenarios raise a hard question: If it is morally troubling to contemplate abortion to avoid a gay child or a dyslexic one, doesn't this suggest that something is wrong with acting on any eugenic preference, even when no state coercion is involved?

Consider the market in eggs and sperm. The advent of artificial insemination allows prospective parents to shop for gametes with the genetic traits they desire in their offspring. It is a less predictable way to design children than cloning or preimplantation genetic screening, but it offers a good example of a procreative practice in which the old eugenics meets the new consumerism. A few years ago some Ivy League newspapers ran an ad seeking an egg from a woman who was at least five feet ten inches tall and athletic, had no major family medical problems, and had a combined SAT score of 1400 or above. The ad offered $50,000 for an egg from a donor with these traits. More recently a Web site was launched claiming to auction eggs from fashion models whose photos appeared on the site, at starting bids of $15,000 to $150,000.

On what grounds, if any, is the egg market morally objectionable? Since no one is forced to buy or sell, it cannot be wrong for reasons of coercion. Some might worry that hefty prices would exploit poor women by presenting them with an offer they couldn't refuse. But the designer eggs that fetch the highest prices are likely to be sought from the privileged, not the poor. If the market for premium eggs gives us moral qualms, this, too, shows that concerns about eugenics are not put to rest by freedom of choice.

A tale of two sperm banks helps explain why. The Repository for Germinal Choice, one of America's first sperm banks, was not a commercial enterprise. It was opened in 1980 by Robert Graham, a philanthropist dedicated to improving the world's "germ plasm" and counteracting the rise of "retrograde humans." His plan was to collect the sperm of Nobel Prize-winning scientists and make it available to women of high intelligence, in hopes of breeding supersmart babies. But Graham had trouble persuading Nobel laureates to donate their sperm for his bizarre scheme, and so settled for sperm from young scientists of high promise. His sperm bank closed in 1999.

In contrast, California Cryobank, one of the world's leading sperm banks, is a for-profit company with no overt eugenic mission. Cappy Rothman, M.D., a co-founder of the firm, has nothing but disdain for Graham's eugenics, although the standards Cryobank imposes on the sperm it recruits are exacting. Cryobank has offices in Cambridge, Massachusetts, between Harvard and MIT, and in Palo Alto, California, near Stanford. It advertises for donors in campus newspapers (compensation up to

$900 a month), and accepts less than five percent of the men who apply. Cryobank's marketing materials play up the prestigious source of its sperm. Its catalogue provides detailed information about the physical characteristics of each donor, along with his ethnic origin and college major. For an extra fee prospective customers can buy the results of a test that assesses the donor's temperament and character type. Rothman reports that Cryobank's ideal sperm donor is six feet tall, with brown eyes, blond hair, and dimples, and has a college degree—not because the company wants to propagate those traits, but because those are the traits his customers want: "If our customers wanted high school dropouts, we would give them high school dropouts."

Not everyone objects to marketing sperm. But anyone who is troubled by the eugenic aspect of the Nobel Prize sperm bank should be equally troubled by Cryobank, consumer-driven though it be. What, after all, is the moral difference between designing children according to an explicit eugenic purpose and designing children according to the dictates of the market? Whether the aim is to improve humanity's "germ plasm" or to cater to consumer preferences, both practices are eugenic insofar as both make children into products of deliberate design.

A number of political philosophers call for a new "liberal eugenics." They argue that a moral distinction can be drawn between the old eugenic policies and genetic enhancements that do not restrict the autonomy of the child. "While old-fashioned authoritarian eugenicists sought to produce citizens out of a single centrally designed mould," writes Nicholas Agar, "the distinguishing mark of the new liberal eugenics is state neutrality." Government may not tell parents what sort of children to design, and parents may engineer in their children only those traits that improve their capacities without biasing their choice of life plans. A recent text on genetics and justice, written by the

bioethicists Allen Buchanan, Dan W. Brock, Norman Daniels, and Daniel Wikler, offers a similar view. The "bad reputation of eugenics," they write, is due to practices that "might be avoidable in a future eugenic program." The problem with the old eugenics was that its burdens fell disproportionately on the weak and the poor, who were unjustly sterilized and segregated. But provided that the benefits and burdens of genetic improvement are fairly distributed, these bioethicists argue, eugenic measures are unobjectionable and may even be morally required.

The libertarian philosopher Robert Nozick proposed a "genetic supermarket" that would enable parents to order children by design without imposing a single design on the society as a whole: "This supermarket system has the great virtue that it involves no centralized decision fixing the future human type(s)."

Even the leading philosopher of American liberalism, John Rawls, in his classic *A Theory of Justice* (1971), offered a brief endorsement of noncoercive eugenics. Even in a society that agrees to share the benefits and burdens of the genetic lottery, it is "in the interest of each to have greater natural assets," Rawls wrote. "This enables him to pursue a preferred plan of life." The parties to the social contract "want to insure for their descendants the best genetic endowment (assuming their own to be fixed)." Eugenic policies are therefore not only permissible but required as a matter of justice. "Thus over time a society is to take steps at least to preserve the general level of natural abilities and to prevent the diffusion of serious defects."

But removing the coercion does not vindicate eugenics. The problem with eugenics and genetic engineering is that they represent the one-sided triumph of willfulness over giftedness, of dominion over reverence, of molding over beholding. Why, we may wonder, should we worry about this triumph? Why not

shake off our unease about genetic enhancement as so much superstition? What would be lost if biotechnology dissolved our sense of giftedness?

From a religious standpoint the answer is clear: To believe that our talents and powers are wholly our own doing is to misunderstand our place in creation, to confuse our role with God's. Religion is not the only source of reasons to care about giftedness, however. The moral stakes can also be described in secular terms. If bioengineering made the myth of the "self-made man" come true, it would be difficult to view our talents as gifts for which we are indebted, rather than as achievements for which we are responsible. This would transform three key features of our moral landscape: humility, responsibility, and solidarity.

In a social world that prizes mastery and control, parenthood is a school for humility. That we care deeply about our children and yet cannot choose the kind we want teaches parents to be open to the unbidden. Such openness is a disposition worth affirming, not only within families but in the wider world as well. It invites us to abide the unexpected, to live with dissonance, to rein in the impulse to control. A *Gattaca*-like world in which parents became accustomed to specifying the sex and genetic traits of their children would be a world inhospitable to the unbidden, a gated community writ large. The awareness that our talents and abilities are not wholly our own doing restrains our tendency toward hubris.

Though some maintain that genetic enhancement erodes human agency by overriding effort, the real problem is the explosion, not the erosion, of responsibility. As humility gives way, responsibility expands to daunting proportions. We attribute less to chance and more to choice. Parents become responsible for choosing, or failing to choose, the right traits for their children. Athletes become responsible for acquiring, or failing to acquire, the talents that will help their teams win.

One of the blessings of seeing ourselves as creatures of nature, God, or fortune is that we are not wholly responsible for the way we are. The more we become masters of our genetic endowments, the greater the burden we bear for the talents we have and the way we perform. Today when a basketball player misses a rebound, his coach can blame him for being out of position. Tomorrow the coach may blame him for being too short. Even now the use of performance-enhancing drugs in professional sports is subtly transforming the expectations players have for one another; on some teams players who take the field free from amphetamines or other stimulants are criticized for "playing naked."

The more alive we are to the chanced nature of our lot, the more reason we have to share our fate with others. Consider insurance. Since people do not know whether or when various ills will befall them, they pool their risk by buying health insurance and life insurance. As life plays itself out, the healthy wind up subsidizing the unhealthy, and those who live to a ripe old age wind up subsidizing the families of those who die before their time. Even without a sense of mutual obligation, people pool their risks and resources and share one another's fate.

But insurance markets mimic solidarity only insofar as people do not know or control their own risk factors. Suppose genetic testing advanced to the point where it could reliably predict each person's medical future and life expectancy. Those confident of good health and long life would opt out of the pool, causing other people's premiums to skyrocket. The solidarity of insurance would disappear as those with good genes fled the actuarial company of those with bad ones.

The fear that insurance companies would use genetic data to assess risks and set premiums recently led the Senate to vote to prohibit genetic discrimination in health insurance.

But the bigger danger, admittedly more speculative, is that genetic enhancement, if routinely practiced, would make it harder to foster the moral sentiments that social solidarity requires.

Why, after all, do the successful owe anything to the least-advantaged members of society? The best answer to this question leans heavily on the notion of giftedness. The natural talents that enable the successful to flourish are not their own doing but, rather, their good fortune—a result of the genetic lottery. If our genetic endowments are gifts, rather than achievements for which we can claim credit, it is a mistake and a conceit to assume that we are entitled to the full measure of the bounty they reap in a market economy. We therefore have an obligation to share this bounty with those who, through no fault of their own, lack comparable gifts.

A lively sense of the contingency of our gifts—a consciousness that none of us is wholly responsible for his or her success—saves a meritocratic society from sliding into the smug assumption that the rich are rich because they are more deserving than the poor. Without this, the successful would become even more likely than they are now to view themselves as self-made and self-sufficient, and hence wholly responsible for their success. Those at the bottom of society would be viewed not as disadvantaged, and thus worthy of a measure of compensation, but as simply unfit, and thus worthy of eugenic repair. The meritocracy, less chastened by chance, would become harder, less forgiving. As perfect genetic knowledge would end the simulacrum of solidarity in insurance markets, so perfect genetic control would erode the actual solidarity that arises when men and women reflect on the contingency of their talents and fortunes.

Thirty-five years ago Robert L. Sinsheimer, a molecular biologist at the California Institute of Technology, glimpsed the shape of things to come. In an article titled "The Prospect of Designed Genetic Change" he argued that freedom of choice would vindicate the new genetics, and set it apart from the discredited eugenics of old.

> To implement the older eugenics ... would have required a massive social programme carried out over many generations. Such a programme could not have been initiated without the consent and co-operation of a major fraction of the population, and would have been continuously subject to social control. In contrast, the new eugenics could, at least in principle, be implemented on a quite individual basis, in one generation, and subject to no existing restrictions.

According to Sinsheimer, the new eugenics would be voluntary rather than coerced, and also more humane. Rather than segregating and eliminating the unfit, it would improve them. "The old eugenics would have required a continual selection for breeding of the fit, and a culling of the unfit," he wrote. "The new eugenics would permit in principle the conversion of all the unfit to the highest genetic level."

Sinsheimer's paean to genetic engineering caught the heady, Promethean self-image of the age. He wrote hopefully of rescuing "the losers in that chromosomal lottery that so firmly channels our human destinies," including not only those born with genetic defects but also "the 50,000,000 'normal' Americans with an IQ of less than 90." But he also saw that something bigger than improving on nature's "mindless, age-old throw of dice" was at stake. Implicit in technologies of genetic intervention was a more exalted place for human beings in the cosmos. "As we enlarge man's freedom, we diminish his constraints and that which he must accept as given," he wrote. Copernicus and Darwin had "demoted man from his bright glory at the focal point of the universe," but the new biology would restore his central role. In the mirror of our genetic knowledge we would see ourselves as more than a link in the chain of evolution: "We can be the agent of transition to a whole new pitch of evolution. This is a cosmic event."

There is something appealing, even intoxicating, about a vision of human freedom unfettered by the given. It may even be the case that the allure of that vision played a part in summoning the genomic age into being. It is often assumed that the powers of enhancement we now possess arose as an inadvertent by-product of biomedical progress—the genetic revolution came, so to speak, to cure disease, and stayed to tempt us with the prospect of enhancing our performance, designing our children, and perfecting our nature. That may have the story backwards.

It is more plausible to view genetic engineering as the ultimate expression of our resolve to see ourselves astride the world, the masters of our nature. But that promise of mastery is flawed. It threatens to banish our appreciation of life as a gift, and to leave us with nothing to affirm or behold outside our own will.

From *The Atlantic Monthly*, Vol. 293, No. 3, April 2004, pages 50-62. Copyright © 2004 by Michael J. Sandel. Reprinted with permission of the author.

A Politics for Generation X

Today's young adults may be the most politically disengaged in American history. The author explains why, and puts forth a new political agenda that just might galvanize his generation

by Ted Halstead

EVERETT Carll Ladd, a political scientist, once remarked, "Social analysis and commentary has many shortcomings, but few of its chapters are as persistently wrong-headed as those on the generations and generational change. This literature abounds with hyperbole and unsubstantiated leaps from available data." Many of the media's grand pronouncements about America's post–Baby Boom generation—alternatively called Generation X, Baby Busters, and twentysomethings—would seem to illustrate this point.

The 1990s opened with a frenzy of negative stereotyping of the roughly 50 million Americans born from 1965 to 1978: they were slackers, cynics, whiners, drifters, malcontents. A *Washington Post* headline captured the patronizing attitude that Baby Boomers apparently hold toward their successors: "THE BORING TWENTIES: GROW UP, CRYBABIES." Then books and articles began to recast young Americans as ambitious, savvy, independent, pragmatic, and self-sufficient. For instance, *Time* magazine described a 1997 article titled "Great Xpectations" this way: "Slackers? Hardly. The so-called Generation X turns out to be full of go-getters who are just doing it—but their way."

Stereotyping aside, some disquieting facts jump out regarding the political practices and political orientation of young Americans. A wide sampling of surveys indicates that Xers are less politically or civically engaged, exhibit less social trust or confidence in government, have a weaker allegiance to their country or to either political party, and are more materialistic than their predecessors. Why are so many young people opting out of conventional politics, and what does this mean for the future of American democracy? Might it be that today's political establishment is simply not addressing what matters to the nation's young? And if so, what is their political agenda?

THE DISENGAGED GENERATION

ALTHOUGH political and civic engagement began to decrease among those at the tail end of the Baby Boom, Xers appear to have enshrined political apathy as a way of life. In measurements of conventional political participation the youngest voting-age Americans stand out owing to their unprecedented levels of absenteeism. This political disengagement cannot be explained away as merely the habits of youth, because today's young are markedly less engaged than were their counterparts in earlier generations.

Voting rates are arrestingly low among post-Boomers. In the 1994 midterm elections, for instance, fewer than one in five eligible Xers showed up at the polls. As recently as 1972 half those aged eighteen to twenty-four voted; in 1996, a presidential-election year, only 32 percent did. Such anemic participation can be seen in all forms of traditional political activity: Xers are considerably less likely than previous generations of young Americans to call or write elected officials, attend candidates' rallies, or work on political campaigns. What is more, a number of studies reveal that their general knowledge about public affairs is uniquely low.

The most recent birth cohort to reach voting age is also rejecting conventional partisan demarcations: the distinction between Democrats and Republicans, which has defined American politics for more than a century, doesn't resonate much with the young, who tend to see more similarities than differences between the two parties. Even those young adults who are actively engaged in national politics see partisan boundaries blurring into irrelevance. Gary Ruskin, an Xer who directs the Congressional Accountability Project, a public-policy group in Washington, D.C., puts it this way: "Republicans and Democrats have become one and the same—they are both corrupt at the core and behave like children who are more interested in fighting with each other than in getting anything accomplished."

Surveys suggest that no more than a third of young adults identify with either political party, and only a quarter vote a straight party ticket. Xers are the group least likely to favor maintaining the current two-party system, and the most likely to favor candidates who are running as independents. Indeed, 44 percent of those aged eighteen to twenty-nine identify themselves as independents. Not surprisingly, young adults gave the strongest support to Ross Perot in 1992 and to Jesse Ventura in 1998.

More fundamental, Xers have internalized core beliefs and characteristics that bode ill for the future of American democracy. This generation is more likely to describe itself as having a negative attitude toward America, and as placing little importance on citizenship and national identity, than its predecessors. And Xers exhibit a more materialistic and individualistic streak than did their parents at a similar age. Moreover, there is a general decline in social trust among the young, whether that is trust in their fellow citizens, in established institutions, or in elected officials. These tendencies are, of course, related: heightened individualism and materialism, as Alexis de Tocqueville pointed out, tend to isolate people from one another, weakening the communal bonds that give meaning and force to notions of national identity and the common good.

EXPLANATION X

MANY explanations have been advanced for the political apathy of Generation X, but none seems to tell the entire story. One theory holds that television, which the average child now watches for forty hours a week, is to blame for the cynicism and lack of civic education among the young. Another is that growing up during the Reagan and Bush presidencies, when government-bashing was the norm, led many Xers to internalize a negative attitude toward politics and the public sector. A third theory blames the breakdown of the traditional family, in which much of a child's civic sensitivity and partisan orientation is said to develop. And, of course, the incessant scandals in contemporary politics deserve some blame for driving young people into political hiding. Each of these theories undoubtedly holds some truth, but a simpler and more straightforward explanation is possible—namely, that young Americans are reacting in a per-

fectly rational manner to their circumstances, at least as they perceive them.

As they enter adulthood, this explanation goes, Xers are facing a particularly acute economic insecurity, which leads them to turn inward and pursue material well-being above all else. They see the outlines of very real problems ahead—fiscal, social, and environmental. But in the nation's political system they perceive no leadership on the issues that concern them; rather, they see self-serving politicians who continually indenture themselves to the highest bidders. So Xers have decided, for now, to tune out. After all, they ask, what's the point?

To be sure, today's young have a great deal to be thankful for. Xers have been blessed to come of age in a time of peace and relative material prosperity—itself a significant historical aberration. And the positive legacy they are inheriting goes much deeper: Generation X enjoys the fruits of the civil-rights, women's-rights, and environmental-conservation battles waged by its parents. Finally, who could deny that today's young are benefiting from significant leaps in technology, science, and medicine? But for all these new opportunities, the world being passed on to young Americans is also weighed down by truly bedeviling problems. Prevailing ideologies have proved incapable of accommodating this seeming contradiction.

Ever since the pioneering work on generational theory by the German sociologist Karl Mannheim, in the 1920s, political generations have been thought to arise from the critical events that affect young people when they are most malleable. "Early impressions," Mannheim wrote, "tend to coalesce into a *natural view* of the world." At the very heart of the Xer world view is a deep-seated economic insecurity. In contrast to Baby Boomers, most of whom came of age during the period of unparalleled upward mobility that followed the Second World War, Xers grew up in a time of falling wages, shrinking benefits, and growing economic inequality.

Since 1973, while the earnings of older Americans have mostly stagnated, real median weekly earnings for men aged twenty to thirty-four have fallen by almost a third. In fact, Xers may well be the first generation whose lifetime earnings will be less than their parents'. Al-

ready they have the weakest middle class of any generation born in this century.

Falling wages and rising inequality have affected all young Americans, regardless of educational achievement. During the said-to-be economically strong years 1989–1995 earnings for recent college graduates fell by nearly 10 percent—representing the first time that a generation of graduates has earned less than the previous one. And circumstances are far worse for the roughly 67 percent of Xers aged twenty-five to thirty-four who don't have a college degree. In 1997 recent male high school graduates earned 28 percent less (in dollars adjusted for inflation) than did the comparable group in 1973, and recent female high school graduates earned 18 percent less. When politicians and the media continually extol the economy's performance, many Xers just scratch their heads in disbelief.

The economic hardship facing today's young cannot be overstated: America's rate of children in poverty—the highest in the developed world—rose by 37 percent from 1970 to 1995. During the same period the old notions of lifetime employment and guaranteed benefits gave way to the new realities of sudden downsizing and contingent, or temporary, employment. Forty-four million Americans lack basic health insurance today, and Xers—many of whom are part of the contingent work force—are the least insured of all. To compound these problems, many Xers received a poor education in failing public schools, which left them especially ill-prepared to compete in an ever more demanding marketplace.

A LEGACY OF DEBT

BESIDES struggling against downward economic mobility, Generation X is inheriting a daunting array of fiscal, social, and environmental debts. Although most media reports focus on the national debt and the likely future insolvency of Social Security, the real problem is actually much broader. When they envision their future, Xers don't just see a government drifting toward the political equivalent of Chapter 11; they also see a crippled social structure, a dwindling middle class, and a despoiled natural habitat.

Despite bipartisan fanfare about balancing the federal budget, the fiscal outlook remains quite bleak for young adults—and for reasons seldom discussed. Long before Social Security and Medicare go insolvent under the burden of Boomer retirement, entitlement payments will have crowded out the public investments that are essential to ensuring a promising future. Government spending on infrastructure, education, and research has already lessened over the past twenty-five years, from 24 percent to 14 percent of the federal budget, and the downward squeeze will only worsen. In other words, Xers will be forced to pay ever higher taxes for ever fewer government services.

Financially most frightening, however, are the nation's skyrocketing levels of personal debt and international debt. With all the focus on balancing the federal budget, not enough attention has been paid to the fact that American families, and Xers in particular, are increasingly unable to balance their own books. Xers carry more personal debt than did any other generation at their age in our nation's history; in fact, a full 60 percent of Xers carry credit-card balances from month to month. In addition, those who attend college face the dual burden of soaring tuition bills and shrinking federal education grants. From 1977 to 1997 the median student-loan debt has climbed from $2,000 to $15,000. The combination of lower wages and over-leveraged lifestyles is doubly worrisome to a generation that wonders if it will ever collect Social Security.

Then there is America's ballooning international debt. For the past two decades the nation as a whole has consumed more than it has produced, and has borrowed from abroad to cover the difference—nearly $2 trillion by the end of this decade, or more than a fifth of the total annual output of the U.S. economy. In the short life-span to date of most Xers, America has gone from being the world's largest creditor to being its largest debtor. At some point in the future, especially as interest on our international debt accumulates, investors in other countries will become reluctant to keep bankrolling us. When they do, we will have no choice but to tighten our belts by cutting both investment and consumption. In other words, just as Xers start entering their prime earning years, with their own array of debts and demo-

graphic adversities awaiting them, they may well find themselves having to pay off the international debt that Boomers accumulated in the 1980s and 1990s.

Despite the penumbra of long-term debt, the U.S. economy remains the envy of the world; U.S. social conditions, however, are certainly not. America has some of the worst rates of child poverty, infant mortality, teen suicide, crime, family breakup, homelessness, and functional illiteracy in the developed world. In addition, many of our inner cities have turned into islands of despair, a frightening number of our public schools are dangerous, and almost two million of our residents are behind bars.

Many Xers sense that the basic fabric of American society is somehow fraying. Traditional civic participation, community cohesion, and civility are in decline, and not just among the young. The long-held belief in the value of hard work is under assault, as many Americans work longer hours for less pay, watch the gap between rich and poor grow ever wider, and see their benefits cut by corporations with little allegiance to people or place. The result is a fundamental loss of trust: between citizens and elected officials, between employees and employers, and, ultimately, between individuals and their neighbors. Yet trust and civility are the pillars on which any well-functioning democracy and free-market economy depend.

Finally, Xers face large environmental debts that stem from the use and abuse of our natural resources. Well over half of the world's major fisheries are severely depleted or overfished; loss of species and habitat continues at an unprecedented rate, with some 50,000 plant and animal species disappearing each year; freshwater tables across the globe, including parts of America, are falling precipitously; each year America alone loses more than a million acres of productive farmland to sprawl; and emissions of carbon dioxide and other greenhouse gases continue to rise, threatening to raise global temperatures by two to six degrees within the next century.

Global warming is a revealing case study from the perspective of Generation X. There is nearly unanimous scientific agreement on the problem, and a consensus among economists that the nation could reduce its greenhouse-gas emissions without harming its economy. In

addition, there is ample evidence—ranging from temperature increases to abnormally frequent weather disturbances to icebergs breaking off from the poles—to warrant deep concern. Yet our political establishment has resigned itself to virtual inaction. Why act now, politicians appear to reason, when we can just pass the problem on to our kids?

How, Xers have every right to ask, can one generation justify permanently drawing down the financial, social, and natural capital of another?

But whining will do no good. The only way for Xers to reverse their sad situation—and to realize the promise of the economic opportunities and technological innovations of the next century—is by entering the political arena that they have every reason to loathe. After all, collective problems require collective solutions. Xers cannot reasonably expect the political establishment to address, let alone fix, the sobering problems they are to inherit unless they start participating in the nation's political process, and learn to flex their generational muscle. Whether or not they do so will depend on two more immediate questions: Does this generation share a set of political beliefs? And if so, how might these translate into a political agenda?

"BALANCED-BUDGET POPULISM"

THREE quarters of Generation X agree with the statement "Our generation has an important voice, but no one seems to hear it." Whatever this voice may be, it does not fit comfortably within existing partisan camps. "The old left-right paradigm is not working anymore," according to the novelist Douglas Coupland, who coined the term "Generation X." Neil Howe and William Strauss, who have written extensively on generational issues, have argued in these pages that from the Generation X perspective "America's greatest need these days is to clear out the underbrush of name-calling and ideology so that simple things can work again." If Xers have any ideology, it is surely pragmatism.

In an attempt to be more specific Coupland has claimed, "Coming down the pipe are an extraordinarily large number of fiscal conservatives who are socially left." The underlying assumption here is that the Xer political world view stems simplistically from a combination of the 1960s social revolution and the 1980s economic revolution. This kind of thinking has led some to describe young adults as a generation of libertarians, who basically want government out of their bedrooms and out of their pocketbooks. As it turns out, however, the political views of most Xers are more complex and more interesting than that.

Xers appear to be calling for a synthesis that unites components thought to be mutually exclusive. Like conservatives, they favor fiscal restraint. Like liberals, they want to help the little guy.

To say that Xers are fiscal conservatives is to miss half the economic story; the other and equally powerful force at play can best be described as economic populism. In fact, the Xer consensus represents a novel hybrid of two distinct currents of economic thought that have rarely combined in the history of American politics. It might well be called "balanced-budget populism."

On the one hand, many Xers are worried about the debts being loaded onto their future, and therefore support fiscal prudence, balanced budgets, and a pay-as-you-go philosophy. On the other hand, Xers are more concerned than other generations about rising income inequality, and are the most likely to support government intervention to reverse it. The majority believe that the state should do more to help Americans get ahead.

What makes the Generation X economic agenda so surprising is that its two main components have thus far proved to be mutually exclusive in contemporary politics. Fiscal conservatism, widely viewed as the economic philosophy of the Republican right, has generally been accompanied by calls for lower taxes, smaller government, and reduced assistance to the neediest. Meanwhile, concern about the distribution of wealth and helping low-income workers, customarily a pillar of the Democratic left, has been associated with notions of tax-and-spend liberalism and big government. Xers appear to be calling for a new economic synthesis. Like conservatives, they favor fiscal restraint—but unlike the conservative leadership in Congress, only 15 percent believe that America should use any budget surplus to cut taxes. Like Democrats, they want to help the little guy—but unlike traditional Democrats, they are unwilling to do it by running deficits.

The Generation X social synthesis is no more conventional. Although the young are presumed to be more tolerant and socially permissive than their elders, today's young are returning to religion, have family-oriented aspirations, and are proving to be unsupportive of some traditional liberal programs, among them affirmative action. There are numerous indications that Xers—many of whom grew up without a formal religion—are actively searching for a moral compass to guide their lives, and a recent poll suggests that the highest priority for the majority of young adults is building a strong and close-knit family.

Wade Clark Roof, a professor of religion and society at the University of California at Santa Barbara, who studies the religious life of Generation X, says, "It is too early to predict whether today's young adults will form lasting commitments to particular religious denominations or institutions, but it is quite clear that there is a renewed level of interest in religion and spirituality among the post–Baby Boom generation. Many, in fact, have embarked upon a spiritual quest." As if they were spiritual consumers, young adults are shopping around among a wide range of religious traditions. In the process they are finding new ways to incorporate religion into their daily lives: for instance, church socials are rapidly becoming the new singles scene for Xers who want to combine their devotional and romantic ambitions. A clear majority of older Americans believe that a more active involvement of religious groups in politics is a bad idea, but Xers are divided on the issue.

This revival of spiritual and family-oriented aspirations represents a partial repudiation of the moral relativism that took hold in the 1960s and has since become a mainstay of American pop culture. In essence, many Xers are struggling to find a new values consensus that lies somewhere between the secular permissiveness of the left and the cultural intolerance of the right.

When it comes to race relations, Xers are particularly difficult to categorize. They are the cohort most likely to say that the civil-rights movement has not gone far enough. Yet, like Americans of all ages, they register a high level of opposition to job- and education-related affirmative-action programs. The American National Election Survey has reported that 68 percent of Xers oppose affirmative action at colleges. This seeming paradox can be explained in part by the fact that most Xers—though genuinely concerned about improving race relations—are among the first to have felt the actual (or perceived) bite of the affirmative-action programs that their parents and grandparents put into place.

Improving public education is one of the highest policy priorities for Xers. In fact, when asked what should be done with any future budget surplus, nearly half favor increased education spending. They seem to understand that knowledge will be the key to success in the information- and service-based economy of the twenty-first century. Their strong emphasis on education betokens a larger belief in the importance of investing in the future. Rather than maintaining the social-welfare state, the Xer philosophy would favor the creation of a social-investment state.

Although Xers have forsaken conventional political participation en masse, it would be a mistake to assume, as many do, that they are wholly apolitical. There is considerable evidence to suggest that volunteerism and unconventional forms of political participation have increased among young adults. Local voluntary activities, demonstrations, and boycotts all seem to be on the rise within their ranks. Heather McLeod, a Generation X co-founder of *Who Cares* magazine, has provided the following explanation: "We can *see* the impact when we volunteer. We know the difference is real." The implication, of course, is that the conventional political system has become so ineffectual and unresponsive that young people can make a positive difference only by circumventing it.

Xers may be poorly informed when it comes to public affairs, but they know enough to believe that our political system is badly in need of reform. At a very basic level they recognize that the political system is rigged against their interests. For one thing, Xers continually see a large gap between the issues they care most about and the ones that politicians choose to address. For another, they understand that Democrats and Republicans, despite an appearance of perpetual partisan infighting, collude to favor upper-income constituencies and to prevent a range of issues (including campaign-finance reform) from being acted on. Seeing themselves as the "fix-it" generation, Xers long for leaders who will talk straight and advocate the shared sacrifices necessary to correct the long-term problems that preoccupy them most. But today's elected officials are far too deeply trapped in a politics of short-term convenience to deliver anything of the sort. Not surprisingly, then, Xers are eager to do away with the two-party system. They register particularly strong support for third parties, for campaign-finance reform, and for various forms of direct democracy.

The final core belief that helps to define the political views of today's young adults is their commitment to environmental conservation. Thanks to the advent of environmental education and the spread of environmental activism, Xers grew up experiencing recycling as second nature; many actually went home and lobbied their parents to get with the program. In fact, the environment is one of the rare public-policy arenas in which Xers are fairly aware. Many have incorporated their environmental values into their lifestyles and career choices. For instance, a 1997 *Harvard Business Review* article titled "Tomorrow's Leaders: The World According to Generation X" revealed that most current MBA students believed that corporations have a clear-cut responsibility to be environment-friendly in their practices. This generation does not believe that a tradeoff is necessary between a strong economy and a healthy environment.

Fiscal prudence, economic populism, social investment, campaign reform, shared sacrifice, and environmental conservation—this constellation of beliefs transcends the existing left-right spectrum. It should be immediately apparent

that this generation's voice is not represented by any of the established leaders or factions in the political mainstream. And Xers seem to recognize as much—61 percent agree with the statement "Politicians and political leaders have failed my generation." So how would American politics change if the voice of Generation X were suddenly heard?

A NEW POLITICAL AGENDA

DESPITE its feeble rates of political participation, Generation X has already—if unwittingly—exerted an influence on the substance of our politics. This may seem counterintuitive, but who would deny that young Americans were a major force in pushing the balanced-budget cause to the fore? In part this is owing to the large number of Xer votes cast in 1992 for Ross Perot, the candidate who staked much of his campaign on balancing the federal books. Though Perot lost, his pet issue gained momentum as candidates from both parties scrambled to win over Reform Party voters, and the young ones in particular. Recognizing that Generation X makes up a large and particularly unpredictable voting bloc, candidates from across the spectrum have gone out of their way to woo the youth vote, usually by paying lip service to some of young people's more obvious concerns, including, most recently, Social Security reform. Over time, however, Xer support for issues such as balancing the budget and saving Social Security will turn out to be only part of a much broader agenda, one that could come to challenge the status quo on everything from taxes to social policy to political reform.

For years the nation's tax debate has revolved around the question of how much to tax, with the left arguing for more and the right for less. In keeping with the concept of balanced-budget populism, the Xer economic agenda would start with the assumption that the government's share of national income should remain roughly constant. It would focus instead on a far more profound set of questions: What should be taxed? Who should be taxed? What should we invest in? and Who should get the benefits? Over the past several decades the tax burden has crept further and further down the income and age ladder, with the benefits going increasingly to the

elderly and the well-to-do—the government now spends nine times as much on each elderly person as it does on each child. If Xers had their way, the collection of taxes would become more progressive and the distribution of benefits more widespread.

One would never know it from partisan skirmishes over income-tax cuts, but the payroll tax actually constitutes the largest tax burden borne by 70 percent of working families and by a full 90 percent of working Americans under age thirty. It is also the most regressive of all taxes, because it kicks in from the first dollar earned, falls exclusively on wages, and is capped at $72,600. An appealing solution to this problem would be to replace payroll taxes with pollution taxes, thereby boosting wages, promoting jobs, and cleaning up the environment, all without raising the deficit. Taxing waste instead of work is precisely the kind of innovative and pragmatic proposal that could help to galvanize the members of Generation X, who have been put to sleep by the current tax debate.

Sooner or later Xers will figure out that America could raise trillions of dollars in new public revenues by charging fair market value for the use of common assets—the oil and coal in the ground, the trees in our national forests, the airwaves and the electromagnetic spectrum—and the rights to pollute our air. We currently subsidize the use of these resources in a number of ways, creating a huge windfall for a small number of industries and a significant loss for all other Americans. The idea of reversing this trend by charging fair market value for the use of common assets and returning the proceeds directly to each American citizen plays to a number of Xer political views—it is populist, equitable, libertarian, and pro-environment all at once.

The populist economic leanings of young adults will also lead them to rethink various other elements of the social contract between citizens, government, and business. For one thing, ending corporate welfare would appeal to a generation weaned on the principle of self-sufficiency. The hidden welfare state, composed of corporate subsidies and tax loopholes that overwhelmingly benefit the well-to-do, has grown several times as large as the hotly debated social-welfare state that benefits the disadvantaged through means-tested programs. Yet today's politicians are too much indebted to the beneficiaries of this governmental largesse to do anything about it. Here, then, may be the key to keeping the budget balanced while funding the social investments that are so important to Xers: all of the money raised or saved by charging for the use of common assets, ending corporate welfare, and closing unproductive tax loopholes could be used to make a topnotch education affordable and accessible to all and, just as important, to make every American child a "trust-fund" baby from birth.

Making economic incentives more progressive and redirecting budgetary priorities is only one part of an Xer economic agenda. Today's young adults, more than any other group at a comparable age, are concerned about their economic outlook and their ability to balance the conflicting demands of work and family. If such problems worsen as a result of economic globalization, then the populism of Generation X, which up to this point has been relatively mild, may suddenly become more pronounced. For instance, the 2030 Center, an advocacy group concerned about the economic well-being of Generation X, is launching a campaign to promote a contingent workers' bill of rights, which calls on employers to provide health care and other benefits to more of their workers.

Even as they were being told that education is the key to a promising future, many Xers were learning the hard way how bad our urban schools have become, and how inequitable is the access to a high-quality education. Neither party is providing a palatable solution: Republicans are all but writing off public schools by emphasizing vouchers that favor private schools, and Democrats are perpetuating many of the worst public-school problems by refusing to challenge the teachers' unions. There are no simple solutions to the predicament, but an obvious starting point would be to sever the traditional link between public-school funding and local property taxes, which only exacerbates existing socioeconomic inequalities. (Several states have already begun moving in this direction.) Another significant improvement would be to increase the skill level of our public-school

teachers by imposing stricter standards and offering more-competitive salaries.

Xers would support enacting new policies to advance racial integration and civil rights in America—policies that avoid the divisiveness and unintended consequences of race-based affirmative action. Although such policies made sense when they were introduced, many Xers believe, race is no longer the determining factor in who gets ahead. In the twenty-first century poor black Americans will have more in common with poor white Americans than they will with upper-middle-class blacks. If the goal is to help those most in need, it would make a lot more sense to pursue class-based affirmative-action programs. Doing so would enable all those at the bottom—regardless of race—to get the help they need, in a way that promoted national unity and racial integration. Another promising alternative to race-based affirmative action is the Texas Ten Percent Plan, whereby all students graduating in the top tenth of their high school classes—whether in inner-city schools or in elite private ones—are automatically accepted into the state's public universities.

Fundamental campaign and political reform is the sine qua non of a Generation X political agenda. Like most Americans, Xers would like to see bold steps taken to get money out of politics. But persuading America's young that their individual votes matter is likely to require reforms far more radical than any currently under consideration.

Until recently most political-reform movements in the United States were based on the assumption that the problem was not the two-party system itself but rather its corruption by special interests and incumbency (hence the proposed cures of campaign-finance reform and term limits). But neither the reduction of private campaign contributions nor the implementation of term limits for elected officials will alter what seems to alienate Xers most of all: the political duopoly of Democrats and Republicans. The rules of today's two-party system actively discourage a third or a fourth party. Consequently, there is growing interest among the young in replacing our archaic electoral process (itself a remnant from eighteenth-century England) with a modern multiparty system. With

three or four parties contesting many races, politics might become exciting enough to draw in disenchanted Xers who believe, correctly, that in most elections today their votes do not count.

As the vanguard of the digital age, Xers will also be inclined to support experiments with electronic democracy. For instance, one Xer has launched an effort to make information about the sources of campaign contributions immediately available to the public and the media over the Internet. But the full potential of digital democracy runs much deeper. Already groups are experimenting with electronic town-hall meetings and various forms of deliberative democracy, in which individuals are provided with a full range of information on a particular issue and can register their opinions with the push of a button. It is not hard to imagine a day when citizens will be able to register and vote online, and to monitor the performance of their elected officials with electronic scorecards.

The introduction of electronic communication within corporate America has helped to flatten organizational hierarchies, boost information flows, increase decision-making speed, and, most of all, empower workers. It is at least conceivable that the introduction of electronic forms of democracy could serve to re-engage a generation that has been alienated by today's money-, spin-, and celebrity-dominated politics. And if Xers do eventually enter the fray, their agenda will transform America's political landscape.

THE FUTURE OF AMERICAN POLITICS

REPUBLICANS and Democrats will be tempted to dismiss the Xer agenda, because it threatens their electoral coalitions and the politics of short-term convenience. But both parties will do so at their peril, because many of the issues that Xers care most about are already rising to the political surface.

A glimpse of the future may come, strangely enough, in the election of Jesse Ventura as governor of Minnesota. Much of Ventura's support came from young adults, who took advantage of Minnesota's same-day registration law and stormed the polls, helping to create a record turnout. This suggests that if a political candidate can somehow capture the passion of young adults, they will do their part. Ventura offered young Minnesotans something refreshing: a clear alternative to Democrats and Republicans, and a willingness to take on the status quo. But Jesse Ventura is no figurehead for Xers; he is just an early beneficiary of their pent-up political frustration.

As the Xer political agenda starts to take hold, it will further strain existing loyalties. On the Republican side, the odd-bedfellow coalition of social conservatives and economic libertarians that has defined the party for the past two decades is coming apart as a result of the Clinton impeachment saga, whose most lasting legacy may be that it dealt a coup de grace to the political aspirations of the religious right. The Democratic coalition is just as fragile, particularly since it has been losing its base of working-class white men, and the potential retreat of the religious right may deprive Democrats of an obvious opponent against which to rally. As these de-alignments unfold, major shifts in the makeup and core agendas of both parties become almost inevitable.

The stability of today's political consensus is also contingent on the promise of an economy that continues to expand. Take that away, and the props of the status quo—a balanced budget and the novelty of a budgetary surplus, a booming stock market and stable price structures, low unemployment and rising wages, falling welfare rolls and crime rates, and the illusion of a painless fix to Social Security—all topple at once. No business cycle lasts forever, and the global economic crisis of 1998 should come as a warning of what may lie ahead. The prospect of a significant recession leaves the future of American politics wide open.

Turning points in our nation's political history, occasioned by the collapse of an existing civic and political consensus, have usually been accompanied by rampant individualism, weakened institutions, and heightened levels of political alienation. On these scores Xers are playing out their historic role remarkably well. But such periods of civic unrest have also stimulated new political agendas, which eventually force one or both parties to remake themselves around new priorities and coalitions. Could the Generation X political agenda serve as the basis of America's next political consensus?

Balanced-budget populism, social investment, and other elements of the Xer agenda could resonate with Americans of all ages—and help to create the nation's next majoritarian coalition.

Balanced-budget populism, social investment, no-nonsense pragmatism, and shared sacrifice could resonate quite strongly with Americans of all ages—particularly the increasing number who are fed up with conventional politics. What is more, the Xer synthesis of a middle-class economic agenda with a moderate social one could remake the powerful alliance between progressives and populists that dominated national politics (and brought widespread upward mobility) from the 1930s to 1960s, when it was ripped apart by the cultural upheaval of the Baby Boom. In practical

terms this new politics—based on fiscal prudence, economic populism, family-friendly morality, social investment, campaign reform, environmental conservation, and technological innovation—could eventually take hold in either of the major parties, both of which are now searching for a coherent agenda and a lasting voter base. For Democrats it could mark a return to the party's New Deal roots, and for Republicans it could give substance to heretofore vague calls for a "compassionate conservatism."

Since this new politics could speak to many of those who are alienated by the current political order, Xers and older Americans alike, it could give birth to our nation's next majoritarian coalition. Such a coalition could do a great deal to reinvigorate our nation's democracy, benefit the majority of its citizens, and restore legitimacy to our political system.

When history books are written at the end of the twenty-first century, it is unlikely that the post–Baby Boom generation will still be referred to as a nondescript "X." One way or another, this generation will be judged and labeled by its legacy. Today's young adults will be remembered either as a late-blooming generation that ultimately helped to revive American democracy by coalescing around a bold new political program and bringing the rest of the nation along with them, or as another silent generation that stood by as our democracy and society suffered a slow decline.

The great question of twenty-first-century politics is whether a critical mass of Xers will eventually recognize the broader potential of their agenda, and outgrow their aversion to politics.

Ted Halstead is president and CEO of the New America Foundation, in Washington, D.C.

Index

Index

Test Your Knowledge Form

We encourage you to photocopy and use this page as a tool to assess how the articles in *Annual Editions* expand on the information in your textbook. By reflecting on the articles you will gain enhanced text information. You can also access this useful form on a product's book support Web site at *http://www.mhcls.com/online/*.

NAME: DATE:

_____

TITLE AND NUMBER OF ARTICLE:

_____

BRIEFLY STATE THE MAIN IDEA OF THIS ARTICLE:

_____

LIST THREE IMPORTANT FACTS THAT THE AUTHOR USES TO SUPPORT THE MAIN IDEA:

_____

WHAT INFORMATION OR IDEAS DISCUSSED IN THIS ARTICLE ARE ALSO DISCUSSED IN YOUR TEXTBOOK OR OTHER READINGS THAT YOU HAVE DONE? LIST THE TEXTBOOK CHAPTERS AND PAGE NUMBERS:

_____

LIST ANY EXAMPLES OF BIAS OR FAULTY REASONING THAT YOU FOUND IN THE ARTICLE:

_____

LIST ANY NEW TERMS/CONCEPTS THAT WERE DISCUSSED IN THE ARTICLE, AND WRITE A SHORT DEFINITION:

We Want Your Advice

ANNUAL EDITIONS revisions depend on two major opinion sources: one is our Advisory Board, listed in the front of this volume, which works with us in scanning the thousands of articles published in the public press each year; the other is you—the person actually using the book. Please help us and the users of the next edition by completing the prepaid article rating form on this page and returning it to us. Thank you for your help!

ANNUAL EDITIONS: American History, Volume 2

ARTICLE RATING FORM

Here is an opportunity for you to have direct input into the next revision of this volume.
We would like you to rate each of the articles listed below, using the following scale:

1. **Excellent: should definitely be retained**
2. **Above average: should probably be retained**
3. **Below average: should probably be deleted**
4. **Poor: should definitely be deleted**

Your ratings will play a vital part in the next revision.
Please mail this prepaid form to us as soon as possible.
Thanks for your help!

RATING	ARTICLE	RATING	ARTICLE
	1. The New View of Reconstruction		22. We Need to Reclaim the Second Bill of Rights
	2. 1871 War on Terror		23. What They Saw When They Landed
	3. Little Bighorn Reborn		24. The Biggest Decision: Why We Had to Drop the Atomic Bomb
	4. The Spark of Genius		
	5. Lockwood in '84		25. The Tangled Web: America, France, and Indochina, 1947-1950
	6. A Day to Remember: November 18, 1883		
	7. Where the Other Half Lived		26. From Rosie the Riveter to the Global Assembly Line: American Women on the World Stage
	8. The Murder of Lucy Pollard		
	9. Our First Olympics		27. The Split-Level Years
	10. T.R.'s Virtuoso Performance		28. The Rise of Conservatism Since World War II
	11. And Still Champion		29. The Spirit of '68
	12. The Fate of Leo Frank		30. The Cold War and Vietnam
	13. The Ambiguous Legacies of Women's Progressivism		31. Soft Power: Reagan the Dove
			32. The Tragedy of Bill Clinton
	14. Uncovering History		33. The Pros From Dover
	15. American Biography: Edith Galt Wilson		34. Breaking the Global-Warming Gridlock
	16. The Home Front		35. A Legend's Soul is Rested
	17. From Front Porch to Back Seat: A History of the Date		36. Ending the Fool's Game: Saving Civilization
	18. 'Brother, Can You Spare a Dime?'		37. Pssst...Nobody Loves a Torturer
	19. A Promise Denied		38. The Bubble of American Supremacy
	20. A Monumental Man		39. The Case Against Perfection
	21. The Greatest Convention		40. A Politics for Generation X

(Continued on next page)

BUSINESS REPLY MAIL
FIRST CLASS MAIL PERMIT NO. 551 DUBUQUE IA

POSTAGE WILL BE PAID BY ADDRESEE

McGraw-Hill Contemporary Learning Series
2460 KERPER BLVD
DUBUQUE, IA 52001-9902

ABOUT YOU

Name   Date

Are you a teacher? ❑   A student? ❑
Your school's name

Department

Address   City   State   Zip

School telephone #

YOUR COMMENTS ARE IMPORTANT TO US!

Please fill in the following information:
For which course did you use this book?

Did you use a text with this ANNUAL EDITION?   ❑ yes ❑   no
What was the title of the text?

What are your general reactions to the *Annual Editions* concept?

Have you read any pertinent articles recently that you think should be included in the next edition? Explain.

Are there any articles that you feel should be replaced in the next edition? Why?

Are there any World Wide Web sites that you feel should be included in the next edition? Please annotate.

May we contact you for editorial input?   ❑ yes ❑ no
May we quote your comments? ❑ yes ❑ no